THEOLOGY OF THE HEART

The Role of Mysticism in the Theology of Martin Luther

by Bengt R. Hoffman
edited by Pearl Willemssen Hoffman

Kirk House Publishers
Minneapolis, Minnesota

Theology of the Heart

The Role of Mysticism in the Theology of Martin Luther

by Bengt R. Hoffman
edited by Pearl Willemssen Hoffman

Library of Congress Cataloging-In-Publication Data

Hoffman, Bengt Runo, 1913
[Hjärtats teologi. English]
Theology of the heart : the role of mysticism in the theology of Martin Luther / by Bengt Hoffman ; edited by Pearl Willemssen Hoffman
p. cm.
Includes bibliographical references and index.
ISBN 1-886513-55-4 (alk. paper)
1. Luther, Martin 1483-1546. 2. Mysticism—Lutheran Church—history—16th century. I. Hoffman, Pearl Willemssen. II. title

BR333.5.M9 T4413 2003
248.2'2'092—dc21

2002040660

Kirk House Publishers, PO Box 390759, Minneapolis, MN 55439
Manufactured in the United States of America

In humble gratitude to the Triune God
for Bengt's and my fifty-year pilgrimage
and a sincere acknowledgment of our indebtedness
to our family, to our friends around the world
—not forgetting those who have departed this life—
for love, prayers, deeds of kindness
and support on our journey.

THE LUTHER ROSE

The Luther rose was Luther's seal. In a letter* from Coburg castle to Lasarus Spengler, town notary in Nuremberg, he gave a description of the Luther-rose seal:

> First there is the black cross in the middle of the heart. The heart should have its natural color. I am thereby reminded that it is faith in the crucified that saves us, because one is justified by what one believes in one's heart. The fact that the cross is black signifies that it humbles and causes pain. But the heart's natural color remains, its nature is not destroyed; in other words, the cross doesn't kill but rather enlivens. The justified person lives by faith, faith in the crucified. But this heart should be placed in the middle of a white rose in order to show that faith gives us joy, comfort and peace and quickly brings us into a life which is comparable to the white, joy-filled rose. This is thus not the peace and joy that the world gives. The rose should be white and not red because white is the color of the spirits and all angels. The background of the rose is the blue of the heavens to show that this joy in the Spirit and in faith is a foretaste of the heavenly joy that awaits us. And yet we already have it in the midst of this life. It is included in hope, but it is not yet totally revealed. Surrounding the whole field is a gold ring, suggesting that bliss in heaven is eternal, endures forever, and is more precious than all other joys and treasures, in the same way that gold is the finest and most precious of all metals.

With Luther's permission, in some versions the rose was surrounded by the five letters, VIVIT, meaning "he lives," namely, Christ, as the unseen but living Lord.

* (*WB* 5, no. 1627, 444-445, 1530)

CONTENTS

Abbreviations

CM — *The Church. Mysticism, Sanctification and the Natural, in Luther's Thought.* Edited by Ivar Asheim. Philadelphia: Fortress Press, 1967.

LW — *Luther's Works*, The American Edition. Edited by H. T. Lehmann and J. Pelikan. St. Louis: Concordia Press and Philadelphia: Fortress Press, 1955-1986.

RGG — *Die Religion in Geschichte und Gegenwart.* Wittenberg, 1957.

W — *D. Martin Luthers Werke*, Kritische Gesamtausgabe. Weimar edition, Volumes 1-58, 1883-

WB — *D. Martin Luthers Werke*, Kritische Gesamtausgabe, Briefwechsel. Weimar edition, Volumes 1-14, 1930-1970.

WT — *D. Martin Luthers Werke*, Kritische Gesamtausgabe, Weimar edition, Tischreden, vols. 1-6, 1912-1921.

PREFACE

Theology of the Heart is the revised and expanded version of my late husband's earlier work, *Luther and the Mystics* (Augsburg Publishing House, 1976). This volume appears in English five years after his death in April 1997. Because I worked so closely with him during the last years of his life in preparing the English text, it was suggested that I write a preface, inasmuch as Bengt had not written one. I am pleased to have the opportunity to relate something about the history of this edition and to acknowledge the help I have received in the final preparation of this work.

When *Luther and the Mystics* first appeared, reviews were published in foreign journals, as well as in the United States. Several theologians and scholars in Sweden took note of the book because of its subject matter and also because the author was born and educated in Sweden and was a clergyman of the Church of Sweden. Several Swedish colleagues urged Bengt to prepare a Swedish version of the book to make it more accessible to Scandinavian readers.

After spending another decade gathering more material and reflecting on the changes he wanted to make in the structure of his original book, Bengt wrote a Swedish version, published in 1989. He gave it the title, *Hjärtats teologi* (Theology of the Heart). He thought that this title more appropriately reflected the focus of his revision, i. e., that Luther's theological thinking was deeply influenced by his heart-felt experiences of life in God. Soon after the Swedish book appeared, one of Bengt's friends, Professor Bengt Hägglund, wrote an enthusiastic letter and commented especially on the appropriateness of the title. Professor Hägglund pointed out that Luther, in the *Large Catechism*, uses the word 'heart' twenty-four times in his explanation of the first commandment.

Although *Luther and the Mystics* had a second printing, it has been out of print for several years. In February 1993, at a Lutheran spirituality conference in Illinois, Professor Timothy Lull and other participants suggested that *Luther and the Mystics* be reprinted. However, Bengt (who had had a serious stroke in 1992 and could hardly express himself) made it clear that he did not wish to reprint his original work but wanted his Swedish version to be published in English. It should also be said that Bengt was very touched by the number of conference participants who told him how much they appreciated the fact that he had spoken out about the interior and spiritual nature of Luther's faith and about the prevailing influence of rationalism on Western Protestant theology.

Upon our return from the Conference, we started working on the English version of the book. I say "we" because Bengt suffered from expressive aphasia as a result of the stroke. For many months he could not read, write, or speak. Yet, it was obvious that his store of knowledge was intact. When he did learn to read again, texts in Latin, Greek, German and Scandinavian languages presented no problem. He acquired a laptop computer and gradually learned to write again. (He never regained the ability to write longhand other than brief memos, and these were hand printed with the aid of an alphabet chart.) As he worked it became clear that he still had his gift for expressing himself, but dyslexia was a problem until the end.

Some readers have asked why Bengt wrote his original work on Luther and what had influenced him to do so. Others have wondered how he happened to be ahead of his time in writing about mysticism and spirituality (in this case, especially Luther's) before these subjects enjoyed the wide popularity they have today.

It is not easy to point to very specific influences in a life as rich in diverse experiences as Bengt's, except to observe that surely the Spirit tries to speak to and through each of us. Although Bengt studied the traditional academic theological courses at Swedish universities, he also had an abiding interest in the writings and experiences of Christians that expressed an immediate awareness of the power of God's love, especially as manifested in the life and death of Jesus, the Christ, and of the Holy Spirit. Such writings were usually not required reading in Systematic Theology and Church History.

Bengt was ordained in 1938 at the Cathedral at Skara, Sweden, and his Bishop and other mentors expressed the hope that he might eventually be called to a leadership role in the Church of Sweden after following the usual path of institutional advancement. However, the political tensions and power struggles in central Europe were casting shadows on the lives of Scandinavians as well as creating turmoil for millions of Europeans. Both outer circumstances and inner compulsion lead Bengt to witness and to serve people mostly outside the institutional church for much of the following decade.

It is not possible to go into detail, but during this period of his ministry Bengt did pastoral work in Skara Diocese; served as national travel secretary for the pre-university Swedish Student Christian Movement; did obligatory military service, including serving as a military chaplain in the Swedish army and to American airmen who crashed or landed in Sweden during WW II; became YMCA camp visitor/chaplain to German POWs in England and Canada; and worked for the World Student Christian Federation, Geneva, visiting refugee students in central Europe; and in the Student Christian Movement in China. The latter assignment, also under the auspices of the World Student Christian Federation, ended earlier than anticipated, in May 1949, due to the Communist Revolution in China.

Bengt was then invited to work in Geneva at the World Council of Churches, the center of the modern ecumenical movement. As the Secretary for Germany and Austria in the Department of Inter-Church Aid, his primary assignment was to administer the aid program to German and Austrian churches to help them recover from the devastation of WW II. In addition, time and energy were spent on helping European refugees and serving on Inter-Church Aid committees for Greece and Italy.

In 1953, Bengt asked his Bishop for a parish assignment, and, in the autumn of that year, he moved to Sweden to serve in a large city parish. However, after three years Bengt was again called to serve on an international team, this time as director of Lutheran World Service, Geneva. In this role he traveled the world and met people everywhere who were hungering for both physical and spiritual nourishment. He often spoke about the contrast between the spiritual-intuitive thinking of most Africans and Asians and the more rational-dogmatic approach of many Western Christian leaders.

After earning a doctorate in Christian Ethics at the Divinity School of Yale University and some years as parish pastor in Sweden, Bengt returned to the United States to accept an academic post. In 1967 he was called to the Lutheran Theological Seminary, Gettysburg, to serve as professor of Ethics and Ecumenics.

It is my belief that the opportunities given to Bengt to meet people of virtually all major churches and his conversations with them about spiritual matters only confirmed an insight he had gained very early in his ministry: that there are many paths to the Center, to Christ as God's incarnated Messenger and our Savior, and that following Christ is more than an intellectual, rational decision. In the Translators' Note to *Early Fathers from the Philokalia* (London: Faber and Faber Ltd., 1954) we are informed that, whereas in the West theology means "systematic theoretical knowledge relating to God," in the Orthodox tradition it means "a gift of the Spirit, the gift of speaking about God with deep insight and with powerful and winning words." Bengt's work is an attempt to show that Martin Luther was an ecumenical "theologian."

As Bengt and I worked on translating the Swedish edition of *Hjärtats teologi* into English, the same principles that Bengt delineated on page 5 of his Foreword with regard to Luther's writings apply to this edition. If the German and Swedish works that were cited as references in the Swedish edition are available in English, these editions have been used. The author has translated the quotations from the German and Swedish books or articles that have not been published in English.

Bengt would have wanted to express his appreciation to all those who, through the years, have helped in divers ways, including in his search for relevant material.

In the Preface to his original work he expressed his gratitude to the librarians at the University of Uppsala and the research workers at the Institut für Spätmittelalter und Reformation at the University of Tübingen. In addition to many who will not be named but are not forgotten, let me expressly thank Professor Bonnie VanDelinder, Librarian, and Sara Mummert, Public Service Assistant, and other members of the staff of the Lutheran Theological Seminary Library at Gettysburg, for their cheerful assistance. I also wish to thank Professor Eric Crump, Professor Tim Lull, Professor Gerald Christianson, Pastor Nancy Eggert, Ph.D., Pastor Joanne Stenman, and Pastor Eric Stenman for reading the manuscript and making helpful suggestions, to Andrew R. Crouse and William T. Leslie, computer experts and true friends, for their valuable help with my aging computer, and to Leonard Flachman and the staff at Kirk House Publishers for making this publication possible.

Reformation Day, 2002
Pearl Willemssen Hoffman

That we can know God only in mystical intuition, and not by the conceptual intellect, may seem to make nonsense of theology. For theology consists of propositions about God. . . . For the present we can only say that, as will be generally admitted, religion is not theology. And when it is said that no knowledge of God is possible except in intuition, the knowledge of God which is spoken of is that inner sense of God "within the heart" which is the religious experience, which is in fact religion. A man may know theology without knowing God. And he may know God without knowing theology. And there could not be any theology unless there were first that mystic inner sense. Theology is but the attempt to interpret that experience to the intellect.

W. T. Stace, *Time and Eternity*, p. 46

Christ does not want his kingdom to be characterized by violence, but he wants to be served from the will, the heart, and from feelings.

Martin Luther on Psalm 1, *W* 2,1; 4, 1516

Faith as true knowledge is not only summarized in what I hear and in the story I tell, but to believe is to take possession of, lean on and ardently long for spiritual knowledge, so it can enter the heart and so that I can hope, and not doubt, and find peace and comfort, as Christ has suffered in this world for me. If faith is only historical it can not have this effect.

Martin Luther on Isaiah 53:11, *W* 40, 3; 738, 6-13, 1537

FOREWORD

In the 1970s when I was studying the question of Martin Luther's spiritual experience and its impact on his theological thought, there were two circumstances with which, in fact, I never really counted. However, these became evident later in the discussion around my book, *Luther and the Mystics* (Augsburg Publishing House, 1976).

First, among those who are occupied with the problems of Luther's thought, there are some who harbor a rather deep-seated suspicion of the word "mystic." They would prefer that this epithet not be applied to the Reformer. A good friend noted—with some relief, I believe—that he could completely agree with me when I wrote: "Luther felt little kinship to the kind of mysticism which dealt with speculations, with visions for their own sake or as a method to find God." Further, my friend concurred with my assertion that Luther did not borrow ideas from mysticism but that he rather found some mystics' expressions for Divine presence "by their nature related to his own [Luther's] deepest experience." The letter writer's conclusion was the following: "Therefore it is clear to me that not even your careful study has found any typical mysticism in Luther's theology."

The question naturally is what one means by "typical mysticism." In my study of theologians' views of the matter I found that their interpretations cover a wide range. Therefore I will give some attention to that subject in the Introduction to this book.

Second, it came as a great surprise to read in a review published in an American theological journal that my presentation did not take into consideration "the epistemological problem," that I did not even mention it. But the entire book is concerned with that problem! The fact is that I had decided that I would not use the technical word "epistemology" excessively. For those who are not familiar with this academic term I hasten to say that epistemology is the theory or science about the method and basis for attaining knowledge: strictly speaking, how and by what means one believes that one can "know." An author would rather not enter into a discussion to defend himself against charges in a review. Nor did I. But now I have had the experience of at least one researcher's dependence on certain terms without which he could not recognize the central point at issue. Therefore I decided that I would emphasize, more forcefully than previously, that, as far as religious or "mystical" experiences are concerned, one cannot escape the question of what "knowledge" is. Is it derived only from the intellect or, in addition, also from spiritual experience in feeling and inspiration? Consequently, I will also take up this question in the Introduction. I will explain "epistemology" or "theory of knowledge" in everyday language.

From time to time I read between the lines of comments made by colleagues that I probably should keep to the academic discipline I chose for my doctoral studies and the subject I have taught, namely, Christian and social ethics. In other words, how does it happen that I have abandoned my "last" to try my hand at others' "lasts"? Mystical theology and Luther's contacts with it are not in line with my "specialty," are they?

Two assumptions are hidden in this objection. First, one assumes that one should not enter an area of specialization if one is not a specialist in that field. It is an old academic rule that you had better not stick out your neck in this way. There is always the risk that it might be cut off. I must concede that by taking up, in a published work, the subject of Luther's relation to medieval mysticism and its significance for Protestant thought, I ventured to enter a field where even angels might fear to tread. But it does happen that reverence for specialization can lead to a short circuit, a disruption of scholarly thought. One who does not at every point possess detailed knowledge and therefore, perhaps, omits a fact that would have spread a somewhat different light over certain relations can, nevertheless, contribute to essential illumination.

I have reason to believe that this is the case with my attempt. The fact that there was a second printing of the above-mentioned work certainly is a hint in that direction.

Second, one prefers to assume that that with which I am primarily concerned —penetration of ethical problems —must lie far from an interest in mystical theology. My view is the contrary. The moral and the mystical belong together. For example, the genuine experience of oneness in meeting the Divine always makes an impact on one's sense of responsibility. As a result of the ego's diminishment, which occurs in facing God, a real sense of co-humanity grows.

There is some criticism of my combining the mystical and the moral, the close link between life in God and life in the world. It seems to me that Christian ethics often becomes a process of "rational decision making" without reference to the Christian's source of power. Under the influence of empirical methodology one uses almost exclusively criteria from the social sciences. The underlying premise is the central dogma of mechanical reflection: *existentia* (existence **in** the material world) precedes *essentia* (essence or being **beyond** the material).

The dependence, more or less, on this dogma obscures the Christian basis for moral responsibility which alone inspires to cross bearing and which cannot be limited to purely rational considerations. One can state that theology, thinking about God, is theology-rooted-in-prayer or it is nothing. From a strictly "scientific" viewpoint this description is hardly a ticket, or an invitation, to the salons where the "objectively verifiable" is dealt with and discussed.

At the outset of this enterprise—this study of Luther's contacts with mystics and mysticism—I want to state that, on my view, ethical analysis in Christian theology is interlinked with responsible Christian living. The roots of Christian responsibility go deeper than rational decision-making or making a "reasonable" decision.

Consequently, one should reverse the phrase about *existentia* and *essentia* and assert that essence beyond matter precedes existence in matter. Perhaps that sounds medieval. But who can say that the latest truths are the supreme truths? Against that background one can argue that frequently heard assertions are wrong, namely, that Christian ethics in no way differs from ethics in general.

It is true that Martin Luther declared, "A Christian uses the world in such a way that there is no difference between him and an ungodly man." That is an observation our sensible selves like to hear. And, sure enough, this sentence is quoted as evidence of the Reformer's soundness, discernment, and robust orientation to the world. But one must not forget the continuation, which is, "Yet there is the greatest possible difference. I do indeed live in the flesh but I do not live on the basis of my own self. What you hear me speak proceeds from another source." This happens when one is "touched by the Holy Spirit." In this sense Christians stand at the center of God's work in the world, wrote Luther. No one can assume the burden of Christian moral commitment without constant resource to the incomprehensible power that lies behind and beyond the ordinary logic of things.

In the Reformer's statements of this type we see an aspect of his life and thought that is often forgotten in analyses. Christian thought and life well up not only from the **promise** of the consummation of all things in Christ at the end of time, but also from Christ's **presence** here and now. From the world beyond the "common-sensical" and the linear-logical comes the "knowledge of Christ" or "knowledge in Christ." The invisible presence that leads to such knowledge is hardly "reasonable." But one must take it into consideration. One might even wish to experiment with it in meditation and contemplation. If theological thought about the Christ revelation borrows all of its "tools and models" from scientific materialism it loses its sensibility for supernatural presence, symbol, and power.

In Martin Luther's writings one finds some fascinating references to "mystical theology" and to experience of the "mystical Christ" (*Christus mysticus*). In much analytical literature on Luther's world of thought no notice is taken of such utterances or, using various explanations, an attempt is made to minimize their significance. This effort is so obvious that it becomes suspect. On the following pages there will be reason to point out similar omissions, the result of a rationalistic conception of knowledge, especially theological knowledge.

But a few researchers are of the opinion that Luther's spiritual kinship with mystics was essential, not accidental. I have received considerable help from their work. They have, in many cases, shown me the path. But these scholars are not to be held responsible for my investigations of predominant premises. In many ways I have been more critical than they regarding the rationalistic undertone in prominent representations of Luther's theology and a resultant inability or unwillingness to take Luther's spirituality seriously.

I mention this because this revised and expanded work has been organized differently from my original book, *Luther and the Mystics*. The controversy or debate that I had taken up in relation to epistemology has been placed in the last part of this version. In my first work, that discussion was at the beginning of the book. Therefore the theoretical discussion may not be as evident as in the original. Perhaps that is an advantage.

A great deal of Martin Luther's written works have come to us by way of friends and students who expanded on his abbreviated notes or stenographed some of his oral presentations. For that reason, researchers question the authenticity of some of the works. With respect to my use of such material I wish to state that the quotations I use are consistent with the theme of Luther's life and his entire production.

Original texts that are quoted or made reference to are from the Weimar edition of Luther's works, *Die Weimar Ausgabe*: Luther's commentaries, pamphlets, and sermons are found in sources marked *W*; Luther's Table Talks in *WT* and his correspondence in *WB*. If the quotations are also found in the American translation of portions of Luther's writings, *Luther's Works* (*LW*), this is indicated. If selected texts are not found in *LW*, the translation is mine. Also, in some cases I have chosen to use my own English translation of the German or Latin texts rather than the one found in *LW*. In these cases, I have so indicated in the text or in the footnote. The Bible quotations are from the Revised Standard Version.

Inasmuch as I hope that the readership of this work will not be limited to those with theological training, I have provided explanations for less ordinary terms, such as "epistemology," "Nominalism," and "repristination."

To my women readers I wish to note that I am sensitive to the fact that the use of the words "man" and "he" to represent both genders might be offensive to some; however it is awkward to constantly write "he/she." God is also referred to with the traditional masculine pronouns.

I am aware that in this book I discuss only one aspect of a genius' many-faceted life, namely, the assuredly significant role which religious *Erfarhrung*, experience, played in his life. I am also aware of the criticism often leveled against Luther regarding his attitude toward women, his comments on Jews, and the role of the state and municipal authorities in God's economy. However, we need to remember that Luther, in spite of a remarkable breadth of vision regarding many questions, was a product of his age. What cannot be taken from him is that for 30 years he was at the front lines of a tremendous freedom movement. What he said about law and grace and about Divine presence will endure. In that respect the theologian who said that it is not back to Luther but rather forward to Luther was right. Or even better: not to Luther at all but to that which he wanted to convey. After all, he did not want a movement or a church named after him. It is typical of us ordinary people that we decided not to follow his advice.

Bengt Hoffman

INTRODUCTION

Two perspectives in thinking about God

The Reformation broke with the domination and control of the medieval church in Rome. The Word became the focal point instead of tradition. The priesthood of all believers replaced clerical hegemony. This did not mean that everything that was a part of the old system had to go. For instance, that which the mystics of the church had said about Christ´s presence in prayer and sacrament was still valid. But in the Reformers' thinking one could observe two positions that soon collided with each other.

In Martin Luther's world of thought we have to reckon with a tension between two aspects of faith: faith as a merit, on the one hand, and faith as experience, on the other. When another's deed, for example, Jesus', is imputed to someone, this does not need to mean that one is emotionally affected and personally engaged in the transaction. Quite early, during his revolutionary period, Luther became aware of the danger of the extremely subjective. His interest in a number of medieval mystics was always balanced by his emphasis on "the external Word."

In his struggle against the Roman doctrine of works, against mystical salvation methods, in which Christ was not at the center, and against the almost "discarnate" forms of enthusiastic Reformation piety, Luther used terms reflecting his desire to anchor the gospel firmly in history and in Holy Writ.

He used expressions like "righteousness outside us," "Christ for us," encompassed in the above-mentioned phrase, "the external Word." These expressions pointed away from the human person to the objective fact. They also underline the eschatological character of sanctification, that is to say, completion as belonging to the ultimate, a "not-yet-here."

Through this choice of eschatological and objective terms, Luther wanted to emphasize the part of faith that is called imputed. God imputes to us righteousness for the sake of Jesus Christ and in the power of his deed. *Imputatio* is the Latin word for this description of Divine grace. Since righteousness is imputed or attributed to us, one cannot say that an individual Christian personally has contributed anything to the process. The Christian is encouraged to hold to the promise of forgiveness, given in the Word, not to rely on elevated feelings. The latter are not reliable road signs to God's kingdom.

However, in Luther's world of thought there is another angle, one that opens a perspective toward the personal. His sermons, his biblical commentaries, and his theological treatises reckon with a category of knowledge that belongs to the inner life, knowledge beneath and beyond the external, merely intellectual, assertion of "truth"—"holding-this-to-be-true."

For this inner knowledge, Luther used words that reflect personal experience (*Erfahrung* or *experientia* are terms frequently used) and awareness of Divine power active in faith. These terms convey his conviction that the external symbols and word are a bridge to the internal, to the "heart" and "feeling."[1] Yes, the conviction that Christ's righteousness is imputed to him who believes is without merit, of no avail, if Christ does not "live" within a person—an "indwelling" that can be experienced with "mystical eyes."[2]

Among the expressions that illustrate this theology of the heart belong, for example, the following: *unio mystica*, "the mystical Christ"; *gemitus*, anguish, the pain one experiences when one stands before God without even the ability of knowing what to say; *raptus*, the rapturous joy of being in God's presence; and "the kingdom of God is within you." (In this connection Luther does not translate the Greek word *entos* as "among," which most exegetes favor, but instead Luther prefers "in"—a significant fact.) The word "to feel" and, as we have said, the word "experience" frequently occur in Luther's theology. With these expressions he describes the inner, personal side of God's work of redemption.

The general frame of reference for this inner side of Luther's world is expressed in the word "mysticism."

What is mysticism?

As indicated, the word mysticism (likewise the adjective mystical) gives rise to associations that have a tendency to divert us from the meaning that Luther and some mystics attached and attach to it. In a book about the mystic Johann Tauler, **Gösta Wrede** writes:

> Perhaps we should use another word than mysticism. It can mistakenly lead one's thoughts to divergent individuals or to groups for initiates. However mysticism is not a matter of isolationism or sectarianism. It is rather a matter of a broadening of the whole area of religious experience . . . an experience of harmony, a moment of union with the ground of being . . . it is not easy to bring any other word than mysticism into the context.[3]

It ought to be clear from the outset of this inquiry that Martin Luther never treated "mysticism" as a uniform belief system nor as having one connotation. One of the greatest difficulties in discussing Luther's relation to the mysticism of medieval times is that the term is being used as though everyone would be of the same opinion concerning its meaning and content. Such a mutually agreed-upon opinion does not exist. If the terms "mysticism," "mystical," and "mystics" can in any way be applied to Luther's theology, and to Luther himself, one must come to an agreement that they embrace the non-rational, experiential aspect. The experiential played a major role in the theology of the Reformer.

In his own way, Luther came close to various descriptions of mystical experience. Mysticism has been depicted as "the establishment of conscious relation with the Absolute" (Underhill); "the soul's possible union in this life with Absolute Reality" (Rufus Jones); "the experimental perception of God's presence and being" (Pattison); "the most Divine knowledge of God which takes place in the union which is above intelligence, when the intellect is united to the superlucent rays" (Dionysius the Areopagite); and "as if led by the hands of angels we feel the being of God and attribute to angelic ministration whatever similitude in which the feeling was conveyed" (Bernard of Clairvaux).

Mystical experiences of the kind just sketched are in themselves a negation of the idea that knowledge stems only from physical sensations and psychological common sense. The impressions of the senses, the intellectual processes, the gradual unfolding of ordinary consciousness are not the final, outer limits for the human search for God.

The basis for the "mystical method" does not lie in logic, but in life. This is the reason a mystic often refers to his search as "experimentation." Through personal experience he or she has become convinced that the seeker can "know," in a manner that is different from knowledge that is mediated only by means of the five senses. Through meditation and prayer the mystical seeker unites with his Lord and apprehends the reality, or some of the reality, of that Lordship.

As indicated, Martin Luther was evidently acquainted with the personal, experience-based spirituality that is embraced by many mystics. But he did not have much interest in mysticism as an "-ism," as a composite of ideas that has to be accepted or rejected. He spoke about mysticism as the inner side of the external confession. The external confession of faith can be personally received and personally experienced in feeling. To Luther this personal experience was hardly a system labeled mysticism, but rather mystical theology.

It is noteworthy that when Luther tried to clothe his words in logical categories about something that could, to some extent, be called the mystical way, he borrowed his terms from a so-called mystic, Bernard of Clairvaux. "Mystical theology," Luther wrote with a tone that reminds one of Bernard of Clairvaux, is the "experimental" and "experience-laden" kind. In other words, mystical theology is experience of God.

Luther's use of the word "mystical"—with him, as far as I can see, it is used exclusively as an adjective—grows out of his contemplation about the treasures hidden in the Lord Christ. Wisdom and love are hidden in the suffering and dying Christ, he thought. Hidden? Yes, for these treasures become visible only to "mystical and spiritual eyes."[4] Mystical theology is thus, according to Luther, the inner, spiritual side of Christian faith.

The dominant view of what it means "to know"

In order to understand the treatment that mysticism, in general, and Luther's mystical theology, in particular, have received, one must devote some attention to the theory of knowledge (epistemology), which underlies much scholarship. The epistemology accepted by most scholars is based on rationalism and intellectualism, the exclusive reliance on the witness of the senses and the accompanying use of logic emanating from empirical observation.

It is within this framework that leading theologians often attempt to deal with experiences of an invisible presence and power and awareness of Christ's presence. For such subjects, rationalism and intellectualism, taken in this order, are not of great help inasmuch as they tend to eliminate all phenomena that do not seem to fit the categories of ordinary everyday logic. Rationalism frequently becomes the skeptical antipode to assertions about the miraculous.

The rationalistic mindset insists that if theology is not going to be wholly emptied of its scholarly content, logical terms should be adequate to describe revelations of a Divine extra-phenomenal world. The rationalist's objection to the paranormal is that paranormal language doesn't appear to be "reasonable," "sound," or "understandable."

This is no doubt a valid protest inasmuch as language is most commonly used to convey ideas. Telepathic communication, for instance, has not been universally accepted as a mode of communication.

Now, it is a fact that the rational-linguistic designations can only proclaim and delimit; they do not, however, encompass the subject. Comprehension or understanding requires an assistance that rational propositions do not contribute. The assistance in question comes from an "endowment" within the human being that surpasses its reason. Man has his religious moments that reveal a congenital "drift" toward the beyond. In this presentation the reader will have to accept the fact that the author is of the opinion that we humans have a religious dimension, that the human being is a *homo religiosus*. Yes, in fact, we bear within us an image of our origin. One can safely state that such thoughts were not foreign to Martin Luther, the man who, in certain circumstances, seemed prone to speak about "the gospel of man's sinfulness," as is often pointed out. However, we must be aware that he was, in many respects, a paradoxical person.

Rudolph Otto (1869-1937) devoted much reflection to the tension between rationalism and the "inner knowledge" that recognizes and is familiar with the miraculous. He was convinced that the difference between rationalism and its opposite, the miraculous, is not that the rationalist does not recognize the miraculous. On the contrary, Otto notes that rationalists often create rational theories in an attempt to explain the miraculous. Anti-rationalists, on the other hand, often tend to be quite unconcerned about the very same miracles. The difference between the two types lies rather in their mental attitudes, Otto says. The question is whether one lets the rational dominate and excludes the non-rational, or permits the non-rational tyrannically to dominate the rational.

As used in this book, the definition of rationalism accords little or no room to the non-rational in religion. The symbols for powers and forces beyond the materialistic chain of events are interpreted either naturalistically or intellectually. This inclination toward rationalistic "elucidations" of happenings that defy logical explanations appears in many interpretations of Martin Luther's theology.

The thesis of the book and its three censors

This examination of the Reformer's theology of experience and its links to mystical elements is based on the following thesis: Martin Luther's consciousness of faith was, in essential regards, born of mystical experience. Western dependence on rationalism has obscured or entirely obliterated the mystical interpretation of this faith consciousness.

In other words: what rational theological thinking about God calls his faithfulness and his loving concern and the corresponding realities in man, faith and trust, are suffused with non-rational experiences of a Divine presence—experiences bordering on fear and awe, but there is also a touch of bliss.

When Luther spoke about God as residing in the heart of the believer, he was not only speaking objectively. He spoke from experience. The rational terms for unity between God and man took on meaning for Luther through mystical knowledge. But there were, and are, in Western intellectualism barriers that make it difficult to discover the intimate connection in Luther between educational concepts and those based on experience.

One could speak about three-fold censorship. In the course of this account, the three modes of censorship will become apparent here and there. In this introduction, however, it seems appropriate to treat this censorship as a unit.

First, much Luther research, when it encounters Luther's nomenclature, is inclined to emphasize the theological and logical differences between Protestantism and Roman Catholicism. Mysticism is not considered as having any central importance for non-Roman conceptions of faith and salvation and therefore the subject is discarded from the discussion.

Secondly, Melanchthon's successors interpreted Luther with the use of essentially logical thought categories. The result was that one made short shrift of the Reformer's mystical utterances. This is still true of those churches whose theology can be described as Protestant Scholastic and which belong to what, in church history texts, is generally called "the Lutheran school." Words like "saintliness" and "the wrath of God" carry a largely moralistic ring in those circles. One speaks of the law that chastises persons before they are ready for grace. In these circles there was, and is, little of the realization that both "holiness" and "wrath" can be symbols of the experience that God is present.[5]

Thirdly, during the eighteenth century and forward, theology was a captive of Newtonian scientific philosophy. This precluded doing justice to the supernatural and transrational in Luther's world of thought. Within a thought structure that has no room for anything but the principle of causality, mechanistically understood, it becomes difficult, not to say impossible, to seriously consider the possibility that, in Word and sacrament, Luther experienced faith in the same manner that characterized, in many ways, several of the mystics whom Luther read.

Concerning this third form of "censorship" perhaps a little digression will be permitted. We are here concerned with "modern" man's intellectualism, rooted in the Renaissance and the Enlightenment. We "modern" persons live in a tension between the Renaissance and Enlightenment's concentration on the intellect and a new wave of mysticism, in a broad sense, inclusive of discoveries about the power of the mental over the material. We are also experiencing the miraculous in a new sense.[6]

Renaissance man sought to conquer the world through vigorous exertion of his intellect and he should be honored for that. The machine has been the weapon of conquest. And, almost coincidentally, applied the dream of complete mastery also to that of man's inner world, his total being, his natural instincts, and his intuition. For instance, one wanted to streamline psychology with the help of the mechanistic model —without much success. However, it is true that the world has gained from the insights of Renaissance man and Enlightenment man and technology is certainly here to stay. And yet, there is no doubt that the Renaissance ideal undervalues man's non-intellectual gifts, instincts, feelings, the realm of the intuitive, and there is the assumption that the intellect must totally dominate the non-rational. The ideal is a world—including a person's inner world—under the aegis of the intellect to such an extent that no consideration can be given to the non-rational.

Since World War II we have experienced a strong protest against this reverence for the intellectual. The protest has expressed itself in a growing interest in the mystical and in mystics. Without necessarily clothing this protest in words this has been, nevertheless, precisely a protest against a future where intellectualism continues to hold sway. The majority among the guardians of culture has found it worrisome that this should be the case. It looks like a return to Nazism's and Bolshevism's disastrous flirt with the irrational or subhuman. However, we must understand the revolt as a revolt against intellectualism's all-encompassing, totalitarian claim. This claim is just as precarious as the claim to complete supremacy of the impulses. It is dangerous and insufficient for two reasons.

First, persons of the Renaissance or Enlightenment tradition usually do not accept the "primitive" as an essential part of man. Included in what one regards as the primitive is also the religious bent. "Modern man" is considered to be emancipated from that superstition.

Secondly, in the name of reasonableness, the intellectualistic tradition rejects every hint of impulses from a world that is not connected with the empirical.

Many theological investigations of the meaning of Divine revelation have operated and operate within the Renaissance and the Enlightenment tradition. Thus, theological reflection labors under the conviction that one can only capture the theological by rational ideas or thinking. This persuasion leads to a complete destitution of the aspect of devotion, the unspeakable longing and sighing, the non-rational impulses in the discipleship of Christ that accompanies God's search for us and our search for God.

One can call this limitation theology's dependence on the cultural milieu. But then one has to keep in mind that thinking about God has always taken color from what is acceptable in any given milieu and has borrowed leading premises about the possible. In the present case, one can say that influences from the intellectualists and rationalists of this age preclude much theological investigation from a more generous appreciation of the personal and subjective in Martin Luther's world of thought and his life. An exclusive intellectualization of the messages of our prophets almost always results in toning down the significance of the non-rational, the mystical wellspring of their message. It keeps on flowing, but the noise of machines suffocates its sound.

On the other hand—and this must be said emphatically—the exhortation to give some weight to the reports about the non-rational sources of Luther's life and thought is not equivalent to a defense of the irrational. The emphasis simply means that it would be wise to take note: the concept of the Divine often falters, but the feeling for the

Divine lingers as an osmosis. The experience of a supersensible presence is always, in some respect, characteristic of true faith.

One ought not to put this on the same level as subjective emotions. Luther often used the word *fühlen* (to feel) when he wanted to describe the work and presence of the Spirit. In his struggle against "the Enthusiasts" he showed what he meant by this. He meant what in English is called "feeling" in contradistinction to "emotionalism."

An examination of Luther's mystical inclinations may perchance be interpreted as an attempt at thinking theologically about a matter that has already been declared impervious to conceptualization. But surely reason has to be utilized and certainly one must apply the intellect to experiences of faith, from wherever these experiences emanate. Mystics have always returned from the outer limits and sought verbally to express the unfathomable.

The task of theology, wrote **Rudolf Otto**, is to "deepen the rational meaning of the Christian conception of God by permeating it with its non-rational elements."[7] I do not know who was responsible for the formulation of the English title of Otto's book *Das Heilige* (literally, The Holy). Note that the English title is *The Idea of the Holy.* "The **Idea**"—this implies that we cannot manage without ideas, without stressing mental conceptions.

Organization and method

Two decades ago when I ventured into the field of this investigation with the publication of *Luther and the Mystics* (1976), I thought, in the first place, that the result would be a debate about the question of what constitutes "knowledge," with special consideration given to Luther's theology. Therefore the theological interpretations of Luther's faith constituted Part I of the book.

When I expanded and revised that work for publication in Swedish, I placed the debate with well-known theologians in Part III and abbreviated it. For the new version, I begin Part I with some anecdotal glimpses of Luther's personal experience of the reality of the beyond. Following, in Part II, is an examination of Luther's views on God, man and salvation.

Consequently, the method will be as follows. We peruse first Luther's own words about the reality of the invisible and his experiences in this respect. Then the searchlight is trained on certain theological words and the way in which Luther's personal, spiritual experiences have influenced their meaning. The manner in which the theological world has treated contacts with mystics and expressions about the Divine presence comprises the last part of the book. A summary concludes that section.

A special methodological question is worth some additional lines. As mentioned, Martin Luther did not devote much time to definitions of mysticism. He called the mystical side of faith "experimental" (try it and see how it works) and "experiential" (without feeling it will not amount to much). And he combined the experimental and experiential with the "inner" side of God's gift: justification by faith in Christ. Then the way we deal with our primary subject, mysticism—namely, medieval mysticism—will be significant. The literature on the subject shows two vastly different methods, both from strictly dogmatic angles. In general Protestants apply a frame of reference which excludes the thought of the "indwelling" Christ and concentrates on Christ's deed as grafted, in other words man cannot, in any sense, assert that he has cooperated in or facilitated the act. Roman Catholic research, on the contrary, reckons with a gradual process, advanced by means of acquired and infused grace.

Another viewpoint with respect to the question of the treatment of medieval mysticism and its connection to Luther has to do with phenomenology. Some students of the subject in question seek to find overlapping areas between medieval mystics and Luther. Consequently one draws conclusions after comparing sundry phenomena.

A third approach is the generic one. One categorizes the different mystical authors in whom Luther showed interest. The captions over the categories suggest the general direction of thought, e.g., what the individual in question thinks about the human's kinship to God or what salvation signifies.

The first method, the dogmatic version, would be of little benefit for our purpose. Its use would lock one into preconceived categories.

The second method, the phenomenological, is appropriated here, with a couple of necessary modifications. If one searches for phenomena of mystical purport, common to both the mystics and Luther, one soon encounters the fact that the word "mysticism" is used to describe so many religious attitudes that a common denominator could be meaningless. In this survey the phenomenological approach is going be used while in constant contact with Luther's basic theological tenet, justification through faith.

Lastly, the generic method grows partly out of Luther's own suggestions. Here it will be combined with the phenomenological aspect.

One must, however, be somewhat wary in this regard since the categorizing of medieval mystics does not always do justice to a particular mystic. It frequently happens that, in one context, Luther cites a certain mystic with approval and, in another context, with disapproval. It all depends on the matter that is being discussed. In neither case should one assume that the entire thought system of the mystic in question receives Luther's imprimatur or merits the scrap heap. When it comes to the generic method Luther's teaching about "justification by faith" will be our lodestar. For him this phrase was both experience and dogma.

PART I

LUTHER AND THE REALITY OF THE INVISIBLE

God, my conveyor of promise, loves me,
takes care of me, will listen to me.
I experience this as something that is present
although it is invisible.

Martin Luther
W 43; 554, 30-35 (1545) *LW* 5; 183
(Author's translation)

CHAPTER ONE

ABOUT ANGELS AS HELPERS AND SPOILERS

When we understand the proper place of angels, we will thank God for them.

Martin Luther, *W* 32; 11 (1535)

Good angels and demons

Perhaps because Luther regarded what he called "the historical faith" insufficient, as such, he never tired of pointing out the mystery of faith by referring to God's influence on our lives as "invisible." One might have thought that religious truth would hardly require that designation. But with Luther, and in many biblical testimonies, one frequently sees just this descriptive adjective when religious trust needs to be anchored, so to speak.

God sees in the invisible, Luther pointed out in a sermon on Psalm I, "Blessed is the man who walks not in the counsel of the ungodly." You think that you can avoid his gaze, but that is impossible. The same is true about faith. Faith sees into the invisible. Perhaps the soul is surrounded by the dark world, but faith **sees.**[8]

Psalm 18:11-12 speaks about the darkness with which God hides his glory, but remembers that the glowing fire with which he pierces the clouds emanates from his unspeakable glory. Not to see and yet to see it all —this is God's way with us. Luther applies this metaphor to man's faith. It is, namely, the same with faith. It sees nothing and yet it sees everything. God rules through the written word and through the spoken word, but those who rely on the external word alone possess merely one part of the gospel. The just have faith in the depths of their hearts. To live in the invisible is to trust in God, yes even when outwardly everything appears to be very distressful so that nothing that one sees would seem to confirm faith's vision.[9]

The Word, as Luther saw it, was not only an historical document, but also God's eternal, spiritual self-revelation. In the same manner it is not only an enumeration of facts about redemption, but the Spirit's not only an enumeration of facts about redemption, but the Spirit's invisible influence. When Luther explained Heb. 11:1, "Now faith is the substance of things hoped for, the evidence of things not seen," he emphasized, as was his wont, that when one is involved with God, one is also involved in faith in the invisible.[10]

The oft-used word "invisible" about God and the supersensible sphere was, as it were, a sounding board. Martin Luther was aware of being guarded and watched and led and used by invisible forces.

He writes that after his partly failed conversation with Cardinal Cajetan in Augsburg he lived in both "fear and hope." The pope was threatening with the ban and exile that would be enacted via the dukes. But he felt protected under the canopy of angels. "Many great men" asked him if his tribulations were not overwhelming, but he was able to reply truthfully, "I am filled with joy and peace."[11]

In one of the table talks there is a comment about Erasmus of Rotterdam that breathes the same reverence and expectation. Luther sometimes experienced a foretaste of a greater joy that is being prepared. He could speak about this future like a child. Erasmus, he said, had for some reason become convinced that God was very far away, if he existed at all. He, Erasmus, apparently did not believe that life continues after death. Luther opined that he could not understand this. Erasmus was, after all, a creature of the spirit, but he apparently was as sure in his theological agnosticism "as I know that I see."[12]

In a letter that he wrote from the Wartburg during his "Patmos-year," as he called it, we read about the living Christ who at the moment is hiding but surely he has something in store for him, Martinus. "I am a strange prisoner. I sit here both willingly and unwillingly: willingly, since the Lord wants it this way."[13]

In another letter from the Wartburg, addressed to Melanchthon, he speaks about the unfathomable in fate:

> But who knows whether Christ does not wish to accomplish more by this plan, not only in my case but also in all others? We spoke so many times of faith and hope for the things not seen! Come on, let's test at least once a small part of [Christ's] teaching, since things have come to pass this way at the call of God and not through our doing.[14]

It became clear soon enough for those who met and got to know Martin Luther that he lived in contact with the invisible and that his charismatic emanation had something to do with this awareness. In a pamphlet against Carlstadt, pastor and author E. Alberus wrote that, in his opinion, Luther was a true prophet. "He could turn away God's wrath. No one could more tenaciously and more seriously pray and appeal to God, no one could comfort better."[15]

When Luther was imagining the universe in the hands of good and evil, he thought in terms of personal, invisible entities. The devil ruled over the dark and evil powers, black angels, small devils, and demons. Thanks to the power that flowed and flows from the work of Christ this evil gang possesses no ultimate power, but can certainly cause a lot of unhappiness and misfortune.[16]

According to Luther there are in the world hierarchies of spirits, saints, and helpful angels. They are Christ's messengers to the world. The closer a Christian gets to Christ, the more energetic and cunning "the evil angels" become in their attempt to destroy what has been built up through communion with Christ. One could say that they can be likened to the obsessed in the land of the Gerasenes; they smell catastrophe for their cause at the approach of Christ. From his time at the Wartburg, where he seems to have been more spiritually sensitive than either before or after, Luther wrote to his worldly protector:

> You know that I have the gospel, not from men but only from heaven through our Lord Jesus Christ. The devil read my heart very well when I came to Worms. He knew that even if there had been as many devils as there are tiles on the roofs, I would cheerfully have jumped right into their midst.[17]

But just as there is a personalized world of entities that work against God and feed on all kinds of human lust, there is also a spiritual counterpole in good angelic forces. These protective angels see us when we die, remarked Luther in connection with some comments about the need for the confession of sin. Each person has an angel, of that he was sure. And Christ stands above the host of good angels, which guarantees that the dark forces will not ultimately win.[18]

We are the objects of loving attention from the invisible during our sojourn on this earth. So, for example, the souls of the departed can be aware of their loved ones who survive on earth. In the beginning of the year of his death, Luther wrote the following to a clergyman in Bremen:

> I shall pray for you, and I ask that you pray for me. Just as I have no doubt that your prayer is effective in my life, so I have no doubt that my prayer will be effective for you. If I depart this life ahead of you —something I desire —then I

must pull you after me. If you depart before me, then you shall pull me after you. For we confess one God and with all saints we abide in our Savior.[19]

In September 1530, in the little chapel of Coburg Castle, Luther preached one of his sermons about the world of angels. It was published as a booklet in 1535. This section will be concluded with a short delineation of the contents of this publication. In this context we will engage in a discussion with a skeptical nineteenth century theologian concerning the place of angelology in evangelical thought.

In the beginning of his authorship, the German church historian and dogmatician **Emanuel Hirsch** (1888-1972) embraced a view of Luther that made it possible for him to describe pietists like Spener, Francke, and Zinzendorf as "Luther's true disciples." However, later he found it necessary, with the aid of historical criticism's yardstick, to crystallize Luther's message in the following manner. Hirsch discovered a number of "impurities" and "contaminations" that had to be removed so that it would be possible to detect Luther's "central" concerns. According to Hirsch those concerns coincided with the results of critical research.[20]

Angelology appeared to be one of the "contaminations." Hirsch undertook to interpret, for a "modern" forum, Luther's angelology. The interpretation runs briefly as follows.

Only through faith can one discern Christ in his role as servant. Angels, radiant entities serving God, do not stand in the way for such a faith. But they might be a temptation for humans. When bringing the message that Jesus was born in Bethlehem, their presence does not guarantee that Jesus was the son of a virgin, nor that Jesus was God's only begotten son, descending from the heavens. We stand here before holy mysteries that can become real and meaningful only through faith. Martin Luther believed in Jesus neither on the basis of the dogma that God became man nor on the basis of the assertion regarding the virgin birth. How does one deal with such events? Hirsch answers: "They are helpful thoughts." However, faith in Jesus and the gospel must not be permitted to be drowned in "miracle-lore."

Hirsch delimits his theology in two directions. First, he states that Luther did not believe in Jesus based on the dogma of God's becoming flesh. That is the same as a demarcation line between traditional, orthodox Lutheranism and the more "liberal" kind. Secondly, he says that the stories about angels are only helpful thoughts. This is delimitation from the mystical.

Concerning Hirsch's first objection, it can perhaps be described as an existentialist's attempt to replace, on behalf of Luther, the external symbols for God becoming man with an existential realization through faith. This is almost a distortion of Luther's thoughts about the external signs of God's action through Christ. It was a matter of "history," asserted Luther, and it is important that the wonderful really happened in time and place.

At point number two, Hirsch's rationalism becomes especially apparent. He dismisses angelology as folklore and miracle-tradition, and assumes that he has thereby lifted out Martin Luther's central concern. That central concern was an effort to peel away everything that had to do with mysticism and the metaphysical. Just as in modern critical research, Luther was constantly in the process of eliminating "impurities," that is to say, eliminating the metaphysical, according to Hirsch.

Hirsch focused his attention on **one** fact and isolated it. It is, namely, a fact that Martin Luther assailed the use that the Roman Church made of the belief in angels. Angels and saints became the mediators between man and Christ. Christ was not at the center any more. But from Luther's serious protest to Hirsch's total rejection of the belief in angels, there is indeed a gigantic step.

Now we are back in Coburg's castle chapel. On the Feast of Saint Michael, the 29th of September 1530, Luther preached on the subject of angels. It was not his only sermon on angels. But it was the only one that he had published separately. The publication appeared in 1535.[21]

In this sermon one finds nothing of the psychologizing that Hirsch ascribes to Martin Luther. Among other things, Luther says: "Some say that spirits do not exist. If we really believed that they exist, we would not live in such false security." Without knowing it people "become possessed" by dark angels. He continues:

> But when opinions about angels emerge from popular lore without insight into the purpose for which angels are ordained, then confusion ensues. . . . But we do not observe the Festival [the Feast of Saint Michael] for angel worship's sake. We observe it because in this way we come to know what angels after all do and what their work and office is, for which they are ordained.
>
> When we know the true place of angels, then we also begin to thank God for them. We do so by the same token as we thank Him for having created the sun and the moon, for creating

> and giving peace, unity, justice and whatever else is good in the world. That is to say, we see for what purpose all his works are ordained and what they are intended to be.... We should, in other words, simply perceive them as created and ordained by God. . . . As a consequence, each person must certainly sense and know within himself that there are angels—and not only good angels but also evil ones.... But, although there are many devils with wicked desires in their minds, we must now know, on the other hand, that good angels abound. They defend, guard and keep.... Well, I must keep to the word and say: "Dear God, you know what the enemy has in mind, send your holy angel and put a limit to the foe." ... For as a child is beholden to its parents..., so are we under the protection of the angels and beholden to them.[22]

Luther's teaching about angels gives a picture of the Reformer's dynamic opinion about the relationship between the visible and invisible, between the sensate and supersensible, between the natural and supernatural. In the material world humans are intertwined with beings in the nonmaterial world.

The human drama is being acted out on a battlefield where a struggle is being fought, not only between good and evil forces in the human's physical being, but also between creatures in the world of our senses and beings in a supernatural world. When we are in stressful situations, succor also comes from the beyond. If one can open oneself for possession of unclean spirits from the other realm, one can likewise open oneself to God's "indwelling." We always have to remind ourselves, Luther points out that, "the dear good angels are much wiser than the wicked angels."

As is apparent, there is quite a difference between Emanuel Hirsch's "modernization" of Luther's angelology and Luther's own view of the subject. The modernized version lacks what the theologian **Karl Barth** (1886-1968) calls "God-oriented imagination."

For Luther the angelic is a dotted line from this life to the next one. To him angels are supernatural helpers, not more, but as such they are important and carry out work on Christ's behalf. That they are not normally observable, in the ordinary sense, did not create any greater difficulty for Luther. He continuously assumed that faith itself moves in an "invisible" realm. In this invisible world live beings who contribute with power through faith. As we have seen, the link between the visible and the invisible also includes the possibility of demon possession, that is to say, a kind of "invasion" of the angels of darkness. Life on earth always means that you can, if you wish, untune your soul, so to speak, down to the disharmony of the demons. The obverse is also true: one can always open up to the music that wells up around Christ and his angels in these spheres. Neutrality, in the line of action and in the line of thought that our natural man hopes for, does not exist. Like all great prophets, Luther had seen this and knew this.

Consequently, one totally misses Luther's thoughts about the angelic if one assigns angels, both the light and the dark ones, to the realm of "helpful thoughts," as Hirsch and many with him do. Instead, on good grounds, Luther counted with an ever-living communication between the sensate and the supersensible. That means, among other things, that energy from the beyond permeates our here and now, and this often turns our self-sufficient attitude, i.e., relying only on the testimony of our five senses, on its head.

Rationalistically influenced thinkers hear Luther say that purified Christianity rightly has eliminated angelology and this type of thinking invites him to be the honorary president of the association. Rather, what Luther wanted to say is that the angels who surround Christ, the Lord of our cosmos, certainly do not want to be worshipped, but are acting as sub-leaders in invisible realms and, as such, are indispensable for the management of the visible realm in which we move. The fact that such a view of the matter cannot be accepted in theological circles requires a broader and more profound discussion. We stand here before the fact that "religious supernaturalism" is regarded with skepticism or is summarily rejected by much critical research.

The premise behind this version of Luther's teaching concerning angels which is discussed here is that, up to the scientific era, biblical interpretation and Christian reflection were informed by a pre-scientific world view and the conviction that there was a sacred context in the universe. This supposition embraced the belief in hierarchies of invisible beings and a secret connection between life here and life there. Now the modern world-view has designated such concepts as "metaphysical," in the sense that they cannot be verified empirically and therefore must be relegated to the realm of superstition and hallucination. In order not to offend those of "simple faith," euphemistic terms like "helpful thoughts" or "psychological metaphors" are used. Under these circumstances, the task of theology is to concentrate on those aspects of the gospel and on gospel interpretations, such as some of Luther's, which are regarded as universal and in harmony with sound judgment and modern thought.

Theological mystical insight has found these rationalistic contributions both constructive and destructive. They are constructive in the sense that they point to the need for constant theological sensitivity to changes in man's external conditions. They also underline the incarnational character of the Christian life. This is not wholly without significance and one has to concede that Luther's application of the gospel was formed by a culture and a society partly founded on ideas that man has now outgrown. But the rationalistic contributions have also been destructive to the degree that they have limited man to himself and found no occasion to reckon with the border-crossing impulse and the possibility that it is an echo from a supersensible original home.

The consequence has been that the rationalistic mind approaches biblical and Christian-historical narratives about supernatural, paranormal events in the illusion that they represent supernatural **ideas**, concepts that do not coincide with natural **ideas**. Everything is intellectualized. But these stories are more than mere ideas. They call us to a "before" and to an "after" and beckon us toward spiritual nourishment without which life is lost. Exclusive intellectualization shies away from even a hint that non-rational forces are at work.

However, one cannot entirely get away from the belief that God's revelation contains paranormal elements. "Modern" thought will not be able to remove them without distorting the meaning of revelation. The paranormal in faith's linkage with God belongs to the constantly developing history of God's incarnation. This is proved by a not always observed fact, namely, that the theological intellectualism that otherwise rules out reports about the miraculous and the angelic is inclined to regard the resurrection of Jesus as a bona fide occurrence—a miracle, if anything is.

When Luther took angels seriously as part of the unseen realm where faith lives and breathes, he was not simply under the sway of medieval superstition. On the contrary, as Karl Barth has pointed out, belief in angels is an intrinsic part of "the theme of the Christian faith." In many respects Barth is a Calvinist who debates Luther, but with respect to the teachings about the invisible helpers and spoilers, he is an ally of the Reformer. Angels, he writes, possess an original gestalt and form in Scriptural accounts. Scripture does not regard them as absurdities or curiosities that can be replaced with our own inventions. We will probably survive as Christians and as churches, Barth continues, without conscious resort to the angelic world, but "only at a pinch . . . not without hurt and not without the underlying awareness that something is missing."

Barth called angels objective and authentic witnesses to God's deed through Jesus Christ. It was his conviction that, without angels, God himself would not have been revealed, would not have been perceptible. When God passed over the angels and became human in Christ the angels entered the human sphere together with the Savior.

As we shall see later on in this book, Barth did not think much of Christian mysticism. He considered it to be mostly human-oriented instead of Christ-oriented. According to him, mysticism could not possibly be a piece of Christian revelation. But in the case of angelology he was indeed positive, providing that angelology be subordinated under Christology.

Martin Luther must have been in Karl Barth's thoughts when he wrote down his thoughts about the angelic. Luther was, in Barth's opinion, a good advocate of true angelology. Barth reminds his readers of the "unforgettable conclusion of the evening blessing in Luther's *Small Catechism*: 'May thy holy angel be with me, that the evil foe may have no power over me. Amen.' And then quickly and happily to sleep." Barth added: "This sentence contains the whole doctrine of angels *in nuce* and decisively so on account of the address: 'Thy holy angel'."[23]

Luther was convinced that angels rule in invisible worlds, under God's dominion, that there are light and dark angels, that we can be "apostates from God to angels" and that the holy angels serve God.

Ingemar Franck's investigation about the doctrine of angels in preaching devotes special attention to Luther's opinion. He points out that the Reformer "in contradistinction to Dionysius and other theological teachers . . . preaches that God gives [the light] angels the task of protecting and helping humans even during their life on earth."[24] Their praise before God's throne does not exclude their actions of succor when our death is imminent.

One might ask if such ideas are only theoretical, dogmatic "supernaturalism" or the result of humans' experiences of angels, hence corroboration of biblical information.

Luther's personal psychic-spiritual experiences

It must be emphasized that Martin Luther seldom or never used personal "revelations" or experiences to enhance or, perchance, to strengthen some argument in a sermon. Even in this regard he shows his discrimination. He knew that a personal subjective account of a psychic-spiritual experience soon enough loses its original impact both for the speaker-writer and the hearers and readers. But there is no doubt about the fact that Luther's faith was suffused with the feelings which the seeker gets in the numinous presence of God and on those occasions when both good and evil "powers," in other ways, break through the wall between the "world beyond" and the everyday world.

We begin by posing a question about Luther's thoughts about prayer.

The little pamphlet, *How To Pray*, provides good insight. One cannot say many flattering things about "jabber prayer," Luther writes to his friend, Peter, the barber. The barber had been exiled from Wittenberg because, while intoxicated, he had killed a relative. In a conversation with Dr. Martin, Peter, the barber, complained about his inability to pray. Moved by this comment, Luther penned his advice. During his years in the monastery he had heard enough "jabber prayer" as it was practiced by devotees of the rosary. Instead Luther wanted to recommend inner, concentrated prayer, "a conversation from heart to heart," as he expressed it. It becomes a sort of internal vision, he suggests, but it should be part of "a methodical contemplation." The praying person ought to avoid themes that amount to a sentimental passion meditation or discourse. Nor ought one (in this case the barber—Luther was writing the advice specifically for him) devote oneself to exercises related to visions about hell or paradise. No, he would be better served by solid means: the Lord's Prayer, the Commandments, one of the Psalms, or "several of Christ's words or of Saint Paul."[25]

One ought to surround these texts with periods of contemplation, place their contents before oneself, and immerse oneself in their message. Then one will feel something, Luther contends. He writes: "Warm the heart and render praying enjoyable, filled with desire, that is the purpose of Our Father." But, certainly, the Lord's Prayer can be expressed in other words, "with more or fewer words. I myself do not pay too much attention to fixed terms or habitual phrases, it is one way today and another way tomorrow, it all depends on how warm and filled of longing I feel."

Thus it is obvious that Luther attached considerable importance to the need for feeling. In the little document that is cited here he says the following about "ecstatic"—a word one does not usually associate with the Reformer. However, as a matter of fact, *ecstasis* is a significant theological word in his writings. It implies that the worshiper, the person engaged in prayer and contemplation, is lifted out of himself and experiences Divine peace and joy.

> Frequently, when I come to a certain part of Our Father or to a petition, I sink into such rich thoughts that I abandon all set prayers. When such rich, good thoughts arrive, then one should leave the other commandments aside and offer room to those thoughts and listen in stillness and, for all the world, not put up obstructions. For then the Holy Spirit himself is preaching and one word of his sermon is better than a thousand of our prayers. I have also learned more from one such prayer than I would have received from much reading and writing.[26]

In connection with preparatory meditation around the commandments, Luther offered additional glimpses from his experience of the invisible through "inner prayer." In his inimitable fashion he proposed that

> If the Holy Spirit would come in the course of such thoughts [methodical preparation for worshipful prayer] and begins to preach in your heart with rich, illumined thoughts, do him the honor, let these rationally formulated (*gefasste*) thoughts, reflections and meditations fade away. Be still and listen for he [the Holy Spirit] knows better than you. And what he preaches note that and write it down. In this way you will experience miracles.[27]

One is usually amused and slightly embarrassed about stories that Luther told at the dinner table and, on other occasions, about encounters with devils or the devil.

Various psychological theories have been advanced in attempts to find immanent behavioral roots to Luther's "hallucinations." We should, however, consider if clairaudial and clairvoyant phenomena do, in fact, enter our sensate world from invisible dimensions—that they are not merely imagination or a distortion of the senses. This is a matter worthy of reflection because the experiences of Old Testament prophets, of Jesus, and of his disciples can be described in contemporary parapsychological terminology. Perhaps what we have here are combinations of paranormal invasions and psychological influences. In other words, the voices and visions very possibly symbolize or sum up human situations and, at the same time, they can be the result of influences from a super-human reality. Perhaps we can be permitted to interpret, in this way, the following account from Luther's "captivity" at the Wartburg:

> Two good lads, who brought me food and drink twice a day . . . had brought me a bag of hazelnuts which I ate on occasion, and I placed the bag in a closed box . . . I turned out the light at night . . . and went to bed. Then the hazelnuts came down upon me . . . one after the other smashes against the rafters mighty hard. I am rattled in my bed. . . . I fell asleep briefly, then it begins to make such a noise in the staircase as though someone were throwing a bunch of vats down the steps. But I knew that the staircase was well protected with chains and irons, so that no one could get up. Yet so many vats were falling. I get up, go to the stairs to see what is up. But the staircase was locked. And I said: If it is you, so be it. And surrendered myself to the Lord Christ.[28]

The devil could sometimes take the form of an animal in Luther's visions. "I looked from my cell window," he recalled, "and saw a big black sow running over the courtyard of the castle. But no swine could come into the courtyard. It was the devil."

"Once I saw a dog in my bed. . . . I threw him out through the window. He did not bark. Next morning I asked whether there were any dogs in the castle and the warden said no. Then it must be the devil, said I."

"Believe me," Luther wrote in a letter, "I am subjected to a thousand devils (*Satanibus*) in this uneventful solitude. It is so much easier to combat the incarnated devil, that is to say, people, than evil spirits in celestial realms."[29]

The diabolical must be taken seriously, but not to the extent that one forgets that Christ is stronger.[30] In contradistinction to several present-day exegetes, Luther interpreted Ephesians 6:12-13 and Col. 2:15 as statements about dark forces outside human life. The human is always the subject of their attention, and they take advantage of every opportunity. "The forces of evil in the heavenly spheres"—this was an assertion about metaphysical dimensions. "The princes of the spiritual world" was, to Luther, an expression of metaphysical reality.[31]

The animals referred to above naturally have psychological connotations, but the incidents were also echoes from the metaphysical. It is biblical to assume that a person who is very obedient also becomes the object of attacks on the part of those whose main endeavor seems to be to undo the victories of God's righteousness. Some of these forces must be supernatural.

To return to Paul's words in his letter to the Ephesians, where he spoke about spiritual hosts, one can safely assume that they were more than "helpful thoughts and psychological metaphors" to both Paul and Luther. They were, and are, part of the invisible dimensions. We would do well not to be too supercilious when interpreting Paul's words. "There are more things in heaven and earth, Horatio, than are dreamt of in your philosophy" (*Hamlet*). It is self-evident that the same holds true of the more cheerful and more encouraging visions in Luther's life, the intuited encounters with and meditation about the light angels.

Swedish Archbishop **Nathan Söderblom** (1866-1931) writes that Luther must have had a vision at the age of 22, when he promised Saint Anna during a thunderstorm that he would become a monk. The promise, Söderblom suggests, "had come about in a vision. Perhaps God had spoken . . . through one of his holy ones."[32] During a conversation between Luther and Cochlaeus in 1521 at Worms the subject was, among other things, personal visions. They had before them this passage from Paul: "If a revelation is made to another sitting by, let the first be silent" (I Cor. 14:30). Cochlaeus asked Luther: "Have you had a revelation?" Martin Luther looked at him for a moment and answered: "*Est mihi revelatum.*" Yes, he had had revelations.[33]

It is apparent that Luther had clairaudial and clairvoyant experiences. No doubt he also experienced precognition at some junctures in his life, even if it was not a central concern of his. In the beginning of 1532 Luther became seriously ill. His doctors talked about apoplexy and declared that he probably would not recover. At four o'clock one morning Luther felt a strong roar in his ears along with great pain. A powerful depression gripped his heart. He sent for Melanchthon and Rörer. They were of the opinion that the papists would surely be pleased if the leader of their movement died. That little remark seems to have brought Luther back to life again. From his sick room he announced:

> I shall not die this time, I am certain. I feel that God will not strengthen the hateful cause of the papists by letting me die now. . . . Satan would be happy to see me dead; he is constantly treading on my heels, but he will not be gratified. God's will alone must be done. He controls all things.[34]

Certainly it was a kind of precognition when he uttered at the beginning of his last lecture series: "I shall linger over the exposition of this book and shall die in the process of doing so." He began with the commentary on Genesis in 1535 and finished it, three months before his death, in 1546. Could it be that he spent eleven years over this work in the conviction that it would be his last commentary?[35]

The year of 1538, Luther predicted, would be an evil and perilous one. He based this prediction on two conditions: one a natural and the other a spiritual. The natural condition, said Luther, was a conjunction of Saturn and Mars. He was not especially fond of astrology, but apparently he had listened to Melanchthon this time. The spiritual cause for the bad year was people's increasing wantonness. It so happened that it was a bad year for Luther. He suffered from serious stomach troubles, had to walk with a cane because of problems with a foot, had constant pain in one of his arms, and was forced to spend time in bed on account of fever.

One could have expected predictions from Martin Luther because of his parapsychological sensitivity. He had not a few experiences of the paranormal. It is actually a waste of time to try to make him into one of the heralds of the modern era. He knew what he was talking about when he declared that we humans are living in an energy field between heaven and hell and that those forces extend into realms that are inaccessible to our five senses.

Luther's spiritual experiences deal with worlds beyond this life—both hostile and friendly. Some of his experiences of the benign sort had strengthened his faith in the same way as Paul was strengthened through the clairvoyant or clairaudial experience at Damascus. Without them the Christian faith would have become only an intellectual game. Luther used paranormal references only sparingly in his preaching. The reason grew directly out his communing with the Holy Spirit in prayer and meditation. *Homo mendax*, man's ego-centered "I", tends to convert the extraordinary pieces of new spiritual insights into trophies, which he then proudly exhibits. In addition, it was, and still is, true that some forms of "occultism" are destructive.

CHAPTER TWO

OCCULTISM AND SPIRITUAL HEALING

The person of senses, the person of reason, and the spiritual person are all **one** *person. The first three commandments prepare us for God, so that in heart, speech, and labor we rest in God —that is to say, with respect to the outer, the inner, and the core of the person, in other words, the senses, mind, and spirit. And then pure peace rules.*

Martin Luther, *W* 1; 436, 20 (1518)

Rejection of magical occultism

Luther knew, from his own experience, that human beings, whether they recognize it or not, are linked to invisible forces. But his rebirth through the grace of Christ made him doubly suspicious of any endeavor to attain salvation or achieve power by occult manipulations. This healthy suspicion becomes quite clear already during the early Reformation years when he had to fight against the kind of mysticism that speaks the language of self-salvation. About this he writes: if you wish to soar into heaven, you can easily plunge to the ground.[36] Dionysius, one of the mystics about whom Luther was doubtful, does not seem to have discovered Christ, in Luther's opinion. "Put your trust in Christ . . . Dionysius' mystical theology is sheer nonsense."[37]

He rejects, without further ado, magic via invisible sources of power. Magic implies that one seeks to gain an end or exert one's will by means of magical words and gestures. This only proves the undeniable truth that man is "curved in upon himself."[38]

Of course, Luther harbored no doubt about God being able to perform miracles, but he always made a distinction between the outer miracle and the inner, lest the outer miracle would turn out to be a magic trick. The main question was what God wanted to accomplish with this miracle. That question brings us to the essential: the matter of inner behavior, repentance, and salvation. Miracles belong to the nonessential; they are nothing but "apples and nuts for children." They lead nowhere as far as salvation is concerned.

Luther pointed out that the devil deludes people to believe that they are experiencing real miracles when in fact they were performed by the potentate himself. "I am saying this lest you believe in all kinds of miracles and signs." As we know, Deuteronomy speaks of false prophets and II Corinthians speaks about the miracles of the Anti-Christ. One must judge all miracles and wonders in the light of God's Word. Luther gave his friends the advice that

> If anyone directs you to any help other than the doctrine and the works of Lord Jesus Christ, you can conclude freely that this is the devil's work and his false miracles, by means of which he deceives and misguides you, just as he had done so far under the name of Mary and the saints where Christ was never known and taught aright. . . . Christ alone performs true, divine signs and wonders.[39]

A Christianity that concentrates on miracles is a rather fragile Christianity. "Miracles, of course, are still the least significant works, since they are physical and performed for only a few people."[40]

Although on occasion he made exceptions, Luther believed that all attempts to forecast the future were not biblical. Only God sees into the future. As the Holy Writ says, not even the Son of Man knows the times and the seasons (Acts 1:7); hence Luther viewed astrology with considerable suspicion. He thought that it stood in the way of preaching about sin and grace. No God-oriented techniques can attain salvation. Only God's righteousness and our will do. One often tries different paths. The devil is always conscious about our spiritual situation and plans. He does not mind at all if we would break our neck by our actions. But one is not so easily deceived, if one keeps to Christ, who is in his church—his "mystical body."[41]

Now, one should not be permitted to think that because Luther rejected contact with the invisible, i.e., contact that was not rooted in Christ, he therefore rejected the reality of the invisible. To be saved through justification means that one has become a conscious part of a supersensible energy field, become aware of it—for prior to this one was still unconsciously, with or without willing it, an "extra" in the drama. As we have already stated, Luther was very aware that there can be no neutrality in our daily living. Every significant explorer in the world of Spirit knows that we must make choices constantly.

In Luther's thought about revelation, the "public" external confession of faith had a "private" inner counterpart. The way in which he, in the name of Christ, made claim to power from invisible dimensions gave hints as to the depth of the spring that rippled far below the surface.

Healing and deliverance

In another context in this book there will be an opportunity to discuss further Martin Luther's opinion about the wholeness that flows out of the freedom that ensues being "righted with God." It is then that distortions of many kinds can be rectified, for Christ's healing power makes straight that which was crooked. This healing and unifying process includes the entire man: body, soul and spirit.

It comes as a slight shock, not least in staunch Lutheran circles, when one draws attention to Luther's utterances which show that this theologian who, in many descriptions has become the prototype for earth-bound spiritual power, was, in the case of spiritual healing, an advocate of reliance on power from higher realms.

Perhaps we should say that it would have been surprising if this had not been the case. After all, Luther was a praying man and a serious exegete, especially with respect to Paul's letters. The thoughts about healing and wholeness that are set forth in I Corinthians, chapter 12, found a ready response in Luther's soul. He experienced the gospel about Christ as the activator of the dynamic between body, soul, and spirit. Incarnate existence and invisible grace belong together. It would have been unthinkable if the man who had been released from so much anguish during the so-called "tower experience"—and thus knew what the helping, comforting, invisible presence was—would not have observed and understood the third part of Jesus' instructions to his disciples. For Jesus sent out his disciples not only to preach and teach, but also to heal.[42]

Under the impact of rationalism the church has often relegated spiritual healing, both psychological and physical, to bygone ages. In other words, only in the past could something like that have occurred, only in the past could such psychological and psychosomatic healing have taken place. Healing miracles took place while Jesus was wandering among us, at least according to reports, but that does not happen any more. In more radical accounts one reads that miracles, events beyond the ordinary, beyond the range of causality, were possibly not historical events, but rather faith's understandable adornment of the beloved Teacher's memory.

Martin Luther did not think along those lines, and it would be futile to attempt to reconcile his thinking with "modern" thought in this respect, as some of his interpreters attempted to do and still do. To be sure, at the time of Luther there was a great deal of what we would call ignorance, prejudice, and superstition. Luther shared many of the attitudes and ideas of his contemporaries. But with respect to the charismatic that Paul touches upon in his first letter to the Corinthians, we are dealing with expressions that are not restricted to a certain era. When we see the evidence of psychic power that is released by faith in the Christ and his presence, we are faced with mysteries that are not limited to a specific time frame. Here Luther and we are on common ground. The miraculous healing power of the gospel and of prayer is an integral part of God's gift to humanity. Humans have access to the universe's healing center, the power field that holds the cosmos together, the Sun above all suns, as Luther called Christ.[43]

"We have received the sun allegorically from the Mystical Christ, proclaimed through the apostles," Luther writes in a commentary to Psalm 19:5.[44]

In 1528, during a period of illness, Luther wrote to a friend "Christ has so far triumphed. I commend myself to the prayers of yourself and the brethren. I have healed others, I cannot heal myself."[45] Indirectly Luther poses the question whether prayer and healing must necessarily result in physical improvement. It appears that Luther would answer "no" to this query. The main point is the relation to Christ. The British healer, Dorothy Kerin, writes on this matter: "Our beloved Lord did not come to take away all pain from the earth, but he did come to share it, all of it, whenever he can get to it."[46]

When Philipp Melanchthon lay gravely ill, Luther turned to the window in the sickroom and poured out his soul in a bold and intense prayer for his recovery. About this occasion Luther wrote:

> This time I besought the Almighty with great vigor. I attacked him with his own weapons, quoting from Scripture all the promises I could remember, that prayers should be granted, and said that he must grant my prayer, if I was henceforth to put faith in his promises.

Luther then took the hand of sick man saying:

> Be of good courage, Philipp, you will not die; although the Lord might see cause to kill, yet he does not will the death of

> the sinner, but rather that he should turn to him and live. God has called the greatest sinners unto mercy, how much less, then will he cast you off, my Philipp, or destroy you in sin and sadness. Therefore do not give way to grief, do not become your own murderer, but trust in the Lord, who can kill and bring to life, who can strike and heal again.[47]

It is clear that Luther knew Melanchthon's inner struggle. Melanchthon was blaming himself for too little resoluteness in a certain situation in the defense of the evangelical cause. He allowed his soul to become depressed. He would rather have passed away than have to return to earthly strife. His dejectedness had influenced his physical health. Luther's words that Melanchthon should not be his own murderer sounds like a comment in a contemporary discussion about psychosomatic illness. The exhortation not to destroy himself and the admonition to summon his courage are examples of Paul's words "work out your own salvation" (Phil. 2:12). Is it a question of the psyche's cooperation in the soul's liberation struggle before God's throne? Perhaps, but in that case cooperation with God's heaven above. For with Luther, as with Paul, the first and the last word is God's: "For God is the one who works."

Be that as it may, on the bridge that was created by Luther's burning prayers came power from the same source that strengthened Jesus when he, at the well of Sychar, informed his friends that he had meat to eat of which they knew nothing. Melanchthon recovered. He had returned from death's waiting room to continue the struggle at the side of his spiritual brother, Martin. When Philipp Melanchthon thought back to this episode he wrote: "I was recalled from death to life by divine power."[48]

Luther was often conscious of having been the object of intercessory prayer in times of illness. After an attack in 1537 of what he called "the stone," he wrote to his wife:

> I was all but dead, I had already recommended you and our children to God and our Savior, in the full conviction that I should never see you again. I was greatly affected when I thought of you, thus on the brink of the tomb, as I thought myself. However, the prayers and tears of pious men who love me have found favor before God. This last night has killed my malady; I feel quite as though newborn.[49]

After his recovery from "the stone," about a month later, a good friend asked Luther what remedy he had been using. The friend received the following reply: "Prayer, for in all Christian congregations they fervently prayed for me according to the direction of the Apostle James 5:14-15."[50] Although Luther, in all likelihood, had undergone some kind of treatment in order to relieve pain and had been under the care of a physician, he still was persuaded that intercessory prayer lay at the root of his recovery. As we already noted, this was in line with Luther's mystical conviction that life in faith wells up from invisible, superhuman sources.

Myconius, pastor in Gotha, testified that Martin Luther had healed him through intercessory prayer. It happened in 1541. In a letter to Myconius Luther had written the following: "I will pray with you that God may keep you here long." Myconius had apparently been rather seriously ill with a lung ailment. Martin Luther's prayer for spiritual healing, wrote the pastor, "showed such a power" that he recovered. Six years later, when Dr. Martin had died, Myconius wrote a memorial tract about his friend, as he appeared from Gotha's horizon and from the perspective of an admiring co-warrior.

Thus it was evident, Myconius suggested in his tract, that our friend, Doctor Luther, wanted me to stay on in this life as he felt I was sorely needed. Luther had written: "You must not leave me alone, dear Myconius, then I would be left among these devilish folks . . . would that I, after so many crosses and so much suffering, be permitted to precede you." God brought Myconius back to this life through Martin Luther's healing prayer, Myconius remembers with emotion. Then he adds:

> Now I crawl into my sickbed to await the moment when the Lord bids me to put down my physical burden—I am now only skin and bone—and permits me to follow Luther to the Lord Christ. I would long ago have followed my dear Father Luther, had not the prayers of my brethren in several churches kept me here."[51]

A letter from Luther to Pastor Severin Schultze on the question of healing, written just before his death, makes it clear that the Reformer also reformed thinking about healing as an integral part of the pastoral task of the church. From this letter one learns that Luther viewed spiritual healing as an essential task of the church, not as a curiosity. He did not forget the role of medicine. He himself had received considerable, and much appreciated, help from physicians. But especially when their resources were exhausted, it became more evident than ever that intercessory prayer is a constant need and should be a challenge continually accepted. The petitions ought to be offered regularly and ritually arranged.

One may wonder how the addressee, not a very well known name in Reformation history, reacted upon receiving that message. Take note of the fact that Luther, in his capacity as spiritual counsel to the newly established evangelical congregations, assumes that the recipient ought to be able to lead in a prayer of intercession. Perhaps the petitioners, laymen, received a reply to their requests for intercessory prayer directly from Luther. If so, we have no written evidence of it. However, we have a record of what Luther wrote to the pastor in question. It was the pastor who would, in the first place, execute the mission command. We do not know how the Reverend Schultze reacted. We turn to Luther's letter:

> To Pastor Severin Schultze, Venerable Sir and pastor, The tax collector in Torgau and the councilor in Belgren have written me to ask that I offer some good advice and help for the afflicted husband of Mrs. John Korner. I know of no worldly help to give. If the physicians are at a loss to find a remedy, you may be sure that it is not a case of ordinary melancholy. . . . This must be counteracted by the power of Christ and with the prayer of faith. This is what we do and we have been accustomed to do this for a cabinet-maker here who was similarly afflicted with madness and we cured him by prayer in Christ's name.
>
> You should consequently proceed as follows. Go to him with the deacon and two or three good men. Confident that you, as pastor of the place, are invested with the authority of the ministerial office, lay your hands upon him and say: "Peace be with you, dear brother, from God our Father, and from our Lord Jesus Christ." Thereupon read the Creed and the Lord's Prayer over him in a clear voice, and close with these words: "O God, Almighty Father, who has told us through your son, Verily, verily, I say unto you, whatsoever you shall ask the Father in my name, he will give it to you," who has commanded and encouraged us to pray in his name "Ask and you shall receive," and who in like manner has said, "Call upon me in the day of trouble, I will deliver you and you shall glorify me;" we unworthy sinners, relying on these your words and commands, pray for your mercy with such faith as we can muster. Graciously deign to free this man from all evil, put to nought

the work that Satan has done in him, to the honor of your name and the strengthening of the faith of believers. Through the same Jesus Christ, your son our Lord, who lives and reigns with you, world without end. Amen.

Then, when you depart, lay your hands on the man again and say: "These signs shall follow them that believe: they shall lay hands on the sick and they shall recover."

Do this three times, once on each of three successive days. Meanwhile let prayers be said from the chancel of the church, publicly, until God hears them. To the extent to which we are able, we shall at the same time unite our faithful prayers and petitions to the Lord with yours.[52]

The ailment that Luther describes in his letter was mental. The prayer for healing here is consequently partly "exorcism," the driving out of unpalatable spirits, in English sometimes called "deliverance." If we, like Luther, accept the existence of a "peopled" dimension just beyond the borders of our five natural senses, then we must also reckon with the possibility of obsession, *obsessio*, or possession, *possessio*. In this context obsession is defined as a partial and possibly temporary, non-corporeal invasion of the ego, whereas possession is a total takeover in which the invisible power replaces the entity that used to occupy it. In other words, the "tenant" has abandoned his abode and an entirely new personality manifests itself. The assumption that there is a suprahuman power field of created but invisible creatures and of constructive and also destructive "possession" lies behind Luther's sermon on the angels mentioned above.[53]

To a mind trained in the scientific empirical method—which regards the Western rationalistic human as becoming increasingly intellectually developed—a discussion about the possibility that there might be a connection between mental illness and suprahuman powers is a throw-back to the "dark middle ages" or "biblical superstition." But the experiences of Western missionaries in the mission field and the dormant but waking intuition for the transcendental overtones in the Occident have moved, somewhat, the prevailing climate toward a less rigid frame of mind. In other words, the mechanistic theories do not seem to be as much in vogue as before.

The change does not mean that psychological or medical thought must be discarded. It is obvious, and nowadays commonly recognized, that negative mental attitudes lead to bodily and mental disorder. However, from the transcendental aspect it can be argued that in individual cases moral-psychological development can be described as an adaptation process for suprahuman destructive forces.

Now, at the end of the twentieth century, "exorcism" is not as impossible a word as it was fifty years ago. Not a few priests and clergymen in the churches of the West now function as part-time exorcists in an atmosphere of prayer and intercession in the name of Christ. Not a few psychologists and psychiatrists frequently find themselves in the border area where the question of "spiritual hosts of wickedness in the heavenly places" (Ephesians 6:12) must be posed in earnest. But more common than this attempt to try in pastoral ways to deal with "mental sickness" are healing services, not least in Great Britain and America. Intercessory prayer for the sick and the laying on of hands, occasionally with oil, takes place at special services. Even Lutheran churches have added such worship services to their program. Some base their ritual on the one that we find provided by Martin Luther in the letter presented above. One should acknowledge, in this context, that the laying on of hands and prayers for healing and wholeness have always been a part of the ministers' and lay peoples' ministry while visiting patients in homes and hospitals.

The reality that opens up through contact with the Christ—which is salvation, which means freedom—contains discoveries of the kind described above. Luther's thoughts about life after death support our assertion that the Reformer's view of "spirituality" included the idea of a more subtle, optically invisible zone that surrounds and penetrates material existence.[54]

The comments on the subject, in the chapter that follows, ought not to be taken as anything else than just "notes," sketches on the path of an investigation of Luther's relationship to medieval mystics. Through faith Dr. Martin came to **know** that the Master described reality when he announced that God is not a God of the dead but of the living, for to him all are living.

CHAPTER THREE

LUTHER ON LIFE AFTER DEATH

In a twinkling of the eye
you will come out of death into the next life.

Martin Luther, *W* 45; 494, 37-38 (1537), *LW* 24; 42

Someone asked Luther once what he thought of the soul's destiny after death. He wrote a reply, but hastened to add that he was not satisfied with his own answer. Was it not true, the questioner had asked, that the souls of the justified "sleep" after death and, furthermore, that they "remain oblivious as to where they are until judgment day?"

Luther was "inclined" to believe this, he wrote. A word in II Samuel 7:12 influenced his opinion, which in his translation stated: "They sleep with their fathers." (In the American Revised Standard Version we find this translation: ". . . You lie down with your fathers.") Luther zeroes in on the word "sleep" and comments:

> And the dead who were raised through Christ and the apostles testified to the same when they were awakened from sleep, as it were, namely, that they were unaware of where they had been. To this come the ecstasies of many saints. So that I know of nothing by which I might nullify this opinion.

But then Luther had second thoughts on the subject. He continued:

> However, whether this is universally valid for all souls I dare not insist. I think of Paul's, Elijah's, and Moses' rapture); the latter certainly did not appear to be creations of fantasy on Mount Tabor. For who can know how God may act with respect to departed souls? Could he not intermittently permit them to sleep, or rather as long as it pleased him? After

> puts them to sleep while they are in the body. Moreover, that passage from Luke 16 about Abraham and Lazarus attributes consciousness to them both. Although this text does not claim universal applicability, it is unacceptable to distort it to make it apply to the final judgment day.[55]

When Luther thought about the beyond, he apparently used two concepts: the Hebrew concept of Sheol, the shadowy abode of the dead, and Jesus' teaching of life after death, a life of conscious spiritual perception.

Since time does not exist on the other side, it is difficult for us to get an idea about it. Luther discussed this in a different context. When the day of Resurrection arrives, Adam will believe that he has been asleep only a little while. As to himself in that situation, Luther thought that he would be able to sleep until Christ knocks at his grave's door and says: "Arise, Doctor Martinus." Then he, Luther, would immediately rise up and be with the Lord in the sweetness of the eternal.

Did Luther, perchance, paint the dotted line after the earthly existence as a sleep because he more or less unwillingly did not want to imagine the picture as anything but the popular image of life beyond? But, on the other hand, at various times and in several connections, he indicated that he did not hold the opinion that the main occupation in life on the other side would be to sleep. The latter perception is more in line with the Old Testament thought about Sheol, which we find in the Old Testament, but also, occasionally, in the New.

In other situations, Luther followed suggestions from the New Testament. There the picture is brighter. Those who die in Christ get to experience joy, in other words, their consciousness is still active and alive. It is hard to imagine that Paul longed so intensely to be with Christ only to sleep. If one speaks about an intermediate stage between the death of the body and the final consummation or resurrection, there is room for such an idea in the dominant New Testament viewpoint on "life beyond," according to which impressions can be received, conscious decisions made, and spiritual development and change occur.

Perhaps the real possibility is that, after death, humans discover that life beyond is really to live and that this earthly life is to be as dead. Luther expressed this thought about the existence of life after death thus:

> When we are dead we will have different eyes. Then we will perceive that the whole world is dead. That is why the Lord

said to a learned scribe who wanted to go and bury his father: 'Follow me and let the dead bury their dead'. [56]

In Martin Luther's writings one finds much evidence his faith also embraced the conviction that life continues after death, not in sleep or semi-sleep, but in a wakeful condition. This thought often emerges when the Reformer wants to depict a true Christian's martyrdom. Most of the time we are probably unaware that for decades Martin Luther lived under the constant threat of plots against his life and therefore martyrdom became a part of his picture of the lot of a Christian. A part of faith's triumph over a world that seems to have all the advantages on its side is precisely the "knowledge" that life continues after physical death. Perhaps the martyr awaits a sentence.

> He is to be hanged, beheaded, burned, or drowned. Then, too, a road stretches out before him that he must walk. . . . a way that he cannot see, on which feet cannot tread, on which he cannot travel by wagon. Yet, one commonly says: "He is departing, he is gone." But this is not to be taken in a physical or literal sense . . . our reasoning ceases to function and neither knows nor understands how the transition from this life to that one takes place, much less how and by what means it is to be attained.[57]

The transition from the natural earthly life to the supersensible invisible is, doubtless, a transition from one form of consciousness to another.

> For faith does not err and does not stray; but wherever the Christ is to whom it [faith] adheres, there faith must be and remain. And the stronger the faith is, the more surely this Way is traveled. For this walking is nothing but a constant growth in faith and in an ever-stronger assurance of eternal life in Christ. If I persist in this faith and death attacks me and throws me down, if it chokes me in my prime or takes me by sword or fire and takes away all my five senses, then the journey is over, and I am already at my destination as I leap into yonder life. [58]

We see here the same persuasion as in Luther's notes about his daughter Magdalena's death, namely, the conviction regarding a continuing consciousness and memory, in what is otherwise a totally different surrounding. The fourteen-year-old daughter died in 1542. His wife Katherine—Kate, as he called her—wept bitterly and disconsolately. Luther had prayed intensively for his daughter's recovery. This time apparently the Lord did not listen to the prayer of his prophet. Magdalena crossed the boundary. Luther felt that his role now was that of the comforter. He turned to Katherine:

> Dear Katherine, console yourself; think where our daughter is gone, for surely she has passed happily into peace. The flesh bleeds doubtless, for such is its nature. But the spirit lives and goes to the place of its wishes.

When they placed Magdalena's body in the coffin Luther said:

> Poor, dear little Magdalena, there you are, peace be with you. Dear child, you will rise again, you will shine like a star, yes, like the sun. . . . I am joyful in spirit, but, oh, how sad in the flesh. It is marvelous that I should know that she is certainly at rest, that she is well, and yet that I should be so sad.[59]

The tenor of these words is the belief that man enters a restful existence after death, but certainly not a continuously somnolent one.

As the people came to carry the coffin and expressed sympathy for Martin and Katherine in their grief, Luther said: "Friends, be not grieved. I have sent a saint to heaven." Perhaps Luther and Katherine were strengthened in their belief in an afterlife of a conscious order after a dream that Katherine had had the night before Magdalena's death. Katherine had seen two beautiful, exquisitely dressed young men come to her, asking for her daughter in marriage. Philipp Melanchthon, the good friend and co-combatant and a close neighbor in Wittenberg, attempted to interpret the dream. The young men, he said, were a vision of holy angels who were preparing to take away the dear girl to the true nuptials in the heavenly kingdom.[60]

A good summation of the deepest meaning of this personal experience we find in the following words of Luther about eternal life: "The human is a unique being and created to be a participant in divinity and immortality."[61]

Of the two views about life after death that have struggled and struggle for dominion over theological thought, the Hebraic and the one that is derived from the Jesus tradition, the latter prevails in Luther's world of thought. Memory and consciousness remain after physical death. But life—the present life—is not something to be desired under all circumstances. It is important to distinguish between immortal life and eternal life. Properly speaking, the New Testament makes a distinction between those two. Immortal life is regarded as a natural fact. To use a spatial category, the term immortal life refers to "quantity." In contra-distinction, eternal life has its center in Christ and belongs to the category "quality." The soul continues beyond death as a "natural" state of affairs. But that, in itself, has nothing to do with salvation, liberation, or walking on the path of God. On the other hand, regeneration through Christ makes the miracle possible. That is eternal life. We encounter eternal life in the midst of natural life, and these glimpses of eternal life lead us to the beyond. Martin Luther did not make exactly this distinction—but almost.

> Christ's believers are most properly called heavenly because if "the soul is present more where it loves than where it lives," and if it is the nature of love to change one who loves into what is loved, it is true that those who love heaven and God are, and are called, heavenly and divine, though not because they are heavenly by nature or in a metaphysical sense.

To Luther there was a difference between this spiritual heavenliness and a natural-metaphysical heavenliness. In the latter sense one can speak of "immortality" as a fact. "Even the demons and certainly all the souls of humans would in that sense be heavenly, since their nature possesses a heavenly, that is, incorporeal, nature."[62]

It should be pointed out that these remarks belong to Luther's earlier period, the one that preceded the final break with Rome. This is also true of a later passage in the lecture series, quoted above, on the Epistle to the Hebrews. Here Luther is of the opinion that "God points out, in somewhat oblique words, that the soul is immortal and that there is eternal life." In other words, incontestably, immortal life awaits the soul. However, that is not the same as eternal life. The latter is a life oriented toward God and Christ. Abel who, during his earthly life, was incapable of teaching his only brother through faith and example, is dead, it is true, yet "lives more vitally as a teacher for the whole world."[63]

Luther was not particularly eager to deal with theoretical anthropology and has not enriched us with many expositions concerning the theological meaning of "substance." The above comes to us mainly from earlier years when he still discussed Scholastic terms, partly as a Scholastic, and took the discussion of "immortality" seriously. More than twenty years after the exposition cited above Luther had fairly negative words to express about the discussion. He then wrote "the conclusion that the human is an extraordinary animal, created for immortality, is almost useless."[64]

However, he does not escape the subject that easily even during later decades, which brought him many disappointments in association with human beings. He often became rather cross and cantankerous and less sensitive to the mystical presence. He could not, however, abandon entirely the question of life after death.

In 1535 in some comments on Matthew 22:31-32, Luther writes about Moses:

> Moses himself testifies (Exodus 3:6) with a strong argument that there is another life after this one, for God was Abraham's God. This they had to concede, but they did not understand. So he asks: Do you wish to make God a God of the dead or any other thing, which is nil or has no being? . . . Since Moses says that God is Abraham's God, Abraham must be something and be alive. But reason speaks: Oh, Abraham has been disintegrated a long time; how can God then be his God? If I now were to say that God is Abraham's God according to the manner of the soul, this is not enough . . . Abraham has body and soul . . . there is a resurrection of the dead, especially of the just . . . Christ says: he [Abraham] shall remain, rise . . . Abraham and all saints live even though they die . . . How this occurs, reason cannot see, nor conceive . . . the soul does not know . . . yet it shall not be dead. For the rising of the dead will surely take place . . . Moses . . . says . . . that we shall rise again for life shall prove stronger than death . . . Abraham . . . has body, and soul, which the order of death shall touch only a moment. . . . Twenty years ago I heard Cardinal Cajetan speak of the Christian faith so that I shuddered. . . . Under the pressure of such views, each burgher and peasant will become a doubter of the resurrection of the dead; into blindness they are led."[65]

In his lectures on the Pentateuch Luther refers to Augustine with regard to the subject of immortality. Augustine tells about a physician who very much doubted the existence of an invisible continuum. It is a most uncertain proposition, this teaching about resurrection and immortality, the doctor argued. Then he had a dream one night. A young man appeared in his dream, turned to the doctor and said: "How can it be," the youth asked, "that you can see me when your eyes are closed in sleep? How is it that you can hear me when your ears are not open, but you are asleep?" To this Luther adds a few reflections: "Therefore learn and believe that there are other spiritual eyes with which those who believe in Christ can see when the eyes of the body have been closed by death."[66]

In his major commentary on the Epistle to the Galatians Luther pointed out, once again, that after the death of the body, life is conscious "existence."

> It is as though he [Paul] were saying: "It would indeed be fine if someone kept the Law. But since no one does so, we must take refuge in Christ, who was put under the Law to redeem those who were under the Law (Gal. 4:4). Believing in Him, we receive the Holy Spirit and begin to keep the Law. Because of our faith in Christ what we do not keep is not imputed to us. But in the life to come believing will cease, and there will be a correct and perfect keeping and loving. For when faith ceases, it will be replaced by glory, by means of which we shall see God as He is (I John 3:2). There will be a true and perfect knowledge of God, a right reason, and a good will, neither moral nor theological but heavenly, divine, and eternal."[67]

The aspect of "sleep," consequently, does not appear at all—not even implicitly—in this description. This becomes especially apparent if one assumes, and any other interpretation is hardly possible, that "the life which follows" most likely means "the intermediate stage," that which precedes the final completion of the last judgment.

We know, for a fact, that Luther rejected the commercial sale of indulgences. That is evident from his *Resolutiones* on the matter. But it is hardly as equally well known that, several years later, he declared that, on his part, he reckoned with purgatory as a reality—although one cannot perhaps always prove it with passages from the Holy Writ. Under certain circumstances, purgatory begins already here and now, Luther added.

In a note in the Table Talks of 1540, we read that he regarded his book on John 14-16, "as the best book I have ever written." In that book he takes up, among other things, the question of "life beyond" in commenting on Jesus' words that he is the Way, the Truth, and the Life. When the time comes that one must say farewell to activities on earth, it does not serve much purpose to rely on one's bygone thoughts and deeds. One must rather hold fast to Christ's words that he is the Way. One must seek to know him and his presence, he who is the mystical Christ.

> Make sure that then these words are firmly imbedded in your consciousness, so deeply that you can feel Christ's presence and He can say to you as He does to Thomas here: "Why are

> you seeking and looking for other ways? Look to Me, and reject all other thoughts regarding ways to heaven. You must expunge these completely from your heart and think of nothing but these words of Mine: 'I am the Way.' See to it that you tread on Me, that is, cling to Me with strong faith and with all confidence of the heart. I will be the Bridge to carry you across. In one moment you will come out of death and the fear of hell into yonder life. "[68]

Through faith in the Christ you have a foretaste of that which will certainly come. True, generally speaking, one must reckon with life after death, but confidence grows only from faith in Christ. According to Luther's comments on the eleventh chapter of the Epistle to the Hebrews, this faith is synonymous to life in God; only from this comes trust as one faces the journey to the other dimension. He writes:

> God be praised, as a Christian I know where I will go and where I will abide. I was assured of this in Baptism, in absolution, and likewise in the Sacrament.... Christ calls Himself the only Way. . . . He wants our heart and our reliance to rest completely on Him when we are to depart from this life; and He promises to transport us safely across and take us to the Father.[69]

It has been said that one should not draw too many checks on Luther's comments on the Pentateuch because they were published in transcribed form. Here we have found that, when it comes to "immortality," the ideas are similar to those in other material. The idea has also been advanced that in all discussion about the Reformer's belief in future life, one must make a distinction between his "transcendental theological thought" and "the psychological." Luther spoke of the "soul's and body's resurrection," the critics demur when discussing Luther's eschatology. Some theologians insist that it was Melanchthon who changed the agenda by introducing the question of the "immortality of the soul."

True, Luther speaks of both the body and the soul when he theologizes or preaches about the continuation of existence. But you must remember that Luther, like Paul, represents the idea that the body, which a human being possesses at the resurrection-as-continuation-of-existence, is a subtle body, the life-giving model that leaves the copy when the material life has ended. As far as I can see, in Luther's case, there is no reason to contrast the concepts of resurrection and immortality.[70]

It has already been noted that it is difficult to know on which side Luther comes down regarding the question of immortality, whether it is on the side of the Hebraic, more existential, immanental view, or on the side of what has been termed here as the Jesus-view of continued existence. As far as I can see from my reading of Luther material, he leans toward the Jesus position. That is to say, life after death is characterized by consciousness, albeit within a framework that the earthly mind can neither utilize nor understand. It is not the stupor of Sheol. However, this conscious life, which includes memory, is from a spiritual point of view unqualified. Eternal life, as represented by Christ, has to do with quality. One can thus, under certain circumstances, enter immortality without knowing anything about eternal life.

Luther's treatment of the parable about Abraham and Lazarus provides a good insight into his way of dealing with the immortal life-eternal life question. The soul does not die, but it must be renewed by spiritual life in Christ, so that there may be meaning with what we call immortality. And Luther's conviction about the reality of a world of angels also gives an inkling as to the main direction of his thoughts about immortal life and eternal life.

In a sermon on the right preparation for death, we read that when a Christian dies, he should know that he is in invisible company.

> The Christian should be convinced that—as the sacraments show—numerous pairs of eyes are turned in his direction: first and foremost God's eyes and the eyes of Christ himself . . . then also the eyes of the dear angels, the saints and all the Christians. . . . The sacrament of the altar shows us that all these together speed towards the dying Christian as if to one of their own, help the dying one to conquer death, sin and hell. All bear the Christian's burden with him or her. In the hour of death the love of the saints and their communion are mightily and eagerly present and at work. In the honored and revered sacrament of Christ's body we are promised the love, comfort, support, and communion of all the saints, at all times of want and need.

Elisha is one among many who knew this to be true. He said to his servant: "Fear not for those who are with us are more than they who are with them" (II Kings 6:16). Certainly, this was not true as far as the testimony of most **external eyes** was concerned. The prophet's servant had seen, with his own eyes, the enemy who had encircled the Israelites at Dothan early in the morning. It was obvious that those who were with the enemy were more than those who were with the Israelites. Then Elisha prayed: "Lord, open his [the servant's] eyes that he may see." Then the servant also **saw** the invisible reality: they were surrounded by friendly forces. "The mountain was full of horses and chariots of fire round about Elisha" (2 Kings 6:17).

It is wholly in line with Martin Luther's inner vision and mystical faith that he selects precisely this narrative in order to show how superficially, and therefore erroneously, we humans judge our own affairs. Practically all that the external eyes could see were enemies, and the enemies were many. But the Lord listened to Elisha's plea, writes Luther, and opened the servant's eyes. In other words, the servant had a momentary glimpse into the inner mystical realm. He could suddenly see into the other world. And then he discovered that he, Elisha, and their minority crowd were surrounded by invisible, helping beings.

Thus it is, Luther thought, that we humans in the so-called visible world are surrounded by helpers—**and** spoilers—in an invisible realm. At the end of life we will go to the other world in order to participate in a life of a more enduring kind. To him such knowledge was not a symbolic, immanental, faith-strengthening process conjured up by the human mind when it faces the challenges of life. The inner knowledge was rather a representation of a comforting, supersensible fact for which faith in Christ and Christ's presence in prayer and sacrament open the door.[71]

Like many mystics, Luther obviously counted with three kinds of beings who, from the invisible, support and guide humans: the spirits of those who have recently died, as well as saints and angels. About these you cannot, or should not, say that they sleep. On the contrary, they are eminently awake, powerfully active, and ever ready to be of assistance to humans, especially in times of tribulations.

In Bible passages concerning the angels, which we touched upon briefly in the preceding chapter, there is also an assurance about eternal abodes. Luther advised his readers to look up Psalms 34, 91, and 125 to be persuaded of the living angelic world around human beings. He drew the reader's attention to the Psalmist's firm belief that God leads his angels to protect the faithful in all vicissitudes and trials. The English translation of Psalm 91:16 reads: "With long life I will satisfy him, and show him my salvation." Luther writes: "I will fill him with eternity." Who is right may be immaterial. The significant point in Luther's version is his concentration on the Christ-life as eternity's beginning in a human life. The soul is immortal—but the most important thing for us is acquaintance with eternal life, life in Christ. The eternal is **not** infinite time. It is not the kind of time that begins when earthly time comes to a close. It bears repeating that eternity, according to Luther, is to be seen from the point of view of "quality," not from the angle of "quantity." Eternity begins now, not immediately after physical death—an otherwise popular notion. We encounter eternity and eternal life in Christ, and in "such [on the surface] insignificant signs as the sacraments."[72]

According to the gospel, one is called to prepare for life after this by surrendering his self-centered ego (*involutus in se*) to the eternal and mystically present Christ here and now. In Luther's thoughts about Christ we have noted that the two sacraments, baptism and holy communion, stand out as the main bridges or channels for hints about life beyond the five senses. This life beyond, in similarity with the earthly, is under Christ's dominion and, at this very moment, is suffused by his love and power. Christ's dominion is an "in spite of," and a "consummation" that is not yet "complete." This "incompleteness" is due to man's unwillingness. He does not submit himself to the Word. He does not avail himself of the sacraments. He neglects everything that would create a greater unity between body, soul, and spirit and promote greater justice on earth. The human does not want to contemplate his own demise.

But the invitation still stands. The outward signs of the involvement of the divine with the human—the Word about and by Christ and the sacraments—exhort us "to call upon the holy angels, and especially our own angel, and entreat the Mother of God and all apostles and saints."[73] In the sacraments one meets God's "angels, all the saints, all beings" and they "unite with God in watching over you, in caring for your soul and in preparation for receiving it."[74]

To "watch" and to be "solicitous"—these words indicate that the realm to which the soul goes is not regarded as a place for sleeping in waiting for the latter day. The ultimate day will come, but the "sleep," from which all creatures will waken, is spiritual. The metaphor of earthly sleep does not do well in this context.

The feeling of this constant connection with the other world kindles faith. That feeling and that faith are given a wonderful description in Martin Luther's last sermon, preached at Eisleben in February 1546. The text is Matt. 11:25-30, Jesus' prayer of gratitude, that it is to the simple and unlearned that God has chosen to reveal himself, instead of to those who think highly of their own wisdom. As a foretaste of the world that receives the departing soul, bidding farewell in death, a person who lives in God can experience God's love in the midst of tribulations. The world looks disdainfully on those who are "hidden with God." They sneer at them with hatred and scorn. The great dukes, the Emperor, the Pope, cardinals and the bishops are all hostile on account of what he, Luther, had said. Such calumnies must be endured. The matter itself lies outside the world's range and its ultimate ability to influence. Christ, the Lord of the invisible host, invited those who were heavily laden to come to him. Luther paraphrased as follows:

> Just cleave to me, hold to my word and let go whatever thereby goes. Should you be burned or beheaded for it, have patience. I will render it so sweet for you that you shall sustain it well. As it has been written about the virgin St. Agnes, when she was led to prison to be killed, she had the feeling that she was on her way to a dance. From whence did this come to her? Ah, from this Christ, from believing this word: "Come to me all who labor and are heavy-laden, and I will give you rest." If evil befalls you I, the Christ, will give you the courage so that you will even laugh about it all, and the pain shall not be so great for you, and the devil not so bad. Even if you walked on live coals, you will have the feeling that you walk on roses. I will give you the heart to laugh . . . Only come to me . . . If you face oppression . . . do not be afraid, it will not be heavy for you, but light and easy to bear. For I give you the Spirit, so that the burden, unbearable for the world, becomes a light burden for you. For when you suffer for my sake, it is my yoke and my burden laid upon you in grace so that you shall know that your suffering is pleasing to God and to me and that I myself am aiding you to carry it, giving you power and strength. . . . Waiting upon the Lord in faith you have already conquered and escaped death . . . and by a large margin left behind you the devil and the world.[75]

We have had some glimpses of Martin Luther's personal reflections about his own experiences of and thoughts about the invisible Christ-presence, in differing ways and in various forms. We have seen, for example, how Luther reacted to the powers that were enemies of the Christ-presence. In the following chapter illustrations of the personal and the subjective in the theological formulas are presented.

But before that, just a word about the "objective" and the "subjective." As indicated at the beginning of this presentation, tension prevails about the views of Luther and of his followers concerning "objective" and "subjective." In much Lutheran theology the spokesmen for "objectivity" fought against attempts to interpret the gospel and Luther "subjectively," "personally." On the other hand, the "subjective" group looked askance at thought structures which include only the "objective," the "ritualistic" and the "institutionalistic."

As I write this, my eyes fall upon a remark made in an interview by an inner-city pastor in Sweden, part of whose time is devoted to an "on call" chaplaincy service for persons in dire need of pastoral care. His comment is very relevant to our discussion: "A person who has a personal, private faith finds God within him or herself . . . whereas the basic view of Christianity is that the message comes from the outside, is objective, and is received independently of the self."

Here the "privately religious" has been put in stark contrast to the "objective" in a tension that does not harmonize well with the reality that the Christian revelation encounters in the world. No "objective" music can come from "the outside" and resonate within, without an echo from a "private, personal" sounding board "inside." In other words, God is not only "out there." God is also "in there." The words of Blaise Pascal could serve as a theme song for an investigation of an "objective" Reformer's "subjective" checks-and-balances or, conversely, a "subjective" Reformer's "objective" check-and-balances on the subject matter. "*Le coeur a ses raisons, que la raison ne connait point.*" ("The heart has its reasons that reason knows nothing of.")

PART II

LUTHER'S VIEW OF GOD, HUMAN BEINGS, AND SALVATION

"But the Spirit himself intercedes for us with sighs too deep for words (gemitus inenarrabilis)" (Rom. 8:26). These thoughts can be felt, like all other spiritual thoughts. But they cannot be expressed in words, and they can be learned only through experience. . . . For the Holy Scripture's inseparable companion is the Holy Spirit, who moves hearts in more than one way and consoles them through the Word.

Martin Luther
W 40, 3; 542, 27-31, 543, 8-12, 29-30 (1534-1535)
LW 13; 110-111

CHAPTER FOUR

ABOUT GOD AND GOD IN CHRIST

All treasures and all knowledge are hidden in Christ. They are called "hidden" because they are only visible through mystical and spiritual eyes.

Martin Luther, *W* 1; 341, 1-3 (1518)

As pointed out, Martin Luther did not speculate too much about God's "substance." In that sense he distanced himself rather quickly from the Scholastics, whom he had studied during his university years. His concern was not in the first place with God as subject, as being, as substratum. It was a question of how God relates to the person. Is the Divine Power "irate" or "benevolent"? Does it meet us in the first place as "death" or "life"? Does it govern primarily through the "law" or basically through the "gospel?" Shall one say that Luther dealt with the problem of God's nature; was it with these questions that his thoughts were occupied? To the extent to which the "problem of God" can be solved within our human existence, for Luther it was "solved" in the manner in which he "experienced" God. "Since God lives in my heart, I am courageous . . . I cannot be lost."[76]

God's life touches our lives in two ways, Luther pointed out. First, God is the hidden God. We see God in creation's "masks" (*larvae*). That is to say that all created things are God's "masked" face. God is in the smallest leaf, in our enemies, yes, in Satan himself.[77] But one also finds God in him who revealed God, namely, Jesus Christ. The only way to enter into the mystery of revelation is to confess "Christ is my life."[78]

Behind God's masks there is God as mystery—mysterious and incomprehensible. Beyond the revealed God is the hidden God, the non-rational. It is against this background that one has to read Luther's description of reason as a "whore." No intellectual speculation can produce clarity on the question of God because God is hidden from and beyond the reach of reason. One may object that this is a paradox. But this paradox is essential. Luther said: "In order to create a place for faith, everything that is the object of faith must be hidden."[79]

Whenever one discusses Luther's opinion of predestination one ought to remember his manner of introducing the paradoxical in discourses on God. One must keep this in mind when reading, for example, Luther's *The Bondage the of Will*, Rudolf Otto explains. This is not, in the first place, a matter of theological logic. Predestination as logic becomes an absurdity. What you find in Luther's book on the will is rather a "numinous mood" expressed in "religious reverence." Here we are dealing with the non-rational and the mystical in the Christian faith.[80]

Luther's experience of the personal sphere shines forth in his theories about God, theories with a practical-religious bent. God is the *tremendum*, that which causes one to tremble. But he is also the *fascinosum*, the power that captivates and enthralls you. Faith and trust have a real, not an imaginary, source and Christians therefore ought to be a happy breed.[81]

In his commentary on the Magnificat, Luther expresses joy this way: "For no one can praise God, without first loving Him. . . . The heart overflows with gladness and goes leaping and dancing for the great pleasure it has found in God."[82] Thus one's experience of God can be both frightening and joy-filled.

Rudolf Otto claimed that the *fascinosum*-element of the picture we have of God took the upper hand among Western mystics at the expense of the *tremendum*-element. This would mean that mystery became the main part of the God-picture in Western mysticism and that the awe-filled dread before the divine became less common. Among the relatively few that experienced the immediacy of the divine presence, before which one quakes, was Jacob Boehme. He knew the dark night of the soul, just like Luther. Luther's use of words like "wrath," "fire," and "rage," to depict God, reveal to us one aspect of his religious experience. But a verbal phrase does not cover the breadth and depth of subjective experience. Experience, *Erfahrung*, of the divine can include God's terrifying side. But *Erfahrung*, experience, also includes the other aspect of the "picture" of God: his goodness and love. It is an attempt to describe the indescribable that lies behind the imagery. We must remember, however, that verbal expressions can never be exhaustive "dogmatic" descriptions, cannot capture the experience of the numinous.

The Scholastics, Lutheran orthodoxy (in old and new garbs), and "liberal" rationalistic theological systems (Lutheran or not in their intention) frequently omit making a distinction between the rational idea and the innermost "ground"—accessible to feeling and intuition. Luther was very aware of the insufficiency of language. One sees this in his method of distinguishing between the "external Word" and the "internal Word" or in his insight into the nature of miracles. The latter must be regarded as only an analogy for something much deeper, namely, God's power and love. Spiritual facts cannot always be formulated, but they can indeed be experienced, says Luther in a commentary to a Psalm.[83]

Since it has become a theological cliché that one must presuppose strict polarity between Luther and the mystics in regard to the question of image of God, it could be useful to stop for a moment and consider Luther's and Johann Tauler's ways of treating the issue.

In a book on Tauler (quoted earlier in this work), Gösta Wrede, a Swedish expert on Tauler, comments on my comparisons between Luther and Tauler. Wrede finds that, although the spiritual communion between the Reformer and the 14th century mystic became unmistakable, nevertheless, it is clear enough that Tauler was a Neoplatonist in the way in which he thought of the relationship between God and man. With Tauler it was a matter of "stealing" into the Godhead. For Luther it was much more like a thunderclap. Despite the fact that both of them reckon with dualism between man and God, "it is not the same kind of dualism."[84] This is no doubt true. When it comes to the question of the view of God, the main issue becomes whether Tauler was a pantheist or not. Not least in Protestant theology the statement is often made that the mystics have abolished the distance between the Creator and the created so that God and man become, theologically speaking, indistinguishable. In his thorough Tauler study, *Unio Mystica*, Gösta Wrede has shown clearly that Tauler's thought was **not** pantheistic. He writes that Tauler differentiates between the created and the uncreated in God's being. Thus Tauler's ontology, that is to say, his thoughts about the very nature of "being," give room for a kind of dualism in the relationship between God and man. In addition, Wrede submits, Tauler's conception of God contains a personal, will-oriented characteristic. This trait is also the distinctive characteristic of the human being in its search for unity and wholeness. The human is an image of God and at the same time "an independent creature."[85]

In an enumeration of the various kinds of captivity that distance the human from God, Johann Tauler wrote that "the third captivity is natural reason." People "vaunt of their learning, of truth . . . they become pompous over their ability to reason." Reason cannot embrace God in its grasp. No, between the human and God there is "an enormous distance." Tauler wrote: "In the face of the enormous distance between the puny being and the great, overwhelming God, it becomes clear that man must mention God with trembling awe."[86]

One can speak of a pervading religious sentiment with Tauler that stems from the "radicalness" of the experience of "dying away from oneself and to be filled with God's life."[87] Luther felt and knew this. The prevailing Protestant interpretation of mysticism assumes the opposite, namely, that all mystics nullify the gulf between man and God. In the last section of this study there will be an opportunity to scrutinize some representatives of this generally accepted assessment. In the present context only one comment will be made to illustrate the Luther-Tauler question.

Steven Ozment, an American scholar, agrees with the traditional Protestant view of mysticism. In his study of Tauler, he has reached the conclusion that "The 'likeness' of created and uncreated spirit, of created and uncreated 'grounds,' is an established presupposition in Tauler's thought."[88] I agree with Wrede when he calls that utterance of Ozment's "a cliché." One can, of course, read different things into Tauler's formulations. But **one** distinction must always be kept in focus in discussions about the mystical traits of Reformation theology. It is **one** thing to say that man has **relations** with the ultimate reality, and thus not be satisfied with just stating that one is **separated** from it. If that were not the case there would be no awareness that one is really separated from it. It is a totally **different** matter to say that there is no distance separating the little human from the great God. As we have seen, Tauler does not assert the latter. Tauler's consistent distrust of the dogmatic Scholastics should be sufficient warning against the temptation to build a defensive position from which the Lutheran image of God could be defended with attacks against mysticism in general, and against Tauler's in particular.[89] Luther found in Tauler the same kind of feeling of guilt and melancholy as he himself came to know in the presence of God and Christ. For Luther, as for Tauler, this experience became an analogy, on a human level, of the frightening aspects of the "God-beyond-God" faith.[90]

About Luther's connections with mysticism's doctrine of God, one can say he said "yes" to the mystical knowledge about God, as *tremendum* and *fascinosum*, when he was of the opinion that the mystic in question had had the experience of what it was like to be justified by grace through faith. That observation is reinforced when we turn our attention to Luther's view of God-in-Christ and then compare it with expressions from kindred souls among the mystics.

Erich Vogelsang deserves credit for his investigations of medieval mysticism and Luther's relationship to it. It was done with great sensitivity to the aspect of religious "experience." But on one point Vogelsang seems to have overlooked part of the text. He asserts that the "mystic" never said: "When we hear the gospel, we hear Christ."[91] Here Vogelsang has momentarily abandoned his basic theory about the three main forms of medieval Christian mysticism. That theory arose out of an academic protest against all the free and easy generalizations concerning mysticism's content. Tauler and the anonymous author (sometimes called the Frankfurter) of *Theologia Germanica* offer material that gainsays the thesis with regard to the absence of Christ in mystical utterances about the gospel. In the exposition of a Bible text concerning a *pater familias*, Tauler writes that the housefather naturally is "the Lord Jesus Christ."[92] In a meditation on the human-God relationship, the Frankfurter declared:

> It is therefore an undeniable truth that the creature as creature is in itself unworthy, has no real claim on anything, no one is indebted to it, neither God nor fellowman. The creature should rightly be surrendered to God's hands, subject to Him. . . . What is thus—or should be—turned over into God's hands and subject to God must also be surrendered to all creatures and fellow beings (and, briefly, not in terms of outer activity but in terms of inner compassion). . . . From this [submission] . . . comes true humility. . . . If this were not the truth and the best and the highest divine righteousness, Christ would not have taught it in words and fulfilled it in His life.[93]

With both of these mystics one finds several similar comments indicating a theology in which the gospel and Christ are linked and mentioned simultaneously.

I remind my readers that Luther thought of God's work with people as twofold: it is objective and subjective; objective in that it imputes to us a "for you," and subjective in the sense that it always remains "in us," if we so wish. This dual "happening" can only take place through Christ. He is the "door." If that is "illumination," it is certainly the only way I know. But the road traveled can be another path. However, no one "escapes" the Christ. In one shape or the other he meets you. It might take time. Sooner or later it happens. Then Christ appears as the "mystical Christ."[94]

Sometimes Luther described the inner process in fellowship with Christ using words expressing tactility, such as *adhaesio*, cleaving to; *conglutinatio*, bonding together. Christ's mystical presence engenders this inner transformation. In Chapter 6, Salvation, we will return to the subject of bride-bridegroom analogies and the aspect of "clinging to" and "bonding."[95]

Those mystics who were approvingly cited by Luther never developed a systematic, coherent Christology. But there was never any doubt about Christ's central place in their world of thought and in their interpretations of Bible passages.

Just as God is everywhere, so Christ is everywhere. He is in all beings, in the stones, in the fire. But do not tempt God by seeking him outside the Word. This was Luther's urgent admonishment, not least after the struggle against the so-called Enthusiasts had begun.[96] It is through Christ that God enters into the soul. This entry influences morality and feeling. It is not only an imputation, not only utilization of someone else's credit or deed; it also means that feeling and will come into play.[97] That assurance which asserts "God for me" is also included in the phrase "faith justifies." And the expression "Christ in me" is a word about the conviction that "Christ is present." The God who can be the object of a person's intellectual speculations comes into one's heart as Christ, and "Christ lives in us, works, and speaks." It is not a question of life in matter, "flesh," although our life is lived in the flesh. No, "it is Christ's life."[98] According to Luther's conviction, this is, after all, a supernatural sequence of events.

At one time Melanchthon had written a letter to Luther about a youth who, after an accident, had sunk into a coma and then recovered his consciousness. The young man resumed breathing again and he was heard to say, with joy in his voice, that he had indeed seen Christ and that he knew that another life awaited him after this life. Christ, he said to those surrounding him, had shown him the wonderful joys of the other life. After some hours the young man sank back into a coma and soon died. Melanchthon wanted to know whether Luther was of the opinion that the anecdote would be useful to others. Luther answered that certainly he thought that the young man's testimony would be helpful in connection with the preaching of the gospel. First, however, one ought to get the matter thoroughly examined. If everything proved to be authentic, one should have the story published. An examination followed. It had a positive result. At Luther's and Melanchthon's suggestion the description of an encounter with Christ in another dimension and a report about possession were published in a pamphlet in 1530.[99]

God-in-Christ is both sacrament and example, Luther pointed out. Christ has carried our human nature through death to victory. By participating in his death and by taking part in his victory, we are integrated with his divine life. The example was transformed to sacramental power. Christ is the original sacrament. His resurrection is not only a symbol, a sacramental symbol of our justification, of the fact that we have been made righteous before God. In the example there is also dynamic power. Luther writes, "Augustine teaches that the suffering of Christ is both a sacrament and an example—a sacrament because it signifies the death of sin in us and grants his power to those who believe, an example because it also behooves us to imitate Him in bodily suffering and dying."[100]

Some mystics experience the godhead as only unfathomable depth, as abysmal darkness, and persist in that view. This has been called "negative theology." Luther and some mystics knew that side of the experience as well. However, when this "negative" theological mysticism occasionally turned out to be pure and unadulterated intellectualism, Luther objected. He was of the opinion that any effort to dogmatize about God's averted gaze is a futile attempt to "understand" God. To Luther the hiddenness of God did not mean that humans are incapable of sensing, observing, or understanding God. Nor did the hiddenness lie in the experience of darkness. Rather, the hidden, secret mystery lies in the story of Christ's advent. A word came to us from God, unbelievably far beyond the reach of our understanding, yet lovingly near. But this "negative" theology of several of the mystics with whom Luther felt a spiritual kinship resembled in various ways his own experience of the divine.[101]

Professor Bengt Hägglund points out, in a publication dealing with justification by faith against the background of medieval thought, that there were close links between the Reformer, on one hand, and, particularly, Tauler and the author of *Theologia Germanica*, on the other. That affinity finds expression not least in Christology. Hägglund writes: "It is therefore not true when it is said that mysticism knows Christ only as an example and emphasizes in this connection only the imitation of Christ." Yet, Tauler and the author of *Theologia Germanica*, Hägglund adds, did not view justification as imputation of Christ's righteousness, as something that is being done "outside me." The emphasis was no doubt different from Luther's. Luther placed more stress on *imputatio*, the objective and declarative in the propagation of the gospel. He never meant that the "credit," the imputed "asset," ought to or should be separated from God's birth in the soul. It is here that the "mystical faith" comes in. Hägglund quotes W. Preger:

> As for the redemptive act in Christ's death itself, Tauler emphasizes at times its fundamental importance in so clear and exclusive a manner that one must assume that also when he speaks of God's being born in us or when he stresses the way of discipleship of Christ as the way of salvation . . . it constitutes the self-evident basis."[102]

The numinous, the awe-inspiring, and the sentiment inherent in the experience before the burning bush—all are present in Luther's thought world, as in much mystical reflection. When the conceptual and the doctrinal begin to predominate over the ineffable and the indescribable in the encounter with God, the church communicates with the surrounding world only through narrow embrasures of intellectual insight. The God and the God-in-Christ thus conveyed become much too limited.[103]

CHAPTER FIVE

THE NATURE OF THE HUMAN BEING

I am a human being;
that is indeed more than to have the title of prince.

Martin Luther, *W* 45; 15, 3-4 (1537)

Ought one to reckon with an essential continuity between man and God? As we shall see in the last main division (Part III) of this book, most Protestant Luther scholars start out with the premise that it is "evangelical" to reckon with a sharp divide—a fundamental break, a discontinuity—between the being of man and God's being. On the other hand, it is Catholic to assume a likeness of being, an essential affinity, that is to say, continuity between God and man. If this were the case, mysticism would belong to the Catholic camp. We will consider this problem by looking at three concepts: the soul, the "conscience" (*synteresis*), and reason.

In his reading of Tauler, Luther noted that God has created us in three parts: body, soul and spirit. In his exposition of the *Magnificat* he described the spirit of man as the noblest part. The spirit, he maintained, enables man to understand incomprehensible, invisible, eternal things. The spirit is the house in which faith and God's word live. The soul vivifies the body and is the place for rational knowledge and feelings. The spirit is potentially the power that makes man whole.

Luther, in other words, does not regard the spirit as a separate faculty. As body and soul, man's sensory and rational faculties are ruled by the spirit and by the flesh. Spiritual man, according to Luther, is governed by God's spirit in faith. When God thinks about the human, he thinks of the person as one—body, soul, and spirit. In order for the human to become what he is in God, a whole being, he must necessarily be ruled by God's spirit in faith, which then works through man's spirit.[104]

Some mystics speak in a similar fashion about unity or wholeness in God. The fact that some mystics do so invalidates the sweeping generalization that all mystics accept the concept that "the ground of the soul," inappropriately and heretically, divides the physical body, as something lower, from the soul or spirit, as something higher. On the basis of this generalization, the mystic is supposed to strive for "divinization." But this is not the perpetual goal of all mystics.

It is beyond the framework of this investigation to scrutinize all the mystics about whom Luther had knowledge, and whom he cited, in order to establish how close to or distant he was from each of them regarding views of the soul. One, already named, will be mentioned here: Johann Tauler.

Tauler's theology of the soul does not coincide with the generalization referred to above. In his ingenious examination of Tauler's view concerning "experience," **Gösta Wrede** inquires into the meaning of the word "ground," as in "the ground of being." For lack of space we cannot here give an account of the lines that lead back to Proklos, Dionysius the Areopagite (Pseudo-Dionysius), Saint Augustine, Thomas, and Eckhart and the points at which Tauler differs from those who were his mentors to various degrees. Tauler learned from Thomas Aquinas that "the ground," as the image of God in man, "longs for God," is created to be with God. However, Tauler came to emphasize the God-image's **love** for God and hence distanced himself from Thomas, who believed that **reason** was the seeker of God in the soul. Tauler was an ally of Eckhart's because the latter spoke about "the ground of soul," but he distanced himself from Eckhart in that Tauler accorded the intellect a less determinative role when it came to the "image of God." Instead of Eckhart's words about "analogies" between human existence and God, Tauler preferred the expression "God's essence in the soul." Wrede writes: "The latter is both the origin and the goal of the soul."

Gösta Wrede draws attention to the fact that Proklos is the author of the statement that God's image in man points beyond itself and that the "ground," therefore, is also a place for spiritual rest, "still, quiet, dormant." "Here we have," Wrede notes, "the **turning point in Tauler's world of thought**, where the human being in its ground of being has come so extremely close to its ultimate goal that nothing else remains but to meet God." According to Wrede, it is—as I have already had reason to state—the Neoplatonic view of the destiny of man that is the background for Tauler's opinion about the "ground." However, "he postulates the preparatory work which especially Augustine and Thomas [Aquinas] had urged." In this entire process Eckhart played a significant role thanks to the fact "that he communicated influences from both sides." The Neoplatonic background to Tauler's ideas about the human being as an emanation from God, and man's destiny to reunite with God, is not found with Luther. Luther spoke of the "old" man and the "new" man, Tauler of the "lower" man and the "higher" man.[105]

However, there remains Luther's great appreciation for Tauler's thoughts about the Christian's path. As some theologians do, one can assert that Luther did not understand his own best in this matter. Or one could say that Luther, with his comparatively little interest in speculation about the "ground" and "God's image," seized upon Tauler's testimony about the encounter with God.

The "ground of the soul" is therefore, according to Tauler, the inner space where the human meets God. Tauler used the metaphor of the mirror and the sun to illustrate the relationship.[106] Luther spoke of the spirit as the house, the abode for God. As pointed out, Tauler's term for God's dwelling place in man was "the ground of the soul." Both of them maintained, however, the dualistic tension between man and God.[107] Tauler also referred to the ground of the soul as God himself. The life of the kingdom eventually leads to a state in which "the spirit in this person . . . becomes so imbued with the divine that it is lost . . . in God."[108]

Man must be born anew in order to experience the fullness of the union with God, according to Tauler. Faith and justification were, as a matter of fact, included in this Taulerian conversion. Luther spoke of the indwelling of the triune God in the faithful person. The choice of words is not the same, but the mystical, non-rational overtones are essentially the same with Tauler and Luther.[109]

According to Luther, the human spirit has a side turned or oriented to nature. He calls this side the "soul." The soul possesses *a priori* knowledge of God. This question came up in one of Luther's table conversations. Luther asserted that

> Knowledge of God . . . is divinely imprinted upon all men's minds. Under the sole guidance of nature all men know that God is, without any acquaintance with the arts or the sciences. **There has never been a people so wild and barbaric that they did not believe in a divine power of some kind that has created all things.** It is for that reason that Paul says: "Ever since the creation of the world his invisible nature, namely, his eternal power and deity, has been clearly perceived in the things that have been made" (Rom. 1:20). Although humans have lived their lives as if there were no God . . . the con-

science witnesses to the fact . . . that God is (Author's translation and emphasis).[110]

Rudolf Otto, basing his conclusions on this and similar statements, asserted that Luther reckoned with "an *a priori* factor in religion" and that this thought on Luther's part is more basic to his thought than his occasional attacks against the idea. The attacks occur mostly when Luther is busy assailing Scholasticism's application of "reason," which in this context, in Luther's eyes, was a "harlot." Theological knowledge, Luther thought, comes only afterwards, *a posteriori*. Otto cites Luther in this connection, without, alas, giving chapter and verse:

> It is a knowledge *a posteriori*, in that we look at God from without, at His works and His government, as one looketh at a castle or house from without and thereby feeleth (*spüret*) the lord or householder thereof. But *a priori* from within hath no wisdom of men yet availed to discover what and of what manner of being is God as He is in Himself or in His inmost essence, nor can any man know nor say aught thereof, but they to whom it has been revealed by the Holy Ghost.[111]

The Roman Catholic researcher **Jared Wicks** has devoted much time and successful labor to Luther's spiritual heritage. Wicks draws attention to Luther's utterance about "God's work as the battering and humiliating of the flesh, so that the soul might rise more freely." Luther's notes suggested that God might need to destroy the original imprints in our soul to introduce the new. Wicks is of the opinion that the contact with Tauler thus served to strengthen Luther's conviction that "God works [in our lives] contrary to our wishes."[112]

Wicks suggested that Luther, in his early writings, was "overly dualistic" in his view of man as spirit and matter, thereby jeopardizing a holistic view. There is, nonetheless, in his theology the conception that we have

> invisible realities . . . within the human spirit; they are reached when a person turns within to consider what manner of goods correspond to his own spirit. . . . When one turns within, one 'finds oneself' and then is open to the word of God, which itself speaks of invisible goods, of the true goods of the human spirit.[113]

During the 1970s and the 1980s several Nordic scholars devoted themselves to studying the significance of mystical terminology in Luther's writings. Here we note their contributions to the question of man's nature in the matter of mysticism and the Reformation.

Herbert Olsson has come to the conclusion that Luther's doctrine of salvation, his view of imputation, and the gift from heaven as something that comes from the "outside," cannot exclude the created, innate inclination toward God. This natural knowing, as Gösta Wrede points out, was not identical with Tauler's way of speaking about the link to God as the "uncreated in the created" returning to the source. This becomes evident in the difference between Luther's description of God, as the righteous one, and Tauler's confrontation with God, as the perfect one. But both speak about "nature" in a positive vein. Olsson writes that one must assume—irrespective of the Christian viewpoint one chooses—that God created man with his own essence (*Wesen*). For this reason man controls his own life to a great extent and, consequently, is capable of making his own decisions. Otherwise one would have to assume that man's existence as a created being—and that would mean God's created being—would be only sinful.[114]

In his examination of Johannes Arndt's theology, **Christian Braw** wrote: "Where Tauler speaks of the image of God in the soul, Arndt speaks of the soul." The nobility of the soul rests in the "ground," according to Tauler. Arndt, on the other hand, is of the opinion that the nobility of the soul arises in the union of Christ with the soul, which occurs through faith.

Wrede sums up Tauler's view of human nature with these words: "It is the human being's nature to want to possess, to know, and to will. This nature is already directed to God and may not be inhibited by self-will . . . **if only self-will could be eliminated, nature would be good.**" Braw opined that for Arndt—and, one assumes, also for Luther—the soul is "fallen, possessed by sin," whereas Tauler, and in this respect he was undoubtedly not a Neoplatonist, saw the soul as poisoned. Yet, through his very essence, God is always present in the "ground," in the bedrock of the soul. God is "born" in the soul, says Tauler. God "lives" in the soul, says Arndt.[115]

Fredrik Brosché has written about Luther's thinking on predestination. Brosché maintains that when Luther uses the word "knowledge" he refers to knowledge born in and of faith. There is also an "inborn" knowledge about God, according to Luther. Brosché makes it clear that the two kinds of knowledge do not stand in "genetic" relationship to each other.

> Luther attributes to all mankind . . . a sufficient knowledge of the divine predicates, that God exists and that God is the refuge who offers support and help in time of need. . . . Reason

perceives certain divine predicates, but not, without Christ, the specific form of the divine subject.[116]

The prevailing tendency in Luther's thinking about the nature of man was to regard the soul not necessarily as "higher," but as more lasting than the body. To that degree the soul, as an invisible part of us, is more closely linked to God. The soul, as an emanation of God, therefore survives physical death. The distinction between the body ("a bag of worms") and the soul seems to have been more antithetical in Luther's younger years. In any case, the dominant idea was that humans belong to God. The soul bears this kinship within it in a special way. It is therefore perfectly in keeping with Luther's predominate view when he said, "Let us say that a person is lying on his deathbed and the soul is about to depart from the body," no one "knows nor understands how the transition from this life to that one takes place."[117] In other words, Luther was convinced, as has already been pointed out, that the life of the soul continues in other, invisible dimensions after death. But, at the same time, he regarded this soul as a participant in the life of the invisible kingdom during its earthly sojourn.

It is thus clear that Luther assumed a certain continuity between the human and the divine. This "natural" continuity is, of course, not qualified—the new birth in Christ must be experienced—yet, it is there. In this respect Luther was close to Tauler. Tauler asserted, as we know, that God's essence is part of the ground of the soul. At the same time he spoke of the soul's "nothingness." Some people, he thought, call attention to their own nothingness "as though they were in possession of this noble virtue of humility and in their self-appreciation thus think of themselves as loftier than the town's cathedral." But, alas, they deceive themselves. Few are those, "perhaps only three of those sitting here today," who know the Naught or Nothingness. Whenever you find that you desire the attention of others, sink yourself down "to your deepest ground."[118]

In his endeavor to establish a completely antithetical relationship between Luther and the mystic Tauler, Ozment argued that Luther's theology was faith-based, concentrated on faith, and that this implied that the psychological and the naturally anthropological could not be a part of Luther's theology. Tauler's theology, on the contrary, is called "mystical anthropology," a theological stance totally other than the reliance on faith that inspired Luther, Ozment asserts with great certainty.

The intention to demonstrate enduring polarity between the Lutheran and the Taulerian positions becomes apparent, *inter alia*, in connection with a Luther notation on a sermon of Tauler's. A Tauler statement causes the Reformer to write, in the margin: "We dictate the mode of God." To Ozment this spells criticism of Tauler. But the contrary is the case. Luther agreed with Tauler's assertion, hence the gloss in the margin. Ozment argues that Luther is, hereby, giving Tauler a lesson in correct Christian dogmatics. Faith, and not a natural anthropological source, determines the relation to God. Ozment averred that Tauler is guilty of Pelagianism because he assumes that there is a natural, in creation grounded, covenant and because he ascribes to the human soul important resources in the matter of salvation.[119]

To attribute to oneself such resources can very well be equivalent to Pelagianism, the idea that we ourselves are the origin of our salvation. But one cannot, as Ozment does, use the quotation from the Tauler sermon, cited by him, and Luther's marginal notes as proof of any polarity between Luther and Tauler regarding the nature of the soul. As we have seen, Tauler knew and acknowledged both affinity and continuity between God and man, on one hand, and the dualistic relation, the distance, on the other. If Luther had not sensed this, he would not have written in the margin: "Thus as he [Tauler] says here, salvation is through resignation of one's will in all things."[120]

A theology that must presuppose confessional contradiction at each significant dogmatic locus has difficulty eliciting a certain measure of continuity between the human and the divine in Luther's teaching. Luther was, to tell the truth, ambiguous in the matter. It depends a great deal on the context of the statement whether a dictum from him comes out on the side of continuity or discontinuity. On the subject of salvation, he was concerned that theology should not sound like synergism, the idea that the human essentially contributes to the act of liberation. In these cases the theological language is that of discontinuity. When he dealt with the question of divine omnipotence, he thought that man and the rest of the created world were accorded divine "substance," the interlinking power that lies under all outer manifestations. To that degree Luther counted with continuity.

A second topic under the rubric the "nature of man" or man's continuity or discontinuity with God is the conscience or *synteresis*, "knowing with God." In a goodly part of the medieval thought-world *synteresis* was considered to hold the highest place in man's endowments. Is this gift, "to know with God," something of a divine substance in the human or was it completely eradicated both formally and materially, both as frame and as content, when Adam fell? Luther seems to have discarded the term *synteresis* from his vocabulary, especially when the struggle hardened in the dogmatic arena. Perhaps the word in question, *synteresis*, carried with it a bit of salvation "philosophy." In his vocabulary it was consequently replaced with *fides*, which meant trust and reliance, even mystical union with God. But despite the change in terminology, Luther always had the opinion that God revives his own substance, emanates his own being, when the human is "born again." Man's "conscience" binds him to God, without him being aware thereof and points to the goal to be "righted with God." Points to the **goal**, yes, but the conscience does not offer the **way**. The role of *synteresis*, according to **Heiko Oberman**, is that of a "continuous, never ceasing appeal in the will of man."[121]

This, at times, anguish-filled longing for God, *gemitus*, meant to Luther that man is born to this earthly life with a *synteresis*, a conscience, which has a spiritual or religious function. In that regard, Luther did not change his opinion later in life when he preferred the terms *fides*, faith, and *adhaesio*, a spiritual cleaving to—a union with God, rather than the term *synteresis*. The essential fact remains: *synteresis*, this constant appeal to the human will, from within and from without, is a part of one's being. Bonaventura had spoken more clearly than many on this point, and Luther interpreted his own spiritual rebirth in a similar manner. *Synteresis* belongs to our essence, our being, in the sense that it enables us to "understand and love the invisible things." To be sure, this longing is helpless without Christ's righteousness and his leadership as the "Sun" of life, of existence, but the longing is there. "*Synteresis* signifies man's being, not his good being."[122]

Heiko Oberman thinks that this *synteresis* is the anthropological "domicile" for the Spirit in the manner that Paul speaks about it in Romans 8:26: "Likewise the Spirit helps us in our weakness; for we do not know how to pray as we ought, but the Spirit himself intercedes for us with sighs too deep for words."[123]

Within natural man there is material that can be molded by God. The "old" man—in the sense of former—provides the "stuff" for the new man. Luther, on the one hand, and Tauler and the *Theologia Germanica*, on the other, agree on this point. Bengt Hägglund maintains that Tauler's expression, the ground of the soul or "the ultimate essence of the soul," ought to be partly understood as "the original image of God in man." Here, adds Hägglund, it is not a question of a "synergistic conception," that is, a human claim to essential cooperation in spiritual rebirth.[124]

The question of "divine substance" in the soul came up once at Luther's dinner table (By the way, with the host's consent and Katherine's patient support, not a few visitors often frequented this dinner table). Luther said: "God is not bound to a locality. He cannot be excluded from any place nor can he be limited to or locked in any place.... He is in even the lowliest creature, in a leaf or a blade of grass, yet God is nowhere." Since there were apparently some professional theologians present, the question arose whether God is everywhere *potentialiter* or *substantialiter*, as a question of whether God was a potential or an essential ground. Luther: "I answer: in both ways in each creature. The creature acts by virtue of its *qualitas*, his qualities, but God acts . . . *essentialiter*, from the depth of his essence." The recorder of the chronicle continues:

> When someone said: "That I don't understand," he answered: "Don't you believe that God is at the same time present on the cross and in the virgin Mary's womb? In either case it is impossible for our reason to believe. In the same way that God can be lodged in the virgin's womb, he can also live in every creature." Another person said: "Would God consequently be in the devil?" "Yes, certainly in substance even in hell . . . as Psalm 139 says: 'If I make my bed in Sheol [the abode of the dead], thou art there'." [125]

Tauler spoke in a similar vein about what he called the innermost ground, that which is always there as a bond, a link. He spoke on the basis of personal conviction and also partly against a Neoplatonic background.

> Man must go into his own ground, into the innermost, and there seek the Lord, as He himself has demonstrated when He spoke: "God's kingdom is in you." . . . seek in the innermost ground where God is closer to the soul and more intimate, closer than the soul is to itself.

But whereas Luther experienced this "natural" link with God as unqualified from the gospel's viewpoint, Tauler taught about the radically life-changing encounter with the divine, which reduces human pretensions to zero. Tauler: "When a human being enters this house and has sought God in his innermost ground, God appears and turns everything upside down, in toto."[126]

How do Luther and the mystics who were closest to him, spiritually speaking, agree on the subject of reason? That is the third subject we have chosen to examine under the rubric the "nature of man," especially the question of continuity-discontinuity in relation to God.

When they have accepted Luther's decided opinion that reason cannot serve as a bridge to rebirth or God's birth in the soul, many of his interpreters have over-rationalized it. A look at the question of continuity and discontinuity, the nature of the soul and of the conscience, makes this plain for anyone who occupies himself ever so little with Luther's kinship to mystics.

It is true that in his disputes with Scholastic thought and humanistic Catholicism on the means of salvation Luther rejected reason. This fact is then interpreted as though Christian faith, in general, and Luther's faith, in particular, have nothing to do with the psychological and with the anthropological in man's search for a gracious God or for meaning to life.

True faith realizes that its links to God include a non-rational element, but that this component in the equation must also be combined together with *ratio,* the rational, the working of the intellect. Otherwise the power of the spiritual life wanes. There is an *a priori*-factor in all religion that can be called the divine nature's unity and goodness. It is rooted in "an a-priori knowledge about the mutual dependency between the rational and the non-rational factors in the concept of God." This is the way that Rudolf Otto puts it in the book, *The Idea of the Holy*. He is of the conviction that there is a necessary link between intuitive knowledge and intellectually derived information. To recognize the presence of knowledge via supersensible overtones, latent divine signs in the human spirit, is to make use of the faculty that we possess in embryonic form, namely, the power of what Otto calls (with perhaps not a wholly felicitous word) "divination," because our thoughts are led to "soothsaying." Otto wanted to coin a phrase for the intuitive experience of the "numinous," the Divine's awesome and rejoicing presence.[127]

One can perhaps dare to say that reason includes a non-rational factor, a "sense" in addition to the five senses, with roots in the suprahuman. Such a possibility forced Luther to make a distinction between purely human reason, which in Scholasticism was elevated to the voice of God, and reason, which is a symbol and a presentiment of God—points toward God—and is imbedded in our existence.

On the one hand, Luther thus criticized our application of reason. On the other hand, he valued reason in positive ways. He could say: "If you wish to live for God, you have to die entirely to the law. Reason and human wisdom do not understand that doctrine."[128] Then again, about the first article of the Creed, he could write: "Intended is that I shall believe that I am God's creature, that he has given me body, soul, normal eyes, reason."[129] And another example: "No one is so morally perverted that he does not feel reason's call and his *synteresis* (sense of the divine, conscience) . . . in accordance with Revelation 3: 'See I stand at the door and knock'."[130]

In another context Luther wrote:

> Natural reason itself is forced even here where there is no Holy Scripture to grant it [namely, the truth that the general human reason possesses many true cognitions of what 'God is in himself or in his inmost essence'], convinced by its own judgment. For all humans, as they hear it treated of, find this belief written in their hearts, and acknowledge it as proven, even unwillingly: first, that God is omnipotent and can neither err nor be deceived. . . . These two things are admitted by heart and feeling.[131]

From the above survey of Luther's and two mystics' thoughts on the soul, conscience, and reason, the following conclusions can be drawn. First, Luther presupposed that a knowledge of God was impressed upon man's spirit and soul from invisible spheres. Second, Luther assumed that every person knows that God is, thanks to the manifold evidence of God in his creation, even without access to the arts and sciences and without the aid of the Holy Writ.

By and large, Luther and his friends among the mystics had the same convictions in these respects. Together with some mystics he took for granted that supersensible knowledge, imprinted in nature, has its sources in extraterrestrial, invisible dimensions. Like some mystics before him, Luther took for granted that man's denial of God is an indirect admission that he is. For one cannot, said Luther, deny that about which one has never heard and of which one has never had any knowledge whatsoever. Man's conscience testifies to and affirms his potential, integral relationship to God. That vestige of the eternal, which has remained with us after the Fall, is perhaps not worthy to be called *imago Dei*, the image of God. The fact remains, however, Luther insisted, that a person "is God's work and creation . . . a created being and that is in truth more than having the title of a prince."

Luther's tendency to include, at times, the self-preservation instinct in the idea of total corruption seems to distance him from the *imago Dei* thought. But the fact that Luther described the human as *incurvatus in se*, egocentric, curved in on himself, does not mean that Luther dismissed the thought about the "natural" connection between man and God. The link, perhaps almost destroyed and of little effect in and of itself, can nevertheless be strengthened and restored by Christ. "The natural law is born with us," testifies Luther, "in the same way as heat is part of fire. The natural law is with us as fire belongs to the flint." Therefore Luther can also say that "man is oriented toward *imago Dei*."[132]

The mystical experience—the experience of God's presence here and now—is in some sense dependent on a certain continuity between man and God, a "substance" in man that is from God. This grows into the ability to make spiritual discoveries in which God's patterns and things that are of God become manifest. It seems to be quite clear that Martin Luther shared this gift with his friends among the mystics.

The danger in much theological treatment of Luther's utterances on the human being is that—and this bears repeating—in the writings of the interpreters of Luther he is depicted as a rationalist, whereas his non-rationalism—spiritual intuition—is ignored. Hence Luther's "dualism" is not as free from ambiguity as it may appear when many establishment theologians suggest that the only abiding contribution by the Reformer was in defense of the **rational theological** line—in contradistinction to his lack of interest in **mystics** and **pietists,** who supposedly follow misleading paths that are psychological and anthropological in nature.[133]

This theological bifurcation would then mean that faith in an evangelical and Protestant tradition now, once and for all, had distanced itself from the psychological and the anthropological whenever there is a question about theological considerations concerning God's activity with and among humans.

To Luther, the question was actually a different one. He asked himself where the point of gravity lay in a true Christian religious life. He found that this point of gravity was not "located" in the soul or the conscience or reason. The natural vitalities and qualities have no power to liberate us. On this decisive point Luther and the mystic Johann Tauler were of one mind. Tauler said: "In us the human must always die."[134] But if, on the other hand, one wants to argue that the theological search for Luther's guidance cannot have anything to do with what we call the psyche—the emotional, the intuitional, and the numinous—as means for inner growth in God, or that theology should not concern itself with the likelihood of divine patterns in nature and in human existence, is to misunderstand both Luther and his mystical kin. Christ can become our substance, our deepest essence, wrote Luther.[135]

It would not have been possible any other way. Luther's own notes certainly have plenty of passages that bear this out. The perception that a person could be without "spiritual experiences" was very foreign to him. "Theology" must therefore include the possibility that the human and the spirit might grow beyond the limitations of time and space. I think that one has largely misunderstood Luther's relationship with the mystics. Luther said that God is our substance, our deepest being. But did he, thereby, also say that we are denuded of that substance by means of which we are able to invite Christ and the Holy Spirit? The soul, the psyche, and the psychological must be involved. How else could Luther have pointed out that in communion with Christ he had entered paradise itself? Was not his psyche moved by that experience? And did he not have the perception, the impression, that in his hidden recesses he, Luther, sensed a feeling of belonging, of "home," when he received a message from an invisible, spiritual home.

Sadhu Sundar Singh told the following: "It became clear to me that the heart of man is God's throne and castle. When he deigns to live there heaven begins, and God's kingdom is there." Luther translated Jesus' words about the Kingdom in the manner of the mystics: *entos hymon* means "inwardly in you." In spite of fact that the words were directed to a group of insensitive Pharisees—or perhaps just because of it—Luther took for granted that an echo from that world always lingers in the valleys of our heart. However, for lengthy periods the sound of that echo is distorted by our sinful acts. Nevertheless, we can hear that tone not least from Luther's own story about his mystical salvation experience, his liberation from the difficult struggle with the meaning of "God's righteousness."[136]

CHAPTER SIX

SALVATION

Since I have been justified and have received the forgiveness of my sins without any merit, through grace, it becomes necessary to feel, in order to understand in some measure.

Martin Luther, *W* 40, 2; 422, 3-5 (1532)
(Author's translation)

We have observed that outer similarities between Luther and the mystics may decrease in number, but that some deeper concerns unite them. The analyses of the picture of God and the view of man gave some illustrations of such spiritual ties. Now that we turn to descriptions of salvation and its meaning we shall find the same essential unity. According to an old adage, saints do not contradict each other. This saying proves to be founded on sound wisdom even when it comes to the question of salvation.[137]

With the aid of the following procedure we are going to consider our theme, Luther and mysticism, and its bearing on the meaning of salvation. First, we take up the question of the (passive) unity with God; second, the question of faith as a *mysterium*; third, the mystical meaning of the words *gemitus* and *raptus*; fourth, the bride-bridegroom analogies; fifth, salvation as *Erfahrung* (experience) and personal change; sixth, participation in God; and lastly, seventh, the supernatural moments in salvation: salvation as confirmation of and as a testing realm for the supernatural dimension.

Unity with God

That which unites us with God is just as important to Luther and his mystical friends as that which divides. The second article of the Apostles' Creed makes this clear to the Reformer. Christ is our salvation and, therefore, the basis for our unity with God. But, as we have pointed out, the first article of the same creed also gave Luther occasion to declare that knowledge of God has been imprinted in the hearts, minds, and souls of humans, in creation itself. Man's mind and soul knows this *proprio suo iudicio convicta*, persuaded thereof by its own autonomous judgment. When the truth about "God in himself" is expounded, man grasps it by dint of reason—that is, of course, to the extent that the intellect can grasp the Being who is its creator.[138]

Luther could say about this potential unity with God, or acknowledgment of the God-fact, that *homo conditus est ad imaginem Dei*, man is created as an image of God.[139] We are potential temples of God and therefore have a predilection for God (but not necessarily a predilection for the good).[140] Tauler declares something similar: just as there is an "unrighteous ground of the soul" so there is also a genuine, longing-for-God ground.[141]

One can paraphrase Luther's thought on the matter and say that natural life is the beginning to eternal life, in so far as it is in the world of the "law" in which we feel the need of salvation, the need of grace. The apostle Paul knew the situation: "Wretched man that I am! Who will deliver me from this body of death?" (Romans 7:24). Yet, we can still count on the latent unity between man and the Divine (see Matthew 10:28). "Also after having lost the supernatural grace, *gratia supernaturalist*, in the Fall, he is still God's image, *imago Dei.*"[142]

According to both Luther and some of the mystics the soul "knows" those things that are of God, although the "knowing" is as if one were looking in a mirror. However, "knowing" or recognition is not the same as salvation. Nor does it mean that this knowledge is a preparation within the soul for receiving the Holy Spirit. (This is the description rendered by Ozment, who, in our accounting, is typical of a group of scholars that represent an almost exclusively intellualistic-dogmatic interpretation of the Luther legacy.)

What it means here is a long forgotten kinship with the power that has created us. When God saves, that which in its fundamental structure or character belongs to God is liberated. Here we stand before significant common ground when it comes to the subject of salvation.

Against this background we can speak of mystical unity between the Savior and the saved when rebirth has occurred. Then the passive heritage in man becomes actualized, and he becomes more actively a "part of the divine nature."[143] God's "being becomes our being."[144] One finds statements of this kind both with the younger and the older Luther.

His basic attitude to the question of the creation-conditioned unity between man and God prevails all through Luther's life.

The mystery of faith

Luther's "faith" was *fiducia*, trust, but also *adhaesio*, a clinging to God, *conglutinatio*, literally, bonded to God. These terms possess more of feeling and personal engagement than the usual word for faith, *fides*. That was the way Luther meant it. It was not only a matter of an old-new doctrine about justification. It was like a child's trust in his parents. Faith is a gift that generates *Gelassenheit*—a liberating, spiritually confident surrender that grows out of trust in God's eternal love, trust in his everlasting arms.

To Luther, justification—to be "declared righteous," to be "liberated"—meant that the human being has been righted, straightened out, by God working through Christ. When you are freed from the conditions or demands of the law that you could never completely fulfill anyway, it does not mean that you have legitimized yourself morally or have produced acceptable humility via spiritual exercises. To have experienced justification was the same as God's birth in the soul. Luther maintained that rebirth was a mystery. God granted him faith when he felt lost. The struggling monk felt that he had contributed nothing but his own despair, somewhat like the tax collector in Jesus' parable. For him faith became devoted trust in God's mercy and this was in itself a mystery. Luther wrote: "He who relies totally on God . . . gets from God everything he needs."[145] But one could not account for the gift. God came even if the recipient was unable to understand. Faith existed in an "independent spiritual life," so to speak. It was so much more than an intellectual acceptance of Christ's deed, imputed to man, an *imputatio*.

Because faith was so much more than a mere cognitive appropriation, Luther could speak of a **spiritual** use of the sacraments and of the institutional church as housing the hiddenness of the Christian life.[146] In other words, faith is more than that which is represented by outward signs, such as the elements and the ceremonies.

Luther's Psalter glosses of 1513 dealt with the mysterious aspects of faith by employing the following revealing terms: the secret of faith, the mystery of faith, the invisible grasped in faith, the calling to the invisible, the secret spiritual force, God as all in all, the conjuncture of soul and God.[147] To have all and yet have nothing, to mourn yet not to mourn—such antinomies emerged from corresponding experiences that later crystallized into dogmatic verities. Luther included in his theology the relation between the invisible and the presence of the Holy Spirit. Both of these aspects are shrouded in mystery.[148]

As there will be occasion to point out during this inquiry, Luther spoke about two sides of faith. This conjunction between two realities was and is necessary if you are not to lose sight of that which one wants to preserve. On the one side is "historical" faith; on the other is "true" faith. Together they make up what can be called the outside and inside, and they should not be separated from each other.[149]

Without hesitation historical faith affirms the creedal confession "Christ has suffered and surely also for me." This is true, historical faith says, and true as an undeniable external fact. But, Luther continued—and here one cannot always find the two components in the same book—if historical faith is allowed to stand only as an affirmation, it often enough fails to be open to feeling-laden, experience-based knowledge: the "**in** me" in conjunction with the "**for** me" makes faith into "true" faith in its spiritual meaning.

The marriage union is an illustration of what one is dealing with here. True faith is the necessary inner, non-rational urge that prompts the faithful to exclaim: My beloved is mine and I reach out to him in gladness. This feeling-side of faith is not grounded in our natural capacity for feeling, but rather in the discovery of our own sinfulness. The important point to make in the present context is that spiritual knowledge, knowledge that grows from faith, is more than to know Christ as a kind of mathematical cipher, as an aid to our self-analysis, or as an assurance of eternal life. Faith is also knowledge derived from experience, according to Luther. The justified knows, based on experience.

Faith, then, in Luther's world of thought, embraced more than "I-hold-this-teaching-to-be-true." There was also a strong tone of mysticism in Luther's experience. Faith was to him the kind of trust that engenders feelings of divine presence. It can, as we have seen, be a question of a feeling of awe or an awareness of a "presence" that makes you tremble. Luther, according to established usage, named this God's *tremendum*. It can also be a question of a joyous shiver, which is called God's *fascinosum*. In each stage of faith's experiential register there is a hidden, a non-rational element.[150]

This is the mystery of faith. It was akin to Tauler's mystical language. Tauler characterized the birth of faith as those moments when a person has reached "his radical Nought" and could "throw himself in the abyss of the divine will . . . sink down on his smallness, incapacity, and ignorance." Tauler advised his listeners to repeat the words of Peter to Jesus: "Lord, depart from me for I am a sinner." Then the mystery of faith will enfold the supplicant.[151]

Faith in its mystical dimension—and this goes for Luther as well for the mystics he cherished—was not only an acceptance of a public, external creed. Faith was also a private, personal surrender and—however unacceptable this may sound to those who speak about the danger of "privatization" of church and religion—a personal, private experience.

In a sermon in the so-called Wartburg Postil, Luther cited Mark 3:35 and Luke 8:21 about Simeon's predictions and the bewilderment of Jesus' parents. Luther asserted that Christ here invites his companions and followers to precisely an inner event. He posed the rhetorical question: "Who is Christ's spiritual father and mother?" The answer was: "Every faithful person is Christ's spiritual mother." The faith of the Christian and the mystical, private, intimate nature of the Christian faith and mission shines forth in one segment of the same sermon: "As often as a person comes into faith anew, so often Christ is born in him."[152]

Gemitus-raptus

The terms *gemitus* and *raptus* are used by Luther and some mystics about salvation. Heiko Oberman has devoted some instructive inquiries into these two poles of a hidden, mystical life in God. He qualifies his conclusions by terming the problem thorny, yet insists that we are now able to discern patterns in Luther's thought with sufficient balance and clarity to venture the claim that the *gemitus-raptus* complex belongs at the center, not to the periphery of Luther's theology.

Gemitus signifies the religious, inner affect, the anguish, engendered by the awareness of God's awesomeness, his "frightening" nature. "It is a fearful thing to fall into the hands of the living God." These words we find in the Letter to the Hebrews 10:31. They point to that reality depicted in Romans 8:26, a previously cited text. It deals with the Spirit, how it strengthens and fortifies us in our weakness and how "the Spirit himself intercedes for us with sighs too deep for words." *Gemitus* is the umbrella word for the inexpressible. There are no adequate words to describe this type of awesome meeting with the exalted one, an encounter that would cause us to tremble. In medieval Scholasticism and mysticism the *gemitus* had its anthropological domicile in *synteresis*, the root of conscience or the "window" to God.

In Luther's thought about salvation, anthropological theory played an unimportant role. He soon supplanted the term *synteresis* with the word "faith" or "trust-filled faith." *Synteresis* provided the goal, but did not offer the way. It is a justified sinner's faith that offers the way, Luther thought. The faith that God infuses into the soul brings man into *gemitus*—the sighing that is too deep for words and which is actually being done by the Spirit on behalf of the human. *Gemitus* is woven into the life of the believer. *Gemitus*, like prayer, presupposes faith. Of course, this was not the case in every mystical accounting. Some mystics would regard *gemitus* more as a practice in the development of humility or as an attribute of a sinless part of man. But for Luther—as for some mystics—God-given faith simply engenders *gemitus* as a sign of the righted relationship with God.[153]

What man knows in the awesomeness of the *gemitus* experience before God is that boasting and self-congratulation do not belong to any genuine man-God relation. This constant reduction to true proportions serves as a counterweight to the other component in a salvatory experience, *raptus*. Luther spoke about that experience, too. A theology of the cross thus prevented the mystical *raptus* from painting the Christian gospel exclusively as a "theology of glory."

The counterpole in this pair of opposites, which could actually be termed a confluence of opposites, is thus the *raptus*—being transportated to another realm. Luther said that one becomes a right theologian—and for him that was tantamount to being "a true Christian"—through *raptus et extasi*. In *raptus* one takes refuge in "the righteousness *extra nos*," from outside us. The *raptus* experience is a spectrum with many colors.

First, in *raptus* one sees Christ with mystical eyes and is overwhelmed. This vision unites within it the experience of the cross with being transported beyond the limits of the visible world. For, whereas the experience engenders life in the soul, it is simultaneously a partaking of Christ's sacrifice, a sense of perishing and being judged, as Luther noted.[154]

Secondly, deep silence prevails at the depth of religious rapture; beyond the Babel of many voices, Luther writes. Right theology and right Christianity grow from absolute silence, "in the highest reaches of the mind," *in summo mentis*.[155]

Third, this spiritual ecstasy changes our feelings and our trust. One's psyche becomes involved. However, this should not be interpreted as an ontological statement, that is to say, not a statement about the essence of being. Salvation comes to us from sources outside ourselves and coincides with *raptus* as an empirical, psychological event. Luther's view of the *raptus* experience thus precludes an exclusively forensic interpretation of salvation, i.e., the thought that the liberation of man is comparable to a juridical acquittal, without a corresponding movement in man's psyche. "If further research would confirm my supposition that Luther's idea about an '*extra nos*', outside us, is connected with '*raptus*'," Oberman writes, "it would take the force out of the main arguments for a 'forensic', juridical, interpretation of Luther's teaching about justification."[156]

Fourth, *raptus* implies passivity with respect to the soul, in Luther's opinion. But, if we read Luther correctly, mystical stillness before God was not an elitist achievement by a few who knew their exercises well, and *raptus* passivity did not mean that the seeker had wedded himself to a completely non-active program. Concerning the exercises, it is clear that Luther did not agree with the kind of mysticism whose exercises for the attainment of an ultimate state of passivity could only be carried out by a few experts. He "democratized" the mystical teaching about passivity. God invites us all, Luther said, to be "transported" and to be "led." This can be expressed in the following: God desires that we "let" him lead us into his grace. Such a democratized mystical theology prevents, rather than promotes, a quietistic interpretation of faith and salvation that urges Christians to withdraw from the world totally. Mystical impassivity is different from mystical passivity that results in participation in Christ. The Christian who surrenders to God in a *raptus* experience is not a dead instrument, nor is his justification an invitation to quietism.[157]

The fifth aspect of *raptus* is its connection with the created word, God's incarnation. Luther avoids linking salvation directly to the uncreated. This is not a question of the uncreated word, not a question of *Deus nudus*, God in his "nakedness," from a material viewpoint. Luther often placed the word *accessus* before the word *raptus*, justification ahead of ecstasy in spirit. This is what he writes in the commentary to Rom. 5:2: "Through our Lord Jesus Christ we have obtained access to this grace in which we stand." The grace in Christ is the *umbraculum*, a shaded, well-protected place. The *raptus* that the mystics spoke of is mediated by Christ.[158]

Sixth, when one experiences God in Christ as a kind of *raptus*, one is also in contact with the reality that Luther called a "hidden circumstance."[159]The witness about God in Christ gets its clarity and its power from the encounters with the hidden and the secret. Paul, in II Cor. 12:2, mentions that he had been caught up to the "third heaven." Luther read this with evangelical earnestness and was of the opinion that the message belongs to the very center of the gospel. He did not assign it to the periphery.

We may draw three conclusions from Luther's commentaries about *raptus* as a foretaste of an ineffable reality. Luther himself had had the same experience as Paul; Luther warned that it was rare and could be dangerous. Finally, without such front line glimpses of the supernatural, the transmission of the gospel would lose its dynamic force. Luther said that he "was once caught up into the third heaven."[160] He pointed out, however, that such events do not occur frequently and that, above all, they are not to be sought for their own sakes. They are, he meant, the fruit and reward of love rather than love itself.[161]

One cannot, however, get away from the fact that Christian witnessing and the Christian life are suffused with numinous experiences that exist far beyond words. Paul is one illustration; Peter, James, and John are likewise. And Luther is in the same category. But like the others he preferred to play down such mystical happenings. Just as in the case of the disciples, mystical knowledge was present by osmosis. The experience gives "power and authority," vibrates between the lines, shines through the spoken word.

But who is there who thinks that he is so pure that he dares aspire to this level (the highest mystical experience) unless he is called and led into the rapture by God, as was the case with the apostle Paul, or unless he is "taken up with Peter, James, and John, his brother" (Matt.17: 1)?[162]

Thus we see that much mystical theology, as personal faith-experience, paints the Christian life as *simul gemitus et raptus*, simultaneous unspeakable sighs and raptures. The common root for this "correspondence between contrasting conditions" is the mystical presence of Christ. The accent falls differently in several regards if we compare Luther with mystics. However, on this point there is doubtless agreement between the Reformer and the mystic about whom Luther said that he had found in him "more solid and pure theology than among all the Scholastics," namely, Johann Tauler.[163]

Tauler spoke of the emptiness and nothingness that one feels before the throne of God.[164] Here we have the *gemitus*-aspect. Tauler wrote that the beginning of the road to blessedness is the awareness or the consciousness that one accounts for nothing in the light of the divine or that what one does, and can do, actually is nil in that light.[165] That is the way in which the *raptus* aspect is introduced. Not that one is asked to follow a certain action or thought pattern to achieve spiritual rapture. This is simply the way it is when one stands even at the outer edge of divine radiance: one is crushed, shattered, and one is joyful, at the same time.

Oberman points out that there will be differing conceptions about the importance and implication of the *gemitus-raptus* comments. Nevertheless one thing is clear: Luther's use of these terms was infused by mystical experience. As a matter of fact, the meditations around the *gemitus-raptus* experience served as a counterweight to the tendency to intellectualize excessively the content of faith. The supernatural element of salvation became evident in using these words just discussed and also in the terms *excessus* and *ecstasis*. We are here dealing with a necessary sequence in divine logic or, perhaps, a fundamental premise —a spiritual counterpoint to God's work of salvation in nature and history.

Luther once expressed the mutual interdependence between mystical awe and rapture, on the one hand, and natural existence, on the other, in the following words: "The eternal majesty submerges himself deep into my poor flesh and blood and unites fully with me."[166]

The bride-bridegroom analogues

When we discussed "faith in God," there was reason to point out how unsatisfactory Luther finds the "historical faith," if it is left to stand on its own. "Historical faith" conveys to us, quite correctly, that Christ suffered and that he suffered for each individual. But "even the devil believes [the historical statement that Christ suffered] and praises God, just as heretics do." Imputed justification must contain experiential insight, empirical spiritual *Erfahrung* (experience), an often-used word in Luther's thoughts about salvation.

It has already become evident, in our previous presentation, that Luther mainly takes recourse to the Bible's and Christian mysticism's bridal imagery whenever he wants to describe the experience of *gemitus-raptus.* This recourse to bridal imagery occurred even toward the end of his life, not only in earlier years. There is reason to make a special mention of this fact. At times, in theological circles, Luther has been depicted as having abandoned, toward the end of his life, all real ties to the world of the mystics and their phraseology (This question will be further discussed in Part III). Luther never stopped reminding his readers or listeners of the fact that there is a way "of knowing" or "having knowledge" religiously, which "historical faith" hardly discerns.

Before continuing my summary of the passages in Luther's legacy that seem to point toward the likelihood that he uses the bridal form of mysticism in order to underline not only the objective element in salvation but, and not least, the personal, affective, subjective, I wish to account for two theological contributions on the subject in which the latter aspect seems to be toned down in favor of a more dogmatic-intellectual emphasis.

In a good and enlightening study of the theological views of Luther and his early followers, Leif Erikson concentrates on the Reformer's and early Lutheran dogmaticians' attitudes to "divine indwelling." Erikson points out, among other things, that Luther did not want to separate the one who is justified from the person of Christ. If that happens, "one is still under the law." In that connection Luther speaks about the essence of faith with the aid "of the most 'mystical' language there is." Erikson cites a Luther quote that suggests that "right doctrine" is "to be so integrated with Christ that man and Christ become as **one** person . . . because we are members of his body" (Eph. 5:30).[167] The question is now what this means subjectively. Does Luther use the language of bridal mysticism mainly to point out objective reality? If I understand Erikson correctly he says that Luther disassociated himself from Dionysius' bridal mysticism that proclaimed that man is able to reach God *sine medio*, without an external medium.[168]

The bridal chamber is a symbol of the "for you" under which a Christian lives. We are lifted beyond ourselves, carried away. But "although Luther emphasizes that Christian righteousness is a passive righteousness and an extraneous righteousness (that comes to us 'from the outside'), he does not deny *inhabitatio*." Erikson continues: "Christ is present in the believer's heart. . . . Luther asserts 'Christ is present, so to speak, in faith itself.'. . . Imputed righteousness outside us (*extra nos*) does not exclude *inhabitatio*."[169]

According to this proposition, it is thus a question of objective acquittal for the justified soul. At the same time, it is a matter of a very personal "indwelling" with all that this means for the soul's transformation and growth. *In corde habitans Christus* (from Luther's *Large Commentary on the Galatians*) means that the indwelling Christ is perceived and inspires.

The process is so intimate that Luther frequently uses the biblical language of bridal mysticism. Martin Lindström, in an interesting comment on the bride-bridegroom metaphor and Luther's affinity for mystical language, raised the following objection. Lindström asserts, namely, that this biblical imagery must be limited to that "intimacy" which is involved in the "blessed exchange" of properties. Christ and the soul "must be left in peace." Of course, this is a matter of justification by faith. To be left alone with Christ in this respect does mean that the "law, one's own achievements and even 'Christ as example' . . . must be done away with." Against this background the word "process" in the beginning of this paragraph becomes less acceptable. I think, however, that it has its place in this context. It is true that the isolation with the bridegroom establishes that my encounter with the Lord occurs without any merits of mine. But that is one step in the pilgrimage. One does not remain forever in the bridal chamber. One does not become a "log" or "stone" in relation to the justifying Lord, as the orthodox "log and stone" Lutherans used to put it. In **this** respect "our theology" is **not** "outside ourselves," to turn the Martin Lindström thesis on its head. When sin and righteousness are exchanged in the Christ-encounter, the soul becomes "pregnant with eternity." Something begins to grow. The event of salvation—whether it is at one particular point in history or is repeated in daily morning prayer—must be put in the context which Luther describes as a series of happenings: *anima formata in Christo*, the soul is formed in Christ.

It is entirely possible that the *Large Commentary on the Galatians* and the book about the freedom of a Christian really encourage the kind of interpretation that Martin Lindström suggests: a "**for** us" with exclusion of an "**in** us." But in order to save this interpretation from static intellectual dogmatism, a mere "holding-this-to-be-true," one must place it in a larger, dynamic framework, the *anima formata* (formation of the soul) context.[170]

The bridal analogies illustrate the "blessed exchange" in which the sinner, without merit or worth, is clothed in Christ's righteousness. The soul, which prior to being justified experienced the law as oppressive, now experiences the joy of God's presence and grows into the law. Now it is not only a matter of treading water in the sea of divine feelings. Growth in deeds of love is expected. Such things do not happen without what Luther called *Erfahrung*, experience, a practiced knowledge that is more than cognition, mental exercise. Here the language of the Bible and the mystic's conjugal imagery fit well together. This is the way it sounds in Luther's commentary on Isaiah 53, which was previously alluded to in the discussion about the nature of faith in this chapter:

> Knowledge is, however, of an empirical nature, and faith has reference to this word: "Adam knew his wife." That is to say, experience-wise through his senses did he know his wife, not in a speculative or historical way, but experientially, *experimentaliter*. . . . The historical faith admittedly says, "I believe that Christ has suffered, and suffered for me." But it does not add this sensitive and empirical knowledge. However, true faith states this, "My beloved is mine, and I embrace him with gladness."[171]

Life with Christ is like "a secret wedding." Both Paul and David complain about the anguish, sorrow, and fear of life. Actually, they ought to "soar high out of sheer joy," says Luther.

> But joy will be prepared for them in that other life. There they will see without scales before their eyes and forever dwell in joy. Now life is like a hidden, secret, spiritual wedding that cannot be seen by mortal eyes and cannot be grasped through intellectual reasoning. Only faith can grasp it, by holding fast to the Word. It is in such a way that faith hears of this wedding—yet understands it only in a dim fashion, since the flesh is so reluctant.[172]

From the same sermon we lift out a sample that again uses the marriage image:

> You may in confidence and joy make claim to the soul of Christ as your own. As a bride in heartfelt trust relies on her bridegroom and regards her bridegroom's heart as her own, so you ought to trust in Christ's love and not doubt that He has the same devotion to you as you have to your own heart.[173]

Further: "Faith . . . unites the soul with Christ as a bride is united with her bridegroom."[174]

As Martin Lindström points out, when Martin Luther speaks about the intimacy and the private nature of the bridal chamber, he illustrates justification by faith. Christ and the soul must be left alone. The law, one's own deeds, even Christ as example, must not be granted admission to the encounter of sin and grace. That is the main reason that Luther uses this imagery at all, Lindström believes. Luther: "This Bridegroom, Christ, must be alone with His bride in His private chamber and the whole household must be shunted away."[175]

One must, however, remember that, although the main object is to illustrate justification, in which all is left in the hands of grace, the significance of the word "private," as well as the character of intimacy, is lost if one restricts the scope of the illustration and its intent to a purely dogmatic assertion: we are certain because our faith and our theology place us outside ourselves. However, even here it is a matter of an inner drama, the Christ drama as it is being enacted within us. Something of this aspect comes through in the following words of Luther:

> For he who relies on Christ through faith is carried on the shoulders of Christ, and He will cross over successfully with the bride, of whom it is written "she comes up through the desert leaning on her beloved" (cf. The Song of Solomon 8:5). [176]

What we have to note is that this is **not** an isolated and static acquittal, exempting one from any resultant commitments and inner growth. This is abundantly evident in many Luther statements on the work of the Spirit. Following is one example:

> Just as life is never idle, but as long as it is present, it is doing something . . . so the Holy Spirit is never idle in the pious, but is always doing something that pertains to the Kingdom of God. [177]

It was, consequently, spiritual sensitivity and activity that was in Luther's mind when he chose mystical bride-bridegroom terminology. It not infrequently bothers some Luther-interpreters that Luther is not shy when it comes to physical illustrations; they find them too concrete and almost indiscreet. **Heinrich Bornkamm**, whose frame of reference will be discussed in the latter part of this book, declared that Luther gives the marriage symbols "a far wider and deeper meaning" than Tauler. One is wondering what this judgment means. Metaphorical language consists of nothing but pictures, it is naturally loaded with "a far wider and deeper meaning" than the immediately literal and natural. This is true about Luther, and it is true about Tauler. A metaphor is not a metaphor unless it points beyond the world of the senses.

Bornkamm wrote that, to Bernard of Clairvaux, bridal terminology was nothing but love-play. But, Bornkamm continued, Luther used nuptial language to indicate transference of Christ's spiritual gifts. But both Luther and many other mystics and biblical writers used all these earthly images in order to describe something heavenly as well as an inner, mystical experience. Under those conditions, therefore, it does not help very much to construct a contradiction between one mystic's "love-play" and Luther's "more far-reaching meaning." The reader should understand that Bornkamm's innermost interest is to separate Luther from every link with "mysticism."[178] The terminology of bridal mysticism was not only individually oriented, not an exclusive "privatization" of God's message and of God's instructions for man. There was also a corporate, communion-oriented element in the images of the man-woman relation which Luther makes use of when he wants to describe the blessed encounter and the blessed "exchange."

As we have heard, Luther spoke about the "mystical Christ" always present as spiritual power. He suggested that Christ lets himself be experienced as "a spiritual essence present in the hearts of the faithful." Christ is not only living in the individual; this is also true of the Christian community, the church. The church as organism can be understood only from the aspect of the gospel about Christ's resurrection and his living presence. If this would not be the case one should not be justified in speaking about the border-crossing task of the church. The church is Christ's body, the bride on behalf of whom he, the bridegroom, has suffered and has risen. The suffering and the victory that was won when Christ was incarnated as a human became the church's example, sacrament, and message of salvation.[179]

Christ guarantees the church's continued life. We ought to count on a perennial "marital" relationship between Christ and his body, the church. In this connection Luther uses Augustine's metaphor about the joy-filled exchange between the Invisible Leader of the church and its members.[180]

In one of the basic passages for the teaching on Christ as the bridegroom of the church, Luther spoke of Christ as the initiator of "spiritual birth" in those baptized in his name and as the founder of the church—"the new manifestation of the gospel."[181]

In Luther's book on Mary, *The Magnificat*, we read about Christ's bridal relation to Christendom.[182] Christ's invisible presence, promised during his earthly life and manifested all through the history of the church, guarantees her survival—even though every thing seems to disintegrate on this globe. As Christ's "bride" the church has always been protected and sustained.[183] About this mystically sustained and miraculously surviving church, Martin Luther said: "Christ has not ever abandoned or given up about his church."[184]

Which kind of "church" did Luther then think of: *ecclesiolae*, congregations growing up around the Reformation message, or the papal church? During the latter part of his life Luther seemed to have come to the conclusion that one must count with Christ's presence in both. According to Luther, there are no sharp boundaries between the churches. For even "the true church" sometimes follows the devil's counsel, mostly unwittingly. Also the true church is "a mixed association." The fact that the church survives when everything else breaks down is a sign of Christ's presence. Even during a time of dishonor and humiliation, the bride is constantly in the bridegroom's thought and care.

While Luther's estimation of the institution, as such, was rather lukewarm as time went on, he continued nevertheless to insist that precisely "continuity" was secured through the preaching of the Word and through the promises in baptism. But—and this bears repeating—to speak of "God's word" and its proclamation, on the one hand, and "Christ's presence," on the other, is not necessarily the same thing. For one must ask oneself: is Christ "automatically" present where the order of regular proclamation of the Word and the administration of the sacraments is maintained? This question is not always clearly posed in interpretive reflection on the Reformation teaching about the church. It was important to defend "order" and answer accusations of notions of independence in Luther's world of thought. As a consequence, it is either assumed that preaching and the sense of "Christ-presence" are mutually exchangeable or that Luther's concept of the church's continuity did not include "spirituality" or "assertions of independence."[185]

Yet, it must undoubtedly be taken seriously, even in theological thinking about the church, that we very often hear Luther say that there is a personal, "experiential" side to the Christian life. He would go as far as saying that the sacrament ought to be celebrated by "a Christian who has Christ's spirit."[186] The mechanical *ex opere operando* is not accepted here, namely, the idea that the act in and of itself guarantees effectiveness.

Hidden within the safely walled-in external church there is "the true church," thinks Martin Luther.[187] You do not see it, but it is there, for Christ is there. Without this faithfulness in the midst of the widespread unseemliness of the external church and the world, there would be no church.

Luther thought of the invisible *ecclesia spiritualis* when he was reminded of Christ's promise that he was going to be present wherever two or three were gathered in his name.[188]

The danger with a goodly number of Reformation interpretations is that the inner dimension, the possibility of "presence," escapes the eye of the expert in the attempt to reduce the evangelical faith to a rational common denominator, or to place it into a pigeonhole for intellectual concepts. Under the pressure of such an endeavor, such phrases of Luther's as the following tend to evaporate: Christians are people who "live from faith and in Spirit, that is to say in recognition of and love for all that is invisible." When he rests in God "man is called internal and hidden as he no longer lives in a worldly manner and in a sensual way." Therefore, every faithful believer is a part of a "tabernacle, which in a mystical way is also the church." (Ps. 27:5: "For he will hide me in his shelter in the day of trouble; he will conceal me under the cover of his tent.")[189] Thanks to the living Christ, "the Lord and the church are one body, head and body one *Christus mysticus* (mystical Christ) and, therefore, **one** beloved."[190]

The Word and the preaching of it are certainly at the center of the commission and mission of the church. But it is a Word that radiates Christ's presence and therefore "exceeds the orders." Words that radiate Christ give "inner" meaning to the individual and to the church body in the idiom of bridal mysticism that Luther used—as did many mystics and biblical forerunners. The magnetism of the biblical word naturally takes hold of the **individual,** in the first place. The imagery of bridal mysticism leaves no doubt about this. But the Christian's institutional setting, the church, transmits the biblical word to the individual through whom the Word is transformed into acts of love.

When we become right with God, when we receive the grace of righteousness, when we at long last cease to struggle as our own saviors, the Savior enters. He comes into that region where stillness reigns, where the claims of the ego do not require an entrance fee. Then it is better for us, writes Luther, that "we remain passive, like a woman before she begets. . . . When grace enters the soul and the soul is being impregnated by the Spirit, she ought to neither pray nor act, but only be still."[191]

This passive waiting is valid and difficult for the individual Christian and, through the ages, it has also been difficult for the church, as bride, to wait before Jesus Christ, the bridegroom. However, the message is equally true for both the individual and the church.

With an exquisite feeling for Martin Luther's personal, mystical conception of salvation, the Roman-Catholic theologian Erwin Iserloh has formulated the following testimony: "After justification there is a something like a (mystical) experience of salvation." He then cites the Reformer:

> After I have already been justified and acknowledged that my sins are forgiven without my merits through grace (*gratia*), then it is essential that I begin to feel so that I may in some measure understand.[192]

The matter to which Luther gave expression with these words was precisely the persuasion that lay behind his use of metaphors of the love between man and woman—although his analogies naturally were colored by the patriarchal culture around him. History and institutions were necessary as vehicles of salvation. But in the last analysis the question is put in a very personal way to the individual. Maybe it comes in the form of Jesus' question to Peter: Do you love me? An affirmative answer is like a confidence-filled nuptial relationship.

Experience and personal change

In one of the most knowledgeable and sensitive analyses of Luther and his spiritual kinship with mysticism, **Hermann Hering,** a nineteenth century German theologian, points to what he calls "Luther's cross vision." He was of the opinion that it was the experience of the cross of Christ that little by little opened Luther's eyes to the need for reform within the church. The church could no longer see the cross. She, the church, was drowning in power, honor, possessions, worldly glory, and was in competition with kings and provincial dukes. The cross vision had faded.

But without that vision the relationship to God had become, and would be, distorted. "The more sensitive Luther's inner being became" the more painfully he experienced that distortion. Hering was convinced that, during the years between 1513 and 1514, Luther discovered, in a more radical and decisive manner than heretofore, that worldly honor and the cross are mutually exclusive.[193]

This new insight coincided with a more discriminating attitude toward mysticism, said Hering. Luther consciously chose as spiritual mentors persons from the past whom he named the "German mystics," discarding much in the writings of the "general mystics." Tauler and the Frankfurter—the anonymous author of *Theologia Germanica*—contributed, in the first place, with answers to questions about the meaning of salvation. Other mystics, such as Bernard, Gerson, Augustine, and Dionysius the Areopagite became the objects of occasional critique on isolated issues.

Why was Luther drawn in a special way to Tauler, the Frankfurter, and Staupitz, Hering asked. His answer: they confirmed and supported Luther's own discovery of the biblical message. They spoke about trust in Christ instead of reliance on one's own merit. Their "German mysticism" was crystallized in doctrines of piety, not in academic or theoretical speculation. Their piety was anchored in the life in God and in experiences of life as a forgiven and a righteous sinner. When they said, "Come to God," they meant it as a personal invitation from a personal Savior. In a moving letter to his mentor and abbey friend, Johannes Staupitz, Luther declares that he prefers "the mystics and the entire Bible" to "the Scholastic doctors." Not that he wanted to reject all the things that the latter have uttered, but one should read "them with discernment." Since he gave expression to such views, Luther adds, his name has "gotten a foul smell" in many nostrils.[194]

Scholastic doctrines offered the world speculation and thought structures about the divine. Having declared that God is unfathomable, they proceeded in the next moment to explain who God is! Luther did not derive too much from this kind of disputation. Nor did he hesitate to share with others his skepticism concerning this sort of talk. No wonder that the established scribes soon enough ganged up against him. In the books on mysticism he discovered people who longed for a life in a not seldom unconscious revolt against Scholastic speculations.[195]

Luther was attracted by the Frankfurter's direct spontaneity. This was also true for Tauler and others among the mystics who sought to relate life in God to life in the world. The adjectives for their approach to the divine were "longing, warm, edifying, and simple." In his introduction to *Theologia Germanica*, Luther declared that he was attracted to this classic because it is so "simple." The Bible and the German colloquial language were also simple. Verbose and artificial language could not possibly serve as a medium for the encounter with God. There was something deeply significant in Luther's observation that the mystical writing in question was "simple." That is the way you talk to God. God sees through flowery talk. God desires that one speak "the language of the heart" with him. A seemingly casual observation about the importance of plain language led Luther to observe the essential simplicity in the mystical experience: God is always ready to meet us, in the stillness of our heart, his own chapel is within, unused because of our sin, available in spite of our sin.[196]

In his comments on the Ten Commandments Martin Luther used terms expressing "interiorization" and *Gelassenheit*—a trustful surrender to God. A Christian should entrust everything to God; he should prayerfully turn to and flee to God. He must meditate on Christ's sufferings. He ought to "go to Holy Communion in a spiritual way," become spiritually poor so that all his works be God's works, not his own. Humility is the fruit of this posture. Humility is also the basis for human fellowship. If the human being knew only a fraction of what God knows about him, he would become "a sweet kindly heart" in his relations to others.

From the experience involved with the "poverty" of the soul comes the desire to share with others. In this spiritual destitution lie the meaning and the secret of the words of Jesus about being harmless as a dove. The concluding commandments speak of salvation from temporal lust, and this is a partially attainable goal for a justified person. But a Christian should know that the perfect lies beyond the bounds of time.[197]

Among Luther's explanations or interpretations to the Apostles' Creed one finds similar thoughts on the place of experience in salvation. Hering points to terms that give expression to feelings of devotion and attachment—terms about the place of experience that Luther had in common with the language of bridal mysticism. The confidence and trust that emerges from the salvation event is characterized as "devoted (*hingebend*) trust." "He who puts all his confidence in God . . . gets from God everything he desires." This means that man has reached the point where it becomes truly genuine to say: I am not putting my trust in any creature "whether in heaven or earth;" I trust "only the mere invisible inconceivable God who is **one** . . . the sole ruler of creation." I believe this, commented Luther, "not less if abandoned and persecuted by all humans. I believe it not less if poor, misunderstood, unlearned, despised or lacking everything. I believe it no less if a sinner." For "my faith (devoted trust, *nota bene*) must soar (*schweben*) above all . . . sin, virtue, above it all, so that he [the Christian] keeps to God single-mindedly and purely in accordance with the first commandment."

About the second article of the Creed Luther wrote that Christ "is risen in order to give me and all His faithful a new life." He "has awakened us with Himself, in grace and spirit, so that we shall not sin from now on, but serve Him alone in all kinds of graces and virtues."[198]
In these Luther statements from 1520, "experience" appears as an ele-

ment in the context of salvation. Here we have also a "for-you" theology that engages the entire self, not only the intellect.

Ten years later, in his *Small Catechism*, Luther did not make use of mystical terms. "But," writes Hering, "in the exposition of the commandments the high standards of the mystical life have remained." Warm, heartfelt feelings and simplicity were signs of Luther's kinship with the mystics. Hering was of the opinion that, as the Reformation was proceeding, Luther's struggle with "distorted mysticism" necessitated a tighter "objective" doctrinal language about the goods of the kingdom and the two sacraments. Yet, the personal experience aspect was still present as part of the salvation event, according to Hering's reading of Luther. In order to undergird the correctness of his interpretation, Hering cited a letter that Luther wrote about the so-called Zwickau prophets, the radical post-Reformation mystics. Luther poses the question: "Have they experienced *Anfechtung* (anguish-ridden doubt), the birth of the divine, death and hell?" God does not normally speak to people directly—and it is **grace** that he does not do so. Mary became frightened when the angel appeared. Luther became skeptical when, for instance, Dionysius the Areopagite described his way to salvation. For Dionysius spoke of a direct connection with the Uppermost, where God's Majesty has its abode. Who can converse with the Uppermost? In Zwickau they are not likely to use Scripture, according to what he has heard. There they read only from their own hearts. But this would never be wise. One knows how it went for Moses. "God speaks through man [indirectly] because not all can endure his speaking."[199] In our case, experience of God's presence comes through the Word, which is Christ, and through it He turns to us. Consequently *sola fide*, faith alone, cannot be understood as a repudiation of mysticism in Luther's theology.

The word *raptus*, discussed above, illustrates how "feeling" becomes an integral part of the mystery of salvation. "Faith with Luther clearly carries mystical traits and, in Luther's theology, it is delineated by one of mysticism's central concepts, *raptus*," Iserloh contends. Luther knew about religious *ecstasis* and his explicating word for this experience was *senses fidei*, the knowledge of faith that includes heart and feeling, not just intellect. This ecstasy he called "the spirit's *Hineingerissensein*," a condition that carries a person beyond himself, beyond the little self, into "a knowledge that grows from faith."[200]

In a lecture on the Letter to the Hebrews, Luther directed special attention to the mystical dimension of faith that can be experienced and that Luther doubtlessly also experienced. He described contact with God as an experience that travels beyond the boundaries of the psyche and the sense organs. Thus he says in the following commentary on the Letter to the Hebrews: "Christ faith is a being-taken-away (*raptus*) and a being-carried-off (*translatio*) from all that is experiential (*fühlbar*), inwardly and outwardly, to that which is experiential neither inwardly nor outwardly, toward God, the invisible, the totally exalted, incomprehensible."[201]

Nevertheless, whether or not near contact with the divine can be reduced to the psychologically registrable or not, one thing is certain, it leaves an indelible mark in "the heart," the symbolic sanctum for feeling. The salvation experience provides an awareness of God's true relation to the heart and the heart's true relation to God. Luther wrote:

> Faith causes the heart to cling to celestial things and in rapture to be carried away to dwell in things that are invisible. . . . For this is how it happens that the believer hangs between heaven and earth . . . that is to say, in Christ he is suspended in the air and earth and is crucified.[202]

Luther's language of feeling made him sound, in certain contexts, like one of those theologians whom he would fiercely attack, the ones that seemed to suggest that man could spin God out of himself and that, therefore, constant positive change and transformation are possible by man's effort. Indeed, Luther's language might have sounded like that from time to time. It is important that we note the soteriological context in which he expresses these obviously unevangelical utterances. He wrote: "It [faith] is the creator of divinity, not in the substance of God but in us."[203] Within which framework was this pronouncement uttered? Obviously, within a framework of a salvation experience where man, in his godlessness, was a corrupt creature and a *homo mendax*, a mendacious being, but where once the power of God's righteousness in Christ had set in, "through faith Christ is called our 'substance,' that is, riches of the spirit, and through the same faith we simultaneously become His 'substance,' that is, a new creature."[204]

When one opens up to Christ's energy-field, one is transformed into the likeness of the Lord. Luther and some medieval mystics were of one mind on this point. Salvation brings with it change, transformation. It is a paradox and a mystery that "remolding" can occur since the *homo mendax* continues to incline toward the devil, even after spiritual renewal has taken place. But conformation with Christ does occur. Mystics knew that something was happening to their existence, as a whole, when they came to the cross. The Frankfurter, one of the closest soulmates among Luther's mystical brethren, called the process of change "divinization," an expression that does not go down too well among some Protestants.[205]

However, a Luther quote in a book by Nathan Söderblom illustrates that Luther thought all persons could change totally through the power of faith. Luther wrote:

> Much has been written about how one shall become divinized. One has made ladders on which to climb to heaven. But such talk is empty nonsense. Here [in the gospel of justification by faith in grace] you are shown the right way and shortest way to get there, so that you will be filled, yes, filled with God, so that you are in need of nothing, but you have everything at once, so that all that you speak, think, undertake to do—to sum up, your whole life becomes completely divinized.[206]

The process of change, a result of salvation, is closely connected with the power of Christ. Is this power mediated only through the two sacraments? Luther's view of the personal experience of Christ certainly transcended mere institutional sacramentalism. A change, that is, a transformation, occurs in a justified person—not only theological but also psychological, a tuning-in to the Savior. The attunement alters man's spiritual-psychological form. The formation takes place in human relations, through contemplating the Word, by prayer and in Holy Communion. Luther's experience of personal salvation (God in Christ spoke directly to him in the midst of his tribulations) broadened his concept of the sacramental, although he was responsible for diminishing the number of sacraments as liturgical acts. He wrote: "All words, all stories in the gospel are sacraments, as it were, i.e., holy signs through which God generates in the believer what these stories signify." [207]

Change as a result of salvation means Christ becomes a power in his follower's life. It then becomes clear that the transforming power of God in Christ was not confined to the two sacraments as administered by new evangelical parishes. Luther maintained that God works in us and builds us up everywhere, in conjunction with the power of the Word, the Word that is Christ.[208]

No special place, no special order emerging from institutional traditions is the condition sine qua non for the work of God in a soul. Places and institutional sacraments are useful—in the case of baptism even essential—but they are not the only channels of grace. In this way one can sum up Luther's thought about the relation between sacramental orders and personal regeneration.[209]

The relatively strong accent on personal experience did not signify that Luther deemed the isolated inner encounter with God as more glorious than the external medium. His pamphlet, directed against the "heavenly prophets," provided evidence of that. Luther did not want the new "Enthusiasts" to assume that their piety would require them to disregard or discard orders and customs. From his knowledge of the human heart it was Luther's view that precisely the setting aside of orders and customs very well could result in a new law, in creating a new yoke. God gives us external signs so that through them one can be brought into faith. He comes in the external, historical Christ who encounters us in the "external," as represented in the words of the Bible, in sermons, in baptism and in Holy Communion, all outgrowths of biblical texts.

However, having made the case for visible signs in refutation of attempts to interiorize and spiritualize the salvation process, Luther turned the question around. One must own and make use of palpable orders, that is taken for granted, but in the area of faith the interior precedes the exterior. The heart names the work; the work does not give the name to the heart. As an institution, the church does not mediate salvation but remembers that "the true Church . . . works and toils in the heavens."[210]

The "external side" of the sacraments and the Word is necessary in order to wrestle the soul away from its tendency to be curved in on itself, but the external arrangement, as such, does not guide us closer to the nucleus of the matter, namely, love as life in faith. Only look at the Enthusiasts (*Schwärmer*) who advocated freedom from all outward order and slipped into a new legalism. God's calling to inwardness and love turned into a new thralldom under the law, where the inner being was not always placed above the exterior.[211]

On the other hand, in 1539, Luther wrote the following to Probst C. Buchholzer in Berlin about ritualistic ceremonies:

> Thus you are free to have a procession in the name of God, carry a cross of silver or gold, and wear a chasuble . . . of velvet, silk, or linen. If your lord the elector is not content with one chasuble . . . put on three of them as did Aaron . . . and if His Grace is not content with one procession in which you go around singing and ringing, then go around seven times, as did Joshua with the children of Israel, who made noise and blew their trumpets. And if your lord the elector is so inclined, let him leap and dance in front with harps, drums, cymbals,

and bells, as David did before the Ark of the Lord when it was brought to the city of Jerusalem. I am well content with it, for such matters, as long as they are not abused, do not add to or take anything from the gospel. But they must not be made a matter of necessity for salvation, to constrain the conscience. Vestments and other liturgical helps should not be consecrated as though the consecration imparted a certain holiness to them, but should be used with prayer and the Word of God.[212]

It became indeed clear that a person of faith had embarked on a journey that touched both Scylla and Charybdis, *mutatis mutandis*. On one hand, the Scylla of built-in legalism and, on the other hand, the Charybdis, the temptation to make a law of "heartfeltness." But the Reformer always returned to the inner, personal crucifixion experience as the gate of entry to salvation. Luther wrote:

I bring the goblet with wine to my mouth, and I drink the wine, but I do not press the goblet down into my throat. So it is with the Word which brings us the voice: it sinks down into my heart and becomes living. But the voice remains outside and dies away. That is why it is a divine power.

About this close connection between the spiritual inspiration and its channel, Luther has furthermore the following to say:

In order properly to understand this sacred hymn of praise [The Magnificat], we need to bear in mind that the Blessed Virgin Mary is speaking on the basis of her own experience, in which she was enlightened and instructed by the Holy Spirit. No one can correctly understand God or His Word unless he has received such understanding immediately from the Holy Spirit. But no one can receive it from the Holy Spirit without experiencing, proving, and feeling it. In such experience the Holy Spirit instructs us as in His own school, outside of which nothing is learned but empty words and prattle.

Seen from the viewpoint of the "School of the Spirit," the law and cross became media and Luther encouraged his readers and listeners to "hold fast to the Word that directs Christ to you in that He says 'See my hands and my feet.' Then shall your heart be filled anew with gladness and you will be able to enjoy his Word in your heart and it will be like sweet honey and fine comfort."[213]

In his thoughts about the bondage of the will Luther included the following words, which give an indication of his attitude to the institutional and the subjective-interior components of salvation.

> Since Scripture testifies that God is present everywhere and fills every thing (Jeremiah 23:24), the pious person asserts, no, not only that, he experiences it and knows it also, that God is present everywhere. Were it not so I would not pray to God if a tyrant should take me captive and throw me into a dungeon or a cesspool and not believe that He is close to me until I come back into a stately church.[214]

To fall into God's arms and begin to change in that embrace—that is the inner salvation story. But, it must be repeated, the orders for the dispensing of the Word and sacraments serve as entry gates and external signs without which there would be no proper growth.

The mystics emphasized the experiential element in faith as well as inner transformation. To Luther the mystical side of Christian life was precisely this experiential side and conformation to Christ. His inner struggle had brought him to the same kind of insight as some mystics. From this came his joy at the discovery that he was not alone (His preface to *Theologia Germanica* mirrors this elation). But did the mystical writers he regarded as co-pilgrims have the same kind of respect for the external and historical in God's work of salvation? One thing is certain: they did not have his strong sense for concreteness and history. Yet, they were by no means unaware of the determinate media through which God works.

Theologia Germanica, which spoke of transformation as "divinization" at some junctures, took pains to point to "the Writ" as primary source. The anonymous author used the phrase "God speaks" immediately followed by the Bible passage to be expounded. The writer enumerated the components of a Christian life: "the word, works, and the way to live." Note he placed the word first.

Johann Tauler described the road of salvation as a total reduction of the ego, an acquaintance with the Nought as antecedent to a tender calm, a loving trust, a friendly confidence, and a holy hope. He was also certain that God communicates through external signs. He wrote:

> When one falls into God's arms one realizes clearly that God contacts us via outward means. In many lands one cannot teach and preach anymore, nor warn. As long as you have the word, there is reason to remember that. . . . The noble, divine Word is little understood. That depends on its getting locked up by the senses so that it does not reach the interior. It is being destroyed by other images . . . the roads will have to be cleared

. . . much of God's word gets lost and remains unapprehended by those who are not yet free.

Furthermore, Tauler placed great emphasis on the outer sign and its observance. In order "to cleave firmly to God" it was necessary, said this mystic, to attend with regularity "the sacrament of the Body of the Lord." This should be done not primarily in order "to attain to a state of great perfection" or on the basis of "great deeds."[215] It rather had to be done in accordance with Jesus' insight into the nature of salvation: those who know that they are sick, know that they are in need of a physician, not those who believe that they are healthy.[216]

As is apparent, the two mystics mentioned above were not unacquainted with the importance of balance between Word and Inner Light. Martin Luther's spiritual intuition concerning the theological soundness of much mysticism proved to be accurate. Therefore, one should be rather cautious about accepting the more or less rationalistic theologies that assert that Luther, in this particular instance, did not know his own best. With apologizing gestures toward the audience they sought to correct the Reformer. He embarrasses them, but the damage could be repaired—by pretending that this is only a slight aberration on the map.

Experience and "formation" were included in Luther's depiction of salvation. When God moves into a person's life, that person feels it and begins to grow in conformity with Christ. As has been indicated, utterances of this kind can easily be misinterpreted as expressions of "enthusiastic" mysticism that seemed to disregard the outer incarnate forms of the gospel or accord undue weight to man's own powers. Thus, if we want to understand Luther's experience-laden language, with its talk about the movements of the "heart" and the significance of the word "feel," we must at regular intervals train the gaze toward the central thought and the central experience: justification, the encounter with God who sees all yet wants to take us into his service.

The other extreme in the history of Luther interpretations is the assertion that the reality behind the words "experience" and "feel" may not be applied to Luther's understanding of faith. Faith has, namely, not any place for an empirical psychic process. "Theologizing" is one thing, "psychologizing" an entirely different one. However, on the other hand, we must point to the experience-side, Luther's joy-filled experience of liberation.

We are standing before a dichotomy in Luther's world of thought: on the one hand, there is the conception that the faith of the Christian can elevate his consciousness and knowledge about life in God and "co-operation" with God. On the other hand, there is the conviction that since grace is all or nothing one cannot speak of any human counterpart or reaction that could result in an actual change. Consequently, we are here dealing with a theological-logical dilemma that clearly becomes apparent on the following pages. On those pages we are going to take up the question about man's participation in God.

Participation in God

Martin Luther spoke of man's participation in God not only as an appropriation of a "for you," but also as an immanental "in you." In the latter instance, we encounter terms like *conformatio*, God's forming, molding, shaping work and *unio*, union with God in Christ. Transformation and unification are accompanied by development toward human wholeness and a growing awareness of the unity with Christ, the spiritual Sun behind the visible sun.

In the following section this subject will be discussed, first, against background of the forensic-juridical and the liberal-humanistic interpretations of a Christian's participation in God. Secondly, we examine the question guided by Luther's use of the term *communicatio idiomatum*, exchange of properties between God and man. Thirdly, we consider this participation in the divine from the point of view of possible contacts with invisible realms. Fourthly, we consider whether this participation might be a source for the integration of body and soul and spirit.

How do orthodox Protestantism and liberal humanistic theologies conceive of man's participation in God? In the last main part of this book some illustrations will be given of the way exclusively rationalistic theologians ignore the psychological and supersensible implications of man's life in God. According to Luther, man is a participant in the divine drama in a two-fold way. In a more distant and a more impersonal way we encounter God in creation's *larvae*, the masks of God. This is to say, God meets us in the guise of his creation.[217] In another more personal way God reveals himself to humans through and in Jesus Christ.[218] Man comes to know God in this dual manner.

In our discussion about the image of God we saw that Luther considers it self-evident that man has been endowed with a general knowledge of God. Luther found it quite proper, theologically, to assert that man, from his own nature and by his own intuition, must concede that he lives, moves, and has his being in God. But this concession commits one to nothing. Before Christ, our Lord, who is both judgment and grace, we are called to a new kind of participation in God. This new kind of participation emerges from a crucifixion that we must undergo in the shadow and power of Christ's crucifixion, namely, to crucify our desire to be our own savior. This leads to participation in Christ's life that implies a growing from glory unto glory, as Paul expresses it. Luther felt at home with Bernard of Clairvaux on the question of our growth as Christians. In the tension between his strong desires, *concupiscentia*, and grace, the Christian knows that "to stand still is to regress," *stare est retrogredi.* [219]

In orthodox Protestantism, natural religious inclination is considered irrelevant to the question of salvation. To say that man is by nature religiously inclined is, to orthodox theologians, an assertion without merit. The same is valid for the statement about links with God, namely, that contact with God can be mystical, experiential. In reaction to the assertion that man can participate in God, orthodox Lutherans become rationalistic.

Thus, for example, *unio mystica* assumes an intellectualistic ring in the hands of theologians of the Scholastic school. Justification becomes only a statement of fact: a deed done for man by Christ. Man is declared guilt-free thanks to a force that emanates from Christ. Then union with God becomes an "I-hold-this-to-be-true" pronouncement, a rational assertion, an intellectually conceived granting of "new life" by the implanting, in the individual and the church, power from Jesus' vicarious deed. Theologians have often used the term *unio mystica* for justification. But orthodoxy's use of this word implies no other expectation than an intellectual recognition of a truth. On this view, justification becomes a basically juridical occurrence in the special theological meaning that when the judge grants the petitioner freedom from guilt that is turned over to somebody else, Christ. Christ's vicarious deed has acquitted man before God's judgment seat. This means, consequently, that grace cannot be thought of as inducing a process of transformation within the human psyche, not least for the reason that orthodox Lutheranism makes a special point of emphasizing Luther's teaching that man is a corrupt creature who lacks the image of God, the "ground" in which spiritual change could germinate. Forensic orthodox theology is closely tied to eschatology, the teaching about the end times. God's gracious deeds among humans, in behalf of man, are described as a fulfillment of the promised redemption. Viewed thus, there is no impact that leads to sanctification, that is, to spiritual change or renewal in daily life with God.

The liberal or humanistic approach to the matter of participation in God discounts the possibility of a mystical sharing in the divine as "only a helpful concept" (Ritschl). If one wishes to speak about participation in the divine, one should turn to our ethical existence. Thus our moral actions are based on rationally determined conclusions, often with guidelines from the social sciences. It is alien to the liberal stance that moral decision making could develop from a non-rational, numinous experience of oneness with God (e.g., John A. T. Robinson's *Honest to God* or Joseph Fletcher's *Situation Ethics.*)

Both the liberal and the orthodox point of view omit, as nonessential, those strains of mystical spirituality that we have found in Luther's world of thought. In his work about Luther's view of *unio mystica,* Erich Vogelsang took exception to these avenues of Luther interpretation as being too rationalistic. Luther, wrote Vogelsang, regarded man's commitment to or participation in God as a gift of grace —but also as a felt response and a contact with a life-giving, invisible power. Luther said "Christ is God's grace . . . given us without any merit on our part." But in delivering the gift he does not remain outside the soul. This, Luther would argue, is "dead justice." No, "Christ himself is there" in the same manner as "the brightness of the sun and the heat of the fire do not exist where sun and fire are not found."[220]

Vogelsang continues: it impossible to think that you possess Christ's gifts without "the real presence, His real presence." According to Vogelsang, Luther's ideas about the "joy-filled exchange" between Christ, as Bridegroom, and the human, as bride, have an enduring prerequisite: Christ's mystical presence. That certainty grows out of faith that emanates from Christ's incarnation.[221]

With partial reference to Vogelsang, **Erwin Iserloh** underscores the same thought. He points out that Luther, in this regard, was in tune with "patristic teaching on redemption," but in disagreement with the Scholastic teaching on satisfaction which "remains tied to the moral-juridical level." The church fathers, and especially Augustine, described man's relationship to God as follows: man has alienated himself from life; he lives in disobedience to God. In fact, he has surrendered to the forces of death. But Christ took upon himself the flesh that was under the dominion of death. Death could not hold the prey that seemed to be lost on the cross. Christ's abundant life was too powerful for death to conquer. Christ's humanity was the bait "on the fishing hook of

Christ's divinity," and this led to the undoing of death. Having emptied himself in obedience through his death on the cross, Christ redeemed human self-glory, rendered death powerless, and brought divine life to man's nature.

Iserloh was of the opinion that Luther had in mind redemption of the kind just described, rather than forensic satisfaction, when he used "the mystical concept of faith as a marriage act between the soul and Christ." In Luther's book, *The Freedom of the Christian (De libertate christiana*, 1520), Iserloh found a striking example of this idea. Luther wrote:

> Faith not only gives the soul enough for her to become, like the divine word, gracious, free, and blessed. It also unites the soul with Christ, like a bride with the bridegroom, and, from this marriage, Christ and the soul become one body, as St. Paul says [Eph. 5:30]. Then the possessions of both are in common—whether fortune, misfortune, or anything else—so that what Christ has also belongs to the believing soul, and what the soul has will belong to Christ. If Christ has all good things, including blessedness, these will also belong to the soul. If the soul is full of trespasses and sins, these will belong to Christ. At this point a contest of happy exchanges takes place. Because Christ is God and man, and has never sinned, and because His sanctity is unconquerable, eternal, and almighty, He takes possession of the sins of the believing soul by virtue of her wedding-ring, namely faith, and acts just as if He had committed those sins Himself. They are, of course, swallowed up and drowned in Him, for His unconquerable righteousness is stronger than any sin whatever. Thus the soul is cleansed from all her sins by virtue of her dowry, i.e., for the sake of her faith. She is made free and unfettered, and endowed with the eternal righteousness of Christ, her bridegroom. Is that not a happy household, when Christ, the rich, noble, and good bridegroom, takes the poor, despised, wicked little harlot in marriage, sets her free from all evil, and decks her with all good things? It is not possible for her sins to damn her, for now they rest on Christ, and are swallowed up in Him. In this way she has such a rich righteousness in her bridegroom that she can always withstand sins, although they indeed lie in wait for her. Paul speaks of this in I Corinthians 15: "Praise and thanks be to God, who has given us that victory in Christ Jesus, in which death is swallowed up together with sin."[222]

In the section on the bride and bridegroom relationship, we had reason to discuss its meaning. Should the exchange imply only an imputation, an admonition, an assertion of a fact, an objective "for you?" Or does the analogy involve, in addition, a mystical **advent** from the living Christ, an **advent** that is experienced as an "in me" by the worshiper himself? As is evident from the next section, Luther speaks about the inner advent in the soul, about continuing visits with the One who invites the soul to prayer and meditation.

From Luther's remarks on participation in God we draw the conclusion that one does not do justice to his view of sharing in divine life by concentrating only on the "for you" of redemption or by a reduction of redemption to the ethical. The freedom engendered by the gospel, according to Luther, was not only a declaration of grace but also an experience that included joy, the beginning of inner transformation, and a new discovery of the law from within.

The second idea chosen to illustrate Christian man's participation in God concerns the spiritual drama that is enacted between God and the soul. The encounter between man and God is often described as a joyful marital union in which there is an exchange of properties. This encounter has been termed *communicatio idiomatum*. Luther suggested that there are qualities in Christ's humanity that belong to the divine. In like manner, Luther said, man harbors aspects of Christ: incarnate man is in part spiritual. The dialectic of this situation emerges in Luther's commentaries on Paul's Epistle to the Romans:

> For in this way there comes about a communication of attributes, for one and the same man is spiritual and carnal, righteous and a sinner, good and evil. Just as the one and the same Person of Christ is both dead and alive, at the same time suffering and in a state of bliss, both working and at rest, etc., because of the communication of his attributes, although neither of the natures possesses the properties of the other, but are absolutely different, as we all know.[223]

Like the church fathers Luther made use of Philippians 2:5 when he wished to describe the exchange of properties between the divine and the human which takes place in spiritual life: "Have this mind among yourselves, which is yours in Christ Jesus." Christ divested himself of God's form and took upon himself the form of a servant. The former is wisdom, power, freedom, and the latter is our sins. Taking onto himself our sins is an expression of God's essential justice or God's innermost righteousness. The fruit of this righteousness is our righteousness. We have cooperated in bringing this about. Again Luther resorted to man-woman imagery when he wished to describe what occurs. We cooperate, we are co-workers, and this is described as the exchange of love between the bride and bridegroom.[224]

Iserloh elaborates on the mystical aspect of this exchange: "The new righteousness is understood as a mystical union with Christ in the depth of the person; yes, in faith the Christian receives in Christ a new person-ground." And Iserloh continues, citing Luther:

> But faith must be taught correctly, namely, that by it you are so bonded to Christ that He and you are as one person, which cannot be separated but you forever remain attached to Him, and declare: "I am as Christ." And Christ, in turn, says: "I am as that sinner who is attached to Me, and I to him. For by faith we are joined together into one flesh and one bone."[225]

Since Luther did not regard redemption through Christ as solely a statement—which one was expected to accept intellectually—we can say that the mystical relationship radiates or emanates works in keeping with Christ's nature. Luther asserted that such deeds are "incarnated faith." In the midst of these deeds is Christ's divinity, a hidden power. Here we are dealing with a secret cooperation between divine power and human aspiration. Humanity, *humanitas*, alone achieves nothing. Only in the union between the divine and the human can one live as Christ's disciple.

The Catholic scholar Peter Manns speaks of a paradoxical unity in Luther's theology, a unity that escapes "Protestant scholars." Luther's "principles" point, namely, beyond the traditional either-or in the matter of grace and deeds. What scholars do not see is that Luther, in fact, speaks about a transformation of the Christian person when he cooperates with God in salvation. Manns writes:

> Along with Luther we understand the mystery of love through grace in terms of the mystery of righteousness to be advanced and revealed. . . . The specific originality of Luther's doctrine of justification is not thereby violated. We go beyond Luther—however, following his basic principles—by simply expanding the *simul* of 'sin and righteousness' by means of this other *simul*: our effort as necessary for salvation and pure grace. . . . Thus . . . faith truly becomes incarnate faith through active charity.[226]

One can thus conclude that *communicatio idiomatum* in Luther's world of thought included experience of Christ's presence and that this presence changes the ego-centered sinner into "a Christ for others."

The third point: man's participation in God was seen by Luther as a reflection of union with invisible realms. To be in God is tantamount to partaking of supernatural power, a spiritual dimension of life which Luther described both in celestial and earthly analogies. Perhaps some of his earlier statements sounded too Platonic in the sense that they divided creation into something higher, the invisible heaven, and something lower, the visible world. Luther said, for instance: "Our invisible spirit is lowered into visible reality." Some people have suggested that such remarks hardly mirrored a Platonic picture of the world but rather, possibly, a Platonic anthropology. But if the idea about the soul's eternal duration in comparison to the life of the body is Platonic thought, then, in this particular regard, Luther must be counted among the Platonists, as we have seen. The soul partakes in the invisible in another way from the body, but this participation simultaneously makes the body and soul one and elevates the body to God's servant and bearer of divine symbols.[227]

Behind the visible sun there is the real Sun, Jesus Christ. The perennial emanations from him make our participation in God possible. It is therefore necessary to maintain a constant communication between the invisible and the visible spheres. *Christus mysticus* as cosmic Lord continues his incarnational work after his redeeming death and his resurrection. This "Sun of righteousness . . . illumines, works, and is all," and the work is carried out by his followers.[228]

In other words, just as there is no life on the earth without the visible external sun, there is no life in a deeper sense without Christ. The natural sun is merely a reminder to our senses of the Christ-power in and beyond the natural sun. "The body is visible heaven and earth, the eyes are stars, the thunder and the lightning are the words of wrath, darkening the forehead, i.e., heaven, and the eyes, i.e., the sun and the stars."

Luther's mystical intuition, under Christ's dominion, led him to such conclusions, perhaps too esoteric for our evangelical interpretations. Man's *vocatio* (call) to conscious resting in God is underlined, according to Luther, by the symbolism of the human body itself. Again we touch here on ideas that are usually dismissed as Platonic and hence are not part of Reformation thinking, namely, that God's invisible world is a world beyond and our world possesses material counterparts to it.[229]

Perhaps, it is not important to be too logical-systematic in the matter of determining what is "Greek and Platonic" and what is "Hebraic" in the Christian concept of salvation. We saw this not least when examining the immortality motif in biblical and Reformation thought.

The fourth aspect concerning the subject of man's participation in the divine concerns the integral unity between body, soul, and spirit. We have already indicated that Luther experienced God's action in his life as a power which brings about a consonance between the physical, the emotional, and the spiritual within us, strengthened by the Lord's Spirit. The Christian faith becomes a pilgrim's journey, during which human wholeness is a promise and a potentiality. If Luther has, in some measure, been correctly interpreted in this depiction, one can say of the Reformer that he thought of mystical participation in God, life with *Christus mysticus*, as a beginning of transmutation of bodily vitality and ego-centered demands into growing harmony with the indwelling Christ. The person who has faith in Christ and converses with him in prayer and meditation is being "formed" according to the Christ-image. This "divinizing" process about which we have been speaking is, consequently, not only a matter concerned with an isolated psychological attitude. It permeates the bodily existence. "Christ is formed in us and we are formed in His image," Luther pointed out. In like manner he declared: "And so is the cross the means through which God wishes to change us . . . so that we daily become increasingly purified." About the influence from Christ, the Sun of the universe, Luther proclaims: Christ is the force that enables us "to flourish (translating Luther literally: to produce green foliage), to blossom, to emit fragrance, to grow, to bear fruit." Contrast similar positive statements about the potentialities of the Spirit with the many dark Luther words concerning the deep-rooted selfishness of the human and you have you before you a paradox that is hidden in all of Christian life.[230] "Not that I have already obtained it . . ." (Phil. 3: 12).

Concerning the subject of unity of the forces or elements within a person as the result of participation in God, it is instructive to read Luther's comments on a mystic's view of the matter. In his notes on a sermon by Tauler about man as three and yet **one**, Luther writes that he shares Tauler's view. Man consists of three mutually dependent, but not often coordinated parts: the sensual based on the five senses, the rational where reason reigns, and the spiritual part which gets its power from faith. Luther saw eye to eye with Tauler on this: "This is all one human being," potentially, if not actually.[231]

Equanimity and peace between the powers that rule our being is in proportion to our participation in God. Here are some Luther words on the three commandments:

> These three commandments prepare man for God as pure material so that he reposes in heart, speech and work, i.e., relative to the interior and the exterior and the central part of man, which has reference to the senses, to reason and to the spirit. And thus pure peace reigns.[232]

The element in Luther's world of thought that we call participation in God—predicated on God's participation in us—is not, in the first place, cognitive but rather intuitive and numinous. This Luther had in common not only with some medieval mystics but also with, for instance, Lutheran mystic Johann Arndt. **Rudolf Otto** wrote about Arndt:

> Johann Arndt says at the commencement of his *Four Books of True Christianity* (Ch. 5): "By this heart-felt confidence and heart-felt trust man gives his heart to God utterly, reposes only in God, surrenders himself and attaches himself to Him, unites himself with God, becomes a sharer in all that is of God and of Christ, becomes one God with God." This is simply Luther's doctrine (his '*fides*' as '*fiducia*' and '*adhaesio*'), clarified and raised to a higher power. These expressions might well be found in Luther's *Of the Liberty of a Christian*—indeed their meaning is to be found there. St. Paul says the same, only more forcibly still, in Gal. 2:20 and I Cor. 6:17.[233]

The typical moments of mysticism are not necessarily pictured by "transcendent quasi-nuptial rapture," Otto maintained. This may well be so. But, judging from the frequency with which Luther resorted to this nuptial metaphor, it must have meant something essential to him about participation in the divine. At times Luther described Christian faith as an *ecstasis*. To be lifted up beyond time and space could very well be part of God's training or education in faith. What Otto described as "the really typical 'moments' of mysticism—'creature-feeling' and 'union'"—point to the feeling of "being lifted out of yourself," depicted by Luther as "ecstasy." It is clear that when Luther resorts to the language of bridal mysticism, he does not wish to limit the act of faith to an intellectual statement. An assertion of fact does not suffice. Feeling and Christ's indwelling are also involved. Otto seems to have taken some of the wind out of his sails when he said that, according to Luther, communion with God "transforms us inwardly and brings us forth anew." Otto reminded us that, to Luther, faith was "the Holy Spirit in the heart, the mighty creative thing."[234]

Participation in God transforms us inwardly, conforms and unifies. It implies that one stands in contact with that which is more than, and beyond, the human. Salvation is a greeting from that world.

Salvation, confirming and testing the supernatural

It is with great hesitation that modern theology uses words like "supernatural" and "supersensible." It is both a sound and understandable hesitation. Much Christian faith has congealed into a kind of dogmatic supernaturalism. Rationalism based on biblical dogmatism maintains that supernatural reports are "true" only because they must be believed, not that the events really occurred.

On the other hand, it is just as unfortunate that some groups demand experiences of a supernatural kind as a condition of "experience-religion." Luther had trouble with both of these approaches. Orthodoxy, which was pretentious enough to make the claim of speaking for the Reformer, denied the experiential in *unio mystica* and instead provided it with intellectual restraints. Justification by faith was dead on arrival, so to speak.

The revolutionaries of the sixteenth century who were against everything external both in theological thought and in liturgies were also convinced that they belonged to Luther's chosen few. They concentrated on the "inner path" and laid claim to certain emotions in the soul in relation to the supersensible and demanded proof that the supersensible had revealed itself. Luther called those people "*Schwärmer*," enthusiasts. They sought direct revelation and did not want to accept that God communicates with us indirectly as well.

But, however one approaches the problem, one cannot escape the fact that faith implies a new feeling of being a part of a paranormal world. Not that extra-sensory experiences and convictions about the supersensible would be unthinkable outside of a faith experience.

Certainly, we find in all religions, and also in groups investigating the paranormal, hints of and experiences about the beyond. But salvation in Christ often intensifies the awareness about invisible worlds. Beyond this, the new relationship with Christ becomes, as it were, a proving ground where the spirits are tested in a spiritual sifting of the grain from the chaff, according to the formula that Christ advised us to use, namely, to think and pray in his name.

Luther's attitude to mystical themes gives evidence of the fact that he was very conscious of the dotted line between this sensory world and the other. He took for granted that this other, non-time-bound, dimension always influences man's existence (We took angelology as an example). This awareness was a genuine part of Luther's way of looking at the history of salvation.

In Part III we will be discussing modernism's rationalistic methods of demythologizing the biblical world's outlook on the supernatural, as well as Luther's view of the subject. The pejorative word "superstition" often became a word that precluded all open, honest discussion. By discarding the experiences of the supernatural from Luther's theology one does violence to his theology and, besides, by extending the demythologizing process to the Bible, one invalidates the Christ-revelation itself.

Without any doubt Luther embraced what "modern thought" would term naiveté or primitive Biblicism, when it comes to the supernatural. However, the question we ought to ask ourselves is whether the inklings and experiences of an invisible "reality" are not, after all, a part of faith. That is, narratives of the other world's "breakthroughs" into our empirical, three-dimensional world ought to be considered an essential part of the theological effort to understand.

Luther regarded the determinate world as a part of a much larger invisible one. On his view it was essential to take "the invisible" into account in theological expositions of faith and salvation-in-Christ. In his evaluation of Luther's theology Rudolf Otto suggested, correctly in my opinion, that Luther shared Duns Scotus' insistence that God was the God of "willing," in contrast to the God of "being," since Luther's own experience resonated to a God who is will, not cognition. In this way, the non-rational or transrational elements in Luther's faith found a theological home. But, Otto added,

> This aspect of Luther's religion was later tacitly expunged, and is today readily dismissed as "not the authentic Luther" or as "a residuum of the Scholastic speculations of the nominalists." . . . In point of fact this is not a "residuum" at all, but beyond all question the mysterious background of his religious life, obscure and "uncanny," and to estimate it in all its power and profundity we need to abstract the lucid bliss and joyfulness of Luther's faith in divine grace, and to see this faith in relation to the background of that mysterious experience on which it rests.

Otto pointed out that it is not significant whether Luther was influenced more by Duns Scotus or by his Augustinian Order and its teachings. Luther's doctrines "stand in most intimate connexion with his own innermost religious life, of which they [the doctrines] are a genuine first-hand utterance, and should be examined as such." Luther made it clear that he did not speak about his theological convictions merely to enter theological disputes but because they are "a central part of the religious experience of the Christian, who must know them in order to have faith and to have life."

Otto asserted, correctly I think, that all through his life Luther was joyful in his faith in divine grace and that this joy was anchored in his feeling that God is a frighteningly awesome majesty, that the Divine is experienced both as hidden, frightening, and as revealed power, brimming over "with pure goodness."[235]

The tacit, on-going expurgation of the motifs, "unfathomable will" and numinous experiences, to which Otto called attention, also applies to the treatment of more specific manifestations of paranormal energy, which we discussed in the first part of this book. The framework of Western culture has influenced much theology so that it relegates such reports, even biblical, to the area of time bound ideas that cannot be accepted in the expanding light of cultural enlightenment. That which is not experienced according to the standards of natural science cannot be the object of scientific investigation. A "supernatural world," a "metaphysical world," cannot be registered to the satisfaction of "scientific theology." The supernatural dimension lives on embryonically in the word "transcendent."

In passing, I should like draw the reader's attention to two words already used, namely, the adjectives "supernatural" and "supersensible." In this study they have been used to mark a standpoint that goes against the grain of the Enlightenment and, therefore, just the opposite of what the Enlightenment had in mind. This is to say, the "natural" contains only empirically observable facts that are linked to the five senses, and "knowledge" can be derived only from such phenomena. "Supernatural" is therefore more of a pedagogical term than a theological one, as far the present account is concerned. It is both possible and likely that the natural harbors the supernatural and, in the last analysis, no definite demarcation can be drawn between them.

It so happens that spiritual occurrences that do not fit the thought patterns of physical causality, which has laid such a heavy hand on the cultural life of the West, are relegated to the category of psychologized angelology or demonology. In other words, the stories about paranormal experiences—events that, according to the "laws of science," cannot happen or cannot normally be experienced by people—are ascribed to man's capacity for symbolization.

Martin Luther's experience of being saved, however, included events of a Beyond, the powers of which are interwoven with human existence. Luther speaks about "Christ's daily arrival" as a real visitation, not merely as a thought-experiment. If one removes the supernatural hints and remakes justification theology into a mere cognitive undertaking, one mutilates Luther's theology.

It has begun to dawn on Western thought—strangely enough less within theology than in other branches of learning—that yardsticks for acquisition of knowledge are perhaps too limited and technical-rationalistic in a doctrinaire fashion. In any case, Luther's life must be seen as a whole. For him the Christ-ruled invisible was not only a lovely thought along the dotted line from the world of our senses to the other world. It was a real world, this invisible world, and without it he would not have had the courage to continue. But "theology of experience" which takes seriously expressions of experiential piety, should not, one might argue, go further than to acknowledge feelings and intuitions involved in faith. One might object that angelology, demonology, faith healing and parapsychological experiences, although present in Luther's world of faith, cannot be considered typical for his thought in general.

As we have noticed in the anecdotal accounts at the beginning of this exposition, one is, on the contrary, forced to assume that the following persuasions were an integral part of his theology: the conviction about living beings, beyond the earthly, invisible to be sure, but real, implicitly "real" in a different sense from the reality of our sensate world; belief in contact, through Christ's name, with invisible hierarchical entities; belief that intercessory prayer reaches invisible worlds and builds bridges for healing; belief in a present *Christus mysticus* who, after his resurrection, lives and governs in eternity.

Luther's spiritual antennae confirmed the accuracy of biblical and church-historical reports along these lines. This means that Luther did not refer to supernatural dimensions and their various manifestations in the determinate world only because such accounts abound in the Bible. Luther did not simply repeat old time-bound myths or biblical information. His insight corroborated Christian experience from biblical times to the present.

Mysticism as feeling and spiritual presence became discernible, as far as Luther was concerned, in experiences of and belief in the proximity of white and black angels and what perhaps one nowadays would term parapsychological phenomena. These Luther integrated with the Christ-drama as it was played out in persons, in the Church, and in the world. Proofs of the unseen reality belonged to Luther's faith in the same sense that they played an important role in biblical revelation stories. Of course, they were not absolutely central. Christ was the center. But they increased his faith. Luther reminded us that life in the Spirit is more than a general undifferentiated "invisibility." We remain in contact with, and must count with, differentiated forms in the invisible realm, precisely as we do here. Salvation guides us toward heaven. When we come to heaven's door we are struck by its multiformity under the dominion of Christ.

How various manifestations of God's interventions and workings on earth are understood by thinkers with respect to revelation will be the object of the next examination of theology's treatment of mysticism, in general, and the mysticism of Martin Luther, in particular.

PART III

THEOLOGICAL INTERPRETATIONS OF LUTHER'S FAITH

Alas, the word "service of God" has nowadays taken on so strange a meaning and usage that whoever hears it thinks not of these works of God, but rather of the ringing of bells, the wood and stone of churches, the incense pot, the flicker of candles, the mumbling in the churches, ... Of such service God knows nothing at all, while we know nothing but this. We chant the Magnificat daily, to a special tone and with gorgeous pomp; and yet the oftener we sing it, the more we silence its true music and meaning. . . . Unless we learn and experience these works of God, there will be no service of God, no Israel, no grace, no mercy, no God, though we kill ourselves with singing and ringing in the churches and drag into them all the goods in all the world. God has not commanded any of these things; undoubtedly therefore, He takes no pleasure in them.

Martin Luther, *W* 7: 596 (1521), *LW* 21; 350

Yet experience alone makes the theologian.

Martin Luther, *WT* 1; 16, (1531), *LW* 54; 7

CHAPTER SEVEN

TRADITIONAL CONFESSIONALISM

In His word God has not promised
to enlighten anyone through ecstasy.

Heinrich Schmid,
Die Dogmatik der evangelisch-lutherischen Kirche, 1853

You will be a real theologian in rapture and ecstasy.

Martin Luther, *W* 5; 163, 28 (1519)

The spirit of Scholasticism broods over Lutheran orthodoxy. With the intention of defending themselves against Roman Catholic assaults, against Calvinist teachings, and against spiritualistic aberrations in their own midst, the Lutheran Protestants made an intellectualized system out of Luther's writings.

The rediscovery of the meaning of the teaching of God's righteousness and man's justification was incorporated into a system of rigid formulations. The same kind of defense mechanism against tendencies of religious dissipation that was built up by medieval Scholasticism now appeared on Protestant ground. Minds of great intellectual acumen formulated the order of salvation inherent in the new experience. The Lutheran revolution was codified in confessions and dogmatic treatises. Rationalism, in principle rejected in its Roman Scholastic garb, made its entry into the world of the Reformation, now dressed in black cape and Luther-coat.

One wanted to reclaim the virgin truths of Christian beginnings. For this purpose the orthodox Protestants tended to regard the words of the Bible as an unerring external means to get at the truth in a verbal, mechanical sense. It was, in that situation, easy to forget that Martin Luther had talked about the Word as the dynamic presence of Christ.

The external sound and symbol became to him a message that radiated God and God-in-Christ.

It has been said that, as a mature reformer, Luther abandoned his thought of the Word as a two-pronged reality: the inner Logos side and the external, incarnated Christ side. The orthodox Lutherans thus should have all the reason in the world to lay emphasis on *verbum externum*, the external Word. Did they not have the mature Reformer in their camp? It is clear that all through his life Luther linked the external Word to the inner by insisting on the priority of the former, so that the latter, the tidings of the Holy Spirit, should reach the hearers of the Word.[236]

The external sound (cf. Paul at Damascus) and the external symbol became a mighty message precisely through the Christ presence or the presence of the Holy Spirit ("the medium becomes the message"). But for orthodoxy the addition of the Spirit became less prominent. It intellectualized something that could not be caught in intellectual categories. The theological password, for the conservative wing of Luther's followers, became "repristination," the recovery of the original, the pristine, in the story of Christ and the formulations around him. Lutheran "repristination theology" wants to be orderly and predictable, but lacks the unpredictability and the spiritual desire for discovery that is part of life in the Holy Spirit.

It is probably significant that Lutheran orthodoxy has always had difficulty in adapting the third article of the Apostles' Creed into its thinking. One is apt to limit the Holy Spirit to sacramental positivism. The step forward to evangelical freedom becomes, in this way, a step backward into the sacramental positivism of the church of the Middle Ages, the target of Lutheran orthodoxy's attack.

Consequently, one can say that the systematicians belonging to the repristination school presumably never were conscious of Luther's spiritual kinship with some mystics. Luther's kinship to the mystics lay beyond the reach of their limited perception. The Lutheran scholastics regarded mysticism with suspicion; therefore they placed it in the same category as what they called "spiritualism," along with Carlstadt, the "Enthusiasts," and the Zwickau prophets, who, as we know, were all objects of Luther's particular displeasure. Strengthened by such observations and in the persuasion that they were on Luther's wavelength, they overlooked Luther's references to mystical experiences as a part of theological faith. This oversight occurred with the good intention of giving the church an *ordo salutis*, an order for grace and salvation with a biblical ground, as an objective description of the nature of faith. The mere idea that Luther should have the likeness of a mystic was irreconcilable to orthodoxy's way of summing up the biblical revelation.

An early Lutheran compendium around the teachings of the faith is *Hypomnemata* by **Abraham Calovius** (1612-1686). Calovius did not refer directly to mystical life nor to Martin Luther's acquaintance with mystical literature. However, his general attitude to spiritual immediacy and intimacy—which is the antecedent of mystical life—makes quite clear that the movements of the soul were considered dangerous. One sees this especially in the way in which Calovius treats the third use of the law, as it has been named. The concern here relates to which commandments should rule a Christian life.

Calovius argues as follows. Lutheran doctrine speaks of a civil use of the law and a religious use of the law. Through civil law God keeps men within necessary bounds. The religious use of the law concerns the chastising effect of interdictions and moral obligations. The religious use is a prelude to salvation—by chastising us it reminds us of our innate sinfulness. Now the Calvinist teaching introduced a third use of the law, depicted as dutiful obedience—holding a promise of growing awareness of God and serving as a vehicle of sanctification. Calovius reports a different opinion. By describing sanctification in that manner the Calvinists are certainly building a false foundation. For that foundation consists of building blocks fetched from the human sphere, whereas the real basis for a Christian life is "universal propositions" about God. According to Calovius, these universal theses deal with faith or the biblical fact that God's mercy concerns everyone and that Christ brought the forgiveness of sins and salvation to everybody. Faith must be born of the universals of Christian dogmatics. Faith cannot possibly be private, as the Calvinist use of the law wrongly suggests. Faith, Calovius maintained, is official, not private, since Christ delivered all.[237]

Two objections to mystical theology are hidden in the conception that faith is a public, universal proposition (the antipode being the private, personal experience).

First, the confessional compendium that we have chosen for study describes theology as a collection of intellectual "propositions." (Parenthetically it may be pointed out that the choice of example, in this case Calvin, does not mean that Calvinism was more open to mysticism than were the Lutherans.) The choice of words is important. One is of the opinion that one has exhaustively caught the biblical message in a number of categorical theses or doctrines. Since mysticism—and in particular those mystics who were within Luther's range of interest—did not think much of the intellectualism of Roman Scholasticism, it is safe to presume that the same feeling prevailed between the mystics and Protestant theologians in the repristination category.[238]

Conversely, inasmuch as the Lutheran scholastic Calovius resorted exclusively to the rational in presenting his doctrine of faith, he thereby ruled out the non-rational, mystical element in faith. Orthodox propositional theology of the Calovian mode was so tightly wed to logical rationality that no room could be found for the mystical within the system.

Secondly, because much mysticism speaks of experience of God on the basis of "experience" in feeling and will and of "immediate" contact with the divine, it falls under the rubric of "privatism," according to Calovius and other orthodox Lutherans. The utterances of Jesus about the possibilities of the unlearned and simple to receive him, in contradistinction to the "wise" and "learned," were hardly words for repristination theology. The "propositions," the doctrinal system, were considered "official," not only because they were valid for all, but also because they are approachable and attainable by all.

Lutheran orthodoxy's battles against Calvinist theology often gave rise to tightly organized and sharp dogmatic statements. This becomes especially evident in the voluminous work on apologetics, *Grundtlicher Beweis*, written by members of the Wittenberg faculty more than a hundred years after the death of Luther. The book asserts in part:

> The faith that leads to blessedness is such a trust in God that I, a poor sinner, condemned by the law, know, trust and am assured by the word of the gospel that God wishes to forgive me all my sins and this from his sheer grace for the sake of Jesus Christ and confer on me my Lord Jesus Christ's righteousness so that I thereby become righteous and eternally blessed.

What man is told in the word of the gospel must consequently be appropriated. One must rely on God's promises. The individual reader ought to include himself in the general assurance of these promises.[239]

The dogmatic treatise is very plain on this point: personal experience does not count. Nothing in me, as a sinner, gives me the right to "include myself in a special promise." According to the words of the gospel there is no *verbum singular*, not a special reference to the individual. "*Verbum universal*, the general promise which applies to all, should be placed as the foundation." Jesus provides "a precious, general merit." Through faith in him we have forgiveness, righteousness and blessedness, not as a personal gift but as an appropriation of a universal offer.[240]

It is clear that the authors of *Grundtlicher Beweis*, the above-mentioned seventeenth century dogmatic work, were quite conscious of the discussion around the question about the place of the heartfelt and the personal in the story of Christian salvation. It is also clear that there is no room in the orthodox inn for the personal, in many ways feeling-directed appropriation. The Christians who thought of faith as, in part, the result a personal address—a "for you," emanating from God's word—were in error theologically and were actually heretics.

"Is it not enough that they . . . in their feelings experience their faith in Christ from the interior witness of the Holy Spirit or in their own inner being?" asked the authors from Wittenberg. "No," they answered, "no proper, firm conviction" can be based on this kind of individualism.[241]

No direct reference is made to Martin Luther—such references are noteworthily rare in the initial stages of the new age of Lutheran orthodoxy. One easily notices Luther's emphasis on the "external Word" and "Christ for us." The repristination theologians concentrate on these ideas from Luther's world of thought. Faith is that mental condition in which one appropriates Christ's righteousness, and this appropriation assumes the form of repeating "Jesus Christ died for me." The earmarks of faith are not of great import, particularly if they aim at feeling God's presence or good deeds and are **not** put into the more essential context: God's objective assurance as addressed to everyone. If anyone stands in isolation from that context the conclusion can be drawn that the person in question is a heretic.[242]

The other and more subjective side of Luther's faith and teaching, the experience side, is hardly noted in *Grundtlicher Beweis*. In the manner of Calovius, the Wittenbergian text equates faith with intellectual acceptance of the doctrine about faith.[243] When one moves from works that emanate from seventeenth-century Lutheran orthodoxy to the same kind of statements of the nineteenth century, one gets the impression, figuratively, that the apartments are different but the furnishings are exactly the same.

In the meantime pietism and Newtonian science made their appearance on the scene, and traditional orthodoxy was compelled to register their appearance. Yet, the formulations of the faith changed very little. **Heinrich Schmid's** *The Doctrinal Theology of the Evangelical Lutheran Church*, well known and widely used, is a case in point. Schmid, in proclaiming which dogmaticians, in his view, are useful, clearly indicates his stance. Hollatius, Schmid avers, must be the last reliable expounder of true Christianity considered in the book. However, Schmid continued, even Hollatius ought to be treated with a certain caution. One should remember that he, Hollatius, authored his works at a time when orthodox theology began to show great uncertainty. One can notice this even more clearly with a theologian like Baumgarten who, according to Schmid, had been influenced by questionable notions, especially those that grew out of pietism. Schmid did not elaborate on this criticism, but simply raised the question whether pietism was a deviation from Lutheran principles. Schmid left no doubt as to where he stood. He asserted, namely, that pietism had exerted a corroding influence on the untainted purity of right doctrine.

Schmid was as confident during his lifetime (mid-nineteenth century) as were his mentors two hundred years earlier, that the accusation that orthodoxy was outmoded had no justification whatsoever. The old dogmatics, he maintained, is not antiquated and will never be antiquated.[244]

Two terms will be considered which have to do with the mystical tradition, *unio mystica* and *illuminatio.* This choice is based on the opinions set forth in Schmid's work which is, in part, an anthology of centuries of Lutheran scholastics: Gerhard, Calovius, Hutter, Quenstedt, Hollatius, and the documents of faith—*The Augsburg Confession* and *The Formula of Concord.*

As far as *unio mystica* is concerned, Heinrich Schmid thought that the term could be safely adopted by orthodox Lutheran theology, provided it was part and parcel of justification by faith, as "forgiveness of sins," and regeneration, as "the faculty of faith." To be made righteous by faith and to born again meant that "God abides in a certain sense in the justified and reborn." In that sense, Schmid assumed, a Lutheran theologian may well speak of "the substance of God" uniting with "the substance of man." However, union could take place only in the believer. Under some circumstances this assertion might also be made by a pietist, and Schmid intimates that he has wrestled with this problem as no one else among his fathers in the faith. Nevertheless, he returns soon enough to firm ground through declaring that the mystical union was neither *illuminatio* nor *personalis*. Thereby Schmid had returned to the sphere of the rational, the conceptually appropriated, a purely cognitive activity, as he also did in the case of *unio mystica*.[245]

At this point I will digress slightly to examine Lutheran orthodoxy's way of using the term *unio mystica*. Orthodox Lutherans have always had a way of employing the term in a manner helpful to them, i.e., using it as though their use of it corresponded to Luther's intention.

Since Schmid was citing thinkers who enjoyed the orthodox imprimatur, we confidently take **Johannes Quenstedt** (1617-1688) as our guide. He was a dogmatician in vogue in theological circles 150 years before Schmid and is mentioned with approval in Schmid's work. Quenstedt wrote, in 1685, "Christ and the believers remain separate persons in the mystical union." Quenstedt was anxious to emphasize the separation because he thought that the passage in John 17:22 so demanded. The passage reads as follows: "The glory which thou hast given me I have given to them, that they may be one even as we are one." In Quenstedt's view this word from Jesus about union was a "union with built-in separation." He emphasized that "even" actually means "in a similar manner." That is to say, that the mystical union would be rather like an analogy. Quenstedt argued that it would, therefore, be heretical to say that man would be changed into a divine person through *unio mystica*. It was by no means a matter of a confluence between God and man in one substance or one person.

The perception of *unio mystica* in Lutheran orthodox theology thus assumed the character of solicitude concerning the purity of the teaching. The orthodox strove after a teaching that would keep intact, as much as possible, the "objective" faith proposition regarding the deed of the revelation, carried out on our behalf and accepted by us without any deeper thought on "the harmony and accord of the feelings." *Unio mystica* had become, on the whole, an intellectualistic part of the order of salvation. According to the scholastic-Lutheran interpretation, there is no place for the experience and language of the medieval mystics with whom Martin Luther was in spiritual contact.[246]

The second word of mystical import in Schmid's dogmatics is *illuminatio*. As we shall see, he has, also in this case, an almost rationalistic mode of seeing theology as "spiritual enlightenment." *Illuminatio* is an old mystical word, representing the second stage toward the path to freedom in God, according to the Augustinian-Platonic stages of development. The first one is purification, and the third one is unification. The path is described in a different way in Meister Eckhart's sermons. In those sermons Eckhart speaks about the positive, the negative, the creative and the transformative stages, elements in an Eckhartian mysticism that embraces the created world in a more positive way than the Neoplatonic outlook. For it was the tripartite, the Neoplatonic, scheme that had the upper hand in the kind of mysticism that Luther encountered in his search for a gracious God. It is sufficient to say that, with Eckhart, "cleansing" corresponds to *via negativa* and "union" with *via creativa.* The reader has perhaps already drawn the conclusion that, for Meister Eckhart, creation was a sacrament more than for Taulerian mysticism. And the reader is certainly right in this assumption. But here it is a question of *illuminatio* in the mystical tradition. That tradition made a profound impression on Luther. As Leif Erikson points out in the investigation already quoted, "Luther seldom uses the concept of *illuminatio*. On the other hand, the matter itself was important to him, namely, that God through the Holy Spirit creates faith in the heart of man." This "faith-awakening occurs . . . through the Word by the power of the Holy Spirit. For Luther it was unthinkable to imagine a direct, i.e., not mediated, relationship with God."[247]

Naturally, Schmid does not refer to the preparation stage of mysticism. On the contrary, his accounting echoes Luther's warnings against the false belief that one can reach God's majesty directly. However, to Schmid, *illuminatio* comes close to an unexalted reading of the Scripture. For Luther the mystical enlightenment was more a feeling of the heart—although connected to an outer "channel." In 2 Peter 1:18, Schmid finds confirmation of his opinion that *illuminatio* must be toned down: "we heard this voice borne from heaven, for we were with him on the holy mountain" (RSV). The point here was supposed to be that the disciples would not have heard the voice from the Eternal if they had not been in the company of Jesus. Light dawned in their hearts **only because Jesus mediated it**. With the aid of that interpretation the scholar then tucks the *illuminatio* away into what is, to all intents and purposes, a rational-logical system, where the original glow has disappeared.

In like manner Schmid handles the question about the "Word from God." It is a "prophetic Word" and as such *verbum Dei auditum*—the word that can be heard through the written word. Direct communication with God does not belong to the promises. The word can be read quietly and rationally. Either Schmid did not know, or did not want to discuss, Luther's use of the word *ecstasis*. If ecstasy would accompany *illuminatio*, then Schmid, for his part, would not go along any more. In that case one would have abandoned "sound doctrine." One finds, he wrote, adherents to such false ideas among "Platonists, Quakers, and mystics." But, he added, ecstasy in connection with illumination could perhaps be tolerated as an excusable heresy.

On the other hand, Schmid rejected totally the thought of *raptus* (rapture) that could be tied to enlightenment by the Holy Spirit. According to him, *raptus* was a greater calamity than *ecstasis* since the former "adds violence." To Schmid and his fellow scholastics among the Lutherans, the experience that Luther and some mystics specified as *raptus* —the experience of being swept into God's arms—was too much of a human attempt to take the kingdom by human force. Although, if one views it superficially, Schmid seemed to agree with Luther in his defense of the primary role of the external means of grace, he, in fact, distanced himself from Luther's interpretation of *illuminatio*. With vigor he represented the idea that enlightenment is a communication of the Word-of-God, but the emphasis became so strong on a purely mechanical level that the overtones of feeling in the presence of the Spirit—which Luther associated with enlightenment —got lost in the process.[248]

A quarter of a century after Schmid, **Ernst Luthardt** (1823-1902) wrote his *Kompendium der Dogmatik* in which he quoted Martin Luther on the question of mysticism's influence in his world of thought. "The Dutch mystic Wessel [Gansfort] and I," the Reformer had written, think so very much alike that "our opponents could begin to think that I have taken it all from Wessel." Apparently Luthardt felt the urge to save Martin Luther from the suspicion of having an essential rapport with a mystic. In point of fact, Luther and Wessel were really vastly different, he assured his readers.[249] It is the opposite, he added, mysticism and Lutheran faith are indeed contrasts. The three-fold way to God leaves much to be desired, if one compares it with the *ordo salutis* in Lutheran orthodoxy. Mystical teaching places purification at the wrong point, Luthardt suggests. The orthodox teachers were of the opinion that enlightenment must precede purification. Knowledge comes first, and then comes will.[250] This is a trust in *ratio* (reason) that is not consonant with Martin Luther's experience. In other words, one must be enlightened by "sound doctrine" in order to be able to speak about purification. Here we meet rationalism in Lutheran orthodoxy—not unlike the rationalistic theories in the Roman church that had been severely criticized. Instead of reason, applied to tradition and natural law, one now had, with Luthardt and others, acquired a rational method which, when applied to the Scripture, generated dogmatic code-words that effectively and automatically excluded mystical theology.

The best contemporary example of repristination theology's attitude to mysticism is *Christliche Dogmatik* by **Franz Pieper** (1852-1931) and **J.T. Mueller** (1885-). This book has been studied by many generations of students at the Lutheran Church-Missouri Synod seminary in St. Louis. Much like other works written by orthodox Lutheran teachers, this book does not discuss mysticism directly. As a matter of fact, one gains the impression that orthodox Lutherans take as a given that mysticism and Lutheran theology have nothing in common. One can speak of an *argumentum de silentio*, an argument against mysticism inherent in the very silence about it.

In a discussion of Schleiermacher's theology, Pieper and Mueller maintain that it is impossible to reach theological certainty as long as a theological system, as in that of Schleiermacher's, revolves around the subjective human "ego." Theological certainty can only be communicated through "the Holy Spirit in the Word." According to these authors certainty lodged in a person's self or his "ego," is "not Christian." The documentation for this assertion the author finds in Luther's pamphlet addressed to the English king. In this text Luther speaks in strong words against man-made systems of salvation (Luther had been the object of attempts to persuade him concerning a certain relaxation of the Confession).[251] The implication for mystical theology—for which, by the way, Schleiermacher had little or no understanding—is that it cannot find room within Lutheran theology because it is "subjective."

Pieper and Mueller bring forward, on behalf of "objectivity," yet another document from Luther's literary works. Luther likens the Word of God to a strong tree. It is shaken by forceful winds but is not moved. Our human nature is not as immovable as God's Word. Without God's Word to lean on, our nature collapses after all the assaults leveled at it from hateful and envious people and from the devil's machinations.[252] They assert that the Christian life must be rooted in the objective certainty that the words of Scripture, statements about God-in-Christ, offer us. We ought to shy away from the natural tendency to look for and to be dependent on any possible, positive changes in the soul.

The pleading for objectivity means that the question of truth overshadows the question of trust. Truth has something to do with the rational, trust with will and feeling. "The acknowledgment of truth," the author contends, is based on "Christ's words." "Modern theology," he continues, has failed in its attempt to clarify this: truth first, only then, trust. It is not only Schleiermacher who is criticized in this connection. Among those who are not accepted one finds, for instance, Ritschl, Barth, and Aulén. The mistake, as far as "modern theology" is concerned, is that it speaks of the certainty of faith that had been whittled down to fit the judgment of the "world." Modern theology has abandoned real faith.[253] Certainty on biblical ground is like a mighty oak that now has been deserted by them that would have been in need of its shade. Instead one turns to human aspirations.

It belongs to the matter under consideration that none of the authors under scrutiny in the Missouri Synod text has shown much interest in the brook that flows into the river of Lutheran theology. However, *Christliche Dogmatik's* criticism of these *personae non gratae* would be leveled with equal force at every attempt to ascribe any importance to Luther's choice of words.

This becomes quite evident from the book's view on Christian "certainty." Christian certainty is based on infallible biblical statements, infallible since the biblical word is infallible in all aspects. One has to appropriate the statements, but the appropriation may not be linked to any kind of spiritual process in the soul of man. The transfer of the gospel from the word to the individual takes place on a purely dogmatic-rational level. The biblical formulas regarding faith were accepted by the reasoning power within man, despite the fact that it deals with truths that cannot be reconciled with worldly reason. Here Luther's emphasis on the "external Word" and the "Christ-for-you" become the Reformation's only theological message. Through their use of rationalism, the authors of the theological work just described deprived themselves of the opportunity of getting to know the significance of Luther's interest in the mystics. One can, against this background, understand the book's silence on the subject of mysticism. There were no receivers for the rays of the mystical life.

To sum up: repristination theology in the Lutheran tradition has to resort to a thought process which, in its attempt to avoid the subjective, comes to describe the biblical message in the form of objective truths: objective in the sense that they are intended to be received and accepted on the level of the intellect, which is probably best described, not as an awareness in the soul, but as an "intellectual holding-this-to-be-true." The dogmatic system worked out in this way, with its focus on the act of justification, reminds one of the formulas of applied science. The religious experiences that are inspired by non-rational forces do not count. Mysticism is considered heretical. Lutheran orthodoxy does not register it. To the people of the "Lutheran school," God becomes "imaginable" in the sense that his work of salvation is rationally comprehensible via the biblical annals. With the aid of intellectual constructions they endeavor to catch the mystery of God-in-Christ.

Lutheran orthodoxy through the centuries has proved to be deficient when it comes to the mystical. In the first place, it lacks antennas for mystical experience. A person with mystical experience becomes aware of indescribable, unfathomable dimensions, whereas Lutheran orthodoxy confines itself to a representation of the revelation and the faith in dogmatic-logical terms, with objectivity as the benchmark. In contradistinction to mysticism, orthodoxy is busy with that which is within its bailiwick, the "intelligible."

Second, Lutheran orthodoxy shows no interest in the question of differentiation between various types of mysticism. That would have made its task more complicated. Accordingly, Martin Luther's interest in this matter has escaped the attention of Lutheran orthodoxy or has been deliberately explained away.

Third, as a consequence of the foregoing, Lutheran orthodoxy cannot see anything significant in the mystical terminology that is part and parcel of Luther's total theology. It is not only "conservative" orthodoxy that finds Luther's mystical leanings difficult to deal with and, consequently, seeks solutions in other intellectualistic ways. "Neo-conservative" and "liberal" theologies have also worked with the problem. In their own way they have applied their *ratio* in order to minimize the importance of something that they regard as a *Fremdkörper*, an alien body, in the theology of the Reformation.

CHAPTER EIGHT

LIBERAL AND NEO-ORTHODOX VIEWS

In the area of the history of spirituality only dilettantes could call Luther a mystic.

Heinrich Bornkamm, *Luther's geistige Welt*, 1947

One overlooks the fact that it is through ordinary words that the mystical is revealed. One does not understand that ordinary words contain hidden meaning, so that, if the Lord had not revealed the meaning to the apostles, not even they would have understood Him.

Martin Luther, *W* 4; 492, 5-8 (1513)
(Author's translation)

In this attempt to probe the nature of Luther's contact with, and understanding of, mystics and mystical theology, we come to an area of interpretation and research which has been more open to cultural change and scientific knowledge than has Lutheran orthodoxy. Not withstanding their mutual antagonism, liberal and neo-orthodox theologies share a desire to relate to their cultural milieu. Common to both theologies is a commitment to rational judgment that hinders and complicates the making of an adequate evaluation of non-rational contributions to the rational.[254]

Because Martin Luther, in fact, actually recognized and accepted the place of the non-rational in theological convictions, the question ought to concern the methods in liberal and orthodox thinking which seem to obstruct or prevent an acknowledgment of the subject.

The following analysis will proceed along two lines and embrace two theses. In the first place, the mystical motifs have been of considerable significance in Luther's thoughts about the gospel. However, this fact has escaped many people since most researchers use the method that generalizes mysticism. Secondly, much research and interpretation uses an evaluation method that has been influenced by certain culturally conditioned assumptions or premises that exclude mysticism.

Mysticism generalized

Theological reflection influenced by **Albrecht Ritschl** (1822-1889) and by the scientific opinions of the nineteenth and early twentieth century made use of the term "mysticism" as though the reality behind it would be an undifferentiated, indivisible totality. This way of looking at this subject I have called mysticism en bloc. This approach, considering all mysticism en bloc, creates the impression that the subject contains no essential divergencies. In the next chapter we will have the opportunity to investigate this more. There is, namely, not a unified conception of the term mysticism; it elicits a variety of thoughts to different people.

One reason for the fact that mysticism often is described as a phenomenon with homogeneous content, and thus, without further ado, can be neglected, is doubtless due to the dearth of scholarly investigations in this area. Until only recently Protestant studies of Luther's relation to mysticism were few and far between and mainly concentrated on the post-Reformation phenomenon called "enthusiastic" mysticism.

A further reason for facile generalization is presumably the tendency in most circles of researchers to simply take over, without independent investigation, magisterial judgments from respected academic leaders. In this way opinions have been carried over from generation to generation without further or continuous work with the sources. Thus, in theological treatises, the definition of mysticism has been generalized and mystics have been regarded as all holding the same views.

A third source of the inclination toward generalization is certainly the Protestant predilection for absolute categories—as distinctions were hammered out in the tension between Protestant and Catholic faith. Protestants have, for example, absolutized the contrast between speculation and faith in their attempts to describe the controversy. Mysticism is frequently classified as "speculation;" in that case it is placed in the non-evangelical camp. Another illustration of Protestant absolutism is discernible in the debate on man's continuity with God as opposed to his discontinuity—a problem already touched upon. Liberal and neo-orthodox theology set aside mysticism in toto to what one considers being the theologically dubious Roman Catholic camp.

Ritschl was once described as a theologian who, despite his rationalistic theology, aroused interest in mysticism. It has been said that "his idea about the uniqueness of the Christian experience" proved untenable and therefore opened a path to the world of mystics.[255] Be that it as it may, Ritschl's treatment hardly drew any recruits to the subject. Ritschl drew a sharp demarcation line between "Catholic mystical" and "evangelical Lutheran." He treated mysticism, in the first place, as a totality with uniform basic thrusts. Secondly, he saw this as a phenomenon that, in the last analysis, is contrary to evangelical Lutheran concepts.[256]

Perhaps **Karl Holl** (1866-1926) does not fit the adjective, which we accorded him here, "liberal." Another German theologian has said that Holl, in his writing of history, gave us a Luther who is "more modern and consistent" than the Reformer was in real life.[257] As a writer on mysticism, and its possible influence on Luther, Holl gave people reason to call him a "liberal." For him, mysticism was an antipode to biblical Protestantism. He, too, treated mysticism as one undivided unit of identical intentions. According to Holl, mystical communion with God and the mystical behavior possessed the same characteristics for all mystics.

Holl was of the opinion that mysticism discovered a kind of affinity with God deep in the soul of man and transformed these religious discoveries into autonomous values.[258] All mysticism is, according to Holl, "a subtle search for enjoyment."[259] In all mystical circles suffering is greeted as a pleasure. The goal of the Christian life is, therefore, **one** thing for Luther, and a wholly different matter for the mystics. Holl asserted that mysticism represented man's desire for happiness, whereas Martin Luther put personal responsibility in the center.[260]

In later editions of his study about religion and Luther, Holl modified slightly his picture of mysticism. He had noticed that a certain difference prevailed between Roman and Germanic mysticism (more about this in the next chapter). But his final conclusion, however, coincided with the view that he had embraced from the beginning: one cannot speak about any essential distinctions within mysticism because all mysticism is grounded in a philosophical notion of God. Mysticism and Scholasticism cannot be separated.[261]

Holl conceded that Germanic mysticism "goes deeper into the consciousness of sin" than other kinds of mysticism. But even after this second look at the subject one cannot say that the mystics' consciousness of sin was akin to Luther's. The German mystics, Holl wrote, assumed that sin was only an "unfavorable or untoward thing." In that way, for instance, Tauler spoke of inner freedom, *Gelassenheit*, in such a way that one could let sin just "float by," not allowing it to "concern the inner man."[262]

It is clear that Holl, a prominent Luther-scholar, could not see any fundamental likeness between Luther's religious experience and that of the mystics. Since Holl has meant more than perhaps anyone else in creating the modern world's Luther-image, we continue the discussion about the generalization of the conception of the mystical. This is emphasized by exposing some central ideas in Holl's authorship, points at which, according to Holl, the path of the mystics and Luther's path lead in opposite directions.

For instance, such a point is indicated by the term *Anfechtung*, the soul's despair and its feeling of being under attack by the powers of darkness. And just here, Holl declares, one can observe the essential difference between Luther and the mystics, if the truth were known.[263]

Perhaps Holl makes too much of the importance of the term *Anfechtung*. There were few among Luther's own followers who knew this term from a general theological viewpoint. Once Luther made a remark about a mystic who really had experienced *Anfechtung*. That person was Gerson. There were probably some more who knew, Luther said, how *Anfechtung* of the body or "the flesh" feels. However, Gerson "was the only one who wrote about spiritual *Anfechtung*, therefore he alone can comfort and edify consciences." Holl's assertion that there is no room within mysticism for the dark moods of *Anfechtung* becomes somewhat less tenable on account of this remark by Luther. If Holl had believed that mysticism could not reasonably understand *Anfechtung*, he would have had occasion to make a clean breast of it. The fact was that the Reformer himself never was sure where one ought to draw the line between his personal gloomy, dark periods and a "normal" feeling of being assaulted by the "powers."[264]

We have here an illustration of liberal theology's temptation to use mysticism as a block-word, the content of which could in all respects be described as non-evangelical. Holl gave *Anfechtung* a central place among Lutheran theology's properties (although Luther himself was less certain of its significance). Holl did so in spite of his conviction that mysticism's goal was enjoyment, and hence could not possibly know anything about the tribulation of the spirit. Holl's generalization is not in accord with the affinity between Luther and Gerson. Consequently, one can state that the generalization of mysticism leads astray. The question is whether reality as the mystic experiences it provides a basis for making the kind of distinctions that we encounter here.

Throughout his work Holl was influenced by his reliance on the generalized definition of mysticism. He took for granted that mysticism en bloc lived in, and of, the Platonic view of our world, i.e., our world as a shadow. That is the reason he placed Christianity and mysticism in contradistinction to each other. Christianity possessed a positive view in regard to the created world and mysticism a negative. Holl tried to prove the validity of that proposition in his defense of the doctrine of divine wrath—God's wrath. How can mysticism that regards this world as a mere shadow have any thought of God's wrath? We have before us two antipodes, Holl argued. On one hand, we consider the view of evangelical Christianity and its teaching of "wrath" and, on the other hand, we have the mystical conviction which does not recognize that there is wrath in the Godhead. Holl points to the attitude of the Reformers by citing some words from Luther: "God hates sin and the sinner, of necessity, for otherwise God would be unrighteous and love sin." Holl was of the opinion that, with these words, Luther showed that he "took this world's reality in earnest." Mysticism, with its Platonic view of life, did not.[265]

If one takes a closer look, the problem is more involved than Holl thought. Martin Luther looked upon the world as a real place where God's wrath was untethered, true, but, on the other hand, he also experienced this life as a shadow. When we arrive on the other side of death, Luther said, we will realize how shadow-like life on this earth truly is. Then, on the other side, "we see that the whole world is dead." Then we perceive that it is the invisible world that lives. The invisible dimension becomes visible to us thanks to a faculty quite different from the one we now use.[266]

If we make a comparison with another mystic, Johann Tauler, we find that although he was of the opinion that "the other world" spelled reality, nevertheless this did not deter him from emphasizing the "reality" of this world. He said: "If I were not a priest I would consider it a great thing to be able to make shoes, and I would like to make them better than anything else." Tauler emphasized how important work was in this world. He wrote: "Man ought to perform good, useful work."[267] Tauler experienced that which the Reformation called "God's wrath" in his deep awareness of his inadequacy before God, for it is God's greatness and our smallness that creates the impression of wrath within our soul.[268]

Once again we note that Holl has used his en bloc concept of mysticism to give the impression of absolute polarity between the evangelical view of the world and the challenges of earthly life, and, on the other side, the mystical view. The mental attitudes that we encounter in both areas do not justify the conclusion that Holl drew.

In this analysis of the place of generalization in theological judgments about mysticism we arrive at the question that announced its presence in other contexts on proceeding pages, namely, the question of man's kinship with God or alienation from God. The crucial point here is the question about the fear of God. What does it mean to say that God is to be "feared?" If there is no fear of God in a person's heart, one cannot suppose that this person takes for granted that there is a link between God and the human heart. On the other hand, if there is fear of God does one know that God is the Wholly Other? Karl Holl stated, on the basis of a not totally improbable characterization of mysticism, that it presupposes

> . . . that we possess an indestructible bridge to God in the depth of our own soul. We can mount it as often as we please, simply by remembering that our origin is in God. Even guilt is not a barrier. By leaving behind our feeling of selfhood we also get rid of our sin. Luther could never understand this line of thought.[269]

Such an idea was tantamount to a derogation of the Christian experience of godly fear, according to Holl, who maintained that these ideas were incomprehensible to Luther.

Holl's dictum that mysticism knows no fear of God, since it assumes a certain kinship with God, loses something of its potency when we are confronted with descriptions of mystical encounters with the divine that are characterized precisely by fear and trembling. Johann Tauler, who truly belonged to Luther's spiritual favorites, declared that the righteous have gone through the fear of God. He spoke also of the tremendous distance between man and God, a distance so great that God's name can be pronounced only with fearful trembling.[270]

As far as the problem of "kinship" with God is concerned, Holl presumably construed every suggestion about an eternal ground of the soul as a mystical attempt to assume an inner presence of an unobstructed bridge to salvation and divinization. But not all mystics belong to this generalized category. Tauler, for one, told his listeners that no one would be able to look into the utmost ground of his being—which is from God—as long as he, through deeds, had created obstacles in the way. For kinship with God, who is the ground of it all, would be worthless unless a person repents. Although the obstacle may seem insignificant, Tauler warned, it would have the same effect as more substantial obstacles, namely, to keep us away from contact with the ground of the soul. "Then the soul's mirror cannot reflect God."[271]

When Luther's eyes fell on these words, the Reformer wrote that man really possesses an inner ground or an inner material that is a gift from God. That material must be indestructible since it is from God. God is the sculptor working with the material. Holl, however, had not found with Luther any understanding for God's "natural" presence. He writes that the claim of mysticism for a natural ground "wholly escapes Luther." With the utterance above, Holl has been swept along by his own generalizations.[272]

The anonymous author of *Theologia Germanica* (a book that Luther edited and published) writes that we humans are provided with a dual capacity: we are able to see into our earthly existence, that is in the category of time; we can also peer into the invisible, that is the dimension of eternity. But the fact that we possess the gift to peer into eternity does not mean that we can arrogate to ourselves independent heavenly substance. If we did that, we should soon perish.

> Note that when the creature assumes for itself some good thing, like being, life, knowledge, power . . . as though the creature were indeed one of these goods, or as though the Good belongs to the creature—in such situations the creature is turning away from God. . . . Remember how it is written that the soul of Christ has two eyes, a right eye and a left eye. In the beginning, when these were created, Christ's soul turned its right eye toward eternity and the Godhead and therefore immovably beheld and participated in divine Being and divine Wholeness. . . . But at the same time the left eye of Christ's soul . . . penetrated the world of created beings and there discerned distinctions among us, saw which ones were better and which one were less good, nobler or less noble. Christ's outward being was structured in accordance with such inner discrimination. . . . Now, the created soul of man also

has two eyes. One represents the power to peer into the eternal. The other gazes into time and the created world, enabling us to distinguish between the lofty and less lofty. . . .[273]

Holl's generalization prevented him from seeing the ambiguity of the situation. To him the question had a simple answer: the very nature of mysticism precludes the experience of "fear of God." But both Luther and some mystics were very well acquainted with fear and trembling before God—at the same time they took for granted a "ground" that man has in common with God. Theologically, one ought to seek the main emphasis, not an either/or. If the search focuses on mysticism en bloc, one moves the investigation too far from reality.

Holl's argumentation also becomes apparent when one looks at the correlation between the mystical and the ethical. Karl Holl entered even this discussion. His treatment of the matter affords us a further occasion to observe his way of applying an undifferentiated definition to mysticism. Briefly put, Holl had reached the opinion that mysticism was not concerned with duty and moral striving. From the point of view of ethics, Holl characterized mysticism as "play." In contradistinction to the alleged lack of moral concern among mystics, Holl spoke of Martin Luther as having contributed "an unremitting earnestness." From an ethical viewpoint Holl pitted two diametrically opposed attitudes against each other.[274]

Holl's contention that mystics lean toward a lack of moral seriousness in their teachings is not in harmony with Tauler's emphasis on the "little humble deed" as an outflow of life in God. Holl's contention is not consonant with the *Theologia Germanica's* reminder of the essence of the moral life: that life does not consist of any anxiously observed moral commands. Yet, paradoxical as it might seem, when man really meets Christ, he inspires him to "abide with the best." The *Theologia* speaks of the good earth, of the ethic of the changed soul, of the given place of moral rules. It is hard to believe that Karl Holl really gave himself time to read this "anonymous" mystic.[275]

According to the mystics to whom Luther was especially linked, life—inclusive of the moral life—wells up from one's life in God. True, the mystic's persuasion in this regard lies far away from Luther's grasp of the matter, as illustrated in a sermon on John 14:12. Here he spoke about the ethical, about the practical-moral aid, that only Christians are able to give to the world. Why only Christians? The reason is that moral life derives from Christ.

> The very greatest works in the world—even though they are not recognized as such—are continuously performed by Christians. . . . the preservation of peace . . . help, protection, and salvation in all sorts of distress and emergencies. All this, says Christ, will come to pass through Christians because they . . . derive everything from him as their head. [276]

The danger in using generalizations is illustrated clearly by the examples just given in the areas of ethics and mysticism.

Holl takes up yet another polarity that he thinks he has detected in his comparison of Luther's thought and mysticism. Mysticism, he writes, becomes pantheistic whenever it speaks about the Godhead. But Luther takes an opposing position. His faith is Christo-centric and is simultaneously a personal faith.[277]

If pantheism is defined as the belief or doctrine that God is not a personality but that all laws, forces, and manifestations of the universe are God, there is no doubt that some mysticism would fit that description. But Christian mystics are hardly pantheists, even though Dionysius the Areopagite and Meister Eckhart sometime appear to be pantheists in the sense here indicated. In Tauler's sermons and the Frankfurter's tract, *Theologia Germanica*, there is scarcely anything that bears out Holl's generalization. Tauler desired that God should be addressed as a person and the Frankfurter spoke of God's "self."[278]

Holl's schema is inadequate. He wanted to prove that pantheism is pervasive in mysticism and that this trait is antithetical to Luther's Christo-centric, personal faith. But his benchmark, the generalized definition of mysticism, left him in the lurch.

Holl's antithetical method induced him to describe the relation between Catholic and Lutheran thought in opposition to each other. Holl argued that all Catholic theology—the Scholastic, the monastic and the mystical—displayed indifference to the created world, failed to have faith in providence, and stressed too much the life to come. At the other end of the theological spectrum was Martin Luther, who introduced to the world a "much higher demand."[279]

This is not the place to discuss the validity of Holl's judgment that indifference to the created world and possessive love inherent in spiritual aspiration are pervasive peculiarities in Roman Catholic life or that, conversely, commitment to the created world and non-possessive faith would be earmarks of Protestant existence. Holl's representation points to that kind of partition.

What most immediately concerns us is the assumption that mysticism was a coherent, monolithic Roman Catholic philosophy that consistently poses the right questions in the wrong way, namely, from anthropological rather than theological points of entry. Not only was mysticism, on Holl's accounting, a uniform body of thought closed to divergent interpretations, but this mysticism en bloc represented a uniform thought structure, closed to divergent interpretations. This structure was secretly united with the larger surrounding spiritual landscape, dominated by Scholasticism and the monastic orders.

Two critical observations should be made in this connection. First, a considerable number of mystics would have to be removed from the company to which they were assigned, if one like Holl (and others among liberal theologians) insists that a mystic is a Scholastic or a monastic. Both Scholasticism and monasticism were criticized openly and severely by some mystics.[280] The agreement in Roman Catholic thinking was surely not as total as Holl assumed. The fact that medieval mystics more or less directly attacked some forms of the establishment weakens the theory that mysticism was an unambiguous, unified thought system. There was, for instance, a mystical movement called the "Friends of God," which consisted of small groups who met for spiritual edification outside established, ecclesiastical ceremonial circles. The Friends of God are evidence that mystics did not always conform to the demands of or work within the established church.

Secondly, the six Luther passages to which Holl referred, in support of his thesis that indifference and possessive love are the hallmarks of Scholasticism, monasticism, and mysticism, do not contain any direct mention of mysticism or mystics.[281] In like manner, other prominent Luther scholars have generalized the perception of mysticism in their attempts to distance Luther's theology from that of the Roman church.[282]

In my first study of this problem (1976) I devoted considerable space to the question of generalization since I found it so remarkable that very few apparently have noticed this phenomenon. Particularly when it comes to the "mystics," there is an almost complete lack of discrimination. Here it may suffice with only a few hints.[283]

Erich Seeberg (1888-1945) was aware of the peril of generalizing descriptions of mysticism. He had observed the fact that Luther talked about spiritual friendship with some mystics. It is, furthermore, worthy of note that Seeberg surmised that Luther's rejection of sacramental positivism ultimately had its genesis in his kinship with mystics. But in his final assessment of the mystic Johann Tauler, Seeberg makes quite clear that, in his opinion, Luther could not, to any appreciable degree, have had anything in common with mysticism.

Seeberg spoke in a critical vein about the Taulerian "ground," that it was the "most fragile bridge between man and God." Tauler's "metaphysical" anchorage provokes Seeberg's sharpest criticism. Seeberg wrote that, in the thinking of Tauler, to "imitate" Christ is a metaphysically derived activity, not ethically inspired. Plato's philosophy dominates the scene, the idea of supersensible prototypes. In contrast to this philosophy is placed Luther's solid, Christian insight.

Seeberg spiritualized Tauler's theology and de-spiritualized Luther's theology. Tauler was familiar with justification by faith and also spoke of the significant role of moral tasks. Luther was ardently conscious of the reality of the spiritual world and knew that the ethical was grounded in the Cosmic Christ. But Seeberg's theological intention was to place Tauler in the "traditional mystical theology," the "substance of which was derived from [Dionysius] the Areopagite." Mysticism, according to Seeberg, "is artificial sublimation, artifice and technique." On the other side—and the right side—stands "Luther's theology on behalf of every person," sound, palpable, and non-technical.

Only a very generalized notion of mysticism could allow Seeberg to make the following statement. Luther embraced the concept of dualism between Creator and created, whereas "for the Anabaptists and in mysticism" the solution to the man-God problem is "monistic."[284] We have here a generalization that entirely overlooks the fact that many mystics knew about *gemitus*, the yearning awe before God, in which man becomes nought and God everything.

Emanuel Hirsch was mentioned in connection with our discussion about angelology. Hence we came to know something of the mystical en bloc thinking that dominates his interpretation of Luther. Mysticism represented, for Hirsch, a part of the vague religiosity and the "theological and ecclesiastical contamination" of the Middle Ages. Mysticism was "opaque" and "dusky." But Luther's "renewal of piety" was significant. This sort of piety found its expression in Luther's hymn "*Aus tiefer Not schrei ich zu Dir*" ("Out of the depths I cry to Thee"). According to Hirsch, mysticism spoke of the opposite: reliance on the human. We have thus, on the one hand, mysticism's "ecstatic and enthusiastic God-passion" and, on the other, Martin Luther's concentration on the genuine and primal in all religion.

Mysticism en bloc was consequently a sub-evangelical phenomenon. Against this Hirsch put Luther's simple, direct, and pure restoration of Pauline Christianity. Mysticism reflected the mood of Roman Catholic life, petitions, *petita*. In contradistinction to this allegedly mistaken notion of petitioning, the Protestant belief—the simple acceptance of a gift—was asserted.

Hirsch was of the opinion that Luther "originally had practiced the religious resignation of Roman mysticism." But ". . . about 1515, while meditating on Rom. 1:17, he rediscovered the Pauline gospel."

To the previous en bloc generalization about mysticism is added yet another generalization, namely, that, after a certain date or after a certain experience, Luther had abandoned mysticism. Hidden in this statement lies the perception that ideas cannot exist outside the logical hierarchy where they have their origin. When a hierarchical structure vanishes, all the separate ideas connected with it also vanish. With this method, in its nature mechanistic, it may possibly seem plausible to say that mystical theology at a certain point had been supplanted with Reformation theology. But when it comes to Luther's relation to mystical theology, the picture was more multifaceted than this.

For Hirsch it would presumably have availed little to look for differentiation among mystics in order to determine who was closer to or more distant from Luther. Because to Emanuel Hirsch it was in the nature of the beast that mystical theology belonged to the wrong logical-theological framework.[285]

Heinrich Bornkamm (1905-1977) found that the most glaring weaknesses of mysticism are the absence of a theological locus for guilt and the teaching about the obliteration of ego-consciousness. For these reasons, he maintained, a true mystic cannot live in true community, and not being able or willing to live in true community reveals a dysfunctional spiritual or intellectual life. A Protestant must regard "the immediacy" of God as an "untruth." Because, according to Bornkamm, the contact between man and God is never direct.

The generalizations—no theology of guilt, no true community—are then compared with Luther's theology. Bornkamm renders this service, he reminds the reader, in his capacity of "theological historian." The historian inside him had discovered that guilt obtained its proper place in theological thinking at the advent of Luther. Man's self was restored to its theological function within the divine "economy" of justification by faith. Historically transmitted faith succeeded the alleged immediacy of spiritual experience. Generalized sets of opposites of this kind were necessary, pedagogically speaking, Heinrich Bornkamm thought. One must, namely, understand that the battle concerned theological truth. "Protestantism," he declared, "must wage a hard and relentless border war against every attempt to persuade it to stage a reformation from within the spirit of mysticism. . . . The difference is one of essence."[286]

We will look at Bornkamm's way of generalizing mysticism en bloc in four areas.

First, Bornkamm dealt with faith as primarily a phenomenon in and of history, based on "objective" events, through which God reveals himself indirectly. Mysticism, on the contrary, is a-historical and claims direct contact with the divine. It is unclear what Bornkamm means by "direct" and "indirect." Does direct communion with God promise a salvation without and outside the Word and Christ? In that case, the mystic Tauler corresponded badly to this description, for to him Christ was the Way and the Truth, and faith was a gift after confession.[287] According to Luther, faith was **both** "historical" **and** "true."[288] The latter embraced "immediate," "direct" feeling. Faith makes of the Christian and Christ one person, and this can be felt immediately and be experienced, Luther believed.[289] By using a generalization of mysticism, Bornkamm's analysis of both Luther and Tauler missed the mark.

Secondly, Bornkamm censored mysticism in toto because it seemed to erase the ego-consciousness. When Tauler said that man is "almost annihilated" when he is lost in God, this must be seen in the total context. For Tauler also said whoever has been "engulfed" in God "finds himself in Him." In God, men may become "masters of their own selves." But preceding this new birth, a seeker has to go through the hell of becoming nothing.[290] Does this imply a complete psychological erasure, a permanent psychological "black out," or a theological religious alteration of consciousness? Naturally, the latter. If that is the case, Bornkamm's generalization loses its validity.

Third, Bornkamm shares with a majority of German theologians the tendency to paint the virile hero, Luther, against the background of a mysticism that is described as feminine, weak, and vague. However, Bornkamm made exceptions for two mystics. He refers to the "manly Tauler" and considers it important to inform the reader that the Frankfurter was a "knight of an order." One finds these attempts at contrast in the first edition of a Bornkamm book about Luther's spiritual world, in a chapter given the heading "the German spirit." In the second edition of the book, this chapter has been omitted. The generalizations—virile, feminine, German spirit—had perhaps become anachronistic.[291]

Fourth, Bornkamm looked at mysticism within the framework of Luther's remarks about the "Enthusiasts." Mysticism that speaks about immersion in God and does not seem to need external support represents all mysticism in this context.[292] We shall return to this viewpoint in the discussion about the role of premises in relation to Luther and mysticism.

Gerhard Ebeling (1912-2001) has reached the following major conclusion about mysticism and Luther's relationship to mystical theology: the use of mystical terms in Luther's writings is just that—terms—and not a matter of essence. Ebeling's treatment of Luther's spiritual relation to Tauler displays this in no uncertain terms.

Ebeling writes that he intentionally avoids discussing "the range of Tauler's influence" on Luther. He draws the reader's attention to "the enthusiastic judgments with which Luther refers to Germanic mysticism in the way he [Luther] understood it." However, Tauler's influence found "an unconsciously objective limit" in Luther's world of thought. Not only that, but Ebeling "also hit upon a temporal limit in Luther's development." Luther, Ebeling said, "withdrew from his admiration for the German theologian [the anonymous author of *Theologia Germanica*] and Tauler already in 1520." After that point in time, Luther never quoted nor recommended either of them. Here the question of generalization appears in two ways: on the subject of Tauler's impact and on the issue of Luther's debt to German mysticism.

Ebeling let it be understood that Luther's spiritual kinship to Tauler and his spiritual influence on Luther were more limited than might be supposed. Although ostensibly leaving the question open, Ebeling nevertheless proffered an indirect claim. He suggested, as noted, that Luther was guided by a built-in, objective, presumably dogmatic "boundary" with respect to Tauler's influence. Moreover, Ebeling alleged, a "temporal limit" also existed which effectively curtailed Tauler's impact on Luther. This is to say, Ebeling proposed that it is possible to chronologically-statistically determine the end of Tauler's sway over Luther's spiritual life. In other words, mysticism would have disappeared from Luther's thought at a certain point in time.[293]

Here Ebeling seeks support for his generalization of mysticism with a fragile argument using numbers and a limited time period. He is grounding a theological assertion—Luther and mysticism belong to opposite worlds—on linguistic statistics. Another thorough research scholar on the subject of Luther and mysticism has produced figures that contradict the Ebeling statement. This researcher maintains that there are in Luther's writings "from 1515 to 1544 twenty-six referrals to Tauler," *nota bene,* positive referrals.[294]

The second question concerns Ebeling's view of what Luther regarded as his debt to mysticism. Ebeling writes that Luther's estimation was an evaluation of mysticism "as he [Luther] understood it." That is to say: Luther's spontaneous evaluation probably would have to be revised by more cautious judges. This is not a wholly unusual attitude in persons who are engaged in Luther research. Luther is supposed to have described the circumstances "erroneously" (O. Scheel) or to have uttered opinions on the matter that are not "decisive" (K. Holl), or to have expressed a view that is not relevant (A. Nygren).[295]

Naturally, some explanations may be required due to cultural changes. Both culturally and dogmatically Luther was, in part, a child of his time. But in the matter of mysticism we are dealing with a subject that in a special way involves spiritual sensitivity and inner judgment. When a generalized picture of mysticism results in attempts to deprive Luther of spiritual intuition, it certainly has been misapplied. For we deal here with more than a conceptual-logical reality, such as an apprehension of mysticism en bloc. When Luther admitted kinship with mystics, it was a question of inner recognition on a spiritual level, beyond the pale of conceptualization. Luther's spiritual sensibilities should have priority with respect to his professions of inner affinity. His positive judgments of some mystics perhaps do not fit our conceptions, yet to become an assessor of a prophet's own assessment of his spiritual debts is a precarious undertaking.

At three other less striking points, Ebeling's method of generalization appears: mysticism is Scholasticism; Luther rejects all mysticism; and Luther knows that mysticism is "false religion." Luther frequently noted that the claim of Scholasticism to be able to apprehend "God" with the aid of intellectual power was a contemptible enterprise. Occasionally he, Luther, had experienced how frightening it is to meet God unprotected, as it were.[296]

Ebeling interpreted this as follows: Luther speaks here about the false knowledge of God, the knowledge of reason; and what he had in mind was doubtless the "speculative, mystical theology of Neoplatonism."[297] Behind this assumption lies the usual supposition that speculative Scholasticism and experience-based mysticism cover the same area and are concentric. But in those passages that Ebeling has consulted, and to which he refers as documentation, there is not one suggestion that corroborates the equating of ideological speculation and mysticism. However, a generalized idea of what mysticism is seems to demand that equation.

Did Luther reject all mysticism? As early 1515-1517 he reminded his listeners and readers that only through Christ can we receive justification through faith and forgiveness of sins. He warned of the danger of seeking religious experience outside of Christ and the Word. Romans 5:2 was before him: "Through him [Christ] we have obtained access to this grace in which we stand, and we rejoice in our hope of sharing the glory of God."[298] Ebeling paraphrased Luther's comments as follows: "The knowledge about God which reason (*die Vernuft*) possesses, is the speculative, mystical theology of Neoplatonism, which teaches a method of penetrating the inner dark spaces and of hearing the uncreated word and of immersing oneself therein."[299]

One notices that Ebeling, in his paraphrase, interpreted Luther as having spoken of all mystical knowledge. However, a closer examination of the Luther passage reveals that Luther was alluding to the mysticism of Dionysius the Areopagite. Dionysius represented the kind of religious effort for which there was no room in Luther's experience and theology. Expounding on Luther's judgment, J. Ficker remarked in the *Weimarausgabe* regarding the Reformer's warning not to seek religious experience outside Christ: ". . . that is to say, the Areopagite's *mystica theologia*. The verses which follow refer to this [the Areopagite's] book with respect to content and partly with respect to certain words or phrases."[300] The impression which one garners from Ebeling is that, on the contrary, no specific mystic is involved but that the clause implies a universal rejection of mysticism as tantamount to "the speculative mystical theology of Neoplatonism." Luther's statement concerned Dionysius the Areopagite, not mysticism. Ebeling has not provided the evidence that Luther rejected mysticism.

Ebeling also analyzed Luther's comments on Galatians 4:8: "Formerly, when you did not know God, you were in bondage to beings that by nature are no gods." Luther elucidated: *Religio falsa* is the kind of religion that endeavors to find a *Deus Clemens*, a merciful God, by works of various kinds. That becomes, in the end, worship of the self. Only Christ's knowledge can save you from that. "Thus everyone who has distanced himself from the knowledge of Christ unfailingly plunges into idolatry." In **this** respect *religiones, observationes* (religious works) are "false." Paraphrasing these remarks Ebeling suggested that they purport to show that "all the ways of religion and worldly wisdom" are "the God-knowledge of reason."[301] The question is if Luther intended to say that religions are false or that reason's God-knowledge under all circumstances is vain, useless. Have "all the ways of religion" been condemned in a statement that proclaims that knowledge of Christ is the cure for idolatry? Mystical theology should be classified in the category of false religion, on Ebeling's view, for according to him, it is doubtless "God-knowledge of reason." A generalization of mysticism has barred mystical knowledge from being anything but "worldly wisdom."

Karl Barth was more radical than any of the other examples now mentioned in his use of the method of generalization. He excluded the possibility of spiritual internalization as a part of salvation. The New Testament passages on death as man's entry into life "have nothing to do with a mysticism of physical or spiritual dying." According to Barth, the Christian kerygma—the message from God to man—does not betoken any unification with Christ in a mystical fashion. Barth declared that mystical unity with God is nothing more than "a deepening of human self-consciousness." He repeated a common critique of Christian mysticism when he maintained that mystical theology privatizes Christian faith, instead of letting it be and remain what it is, "public." Already in early Christian times, said Barth, mysticism was "a privately practicing foreign body." Mysticism, in whatever guise it may appear, is anthropology and disguised cosmology. For Barth there was no doubt about it: mysticism is the opposite pole of the Christian faith. Barth wrote: "The Christian faith is the day which heralded the passing of the mystical night." True, one can acknowledge that mysticism offers experiences, but who can assure us that these do not emanate from "spirits totally other than the Holy Spirit?"

Barth shared the definite opinion of many theologians, whose premises for systematic theology may be very different from his own, that mysticism in toto (including forms that confess Christ) counts with an independent "ground" within man, a "being" of a somewhat autonomous nature. On behalf of the kerygma, Barth announced a dissenting and contrary view. The deed of Christ, so ran his verdict, annuls man's "being." In this sense Barth's view of the relation between soul and God diverged from his fellow-theologian, Calvin. Calvin counted with an *insitio in Christum*, a grafting into Christ, and a *coniunctio*, a process of uniting in friendship and love with Christ. Barth repudiated in the most determined manner a saying from Angelus Silesius that Christ might be born a thousand times in Bethlehem, yet were he not permitted to be born in the soul, that soul would be eternally lost.

However, Barth makes a little concession. One might possibly say something positive about mysticism under the assumption that the proper perspective is being observed. After all, Paul referred to the presence of Christ and his memories of this included experience in the field of feeling and intuition. One could even speak of "Pauline mysticism," Barth thought. But it should be noted, he added, that that was a "mysticism which observes the distance." To be aware of the distance is to interpret man in the light from Christ. Mysticism, Barth was quick to retort, often chooses the opposite way: it interprets God from within man. In mysticism, pietism, and monasticism the accent is on the human, Barth asserted.

Although Barth was not in agreement with Luther's gospel interpretation at important junctures, his view of mysticism nevertheless would coincide with the antipodal thinking about faith versus mysticism frequently ascribed to Luther. This is apparent if you compare Barth's interpretation of the words "overcome by the world" in I John 5:4. Barth averred that these words do not refer to "that mystical emptying . . . an artificially anticipated death." Justification is not man's "task." "God has not created man for such an emptying." Humanly speaking, mystical longing can be a legitimate joy and a human expression of man's love of God. But Christ's deed takes everything connected with man's being away, and that is the decisive point. Theologically speaking, man is totally depraved and the only term that describes his natural relation to God is "discontinuity." For Barth mysticism must be in error since it reckons with continuity of some sort. Against the background of this theological persuasion it becomes less important to find out whether there are differences among the mystics themselves. The very fact that mystics speak positively about the "ground of being," the "soul's longing" or the "image of God" excludes them from serious consideration in a work on church dogmatics. Mysticism en bloc is a *Fremdkörper*, a foreign body, according to Karl Barth.[302]

Many questions arise when one considers Barthianism—both, in general, when one sees it as an understandable reaction to the "new German religion" and, more particularly, when looked at in its role as "anti-mysticism." Is the movement from man to God so exclusively human as Barth seems to think? Can we accept Barth's assumption that man's "religion" has no room for any of God's salvatory work? Is not the longing for which so much mystical theology gives expression also, in part at least, God's longing? Although Barth's generalization of mysticism is unavoidable and logical, given his conception of theology's role, is it possible to excise personal internalization from faith? The kerygma is by its very nature both objective, as history and as sacrament, and subjective. It brings the "eternal now" into the depths of the soul. Because Barth was persuaded that personal experience in faith was theologically insignificant, he would have had difficulty understanding Luther's suggestion that mystical theology is experience of God.

Reinhold Niebuhr (1891-1971), American ethicist and neo-conservative theologian, had found that the greatest problem with mysticism was its attitude toward individuality. He had the impression that "mysticism regards individuality as evil." He was convinced that "all mystic philosophies . . . lose the very individuality . . . they emphasize." The deepest reason for the alleged longing for liberation from individuality is that mysticism, without exception, thinks of sin as involved in physical necessity.

Niebuhr possessed an admirable gift for formulation, but his writings often revealed that he had not thoroughly studied certain subjects, especially the mystics. He had apparently read a book on nature-mysticism and on this basis formed an opinion. Meister Eckhart may have been Niebuhr's prototype for mysticism en bloc. Reinhold Niebuhr made little distinction between the "mysticism of infinity" and the personal mysticism of Christ-allegiance, the "mysticism of personality"—to use the distinction Nathan Söderblom made.

According to Reinhold Niebuhr, **all** mysticism was characterized by the following components: the death of individuality, fear of action for fear of sinning, indifference to history, and the idea that the Holy Spirit is a projection of the human spirit. To the "heresy of mysticism," Reinhold Niebuhr counterpoised genuine Christianity that he described as historical, biblical, and prophetic.

Niebuhr shared with the theological liberals who preceded him a common persuasion that mystical theology could not be integrated with Christian reflection. But in one respect Niebuhr distanced himself from the German mentors who dominate American college and university theology. He differed from them in his treatment of Luther himself. Niebuhr wrote that Luther's influence contributed to "the tragic events of contemporary history," i.e., Hitlerism. And when German scholars of the historical-critical school said that mysticism did not possess a very essential place in Luther's theology, Niebuhr answered that one can, on the contrary, explain the whole Luther-phenomenon with reference to Luther's "mystical teachings about passivity." After having made the conventional separation between, on the one hand, unacceptable non-biblical mysticism and, on the other hand, biblical faith, he parted with his mentors and declared that Luther belonged to the latter category.[303]

Niebuhr used a generalized image of mysticism. In that picture one could hardly recognize any dividing line between nature mysticism and mysticism of personality. The result was an indirect repudiation of the inner, personal element in faith—in itself quite understandable of a social ethicist who witnessed much social-ethical Lutheran quietism.[304]

In conclusion, the generalization of the concept of Christian mysticism, as exclusively manward and subjective, in contra-distinction to the mainstream of Protestant theology, depicted as Godward and objective, has had a distorting effect on inquiries into Luther's relationship to medieval mystics. Three results are discernible in this process:

1. The generalized view of Christian mysticism accords little significance to the suggestion that basic theological differences exist within Christian mysticism and that Luther saw the importance of such differentiation.

2. The generalized view of Christian mysticism encourages oversimplified polarity thinking according to which mystical theology, described as unbiblical and unevangelical, is contrasted to biblical faith considered to be historically and biblically sound, and evangelical.

3. The generalized view of Christian mysticism bolsters the tendency to de-emphasize, as insignificant, certain indications that Luther regarded his affinity with mystical thinkers as essential.

The idea that Christian mysticism, or all mysticism, revolves around **one** leading basic concept or represents **one** thrust, has enabled the person who generalizes about the meaning of mysticism to relegate mystical theology, as such, to an alien, unevangelical, or heretical system of thought. The widespread acceptance of this approach is, I would suggest, rooted in the persistence of an exclusively logical-ideological method for apprehending biblical reality and subsequent Christ-related religious experience.

Mysticism under rationalistic premises: the power of preconception

We have established that liberal and neo-orthodox theological systems often operate under the assumption that mysticism can be viewed uniformly and, therefore, scant attention is devoted to its various forms. Generalizations often replace thorough investigations. Standard judgments concerning mystics and mysticism are accepted as definitive truths from one generation of theologians to the other.

We have also had occasion to suggest that the generalizations serve a confessional purpose. In the realm of "ecumenical dialogue," one is anxious to use the right labels, so to speak. At issue, frequently, is the contrast between a Roman Catholic corpus of faith and an evangelical salvation doctrine. Or put differently, mysticism en bloc is mobilized as support for the argument that a pervading, essential difference exists between the Roman Catholic and Protestant thinking on each important locus in doctrine. Generalizing about mysticism thus serves the purpose of universalizing an historical rift within the church.

In this examination of theological method on the foundation of Luther's theology of experience and of his links to and acknowledgment of mystics, we arrive at the matter of the premises with which one approaches the task. Hence the question is which premises (*Vorverständnisse*) are used. One approaches mysticism with preconceived ideas, either with an open or a closed mind. In the latter case the incitements emanate from the cultural atmosphere of the Western world and its scientific climate. We have already had occasion to take up the epistemological problem, the question of what it means to "know," to have "knowledge." On the following pages this problem will be illustrated with reference to the same theologians who were reviewed under the rubric of generalization. Adolf Harnack will be added in the beginning and Steven Ozment at the end.

Adolf Harnack (1851-1930), a disciple of Ritschl's, thought that the essence of the gospel was "naive eternal life in the midst of time." Culture was the unfolding of individuality and freedom. The process had only one safeguard: the gospel, foundation of "all ethical culture." For Harnack, history was a drama in three stages: "progress" from the Old Testament to the gospel, a fall from the gospel to Greek metaphysics and, through Luther, an "evolution" or a "development" to disposition-ethics.[305]

In the way Harnack saw matters, Christ's message consisted of three truths: first, the message about the kingdom of God as reality close at hand or as future salvation; secondly, the message about Jesus' deeds and thoughts; and thirdly, the new righteousness or the new law.

Harnack adopted the attitude of his mentor, Ritschl, when it came to mysticism. Mysticism was "the Catholic version of individual piety." Thus we find that he took the same stance regarding mysticism as the theologians chosen to illustrate the generalization tendency. Harnack said that he was aware of the "wide-ranging examinations . . . in order to classify the mystics." He considered the inquiries useless. "The differences are essentially irrelevant. Mysticism is always the same. The differences never concern its essence."

Against this background Harnack then described Luther as a person of sober common sense, who naturally found mysticism wholly unsatisfactory. Later, through his religious experience, Luther formulated a theology that is a total refutation of mysticism's way of life.

"Luther hardly experienced the movement of the mystic between rapture and fear for he was too stern with himself," Harnack claimed. In contradistinction to the mystics "who always landed in elevated feelings but seldom attained a pervasive feeling of peace" and soon arrived at "psychological self-destruction," Martin Luther displayed "an active piety" which brought him "a steadier, more blissful certainty."

Harnack declared, "Through a cheerful faith he [Luther] became a hero." True, Luther may have learned "from the old mystics, but what they only sought he [Luther] found." What Luther found about Christ, Harnack deemed, was first and foremost that he is "the historical Christ." Catholic piety talked about a kind of mystical presence that implies Christ would be present even in good deeds. On the contrary, out of protest against this teaching, Luther spoke of "a gracious God in faith." Luther's faith was *kräftig und freudig*, strong and joyful. In Luther's way of looking at things, Harnack thought, there was no mystery in the awakening of faith through the Holy Spirit.

The accent on the historical and the robustly common-sensical in Luther's faith led Harnack to assert that Luther was vastly separated from mystical beliefs "by the totally non-mystical persuasion that trust in God for Christ's sake is the proper content of religion, not to be outdone by any speculation. Trust in God's truth and Christ's deed was rooted in one thing . . . *per crucem Christi*, through the cross of Christ."

Harnack's Luther interpretation excluded every thought that the Reformer's life in Christ was in any sense "immediate." He was of the opinion that the mystic's way of speaking about *imitatio Christi* was entirely alien to Luther's mode of thought. This imitation theology, he pointed out, can after all "often enough drift into becoming a Christ."

Harnack looked at faith, and consequently also Luther's faith, as mediated, not as immediately experienced. Christ and the Christian faith are historical. History mediates Christ. For this reason one must erect theological ramparts against the attacks from the unpredictable and emotion-oriented mystical movement. "Remain in the historical!" that was Harnack's dogmatic testament. But, Harnack asked, how does one remain in the historical when one releases the forces of the imagination and then declares that they are the means for union with the Godhead?

According to Harnack, "sound reason" ought to guide all investigations of history. As a successor to Albrecht Ritschl in the world of thought, he developed an immanental view of the gospel. He thus found it possible to say "that neither mystical contemplation nor the ascetic life style are included in the gospel." Inside this framework, where "sound reason" ruled, Harnack sought to accommodate Martin Luther. Since the gospel, according to Harnack, is at heart a non-mystical message, he praised Luther as an essentially empirical person, guided by common sense.[306]

However, a considerable part of Luther's theological heritage was in this way lost. Luther had really listened to a voice that forced him to a revolt—a revolt that went much beyond what ordinary common sense would want or dare. The voice that he heard came from Christ, and it led into experiences that lay beyond reasonable calculations. Without that "rapture," which sometimes lifted ordinary weekday faith to unimaginable heights, he would have hardly had the strength to be a reformer. This becomes apparent, for instance, in his commentary to Psalm 116. Luther stated that the psalmist wrote out of a feeling of ecstasy—an ecstatic expression of gratitude and faith. Another word for it would be *raptus*, rapture, an indescribable delight, a knowledge that all is well, despite all, Luther added. The word *raptus* came from the treasury of mysticism. This does not have much to do with ordinary reason. The outward signs point to storm, but deep in meditation and prayer, the chosen know that the Lord safeguards the called. The "Lord preserves . . . Return, O my soul, to your rest" (Ps. 116: 6,7).

This is a kind of "ecstasy," perhaps not often experienced, but, in the manner of Paul's Damascus encounter, it is of basic importance for faith. That rapture, or ecstasy, Luther knew quite well. But he also knew the anguish-filled despair that could attack the soul in this "mendacious" world. The state of abandonment, or spiritual exhaustion, was called *gemitus*—anguish, the region of "unuttered or unspeakable sighs." Luther identifies with Paul's experience expressed in II Corinthians 4:8-13, in which Paul refers to Psalm 116:10: "I kept my faith, even when I said 'I am greatly afflicted'."

Luther then gives the reader descriptions of states-of-mind in which a Christian might find himself in times of joy or stress. These mind-states cannot be described in a "reasonable," or purely intellectual, manner. One could say that their origin is non-rational or inaccessible to reason alone.[307]

As we know by now, these, and many similar Luther testimonies, do not derive from the immediately palpable world of pure sense impressions. On the contrary, they communicate an impression that is directly contrary to Harnack's assurances. The models of scientific knowledge, which theologians also feel that they ought to accept, had molded Harnack's picture of Luther. Luther was a reasonable man, to be sure. But he, also, personally experienced a call from God, who is beyond all reason.

Another aspect of the "common sense" philosophy is the question about the "immediacy" of faith. In Harnack's theological world, apologetically dependent on nineteenth century scientific reasoning, Luther could not "reasonably" have anything in common with people who thought that there was theological value in religious imagination and "immediate" experience of seemingly supersensible realities.

The apologetic theologians, among whom Harnack can be counted, naturally claimed Christ as the fountainhead. But because they had been molded, in part, by those who were the objects of their conversion efforts—the empirical skeptics—they neither could, nor would, proclaim Christ as present in a mystical, immediate way. They could not accept that Christ was not only an intellectual concept, but also a personal power continuously involved in the destinies of individuals and the future of the earth.

Time after time Luther returned to the unsophisticated persuasion that Christ's presence could be **felt**. Harnack read, and yet did not read, the words that dealt with this phenomenon. Scientific reason, the yardstick of natural science, provided the building blocks to the premise that nothing invisible can be said to be "immediately" present. Such a confession would be equivalent to the collapse of the "historical perspective " and open the floodgates to the "powers of imagination, fantasy."[308]

Karl Holl presented Luther as somewhat more modern and more consistent than he was in reality, to cite one of his colleagues. He painted Luther as a person whose conscience and conscious thought were always alert and wakeful. It is important that we notice the choice of words. Luther's conscience and conscious thought eventually produced a liberating conceptual solution to a great spiritual dilemma, Holl assumed. In times of great spiritual confusion, most people take their refuge in "visions or miracles which should guarantee . . . grace," he suggested. Luther did not harbor any longing for visions, since he did not like "flings" or "escapades." (Holl used the word *Seitensprünge* = literally, side leaps [fig. extra-marital affairs], not a very felicitous figure of speech, one might think).

In Holl's account, Luther sometimes emerged as a man who consciously guarded himself against feeling and intuition; he was, in the main, intellectually disposed. Rather than being inspired from above, Luther, in Holl's analysis, sets his conscious thought in motion and arrives at a solution. After mature and deep theological pondering, the Reformer emerges with the theological key that opens many hitherto closed doors. The transcendent and mystical intimations in Luther's struggle are absent in Holl's reporting. The illumination depicted by Holl was a conceptual illumination. A new kind of "knowledge" has been added to the store of life's knowledge. This new knowledge was not emotional-spiritual, Holl assumed, but entered the life stream as an idea long hidden under layers of false Catholic anthropology, but now revived. Paul mediated this idea, the concept of justification by faith, according to Karl Holl.

We encounter here an intellectualistic premise. Out of the Reformer's writings steps an intellectual problem-solver, to be sure one of high caliber. First comes the intellectual correction; only in second place comes intuitive experience and spiritual kinship with souls who have had similar experiences. Throughout, Holl's works are dominated by the persuasion that theological thinking is an undertaking that exclusively deals with ideas. As an interpreter of Luther, Holl simply struck from the register those ideas that he considered "folklore" and saw his task as delineating the history of rational theological thought. It was difficult for him to treat the claims of spiritual presence as starting points for any kind of intellectual assessment. In his endeavor to defend Luther's originality, he was forced, because of his rationalistic premise, to explain that "Luther was not under the extraneous influence of mysticism." This is to say, ideas and thoughts are the foundation of the Reformation; mysticism represents another, unfortunately heretical collection of lore. The illumination that radically changed Luther's life was a conceptual enlightenment, according to Holl. The new intellectual insight, the concept of justification by faith, was seen as having been mediated to Luther by Paul. Justification by faith was "a **thought** that became his salvation" (emphasis added). According to Holl, Luther "established," or was the founder of, a new relationship to God based on a rational thought system.

Judging from this "conceptualization," Holl would not have found anything of value in the assumption that non-rational presentiments can serve as sources of theology and that feeling remains where the conceptual ebbs out. Yes, Holl rejects the view that the interlacing of the rational and non-rational is the secret of theological thought. In other words, the idea that theological thinking is "prayed theology."[309]

Holl's rationalistic premise surfaces especially when he seeks to place "the inner life" in his scale of values. To Holl, religion was a series of rational statements. A skeptical, "scientific" society does not accept intuition and feeling as components of a philosophy of life or as objects for rational investigation. But such sources of knowledge **are** a part of the mystical path. A theological premise, composed in deference to the rationalistic values of society, makes light of the significance of feeling and experience in the new relation to the Divine. Therefore Luther's "inner life" came to be treated rather unfairly as an illegitimate child in Holl's account. His intention was limited to registering the ebb and flow of ideas. The "inner life" belongs to a private territory that could not possibly be considered a legitimate research area for a theological analyst. However, the analysis of concepts had to do with a gospel that was the opposite of private; it was public, included concepts, and was accessible to all. In many other contexts, Holl described mysticism as a human being hunting for proprietorship of God himself. In contrast, Luther was depicted as the herald of the certainty of the Word, available to each and all.[310]

With respect to the place of the "inner life" in theological reflection, Holl—a person of liberal-theological stripe—definitely associated himself with orthodox Lutherans. Neither the liberals nor the orthodox thought much of the idea that Christ lives in the believer in a private, subjective, experiential, and psychologically describable way.

In **Erich Seeberg's** case we noted that he generalized the concept of mysticism by describing its spirituality as technique. At the same time he mistakenly portrayed Luther as very little interested in method in devotional life. The rationalistic premise behind this reconstruction of the material was that Luther's theology limited the human's worship of God to methodical fulfillment of vocational duties, thereby rejecting the mystical invitation to further God-consciousness by methodical practice of devotional exercises. In this respect mysticism was over-spiritualized (not much interest in the earthly) and Luther was under-spiritualized (not much interest in spiritual practices). Seeberg's theory of cognition was based on the idea that knowledge that emanates from non-rational dimensions hardly has any significance for theology, due to the fact that theology is primarily a rational activity. The fact that Martin Luther, in reality, put a lot of weight on regular reading of the Scriptures, contemplation, and prayer was omitted—or perhaps was overshadowed by an automatically accepted intellectual premise.[311]

Emanuel Hirsch, world-famous Church historian, was the object of my attention in connection with our discussion about the "angelic host" and the tendency to generalize. In the beginning of his research, Hirsch underlined the personal in Luther's fellowship with God. Luther broke through the institutional faith to a personal experience of a God whose message to the heart is both wrath and grace, Hirsch explained. He described Luther's faith as "a trans-dogmatic measuring rod for the gospel's breakthrough via the medium of conceptual thought." Luther's "true disciples" were not the orthodox teachers, but "Spener, Francke, Zinzendorf and Schleiermacher." Hirsch's studies on Kierkegaard furthered a certain sensitivity to Luther's existential experience and Luther's remarks about divine presence.

However, Hirsch found it necessary, on second thought, to demythologize the Reformer, guided by a desire to make the message of the Reformation more accessible to modern man. Consequently Hirsch applied to Luther's utterances the criteria of modern historical science and of modern biblical criticism. With this approach Hirsch found that, in a remarkable way, Luther's innermost concerns coincided with the results of critical research. One sees this, for instance, in Luther's explanation to the first article of the Apostles' Creed. Here Luther is already on his way from myth and metaphysics to "a trans-dogmatic faith," Hirsch asserted. Luther's choice of words may appear "simple and common. Yet the seriousness of personal actualization makes the difference clear between unadulterated strong faith and all the unclear ecclesiastical contaminations."

As we saw in the first chapter of the present book, Hirsch solved the problem of "angels" by "existentializing" them. He was of the opinion that angels ought to be recognized as "helpful thoughts," but not as metaphysical realities. With reference to the debate concerning angels, we can now say that Hirsch placed Luther in tension between primitive, simple reaction and critical thought. On one hand, we have "the simple mind "of primitive ideas which dominated primitive Christianity and which still meant a lot to Luther. On the other hand, we find "a spiritually clear, thoughtful intellect."

The unreflective, primitive mind-set requires concrete guarantees that include palpable manifestations of the divine. But Luther was closer to modern historical criticism and its values than the simple mind and its values, Hirsch maintained. In that connection he pointed to what he believed was Luther's lack of interest in the popular belief in angels, a lack of interest that Hirsch considered healthy. It stemmed from "a strong faith," he thought. Such a faith had no need of supernatural "knowledge" that cannot be reconciled with the demand for intellectual clarity. According to Hirsch, the effect of modern critical thinking was that "the unvarnished, original faith" had been brought to light. Criticism, in the modern, scientific sense, had peeled away pre-Christian superstition. This had been a painful process, Hirsch conceded, but, in the final analysis, it had been useful and beneficial. That which was truly Christian had in this manner seen the light of day.

The peeling off of years of encrustation resulted in liberation from supernatural lore. This process had also thrown light on Luther's world of thought, according to Hirsch. He was convinced that the methods of historical criticism had dispersed the mists of primitive superstition that still surrounded Luther's statements or those of his theological interpreters. In this enthusiastic apologetic for the potentialities of modern scientific criticism, Luther stood out as a man who, long before the epoch of the modern critical method, was its herald due to the power of his theological style.

However, in order to reach this conclusion and attain that picture of Luther, Hirsch was forced to make energetic use of an intellectualistic premise with traits borrowed from rationalistic philosophies that grew up around modern science before Bohr, Planck, Heisenberg and Einstein. Hirsch gives us a Luther who followed rationalistic man's "sound reason" but who knew very little, or nothing at all, about the world of experiential knowledge from which mystical theology grows.[312]

In the beginning of his career as theologian, Heinrich Bornkamm spoke of Luther's "rich thoughts about the Spirit." He had been influenced by Karl Holl, whose scholarship Bornkamm considered to be the watershed in Luther research. The German philosopher Dilthey had also made a deep impact on him. Bornkamm agreed with Dilthey's thoughts on "understanding," as an intuitive process, and his opinion that the Protestant mystic S. Franke was "the crown of the Reformation." He also noted that Troeltsch's sociological analyses reckoned with mysticism as a power in spiritual life.[313] One finds in his earlier works references to Luther's "Christ-mysticism," as well as the observation that Luther made an analogical use of bridal mysticism.[314]

However—as was shown in the discussion on the generalization of mysticism—Bornkamm's later works suggest an approach that reflected an altered frame of reference and a different yardstick. The possibility of "immediate" experience of God is called into question from an ideological-theological point of view. A proper interpretation of the gospel would exclude anything like that. Bornkamm spoke **for** "Protestant faith," on the one hand, and against mysticism's view of nature and creation, on the other. The latter he simply termed an "untruth."

We have already observed that Bornkamm considered mysticism a collection of theological misjudgments. When it comes to rationalistic premises, one notes especially the tendency to polarize two theological worlds seen exclusively as thought products, as intellectual crystallizations. Theoretical, dogmatic formulations about truth are given a considerable measure of finality. It is obvious that Bornkamm, in his later thinking, assumed a more theoretical, didactic posture than in his earlier production. "Protestant faith" thus came to stand for a system of truths, things one regarded as likely, things that are not going against the grain of what is "known." In this respect one finds, in historical-critical circles, the same kind of trust in the cognitively formulated as among orthodox Lutherans.

In three respects one sees how Bornkamm's premises have an effect on his treatment of the place of mysticism in Luther's world of thought: the question of conceptual truth, the idea of divine presence, and the question of the mystical with Luther.

Bornkamm's thinking about mysticism dwelt increasingly on the logical antinomy truth-untruth. He referred with approval to Ritschl's verdict on the absolute distinction between the Catholic-mystical and Lutheran-evangelical faith. The evangelical truth, as propounded by Luther, took comfort in the seemingly insignificant manger of the Christ child, while Catholic verity, in general, and mysticism, in particular, implied an ascent to divine majesty. Bornkamm described evangelical truth as a sober, wakeful acceptance of a gift that did not require a corresponding inner movement of feeling and inner growth. The Catholic-mystical attitude, on the contrary, was described as a selfish desire to possess the divine in the psychic recesses of the soul.[315] The contradiction was one between Protestant truth and Catholic-mystical "truth." The Luther dictum, "God is in each creature," Bornkamm interpreted as follows: in no way did Luther intend to suggest, with this utterance, that nature brought forth "knowledge of God." The desire for antinomy doubtless actuated the absoluteness of the statement. For, and this has already been pointed out in the present study, Luther's thinking about man's essence with respect to his natural knowledge of God is **not** as unambiguous as it may appear in Bornkamm's theology.[316]

Evangelical "truth" is here contrasted with Catholic-mystical "untruth" in such a way that the contradistinction becomes total. Evangelical truth was pitted against the claims of mysticism, so that the latter is depicted as "untruth," "fraud," or "illusion."[317] Protestant faith assumes the character of a system of truths, a linking together of a series of logical theoretical formulations. Truth, as a logical-theological crystallization of what people say about faith, becomes the dominant concern. Trust as a living, prayer-born relationship to God, which is not always amenable to critical logic, diminishes in theological significance. In Bornkamm's interpretation, the tension between truth and trust has been decided in behalf of objective, logical-theological statements, and trust is exiled to the world of "subjectivity," the home of mystical theology.

The premise that lies behind this way of approaching Luther is intellectualistic. Within its pale there is only room for logical distinctions between "truths." This one-sidedness makes it difficult to understand the trust-filled language and the words about numinous presence that grow out of dynamic spiritual experience. Practically speaking, inside this rationalistic framework, Bornkamm's Luther-interpretation is closed to the component of experience in Luther's, and mysticism's, terms about life in God.

Secondly, in Bornkamm's generalized picture of mysticism, the seeker enjoys "immediate God-experience." Bornkamm's measuring instrument reacted against this aspiration. Not even in the sacraments can immediate God-encounters be experienced, he objected.

Everything hinges naturally on what one means with the word "immediate." With some, it can mean that no "media" are needed. The Holy Word and the sacraments would not, under these circumstances, be needed, as far the Christian is concerned. Luther ruled out this kind of "immediacy." But the word "immediate" can also harbor the feeling-side of faith, the "heart's" experience of God's presence. Much suggests that Martin Luther was familiar with that kind of immediacy, and in this book space has already been devoted to his inner *Erfahrung*, experience. Luther was of the opinion that immediacy as feeling is a part of true theology. To the contrary, Bornkamm asserted that neither immediacy nor immediacy as a part of true theology had very much to do with evangelical theology. According to Bornkamm, Luther's sacramental theology held not a hint of experience in the field of feelings. The sacrament of holy communion is declarative. It declares that Jesus Christ is my God. The sacrament is "not a place for immediate mystical God-encounter in supernatural bliss," he wrote. As Bornkamm viewed the matter, Luther limited man's participation in the sacrament to a confession of fealty to Christ.[318]

As we have seen, Luther said more than this about our participation in the worship of God and in the Eucharist. We are primarily interested in finding out why Bornkamm, occasionally in nearly indignant terms, consistently rejects the immediacy-motif in his reading of Luther. The conclusion must be that Bornkamm's intellectualistic preconception—according to which the evangelical thrust represented the objective and declarative in the gospel and mysticism the subjective and desiring—eliminated the feeling-side of religion. Dogmatic logic and institutional order became the only repository of Luther's legacy.

The third inquiry in our scrutiny of Bornkamm's rationalistic premise is closely connected to the second. Can one say that Luther's theology has any organic links to mystical theology? Bornkamm's answer issues directly out of the previous discourse and is summarized in the following: the Catholic-mystical and Lutheran-evangelical are dogmatically-logically contradictory. The Reformer, who contributed the logical theological arguments to illumine this polarity, cannot very well be expected to abide in that which he proved wrong. The subjective and the experiential in the realm of religion belong to be a man-centered quest manifestly opposed to the objective address of God in word and sacrament, in which he declares, makes known, that we are justified by faith. The Reformer must be on the side of the objective, and he cannot simultaneously take the side of the man-centered and the subjective. Mysticism is a part of an entire system of untruth. The Reformer lifted out the truth. This is a logical-dogmatic evaluation of the question concerning mysticism in Luther's life, argues Bornkamm.

It is only from within the logical-dogmatic conception described above that one can understand this quotation from Bornkamm: "Only dilettantes in the field of spiritual history can call Luther a mystic." But without understanding Bornkamm's rationalistic premise this statement becomes presumptuous.[319]

As in the case of other Luther interpreters, the nature of **Gerhard Ebeling's** presuppositions can be advantageously studied in his treatment of Luther's connection spiritual to Tauler. In his work on Luther's comments on the Gospels, Ebeling asserted that Luther's acceptance of Tauler was limited by "an unconsciously objective limit" as well as a "temporal limit." We discovered those delimitations in connection with Ebeling's inclination to generalize when dealing with mysticism.

This German Luther-expert did not think that Luther was "conscious" of those limits in his relationship to Tauler, but that later research has corrected Luther on this score. Let us, for some moments, assume that this vicarious correction has been inspired by the pervasively Protestant-Lutheran persuasion that Luther's thought cannot, in any essential aspects, be described as "mysticism." The validity of this assumption can be partly tested if one scrutinizes an interesting Ebeling translation of an autobiographical notation by Luther.

In the preamble to a volume of his writings in Latin, Luther told about an inner change, presumably the so-called "tower experience," that transformed his entire life. The most significant words run as follows: *Miro certe ardore captus fueram cognosceni Pauli in Epistola ad Rom.* Ebeling translated the first part: "A very unusual burning desire had gripped me." The adjective for *mirus* belongs to the substantive *miraculum*. It describes something extra-ordinary, something miraculous, filled with wonder, mysteriously strange. The mood is numinous. A stronger, more descriptive adjective than "unusual" is certainly called for.

O. Clemen's German rendering of this passage in the Weimar-edition has caught the spirit and the meaning of the Latin text: "I was gripped by a wonderfully glowing desire." In this translation the mystery, the feeling of the beyond, has been preserved. Presumably in order to more definitely emphasize the dynamic presence of something paranormal, Clemen added: "And it still had me in its command." That is to say, Luther's experience of Divine presence on that remarkable day—when the justification message broke through to him—spread light over his entire life. It was not a question of an isolated sensation. The choice of tense indicates that the original occurred fairly long ago, when Luther had begun his interpretations of the Psalter, possibly 1518. But the sensation of the miraculous persisted.[320]

He had been saved from his fear of Christ as judge to the certainty that Christ is a friend. The grace of the other world had broken through, not primarily as a result of theological pondering, but as an assurance of the "heart." We are reminded of Paul's encounter with the risen Lord at Damascus. In both instances there was a supernatural presence and its nimbus. Ebeling's translation lowers the whole description down to an everyday, ordinary level. To say "unusual" about a Damascus experience is to use mundane language about a transcendental experience, which from the recipient's subjective viewpoint is described with the words *miro ardore* (miraculous ardor).

Ebeling's translation discloses the rationalistic academic climate in which he wrote. It is not so easy in that climate to be open to the possibility that Luther alluded to a metaphysical reality that could also be felt. The contour of a definite "prejudice" presents itself. The contour comes into sharper focus in the following passage where the author delineates the aim of his investigation.

The reader ought not to expect a biography on Luther, Ebeling warned his public, nor, for instance, a "personality-portrait" of Luther as "the eternal German" (In this there is a concealed criticism of colleagues who, inspired by patriotic moods, elevated Luther's Teutonic virtues to the skies). Nor did Ebeling offer a systematic examination of the traditional articles of faith. Instead Ebeling offered an introduction that would bring the reader to an "encounter" with Luther. Isolated facts and thoughts, taken out of context, can be ever so interesting, Ebeling pointed out, but this is a matter of finding the foundation for the thoughts. Hence he intended, he continued, to initiate the reader to the art of ferreting out Luther's **thought**, not his **thoughts**. He, Ebeling, felt himself as part of a movement toward a complete and full understanding of Luther. He was not involved in any attempts at copying, Ebeling asserted. His Luther study was rather an expression of his desire to be responsible, he pointed out.

The aim of the study demanded an antithetical method. Ebeling was of the opinion that Luther could not be understood unless a particular schema for understanding him is accepted. Ebeling's scheme was a dialectical one. Luther's thought, he wrote, developed in antithetical fashion. For example, Luther thought and lived in the tension between philosophy and religion, letter and spirit, law and gospel, faith and love. His thought was assertive and confessional. In the process of the examination, Ebeling declared, the inquirer would remain open "for an encounter with Luther as a language event." For what really fired the Reformer was zeal to find "the right way to bring the Word into language." Luther as a "language event" should be seen, if I have understood Ebeling, as an emergence of antithetical motifs and movements.[321]

With this type of analysis, Ebeling hoped to reach beyond the historically conditioned way of understanding Luther. For instance, it would be necessary to indicate the erroneous images of Luther that Lutheran orthodoxy and Lutheran pietism have created.

Ebeling's pronouncements on **pietism** are of special interest for our examination. He states, first, that persons of pietistic leanings always find a special pleasure in reading about Luther in his early years as a Reformer. For it was during those years that "the so highly esteemed edification literature of German mysticism . . . seemed closely related to the gospel of penitence and grace." According to Ebeling's conception of pietism and its relation to Luther, pietists maintained a certain distance from the "later Luther" whom they regarded as a more unbending Christian reformer, a person who under the pressure of the daily load slipped into some "re-Catholicizing" positions. To Ebeling this was an illustration of the tendency to come under the spell of "general value judgments" in an effort to understand Luther. Ebeling's ambition was of a different order, he said. His method, he claimed, was oriented toward in-depth (*eindringend*) examination of the sources. A scrutiny of the traditions that were part of Martin Luther's life makes it clear that two epochs are battling for his soul. But something dynamic and constructive had emerged in the process of that tension. Luther found that his renewal was a rediscovery of "the antithesis between the old man and the new man." The question is not only historical, he said. It was existential. For its pivot was the antithesis: "the time of law—the time of grace." In other words, Luther posed a question that concerned life in the present, not just a historical one.[322]

However, the timelessness of Luther's renewal and its significance appear only to the "trained ear," Ebeling explained. With that reservation he introduced a piece of elitist intellectualism. Only those who have grasped Luther's deepest concern will escape the disappointment that sets in at the discovery of the Reformer's human weaknesses, at the realization that he was not a "holy man," Ebeling pointed out. Precisely here is the point at which "a trained ear" discovers the essential: the tremendous force of Luther's struggles, "the great burden of historic responsibility." "A trained ear" learns about this Luther inside Luther, less through psychological analysis, dogmatic statements, or simple biography than through "the language event." The language that emanated from his spiritual regeneration coincided with Luther's experience of his faith, according to Ebeling: "Only experience makes a theologian," *sola experientia facit theologum.*

Here we must ask if Ebeling and Luther meant the same thing by "experience." Ebeling's striving was to reveal Luther's "thought" with the aid of a finely honed analytical faculty. Only the trained analyst knows, when all is said and done, what Luther's foundational experience actually was about. That assertion limits to a select minority those who could ever hope to "understand Luther." The analysts would, according to Ebeling, come closer to a real "encounter" with Luther by studying "the language event," an event that indirectly grew out of the traditions around Luther and "the distinctive traits in his approach to these traditions." In the awareness of this background and precisely in the study of the "language event," the analyst perceives how Luther, through "mutations" in his thinking, arrived at something that can be termed "his own."

This was thus the "experience" which Ebeling had in mind when he suggested that the Luther statement, "Only experience makes a theologian," coincided with the analytical understanding of the "language event."[323] But the two ways of looking at things, the two concepts, do not correspond. Luther referred to a physical-spiritual state, Ebeling to an intellectual process. As Ebeling viewed the matter, only the "trained ear" can discern the different traditions surging in on Luther, can really comprehend Luther, and have a genuine "encounter" with him.[324] But the meaning of "experience," as Luther used it has little to do with a purely conceptual process, it would appear. The experience about which Luther spoke was an experience of trust, flowing out of a trust relationship with God.

I ask the reader's indulgence for this digression. However, it became necessary as an illustration to the manner of thought and the premises from which Ebeling sees Martin Luther, yes, as an illustration to a predominant intellectualistic method. Ebeling's choice of words in the translation of *miro ardore* revealed a certain hesitancy before the metaphysical, the miraculous, and the numinous in Luther's use of

Erfahrung, experience. The nature of the premises of Ebeling's theory of cognition begins to take form at this stage. His preconceived opinion had its roots in empirical "common-sense" naturalism, according to which one does not acknowledge the non-rational as a source of the rational. Moreover, we saw that Ebeling, in his plan for his Luther-examination, moved in exclusively intellectualistic categories. In combination with the common-sense attitude, this outlook becomes an obstacle to attempts to understand the content of Luther's *Erfahrung*. It is plainly evident that Luther's and Ebeling's views on that reality are **not** congruent.

One may observe a similar dependence on a rationalistic theory of knowledge in the following areas of Ebeling's discourse on Luther: the meaning of the cross of Christ, love directed to God, the nature of man's "cooperation" with God, and the structure of the human conscience.

Luther's theology of the cross is only seemingly mystical theology, proposed Ebeling. With this assertion Ebeling relied on an enduring argument in Luther-research, namely, that only the "young Luther" could have been influenced by mystical thought. Ebeling asserted that it was only a matter of "a passing concern or a peculiarity of the young Luther." Because the theology of the cross is the core of justification by faith, it could not be combined with the mystical.[325]

My objection to this kind of reasoning is not only that one finds the mystical reality also with the later Luther—a subject which will touched upon later in our exposition—but also that Luther rejected speculative mysticism and ego-centered passion-mysticism. However, in his talk about Christ's sufferings, he took for granted that it brought with it interiorization, a dying and a resurrection in personal life. In this way man welcomes Christ to dwell in him.[326] The mystical language that Luther employed in this case unites him with several other medieval mystics. The unity experienced with Christ under the crosses which life gives us can be likened to a heavenly embrace, when the Bridegroom, Christ, embraces the soul, the bride. This, Luther pointed out, is to accept the cross.[327] Christ's passion is both sacrament and example, Luther maintained. The sacrament was a gift and Christ's example inspires to *imitatio* through suffering and death.[328] The cross-bearing Christ himself becomes, in a mystical sense, both "acting subject" and "humanity's power."[329]

It is clear that Ebeling's premise precludes an acknowledgment of Christian cross bearing as in any sense a psychological reality. His intellectualism impels him to assume a posture that, in some respects, resembles the orthodox forms of rationalism: justification solely as imputed truth existentially corroborated. Faith, Ebeling maintains in refutation of mystical passion theology, is an appropriation of the Word, not "an actual change of man."[330]

Is the expression "love for God" acceptable in true Reformation theology? Ebeling answered the question negatively. Luther spoke about the meaning of this phrase in a comment from 1515-1516. About the question of "loving God," he said, it is a manner describing that which we actually have no power to describe. It sounds like human love, but the love of God is ultimately rooted in the Unspeakable, the Unfathomable. The experience is Luther's personal experience: "a transport right into the midst of innermost darkness."[331] Mystics speak in the same terms. Ebeling explains these words from Luther as follows: Luther gives us here a metaphor of the link between faith and God, with a choice of words that "still" lingers in his mind and is a "loan" from mysticism.

According to this version, mysticism is considered to be a past stage in the Reformer's life. Consequently, mystical terms must be registered as extraneous. Faith is, according to Ebeling, **one** thing, genuine change in the soul quite **another**. Luther embraced theological faith; Catholic mysticism subscribed to the religion of inner change. The assertion that God's love must include love for God in order to be meaningful is, according to this way of looking at things, theological nonsense. According to Ebeling's interpretation of the gospel one ought not to include human feeling and intuition as a part of theological concern. Thereby, he believed that he stood on Luther's side. The words of Thomas Aquinas, that love unites one with the beloved, militate against—as pointed out previously—Ebeling's design for true theology. Talk about internalization, about receiving God in the heart, "points to the extraordinary depths of the confessional difference."[332]

If one considers Luther's statements one must ask: do we really have the right to excise his testimonies, including his statements of later years, about experiences of feeling-in-faith and psychic response? Dare we relegate them to the realm of obsolescent terminology just because these testimonies have no basis in "reality"? Ebeling's rationalistic premise leads to an affirmative answer: we do have this right. But much evidence can be cited to warrant a negative answer: with Luther justification includes a human love for God, an overwhelming awe, the wonderful miracle that one has been justified, forgiven, and liberated.

Ebeling introduced a seemingly orthodox note into his critical-intellectualistic score when, presuming to speak on behalf of Martin Luther, he wrote that man should not be considered as acting or active before God. This should not be interpreted as though man would not be encouraged "to be acting as an agent before God in the face of the world," he continued. But this means that man is not acting when he encounters God.[333] The interpretation in question is a paraphrase of a Luther statement in *The Bondage of the Will*. Let us go back to that statement. Luther wrote that God's mercy is the prime mover. It is the driving force in all. Our own will "activates nothing but surrenders."[334] The significant word is *agere*, to set in motion, to stimulate or to spur to action. Luther wrote, "*asserto . . . Dei misericordiam solam omnia agere et voluntatem nostram nihil agere sed potius.*" Ebeling interpreted *agere* as act, acting in the face of God, and thus obviated the thrust of the remark. If one says that you, as a Christian, are not spurred to action, you indeed are approaching Lutheran orthodoxy's fear of the word "cooperation," expressed in the dogmatic declaration that the Christian, in his relation to God and the world, would best be compared to a log or a stone. Here we return to the influence of the intellectual Stoic premise: a central, "reforming" faith provides no platform for subjective, psychic response and spiritual growth (The latter, however, are considered positive human values). But Ebeling's thesis hardly does justice to Luther's statements about our actions that are a part of God's actions. For Luther wrote these words in indignation and irritation on account of Erasmus' book on the will. The sharpness in many of the book's phrases must be seen against this background. The quotation in question does not fit the non-mystical interpretation that Ebeling gave it.

Another Luther passage, this one from *On the Freedom of the Christian*, lends weight to the suggestion that the idea of complete passivity before God was not an organic part of Luther's thought. The situation in the latter case was naturally entirely different from the former. Luther hoped that the Pope would be able to show greater insight into the Christian cause than the clergy and the theologians. In this book, Luther witnesses about his faith that gives him freedom in Christ. A liberated person has the right to be glad and jubilate. Out of trust the liberated person's faith grows as the will to be of service grows. There is a quality to the Christian life that distinguishes it from the world. The genesis of this quality is the new insight that the Christian is not doing Christian tasks in order to further himself or to please the priests or the world. He does them because he is in Christ.[335] In those statements about the freedom of the justified person to be and act in Christ one finds not a hint to the effect that he is not acting vis-à-vis God. To say the contrary would be to make the Christian into an automaton. One does not defend God's sovereignty by depicting the Christian as a robot.

Luther's intention by the statement containing the word *agere* was not to invalidate the responsibility to act in the face of God, but rather to underline the sovereignty of God as the prime mover and energizer of everything. According to Luther, man is an "agent" who is expected to "act" before God's face—moved by God. The premise that begins with the apprehension that religious sentiments or feelings and creative deeds do not possess a rightful place in justification, have, in this way, largely obscured Luther's opinion about the Christian's ethical collaboration with God. The concept "conscience" became for Ebeling a symbol for those points "where God and the world wrestle with one another."[336] Sometimes it surely seems, Ebeling conceded, that Luther said more about conscience than that. It may seem as though the Reformer assumed that an inner process of appropriation ought to follow, after man has surrendered to God's hands, yes, even a kind of spiritualization or interiorization.

However, Ebeling said, that is an illusion. He assured his readers that Luther took refuge in a nomenclature that in itself does not belong to his theology of justification. Luther's real intention, according to Ebeling, would have been to "locate the God-talk," that is to say, map out the place where this is supposed to have happened. In other words, in large part, Luther would have been engaged in an analysis of an existential situation.[337] In and with this undertaking, Luther would then have found that the conscience offers us a suitable occasion to test the area for study of the human experience or, to express it in a somewhat more learned way, phenomenological observations. Thus Luther's language, Ebeling says, was a mystical language only superficially.

This argumentation points back to a rationalistic premise. Did Luther really think of the conscience purely as a symbol for the points of contact between the world and God? After his liberation from a Scholastic definition of conscience, Luther regarded the conscience as a meeting-place between God and man, a dynamic "knowing-with-God" for souls made righteous. He began describing the life of conscience as Christ's advent into the soul, with all that that means of moral and emotionally tinged alteration.[338] How could Luther avoid the question of the conscience when he wrote that Christ is formed in us and that we are formed according to his image?[339] When he described faith as creative of divine attributes "in us," what else did he characterize, if not the Christian conscience?[340]

Upon a closer scrutiny of Luther's statements about the conscience and Gerhard Ebeling's premise (supposedly faithful to Luther) about the nature of the conscience, one cannot help but draw the conclusion that we have before us two vastly different viewpoints. On the one hand, we have Luther's statements about the conscience as God's growth in man and, on the other hand, Ebeling's opinion that such propositions were merely Luther's way of verbalizing man's ideas about God. Unconsciously guided by his intellectualistic premise, Ebeling sought to make plausible the argument that Luther took refuge in words of mystical internalization, which in the case of the "conscience" had nothing to do with mystical internalization. We see once more how a preconceived perception of Western European academic origin pronounces an anathema on mystical experience from the point of view of evangelical theology and, as a matter of fact, declares war against it.

It may seem that entirely too much space has been devoted to one example illustrating the dominance of rationalistic premises in those theologies that deal with the Reformation and mysticism. But Gerhard Ebeling's learned efforts in this area have, in significant ways, molded the teaching of theological schools about Luther and should therefore demand special attention. In Ebeling's Luther interpretation, reason-centered empiricism has taken the prime place. Thus, according to him, the insight about Luther and Luther's legacy—when the chips are down—rests with the linguistic analyst, and Luther's mission to reform is depicted, in the final analysis, as "analytical." According to Ebeling, Luther's great goal was "to **think** God and world into **oneness.**"[341] (emphasis added). This depiction of Luther's theology presents it as primarily intellectual-reflective renewal, with mysticism as its antipode. We are also given an image of Luther that resembles more the analyst than the inspirer, more the professor than the seeker. In Ebeling's theological world the mystical and Luther have nothing in common.

The American dogmatician **Steven Ozment** (1939-) was cited in the discussion of Tauler and Luther (Chapter 5). Here he will be briefly mentioned as an exponent of a widely accepted school of thought based on rationalistic premises. Luther's and the Apostle Paul's anthropology stands in diametrical opposition to "mystical anthropology," Ozment thought.[342] He asserted that Luther presupposed no continuity between God and man, no uniting "substance." With such an assumption the border between God and man would be eradicated. Therefore Luther's and a mystic's views of salvation are diametrically different. Ozment's thesis was that it was "Luther's conviction that human life is soteriologically de-substantial." In other words, this view assumes that human nature does not contribute in any way to salvation. Mysticism bases its view of man on the assumption that we, in some sense, are taking part in the work of salvation. We possess something within us, something that is in constant contact with God and is "soteriologically substantial." It points to a connection between us and God and a relationship that would not be without importance in God's work of liberation on our behalf.

According to Ozment, a polarity between mysticism—and especially its anthropology—and the thought of Luther prevails. Ozment believed that he had proved this by developing his study of Tauler, Gerson, and Luther in an historical and systematic manner. The former method wards off attempts to make a-historical comparisons of ideas for polemical or ecumenical reasons. The latter method guarantees a holistic approach to a thinker's world and obviates the use of ideas in isolation, abstracted from systematic contexts.

Against this programmatic background, Ozment declared that Tauler's anthropology is basically non-Lutheran. It depicts man's precreaturely status as "one essential being" with God—a concept that cannot be included in Luther's thought, according to Ozment. Furthermore, in Ozment's accounting, Tauler calculates with "human preparatory activity" in salvation. Luther did not. With Tauler mystical union is thought of as "conformity" of the will to God in "preparation for a still higher union with God." This, Ozment maintained, would be far from Luther.[343]

On the question of faith and humility there is a gulf between "the Catholic doctrine of grace" underlying Tauler's mysticism and "the Reformation doctrine of justification." For Luther faith and humility belonged closely together because, as Ozment seems to think, before God man's only assumption could be that he is not of God's substance.[344]

Regarding preparation for the reception of the gospel (*preparatio evangelica*), Ozment had come to the conclusion that Tauler made "human preparatory activity an indispensable condition for divine presence." Ozment imputes to Tauler a universal "natural creational claim to salvation." Against this assumption stands Luther's own utterance, "In Tauler I have found more true theology than in all the university doctors lumped together." It should be noted that although Tauler occasionally spoke of a preparation for God's entry into the soul, he was also conscious of the great distance between God and man and man's nothingness and sinfulness before God. In the Tauler sermon which Ozment uses as justification for the assertion that this mystic —quite contrary to Luther—speaks of "a natural creational claim to salvation," we read that God, from eternity, has imprinted his image in the ground of the soul. That is to say, the soul is tied to God in the sense that the soul, through grace, can receive all God owns in his nature (The text is John 3:11). Ozment is of the opinion that Tauler's view of "the natural covenant" between God and man outweighs "isolated remarks" on "radical sin." But it is obvious that Luther found that both viewpoints on man's relationship to God are valid. They are parts of a huge paradoxical truth about "justified sinners." For him it is essential and meaningful to hear Tauler say that "our renewal must take place in God's righteousness and holiness." "Natural man" cannot understand "the will and the pleadings of the Holy Spirit" since natural man is living in self-generated justification. Even regarded as a whole, Taulerian theology, in spite of Neoplatonic strains, often enough is not too far from Pauline anthropology. One must also remember that Luther, without a Neoplatonic background, reckoned with man's eternal link with God (See Chapter 5 of this book).[345]

Ozment's theory of cognition lets him look at the problem, Luther and the mystics, from within the either/or position of doctrinaire perceptions: "medieval or modern," "Catholic or Protestant," "mystical or theological." The matter is naturally more complicated than this. I will pass over certain critical points of Ozment's propositions concerning Luther's relationship to mysticism or, more aptly, the mystical in faith. Let us only note, finally, this scholar's view of the relation between the cognitive and the spirit.

In addition to the dominant statement about the "soteriologically non-substantial" (that there is nothing in man's nature which participates or contributes to salvation), the following utterance is of central importance for Ozment's reasoning: "Luther secularizes man, not man's justification before God." That pronouncement was made principally in protest against Karl Holl's tendency to secularize justification so that Christianity could be reduced to ethics. But by delimiting himself, Ozment also barred the thought that reckons with immediate life in God and the Christian's potential in God. A static-rationalistic outlook removes from Luther's world of faith the possibility of spiritual growth and kinship with God. In this interpretation of his relation to mysticism, Martin Luther becomes a theologian who is "theological" with the exclusion of the "psychological-anthropological." Thus it is a given that the two areas, the cognitive-conceptual construct and intuitive-experiential construct, should and ought to be separated when one is thinking about divine revelation.

In the case of mysticism, Ozment wished to prove that there is, even in the case of Johann Tauler, an unbridgeable gulf between the mystical and Luther's thought. Is this sharp distinction viable? Even if it is conceded that this expert has read more on the subject than the present author, it can be asserted that the material which he and I have both read may give rise to divergent conclusions and interpretations. In addition, one cannot rule out that Ozment's conclusions might diminish in significance by documentation that the present author has not read or has not chosen to submit.

Ozment gives us an illuminating picture of an exclusively, logical concept-supported treatment of the subject, Luther and mysticism. He is uncompromising in describing the difference between "theology" or "theological faith" (considered as a logical, unitary system, based on professorial manuals along "faith lines"), on one side, and "mystic spirituality" (as an integrating part of religious life), on the other. In order to maintain this categorical, intellectualistic separation, this American dogmatician, guided by studies in Germany, overlooks that common, congruent ground where Christian mystics speak about "theological faith" and Martin Luther speaks about the "mystical" presence, which can be experienced.[346]

The German Walter von Loewenich took a strange, intermediate position. In three editions of his book on Luther's theology of the cross, he determined that mysticism had no part in Luther's thinking. Later, unrevised fourth and fifth editions were published with an author's addendum in which he, practically speaking, sweeps away all that he had previously said! He seems to say, the mystics were right all along. His lack of consistency is certainly glaring.[347]

Conclusions

Protestant orthodoxy's rationalism was mainly a pre-scientific rationalism whose theological concepts prevented both scholars and preachers from including in their thinking non-rational forms of spiritual experience which mystical theology registered. Inasmuch as mysticism seemed to ascribe importance to feeling, Protestant theologians, unconsciously or consciously, hardly noted Luther's mystical utterances. Or they interpreted them as internal, psychological emblems without theological relevance for a more enlightened age. *Unio mystica* was transformed into an idea within the framework of a catechetical order of salvation.

Many Protestant theological structures have had as architects persons whose academic spheres have been permeated by historical criticism and naturalistic empiricism. In other words, the critical evaluation of events in their historical contexts and practical, palpable experience were regarded as the only "reliable" source of knowledge. In Newton's wake, verification codes came from mechanistic science and from philosophical thought according to the model of Descartes: *Cogito, ergo sum* (I think, therefore I am).

Although just as dependent on rational concepts and just as suspicious of feeling in contexts of faith as Lutheran or Calvinist orthodoxy, modern rationalistic theologies were much more apologetically oriented than that of orthodoxy toward a skeptical modern world. It was precisely the skeptical world around them that led rationalistically inclined theologians to dismiss the relevance of Luther's testimony about spiritual kinship with mystics. Liberal theologies correspond to that description, whereas neo-orthodoxy's motif—the exclusively intellectualistic "holding-this-true" proposition—stemmed, not so much from apologetic considerations, but rather from an endeavor to again place Christ at the center. According to confessional Lutherans, Christ had been banished from the core of theology precisely by the liberals. Conservative traditionalists (orthodox) thought that mystical theology concerned itself too much with man's potentialities, too much with subjective moods, and too little with elucidating the articles of faith. In that camp "the mystical Luther" was, and is, an impossible idea.

Yet, both of these groups of past and contemporary Protestant theology place "theological faith," in one camp, and "mystical-anthropological theology," inclusive of "real change," in the other. One does not always detect that orthodox and liberal Protestant thinkers actually proceed from the same starting-point, from the same generalizations, and the same views concerning the nature of knowledge. The idea-bound, the attributes of logical reason, command the scene both in orthodoxy and liberalism. Luther's mystical theology of experience is discounted in both neo-orthodox and historical-critical frame-works.

In both cases one can speak of a confessional ideology filtered through liberalism or text-criticism. The definite categorization of "evangelical theology" and "mystical theology" is thus shared by two groups that, in other respects, are not particularly close allies.

The picture of Martin Luther emerging from the special angle of his relationship to mysticism assumes varying shapes:

1. Luther is depicted by some in the liberal camp as a robust and common-sensical man of a wholly non-mystical bent. The codes of the empirical historian are applied to Luther's thought. Those codes reject mystical "lore" as having any part in the Christian faith.

2. According to other thinkers, it is the conscience that stands in the center of Luther's theology. For them justification by faith became a new, exciting concept, a cognitive key, with the aid of which one cannot, or ought not, open the door to mysticism—to spiritual experience. According to this school of thought, Luther fulfills these criteria.

3. A third group puts the emphasis on Luther as a recoverer of the gospel that sanctifies our material existence. The historical-critical school plays a decisive role here. Writings along this line are primarily interested in the practical-ethical aspects, with the result that Luther's words about mystical "formation" into Christ-likeness have been forgotten.

4. We have noted the assertion from liberal-historical-critical quarters that Luther's main concern as a Christian coincided with the results of critical scholarship. Liberated from supernatural adornments, the Christian faith becomes what it ought to become, namely, a process of inner realization, seen mainly as an intellectual reflection and development. This process was described as the truly Christian element in faith, and Luther is described as modernity's pioneer for the historical-critical view of the Christian faith.

5. We have further noted that, for some systematicians, theological knowledge is given such preferential treatment that trust or *fiducia,* on the subjective plane, is hardly reckoned with in theological calculus. The "holding-this-to-be-true" affirmation of God's "for you" in Christ annuls belief that even natural life offers knowledge about God. Within this framework for theological discourse, the evangelical becomes the antipode to the Catholic, the life of faith contrary to the mystical, and Luther's down-to-earth personality as a counterweight to passion-mysticism.

6. In one area on the historical-critical front, one seeks to systematize Luther's Reformation theology through analyzing it as a "lin-

guistic" or "language" event. Luther's "thought mutations" may be best observed by applying antithetical word-pairs as, for instance, letter and spirit, law and gospel. Luther's religious experience is described as an intellectual-analytical undertaking rather than an inner drama with psychological meaning. Luther's theology about the cross of Christ is described as "theological" in contradistinction to "psychological." Luther, according to this view, does not count with "real change" within man. In addition, in this Luther-interpretation, the Reformer's mystical language is regarded to be only superficially mystical. As a matter of fact, according to this school of thought, Luther's theological language deepens the confessional chasm between evangelical faith and Catholic faith. The latter includes mysticism.

7. The divergence between Luther's thought and mysticism is further emphasized in still another version of systematic theology that deals with the Reformation. With emphasis on Luther's learning and gift for scholarly clarity, it finds in Luther's literary legacy the proposition that, when it comes to salvation, the human being should be looked at as non-substantial, that is say, there is nothing about the human which is related to God, in such a way that it would be able cooperate in salvation. Mysticism is described, on the other hand, as a spiritual movement, which claims to have substantial kinship with God and presupposes a certain cooperation with God as part of salvation. Luther is here called "modern;" the mystic way is called "medieval." According to this theology Luther is a prototype for the "new man;" mysticism provides a pattern for the "old man."

The fundamental train of thought in these samples of theological reflection around the subject Luther and mysticism is intellectualism or rationalism, as it was formed by the so-called "exact" sciences during the nineteenth century. In my comments about Ebeling's view of Luther as analyst—which aimed at "thinking God and the world into unity"—I suggested that Luther's spiritual affinity with some mystics would remain an enigma as long as the *ratio* of naturalistic reflections must guide theological research. *Nota bene*, this is a matter of reason dominated by knowledge and/or experience gained only through the five senses.

Under those circumstances, scant room is accorded in the thought structures to experiences of spiritual presence in prayer and mediation and feelings of sacred trust inspired by the Holy Spirit. It is simply true that theology operates with the unspoken aim of dismissing any suggestion of supersensible manifestations in faith. As was evident from examples under the rubric "Mysticism under rationalistic premises: the power of preconception," one reaches out in attempts to arrange the documentation so that it seems to corroborate both dogmatic delimitation and conviction with regard to the theory of cognition.

In the following chapters an attempt will be made to show that Martin Luther's theology, if it is robbed of its mystical element, runs the risk of losing Martin Luther himself. In that process the discussion will be continued concerning the intellectualistic constructions with regard to Luther's theological intentions.

CHAPTER NINE

IF ONE COUNTS WITH THE SPIRIT: THE PNEUMATIC SCHOOL

The second is a spiritual sight, which only Christians have and which takes place by means of faith in the heart. . . . For I do not recognize a Christian by his external appearance . . . but by the fact that he is baptized and has God's Word. . . . I do not see this inscribed on . . . his forehead, . . . I see it with the spiritual vision of the heart.

Martin Luther, *W* 45; 490-491 (1537); *LW* 24; 33-34

The "Tabernacle" is the church or the body of Christ, that is, the church in a mystical sense.

Martin Luther, *W* 3; 150, 15-17 (1513-1516)
(Author's translation)

The problem: intellectualistic abstraction

We have seen how preconceived opinions or premises about the nature of knowledge almost completely overshadow the experiential dimension in Luther's view of the gospel. This is true of both confessional-orthodox and liberal-critical theology. *Erfahrung* is Luther's word for an immediate God relationship mediated by Jesus Christ. The consequences of the obliteration of this reality give us a picture of Luther and a kind of Lutheran theologizing lacking in power.

First, we only have to consider developments immediately after Luther's death. Then, in many dogmatically engaged circles, there was a return to Scholastic-rationalistic orthodoxy in which the external Word became the focal point among Lutherans, instead of the ecclesiastical tradition as among Catholics. This was the line of Lutheran orthodoxy.

Secondly, theology borrowed its apologetic frame of reference from the Newtonian science of modern times. That which was explainable and scientifically verifiable, according to the codes of "exact" science, also became theology's methodological norm. Luther was brought before the tribunal of modernity's sober causality thinking and, like biblical events and personages, was either found wanting or profoundly modern. ("Post-modern" scientific thinking about apparent a-causality has hardly made an impression on prevailing theologies). The mystical life in God was deemed unessential to modern man. We find here a large group of thinkers which, broadly speaking, one could call the critical-liberal tradition.

Thirdly, we encounter on the scale of theological opinion the view that evangelical-Lutheran faith in each important context stands in diametrical opposition to its Roman Catholic counterpart. As a consequence, Luther's spiritual affinity with some mystics and his conviction that Christian life is partly an immediate experience of life in God meets with scant or no attention. Orthodox as well critical-liberal interpretations of Luther's world of thought have fallen victim to this consistently perpetrated polarity thinking.

The German church historian Ernst Benz has the following to say about the influence of intellectualistic abstraction on the theological enterprise:

> Since the confessional struggles of the 16th century [intellectualistic] theology has accumulated a monopolistic position of power behind which all other expressions of the Christian faith have regressed and languished—the religious experience in mind and heart, religious poetry, meditation, the *charismata*, which extend into the irrational, into the prerational, into the transrational and which played a decisive role in the early church.
>
> Let us not forget that one of the spiritual gifts that Jesus gave his disciples when he sent them into the world as missionaries ... was this: "Behold I have given you authority to tread upon serpents and scorpions, and over all the power of the enemy; and nothing shall hurt you" (Luke 10:19). ... How often has not theology become a sort of abstract mathematics: numbers and mathematical symbols were transformed into dogmatic codes and symbols. On the one hand, this enabled shrewd brains to create all manner of interesting intellectual

combinations. On the other hand, this satisfied only as far as insight and appreciation for such intellectual games extended.

Benz then compares this activity with the vision of the Unreachable, the totally Different, the immediate experience of the beyond, of a world that "no eyes have seen," but about which the prophet and the seer can witness.[348]

Rudolf Otto, previously mentioned, is highly respected by many, but routinely disparaged in the rationalistic school because he has written extensively on mysticism and the mystical. He suggested a special designation for the outlook of those who, in one way or another, receive spiritual gifts by grace and hide their experiences in their heart. Professor Otto called it "the religious conception of the world." Against this religious conception stood, he thought, "the naturalistic, 'mechanical' interpretation of life." It may be a source of wonderment that especially theology should have difficulty incorporating "the religious view" with its way of looking at things. But it happens to be a fact, Otto maintained. In theological discourses it often happens that naturalistic frameworks and religious attitudes prove to be incompatible. The religious grasp of the world, Otto surmised, never grows immediately out of the natural perception of things. Nor, he suggested, could the religious view of the world ever be exhaustively explained by natural perception. That means, in other words, that the religious view of the world will not need to pronounce opinions as to the nature of the world and the meaning of existence. It is enough, Otto declared, if it sheds light over our existence and grants purpose and meaning to personal being.

Otto thought that it is sufficient if in **this** regard reality conforms to religious illumination by corroborating it. Reality does so in signs and in moments pregnant with meaning. The religious view of the world can consequently serve as a defense, an apologetic, for a non-naturalistic grasp on life. But it is an apologetics well aware of its limits. It should be added, however, that theological defense or theological explication must fetch its inspiration in a personal will to believe or a personal will to faith and joy, inherent in faith. Many enigmas will remain enigmas for those who are living in and by religious experience. Religious experience, Otto stressed, is less concerned with explanations than with decision and choice.

Regarding life in God, which should always influence theological thinking, Rudolf Otto also stated that genuine faith does not flee from pain and insoluble enigmas. When faith has struggled, even to a degree, with these questions, it has always been touched by them. But the religious outlook on life does not seek to solve the problems through explanations and analyses about the reason for them. Otto cited Luther: faith involves defying appearances. This means, according to Otto, that the religious conception of the world can never be congruent with a scientific or a general view of things. At times, it seems that the religious or sacred life might flounder when life's apparent contradictions press upon it. But, frequently and paradoxically, faith finds strength. In situations where faith has died under the weight of contradictions and appearances, the person whose faith seems to die might assert that faith—as an attitude of awe and reverence before God—was possible in earlier naive periods, but vanishes when one has gained greater insight into life. This, said Otto, is foolish talk. If faith dies because "science" says so and so, it dies from a childhood disease.

I associate myself with Rudolf Otto when he states that reflection about faith from natural presuppositions and reflection on faith from charismatic or religious experience do not necessarily have to conflict with one another, but often do. The aspects become absolute. Religion becomes irrational and natural reflection becomes rationalistic.

For the subject under review in this book it is important to note that, under the influence of naturalism, "the spiritual sciences," including theology and the epistemology associated with it, in large part have become patterned on natural science. The result is that spiritual inspiration and the movements of man's conscious life tend to be described as having equal value in theological deliberation.[349]

However, that which springs from inspiration and that which is guided by logical reason are two parts of one theological whole. If the conceptual-logical takes the upper hand in scholarship, the visionary who is a scholar becomes a scholar without vision. Martin Luther was a scholar and a visionary. Much depends on where the accent falls. On the following pages two examples are given of intellectualistic abstraction and the outcome of it, on the one hand, and the experience of divine presence, the power of the numinous to spellbind, and the perception of the reality of the supernatural, on the other.

Logic and numen

Numinous is a word that has already been used several times in this account. It derives from numen which means "an indwelling, guiding force or spirit," "divine power." A numinous experience is the experience of supernatural presence, both fear-filled and blessed. Mystical experience is numinous. The main stream of Protestant theology generally regards Martin Luther's theology as wholly alienated from mysticism. It is usually assumed that mysticism is incompatible with Luther's world of thought and that, in any case, it does not qualify for honorable mention in comments about this world.

Pneumatic theology assumes that the Spirit, pneuma, makes itself felt in the soul. Logical dogmatic theology has difficulties with integrating the Spirit as part of the system and has therefore often been reduced to historicism or logical positivism. In order to more closely study the pneumatic attitude I have selected two theologians who have both devoted a great deal of time to Luther's *The Bondage of the Will.*

The one is a contemporary, Harry McSorley, an American Roman Catholic theologian. The other is the German history of religion scholar, Professor Rudolph Otto, to whom several references have been made and whose classic work, *The Idea of the Holy*, has already been cited.

As an illustration of the tension between *ratio* and numen, between logical predictability and the acceptance of the mystery of God's nature and his intervention in our world, I will draw attention to the question of predestination, in other words, to what extent is our life predetermined and predestined in God's counsels. Logically it becomes absurd to think that everything occurs of necessity. How, under these circumstances, do we account for the role of the will in our association with the divine?

When Luther speaks about "predestination," does he think exclusively of a kind of fated *ananke*, a mechanical necessity, *que sera sera*? Some of his critics have gotten that impression regarding his views on the will and felt disturbed on behalf of theological logic. Harry McSorley belongs to this group.

Or, does Luther describe (that which all profound religious experience affirms), in the context of predestination, a mystical experience which does not in any way seek to be or want to be a logical explanation of how omnipotence is built into love and to the fact that some people experience a liberating grace and others do not? Some would want to answer 'yes' to this question. When we encounter God in our life, it is not only that we know that we are unmasked and are always seen, but that we also experience God's pursuit of us as preordained in detail. This does not correspond to logic. It is rather a question of recognizing the limitations of our explanations and of "knowing" in the depths of our hearts. Rudolf Otto is our spokesman for this point of view on the mystery of the numinous.

According to McSorley, Luther underwent a dogmatic development from *liberum arbitrium*, the will is free, to *servum arbitrium*, the view that the will is not free.[350] Between 1510 and 1524, when he had finished his book on the enslaved will, Luther had reached the conclusion that the will was in the talons of necessity, McSorley opined. Yes, Luther even embraced the "necessitarian concept" of man's will, a purely deterministic view of life, including that salvation is given to some and denied to others. In that case, from the viewpoint of historical theology, Luther would have moved from nominalism, which taught that the will is free, to Augustinianism that spoke more about the unfree will. McSorley quoted Luther from *The Bondage of the Will*: "Free will is knocked flat and utterly shattered." He thought that Luther, with an utterance like this, had removed himself from "the entire Catholic dogmatic tradition" which reckons that man, as a natural being, always possesses free will.[351]

In this way Luther seems to make no distinction between a necessitarian view of God's omnipotence, which borders on determinism, and a "biblical" posture, according to which God's grace precedes all. McSorley finds this lack of clarity with Luther "unfortunate."

Two methodological points should be mentioned in connection with McSorley's Luther study. First, he limited his examination to "only one dogmatic point," namely, the question of the will. Secondly, he discounted "the 'existential' aspects" and the role that mysticism played in Luther's life.

The first point raises a counter question. On the subject of "bound or free" will, McSorley accuses Luther of "speculative theological reasoning." Is not McSorley himself, through his one-eyed description, guilty of "speculation?" If you isolate the documentation for the statements on the will, you lose the viewpoint of the experience that lay behind the entire Reformation reasoning about the will, namely, the experience of the dreadful and the joyful encounter with God, who makes righteous that which is unrighteous. It is therefore hardly possible, as McSorley hopes, to register "not only . . . what Luther said but also . . . what he meant," if one limits the examination to words on the will. Furthermore, these words were taken from a small number of Luther's writings (the first lectures on the Psalms, Luther's notes in the margins of Gabriel Biel's *Collectorium*, and, as mentioned, the treatise on *The Bondage of the Will*).

In addition, the understanding of Luther cannot be furthered if one assumes, as McSorley does, that Luther's development toward becoming the Reformer consisted in moving from one doctrine to another, as though the Reformation would have been mainly a series of ideas, where one idea is expected to supplant another idea. The Catholic McSorley shared the confusion over Luther's "lack of clarity" concerning the difference between "theological determinism" and "the biblical" apprehension of the will with Protestant authors who have sought to make Luther more acceptable, in spite of his lack of theoretical, conception-bound clarity in this regard.[352]

A key to Luther's unconcerned indifference with regard to intellectual clarity in the case of the will lies hidden in McSorley's somewhat astonishing utterance: "Luther, very uncharacteristically, makes no effort to give biblical support for this [the necessitarian] argument." Here there is a hint of the implicit conviction that each religious contradiction can be accommodated through additional intellectual effort and more biblical citations. Luther is considered to have slipped up for once on a dogmatic question. There is also the implied suggestion that "biblical" support is equivalent to the number of Bible references that can be produced. Perhaps, on the contrary, Luther felt that he had, in the biblical message, proof for both his theological determinism and for his view of the will as powerless without grace.

Point number two is built into point one. You can, namely, assert that, if the mystical experience is neglected in the study of Luther's life and thought, the seeker or the scholar inexorably will be disappointed over Luther's lack of "clarity" and his "poor terminology." This is ultimately what makes McSorley utter the following distressed judgment: "Luther's doctrine of [man's] responsibility leads him to an anti-rational concept of faith."

But, perhaps, this is exactly the point. To meet God is to know increasingly that he knows and plans everything (even though he, in the most intricate manner, has to make use of our circuitous ways so that he can guide us to the goal that he has set for us). Even if it is irrational, to encounter God is also to know that he needs the human will's assent and the will's gradual accord with his.

When McSorley expressed the opinion that "Luther's rejection of the traditional argument for the freedom of the will" is "questionable," he spoke on behalf of something which most nearly can be likened to a logical equation.

Luther, on the other hand, mediated a message from within the mystical *gemitus-raptus* experience. That experience says simply and straightforwardly that the Pelagians—those who were of the opinion that the free will was capable of achieving righteousness—did not know what they were talking about. In his attempt to rescue "Luther's **intention**" from his "misleading **terminology**" (emphasis added), McSorley declared that Luther actually did not question the fact of the free will with natural man. On the contrary, Luther wanted rather to improve the will's ability to contribute to salvation. This would thus be Luther's basic intention, not a doctrine of predestination. According to Catholic teaching, it is not heresy to state that prior to grace the free will can do nothing but sin, avers McSorley. After all, "it is a thesis of Augustine, the 'doctor of grace,' a thesis which has been accepted by the official teaching of the Roman Catholic Church."[353]

In response it could be argued that this attempt to bring Luther in harmony with the Scholastic tradition, in all likelihood, does not further the cause of ecumenical understanding. There are deep ecumenical affinities between Luther and the Roman Catholic Church, which he cherished for a long time but then chose to fight. The absence of the necessitarian element in relation to the will in much prior Catholic thought, and in subsequent Protestant thinking, tends to remove the mystical experience from the Christian dogma. It was precisely that experience which made Luther's unreasonableness on the necessity-issue "understandable." In one of his dinner table conversations, Luther referred to the difference between Erasmus and himself (which was the impetus for Luther's heated entry into the debate) as experiencing God's Now or not experiencing God. McSorley called statements about experiences of the numinous, about the inner certainty of Christ's mystical presence, "anti-rational" and "exaggerations." But they are components of the spirituality that was at the core of the Reformation, a spirituality that in many ways was akin to the mystical.[354]

In his renowned investigation of the nature of the Holy (English version: *The Idea of the Holy*), Rudolf Otto comments on *The Bondage of the Will.* In that interpretation one finds a dimension that is lacking in McSorley. Like McSorley, Otto noted that Martin Luther regarded his treatise on the enslaved will as belonging to the nucleus of his gospel interpretation. But Otto presented Luther's predestination theory as the meeting place between the rational and the mystical, the numinous (a word that Otto launched into the theological world), whereas McSorley, in a more contemporary work (*Luther: Right or Wrong?*) treated predestination according to Scholastic tradition.

In Otto's portrait of Luther, predestination, "necessitarianism," became an analogy for the evangelical view of man's relation to God. Otto held that, for Luther, a contrast prevailed between *mirae speculationes*—the awe-filled reaction to the unspeakable in God —and the *facies Dei revelata*—God's revealed face, i.e., between God's majesty and his grace.[355]

Luther said that his teaching about the will, as it approaches God, was not only a subject for discussion among philosophically interested, but was grounded in religious experience. In fact, Luther described the awe-inspiring, non-rational character of God and the lovely, human, gracious side of God as a force to be experienced, felt, as a mystical movement of mind and heart.

With a bit of personal biography, Otto commented on this duality: "I grew to understand the numinous and its difference from the rational in Luther's De Servo Arbitrio (*The Bondage of the Will)* long before I identified it in the *qadosh* (the holy, the all-holy) of the Old Testament." The "unapproachable which becomes approachable"—this cannot be grasped by the intellect alone, but by "inwardness." Heartfeltness and spiritual engagement should be added. This inwardness, this interior event, "finds only very dubious expression in the subsequent one-sided doctrine of the schools, where the mystical character of 'wrath'—which is of the essence of 'holiness' infused with that of 'goodness'—is referred simply to the righteousness of God, and taken thus as righteous anger or indignation."[356]

Rational terms must be resorted to, Otto continued, when God's judgment and wrath are to be expressed. But if "we are to recapture the real Luther in these expressions, we must hear sounding in them the profoundly non-rational strain of 'religious awe'." In *The Bondage of the Will*, the mystical presence, the aspect of God's *tremendum*—that which causes one to tremble—as well as that of "fascination" ring through Luther's words. Can the rational attributes of faithfulness and love and their corresponding elements, faith and trust be apprehended in the mind of the worshipper? Is "fascination" missing altogether?

> No, beyond all question it is not. . . . [T]he element of fascination is in Luther wholly interwoven with these rational elements and comes to utterance with them and in them. This can be felt forcibly in the boisterous, almost Dionysiac, blissfulness of his experience of God.

Here we have "the mystical tone of Luther's actual creed."[357]

McSorley represents, despite his Roman Catholic background, a general trend in Protestant theology, namely, the assumption that faith is a doctrine that can be rather exhaustively expressed in rational concepts. Consequently, Luther's spiritual kinship with mystics was not noticed in McSorley's version of Luther. This fact now becomes more understandable. McSorley's logic does not allow any space for nonrational knowledge about the will.

As far as McSorley was concerned, it is "unfortunate" that Luther denies a "free will" to man—not because man is a sinner, but because man is a created being. This means, according to McSorley's way of looking at things, that, if a theological idea breaks with the logic of the order of salvation, then the rational should take precedence over the non-rational.[358]

Otto had the deeper grasp. He wrote that in Luther's religion faith "plays the same essential part, *mutatis mutandis*, as 'knowledge' and 'love' for the earlier mystics: it is the unique power of the soul, the *adhaesio* Dei, which *unites* man with God: and 'unity' is the very signature of the mystical." Faith, argues Otto, is the ground of the soul about which mystics speak. It is also "an independent faculty of knowledge, a mystical *a priori* element in the spirit of man." Otto contended that

> there are definite features in "faith," as the term is used by Luther, which justify us in classing it with the mystical ways of response to which it is in apparent contrast, and clearly distinguish it from the *fides* taught by the Lutheran school with its determinate, well-ordered, unmystical temper.[359]

In faith thus understood, "determinism" takes on another tone than it has within the range of "reasonableness." McSorley is representative of those who attempt to find adequate formulations for predestination. However, in the case of Luther's necessitarian predestination, he found no logical-apologetic way out of the dilemma and rejected, therefore, Luther's words about predestination in *The Bondage of the Will* as "misleading terminology."

On the other hand, Otto pointed out that the necessitarian view of determinism is an analogy of predestination, not a formulation of theological logic. In contrast to McSorley, Otto found an "inner logic" for a necessitarian view of determinism in Luther's thought. He understood Luther's thoughts on necessitarianism in that which happens, as an expression for the numinous feeling of being completely in God's hands. There is within the personal numinous experience an "inner logic," which says: God knows everything beforehand, sees everything, yet he is grace and love. That does not add up logically. That the will is shackled, and yet free, is not logical, does not make sense. One cannot describe Luther's passionate pronouncements in the essay against Erasmus, concerning the determinalistically bound will, as an isolated lapse of an otherwise trustworthy theological acumen. We stand here, instead, before an expectant and apprehensive mystical experience that demands to be clothed in words. The logical conception-bound and the numinous complement each other. They are not congruent. The question of God's omnipotence is not a problem that can be solved. It is mystery that should be worshipped.

In his book, *Luther on Predestination*, Fredrik Brosché suggested that there is reason for the proposition that Luther's experience of God's participation in and the necessity of contemporary events formed his "concept of God's omnipotence." His faith was grounded in the Bible as God's word, which reveals a pattern of God's omnipotence, love and providence. Brosché pointed out that

> He [Luther] seeks to emphasize that reason and the flesh are automatically impelled to sinful impatience and grumbling, and that it is good "practice" for faith to trust that the Almighty God has love as motive even when through agents He sends us that which at first glance appears to be evil.
>
> It is hardly surprising that also in the form of a sermon Luther suggests a way to peace and quiet, consisting of radical acceptance that all things come to pass in accord with the perfect will of God. When the believer is confident that nothing happens by chance, he can abide in the divine will and partake in the total peace. (*W* 10.I.1.315,18ff., 1522)

At the end of his book Brosché hones the argument, I would say justifiably so, with these words.

> The homogeneous notion of God implies, finally, that the Luther interpretation can rightly set Christology, or justification, as a unifying centre of Luther's theology. . . . [However, this center is not] a theoretical doctrine, from which all the other loci could be grouped in a logically coherent system. . . . But *it is deep existential conviction from which, on the basis of the Word concerning justification by faith alone for Christ's sake, the Christian regards God as total love, even in the eternal damnation of predetermination.* (Italics in original).

In this context and independently of each other, Brosché and I have both come to think of Pascal's remark, already cited, about the heart that has its "reasons" of which "common sense" knows nothing.[360]

But if the mystical presence influenced Luther's thought so that the logical and the numinous became interwoven, one must ask oneself the question how Luther distinguished between biblically-oriented mysticism and mysticism that is further from the heart of the gospel.

Mysticism differentiated

Most of the theological opinions of mysticism's role in Luther's thought that have been surveyed reflect either a total disregard or a sweeping generalization of the subject. In some contexts we have had occasion to suggest that a differentiation between varieties of mystical reflection might possibly—all else being equal—lead both the school of total disregard and the school of generalization to a reappraisal of the significance of Luther's mystical terminology.

Martin Luther himself made his relationship to mysticism clear through specific approval or specific disapproval. For, as noted earlier in the analysis of Protestant thought on the matter, there is no mysticism in general. In 1515-1516, in the course of his lectures on Romans, Luther pointed out that "Roman mysticism" devoted too little attention to the incarnated Word. Purity of heart comes only through the incarnated Word, he wrote. Only after the encounter with the incarnated Word, does there dawn the reality of the uncreated Word.[361] In 1519, Luther warned against another kind of mysticism, the one of Dionysius the Areopagite. Dionysius was not, Luther said, "a right mystic" for he spoke of "understanding" as a primary requirement. True theology must, however, go through "death and judgment."

It is clear that Luther felt little kinship for mysticism that dealt in speculation, in visions for their own sake and the use of method to find God. On the other hand, as Vogelsang pointed out, all his life Martin Luther was grateful to Bernard [of Clairvaux] for his references to the Crucified Christ, to the gravity of judgment, and to the awareness of God's presence.[362]

What made Luther repudiate one form of mysticism and give assent to another? The benchmark for Luther in assessing mysticism was the personal experience of justification by faith. The differentiation of types of mysticism, especially Christian mysticism, is a process that Luther himself initiated, and it grew out of his deepest religious experience. However, before looking a little more closely at the distinction that Luther made after his study of various mystics, there is reason to take up two subjects closely connected to mystical typology. They are, first, the question of the personal-individual and the impersonal-infinity in the mystical attitude, and, secondly, the query about the "young Luther" and the "mature Luther" with respect to mysticism.

Mysticism of infinity and mysticism of personality

In his book, *Uppenbarelsereligion* (ET: *The Nature of Revelation*), **Archbishop Nathan Söderblom** uses two terms to define mysticism: "mysticism of infinity" and "mysticism of personality." He explains:

> The mysticism of infinity in its pure form, seeks its way out to the point of union with the divine by leaving, by degrees, the creaturely, divesting itself of all qualities, pushing slowly out beyond the sole distinction of existence and non-existence, being and non-being. . . . How different is the world of personal mysticism! Jeremiah, St. Paul, Augustine, Luther, Pascal, Kierkegaard, cry out: "Lord, spare me! Depart from me! My guilt!" (O, culpa mea!) The miserable human creature quakes and shivers, bleeds and moans . . . [has] liberty in the mighty hand of God . . . a meeting in quiet places perhaps, but also in the desert, in labour, with an attacking living, active Will; with an overflowing, empowering fulness of personal life of holiness and love, . . . a living God unutterably active, who crushes us, but also saves us.[363]

Söderblom pointed out that his distinctions "must not be pressed too far." But the fact is that a good deal of mysticism is classified under the rubric "mysticism of infinity" and much Christian mysticism is imprinted by personal encounters. In the former the ego is lost in the "sea of infinity." In the latter one loses "the limited, selfish ego, but not by extinction, submergence in the sea of infinity, but through realizing its true nature in God."

Söderblom wrote that "Luther has with incomparable richness and clarity described 'the communion of the Christian with God.'" This, he asserted is in contrast "with the sublime mysticism of infinity," not least because the experience of God in "mysticism of personality" contains "a psychological mark of identification, namely, the terror of conscience," as Luther pointed out against the "enthusiasts," the *Schwärmer*. As we have seen in prior pages, many Protestant interpreters of the gospel and of Luther reject the thought that the movements of the "psyche" belong to the area of theological research. Söderblom did not agree with them. In revelation as a personal experience, as a link between an "I" and a "you", "we have here to do with a psychological fact, verified also outside the area of religion, within that of creative art. Insight comes instantaneously. Certainty spreads through the mind like a light from heaven."[364]

A work published in 1919, *Humor och melankoli och andra Luther studier [Humor and Melancholy and Other Luther Studies]*, gave Söderblom occasion to accord mysticism an even more conspicuous place in Luther's life and faith than the strong influence which Ritschl had allowed earlier. Luther's 1518 investigation of indulgences contains an autobiographical sketch about how it feels, especially for a melancholic, to encounter the "wrath of God." The depiction reveals

> familiarity with mysticism's experiences and modes of expression. . . . We shall . . . see, what significance mysticism's cross-theology . . . had for Luther's assessment of his inner abandonment and anguish. . . . Luther has . . . elevated the expressions of mysticism's pain, rather than needing to use imagination and exercises as aids. . . . Luther is the genuine perfecter of the church's tradition of mystical piety in its deepest channel. [365]

In a later book, *Tre livsformer [Three Patterns of Life]*, apparently influenced by contact with the Indian Christian mystic, Sadhu Sundar Singh, and the French Catholic, Imbart de la Tour, Söderblom noted Luther's "inner affinity with medieval piety's golden stream in mysticism." This was not about a mystical stream or movement in which one strives toward "the Neoplatonic immersion into the All-One," but about "influence from the prophets' and the gospel's ethical pathos and Holy God of revelation."

For Luther, faith was not in the first place an "assent to the truth of church doctrine, but it is Christ's own mystical presence with us that effectuates repentance, intention, and deed." Sin, justification and faith—with these three words "Luther has delineated his radical, mystical teaching of salvation." This Söderblom termed "faith mysticism." It was, he thought, precisely "mysticism's inwardness," in which man knows that he cannot do anything to achieve blessedness, that made Luther "mysticism's hero" and his religion "the mysticism of comforting trust."[366]

In a work on the subject of Nathan Söderblom's religious development up to 1894, **Hans Åkerberg**, a psychology of religion professor in Sweden, pointed out that "the mysticism which Ritschl describes and that he so forcefully rejects is what Söderblom later characterized with the term 'mysticism of the infinite'." In other words, Söderblom gradually discovered the limitations of Ritschl, whom he had initially greatly admired. These limitations were empiricism and anti-metaphysics. Söderblom's own "conversion-experience" included "individual fellowship with God and personal experience of divine communication through experiences that gave and give the human person a kind of 'certitude'." Åkerberg argued that Söderblom fathomed that the sense of intimate communion with God is "the innermost driving force of many evangelical, 'genuinely pious' people, for example, Luther and [those of] a certain kind of pietism." Luther was "in Söderblom's definition a mystic."[367]

Åkerberg referred to a Söderblom statement about Luther "as a German mystic . . . he had nourished his soul with mysticism, with *Eyn deutsch Theologia*, with Saint Bernard and Tauler." According to Åkerberg, Söderblom, with his reference to Luther "as a perfecter and a pioneer" among "the Germanic mystics," intended primarily, "with the aid of Luther, to emphasize the more unadulterated 'mysticism of personal life' pole in his distinction." Åkerberg also drew attention to my English translation of the Luther-edition of *Eyn deutsch Theologia* (English title: *Theologia Germanica*). My comments, Åkerberg says, "quite properly emphasize that the little medieval book is manifestly within the framework of 'mysticism of personal life,' besides being rather close to the type of piety, with it special characteristics, which bears the stamp of Martin Luther."[368]

Åkerberg rightly emphasized, in a work concerning different ways of interpreting religious phenomena, that many analyses of mysticism "do not take into account facts of a psychological nature." In his recommendation of Söderblom's distinction, Åkerberg suggested "a model for a solution" which could be of help with the tension between the phenomenological and the psychological way of looking at religion and mysticism. An initial step would be to more sharply distinguish what one means with "experience," "ego," "consciousness," "person," and "religious internalization." In this context "the polarity system" is useful, the two poles being "mysticism of the infinite" and "the mysticism of personal life."[369]

What is presented here, from the viewpoint of the history of religion, is no doubt correct from a religious psychological angle. Too long and too often theology has spoken of religion as exclusively intellectual, ostensibly having nothing to do with the psyche or the soul.

In an insightful essay of 1983 about Luther and mysticism, Åkerberg called attention to my earlier work, *Luther and the Mystics* (1976). He noted that the book raised the "essential problem of Luther's personal relationship to mysticism." Åkerberg also asserted that in much theology "references to [mystical] experience largely fall outside the field of research" with the result that mysticism is not discussed. The same could be said of Luther's "world of religious experience." With Luther, "mysticism of personal life" is illustrated especially by the Reformer's "tower experience," an event similar to Paul's encounter with the Risen Lord on the road to Damascus. It concerned

> "the gate of paradise"—to use Luther's own words—in the **midst** of this life's suffering and cross . . .The majority of the old terms and expressions remain, but the power of their meaning is different. All is colored by the overwhelming experience, and the certainty of living in an immediate, dual relation to God as a living *and gracious* Partner ([Professor Hjalmar] Sundén's terminology) gives to all his future production a key signature that unconditionally must be heeded, if one is not going to fall short of or fail Martin Luther himself. [370]

Åkerberg returned to that particular motif in his study about personal life and mysticism: the "primary variables" on the theme of the infinite and personal life are "God's image" and "relationship to God." "The line of demarcation appears, as Söderblom expresses it, 'in the role of the personality'." In a discussion on the respective roles of structured "exercises" and of "spontaneity," Åkerberg asserted, again with reference to Söderblom,

> the less [spiritual] "exercises" are emphasized, the further one comes from the pure "mysticism of the infinite." If one considers the calibration instrument "spontaneity," the reception of union with the suprahuman through "divine grace" after "self-divestiture" (Söderblom's expression) of all trust in and reliance on one's own indwelling god-oriented power-resources, one has an instrument whose primary sphere of application is definitely within "mysticism of personal life." [371]

Even the mysticism that, in many assessments, has been termed "mysticism of infinity," namely, Meister Eckhart's thoughts about life in God, is a personal address, according to Hans Hof. When Eckhart said that God loves the soul with such intensity that if anyone should take from God this divine love for the soul, that person would kill God, the statement must be seen against the background of the fact that

Eckhart makes a distinction between our existence as the human race and our existence as individuals. The nature of our existence is non-essence, which cannot be identified with that higher world which Eckhart called "God," "righteousness," "the essence of things in their divine motivations (*rationes*)." Hof thinks that Eckhart "made a radical division between a thing in the world of sense-impressions and its idea, its real essence, its being in God or in Logos." As far as is known, Luther did not have direct contact with the writings of Meister Eckhart and, perhaps, would have had difficulties with the great Dominican's mystical schema—creation, abnegation, birth of the soul/ego, and new creation in compassion and justice. Yet, Luther heard something of Eckhart's voice with Johann Tauler where, it is true, the path was described differently—more Platonic: purification, enlightenment, and union. And the voice spoke about God's personal intervention.

The ecclesiastical "trial" against Eckhart in Cologne (1327) concerned, not least, Eckhart's "double-speak" about "being" and God: our being is united with the utmost Ground, about which nothing can be said, and our being is united with the Son, about whose mystical Sonship we can speak. Is our being intended to "break through beyond all that possesses a name" (in which case there cannot be unity with the being of the Son) **or** is our being called to "let the Son of God be born within you" (in which case the essence cannot be united with the nameless God beyond God)? In the former case, we are dealing with a total eradication, where the "I" is neither God nor a being, and yet the source of God and beings. In the second case, man becomes endowed with sonship and gives birth to Christ. The solution is presumably to be found in the assumption that our spiritual powers become identical with the Son's being and simultaneously identical with God. But this does not permit us to conclude that "the Son's individual consciousness is the same as the Divinity or that man is the Son or that man is the Divinity." For man's being is, according to Eckhart, "just as separated from Divinity as Divinity is separated from God." Especially in his ethic of compassion, Eckhart appears to be a "personal life" mystic. "The Son's birth in the heart" is a personal event. "My being is eternal, my becoming is temporal," Eckhart said.[372]

The first distinction we thus ought to make inside that complex phenomenon called "mysticism" is the delimitation between mysticism of infinity and mysticism of personality. We then notice that Martin Luther felt at home in the category of experience that is termed mysticism of personality. This means two things. On the one hand, Söderblom was right when he makes the statement that the Reformation took place through Luther's person; it was not only a question about well thought out, objective logic, in the first place. It was also a question of a spiritual change of direction, beginning in a personal "earthquake." And, partly, it was a matter of an encounter with God that yielded pain and anguish, but ended in joy and trust as with the prodigal son and his father.

We now proceed to an attempt at distinction that is often made in order to remove mysticism from Luther's theological world. I am thinking particularly about the debate about the "young Luther" and "mature Luther" vis-à-vis medieval mysticism. The question is whether one can observe any essential difference between the attitude of the young Luther and that of the mature Luther to the mystical life.

The young and the mature Luther

We often meet the argument that Luther's thoughts might have dwelt on mysticism during his younger years, but in his mature years he made a definite distinction between the mystical and the evangelical. The Reformer's youthful, theological inexperience is contrasted with the later years of theological realism. It is all whittled down to a case of chronology. Some examples from a few systematicians and historians will serve as illustrations of what one could call the "before-and-after school" concerning Luther's relationship to mystics.

The German theologian Adolf Harnack maintained that Luther "during the first period" used terms indicating that he had "learned" from Augustine and the medieval mystics. We noted that, according to Harnack, Luther was a student of the old mystics, but "**he** found what **they** sought (emphasis added). Harnack painted mysticism, in general, as a complex of elevated feelings and a desire for psychological self-extinction. If Luther ever gave expression to such inclinations in his theological vocabulary, he liberated himself later on from moods of this kind in favor of a piety of deeds and a steadfast, blissful certitude, Harnack thought. He experienced Luther as a sound and cheerful hero of the faith. It was, after all, around the historical Christ that Luther concentrated his comments on chapter 8 of Romans. In this way, Luther had reached certainty about salvation and, as Harnack put it, "conquered mysticism." One could consequently, according to Adolf Harnack, speak of a fairly opaque Roman Catholic epoch, followed by a clear and bright evangelical era. The latter completely neutralized the former. Luther totally nullified Catholicism as a fundamental spiritual movement. Catholicism was, in Harnack's view of history, synonymous with "mysticism." Hence Luther, out of theological necessity, must have left mysticism behind.[373]

We turn to Karl Holl. He asserted that those mystics who captured Luther's attention led him to the Apostle Paul, and then disappeared from the picture. This must have been the case, since the mystics entertained the wholly false notion that man could bring order in his relationship to God through meritorious deeds. Paul helped to discard this fallacy, and after that, you cannot speak about any mysticism with Luther.[374]

Archbishop Söderblom began very early to discover the kinship between Luther's experience of faith and mystical strains. In the beginning of his authorship—not least under the influence of Ritschl—Söderblom held that the "mature Luther" did not approve of mysticism which demanded a certain technique for attainment of inner knowledge, a generalization of mysticism which was later replaced with the more realistic distinction: "mysticism of infinity" and "mysticism of personality."[375]

Söderblom's compatriot, Gustaf Ljunggren, in his substantial monograph on sin and guilt with Luther, shared the conventional view that the "fully developed Luther" had had to conquer mystical patterns of thought before reaching this kind of maturity.[376]

Heinrich Bornkamm conceded that "in [his] younger years" Luther had walked the way of mysticism. Luther had tried "to climb into the divine Majesty before he had found comfort for his heart in the humble reality of the infant in the manger." Yet, soon enough his "German spirit" and his "manly" inclinations drove him away from "less virile" mysticism.[377]

Gerhard Ebeling did not go quite that far. He argued that a certain continuity can be found between the early Luther and the later mature Reformer in regard to basic evangelical insight. Only with respect to mysticism is there a discontinuity. Ebeling qualified the presence of mystical elements in Luther's theological vocabulary through his use of "still" and "seemingly" to indicate that—although the words were still used—their integrating role belonged to the "young" Luther's thought world, not that of the "mature" Luther. As we noted earlier Ebeling had a tendency to generalize about mysticism, he also used generalizing judgments in his attempts to apply a dialectic pattern to Luther's doctrine of faith. Mysticism cannot be associated with Martin

Luther's *iustificatio* theology, of this Ebeling was convinced. Mysticism in Luther's life was a stage that later became quite unimportant. In the development of the thinking of a young man searching for truth to the theology of a mature person, the mystical interest was wiped away, since it did not fit into the mature Reformer's later theological discoveries, according to Ebeling. In that sense one has the right to call Luther's mysticism a "passing interest," *ein Augenblicksanliegen*. The pietists, he held, clasped young Luther to their breast—the Luther who was less versed in theology. Hence he could, wrongly, declare that the gospel about penance and grace stands in harmony with mystical edification literature. These pietists maintained that the later Luther had hardened and fallen back into Catholicism. Ebeling concluded that the deficiencies in the opinions on Luther were rooted in a certain set of values. Ebeling, for his part, wanted to submit a value-free, unbiased "in-depth examination of the sources." Thanks to such an analysis, Ebeling was able to inform the world that Luther simply lifted out "the antithesis between the old man and the new man." He wrote that mysticism reflected the "old man's" way of being, whereas Luther's mature Reformation teaching gave us the right teaching about the "new man," which is *simul iustus et peccator*, justified and sinner, at the same time.

The reader will remember that we observed how Ebeling displayed a certain aversion to admitting, or inability to recognize, an interweaving (*Verflochenheit*) of the spiritual motifs of medieval mysticism and Reformation theology. As a picture of this hesitation or unwillingness, I took Ebeling's rather lame translation of Luther's description of his "Damascus experience." In the expression *miro certe ardore*, *mirus*, in Ebeling's version, became "unusual" instead of "miraculous, filled with wonder." The miraculous, the supernatural, becomes the "unusual," without supersensible overtones. If my assumption is correct, namely, that Ebeling's scientific and personal equipment did not register numinous feeling and presentiment which cannot be expressed in intellectual formulas, it becomes fully understandable why Ebeling was guided by the conception that thoughts are formulated ideas which successively replace each other as they develop, rather than spiritual forces that are interwoven. As we know by now, this more mechanistic thinking lies behind Ebeling's opinion that one can speak about "temporal stages" in Luther's development to Reformer and that this means farewell to mysticism.[378]

Wilfred Joest will conclude this collection of examples around the subject "young Luther" and "mature Luther" in relation to mysticism.

First, we note that Joest follows the well-beaten path of all those who have taken it as an axiom that only as a relatively immature monk could Luther have been interested in mysticism. Joest took for granted that all mysticism simply means "the immersion of consciousness in the ground of being." He contrasted this "immersion" with Luther's words that the crucified Christ is the unspeakable Word.

When Luther, in his *Operationes in Psalmos* of 1519-1521, concerned himself with some of the terms of mystical experience, it should, according to Joest, be evident that the "Luther of 1519 cannot mean the immersion of consciousness in the ground of being. . . . Already long before this time, the *verbum innominabile* (the unspeakable Word) had a content: the crucified Christ." Here we encounter again the notion that it is possible to delineate the contours of the young Luther, as distinct from those of the mature Luther, by drawing a temporal dividing line. Certainly he "developed" during his battle against Scholasticism and humanism—but this does not mean that the mystical experience can and should be assigned to only one period and erased from the other. Logic can function this way, but not life. Not least because of this, it is a mistake to declare that all mysticism lacks room for the crucified Christ.[379]

There is a way to look at the mysticism story, "young Luther-mature Luther," that would render the distinction less categorical and less intellectualistic. Whereas the theological majority sees the question from within a dogmatic understanding analogous to abstract mathematics, a theology that is receptive to the unfathomable power of the Holy Spirit emphasizes the spiritual kinship between Luther and several mystics.

For want of a better expression, we can call it "pneumatic theology," emanating from the Greek word, *pneuma*, spirit. The feeling and the experience of God's and Christ's immediate presence then becomes the link between Luther and kindred spirits. As suggested, there is no need to speak here about "influence." Kinship is a better word for the affinity in question. If one puts this perspective on the matter, it becomes difficult to draw a chronological line to separate the young Luther from the mature Luther.

Rudolf Otto represented this way of thinking, not without irritated resistance from prevailing rationalistically oriented theologians. Many points of contact link Luther with mysticism, Otto said. Some of these contact points were strong at the outset, only to be dimmed as time went on. Some disappeared entirely. The explanation is that Luther represented the numinous consciousness that grows out of a direct experience in a personal struggle. It was not a consciousness that he had only read about, not a second-hand knowledge. The message of mysticism, the wonder-filled thoughts about God's majesty, finds a resonance in Luther. It is in harmony with his inner knowledge.

Otto ventured the suggestion that non-rational elements in Duns Scotus' emphasis on God's will rather than on God's being were brought to fruition in Luther's theology. This aspect has, more or less, been expunged from later Lutheran thinking as supposedly a counterfeit product of Luther's religion. This element, the unfathomableness of divine will, was often looked upon as an uncongenial residuum of nominalism, the theological movement that laid a good deal of emphasis on the will in the work of salvation, more particularly what man could achieve from inside himself on behalf of his own salvation. However, it seems to be the case that Luther, throughout his life, thought of God as **will**. Faith becomes "experimental" and experience-based only if it has been formed by the numinous experience of God's incomprehensible, will-infused counsel, a counsel that we very well may find to be both incomprehensible and unjust. Numinous consciousness, said Otto, is at the root; rational dogmatizing is a derivative.[380]

As we continue to deal with the problem "the young Luther" versus "the mature Luther," we find that Erich Vogelsang has the following to say: "There is hardly an alleged 'mystical' statement with young Luther which could not be found with the allegedly 'unmystical' later Luther." That judgment was expressed with reference to Luther's comments on the penitential Psalms. Both with the young Luther and the older Luther, Christ is considered to be mystically present, not just a theological verity. Christ is dynamically present in the Word, which was uttered by him and about him, because he lives in the words he spoke. Christ is consequently present in the tribulations of man as well as in his happiness. Vogelsang pointed out—something that already has been stressed in this account—that Luther never rejected mysticism in general for the simple reason that there is no mysticism in general. I say this in contradistinction to much stubbornly held theological "wisdom." Luther took umbrage at Dionysian mysticism, but he accepted the kind of mysticism that agreed with his own salvation experience.

An absolute delimitation between a theologically "young" Luther and a theologically "old" or "mature" Luther, who obliterated everything that the young Luther said, is far from reality, at least as far as mysticism is concerned. Vogelsang reminded the readers about the fact that Luther received his "definition" of mysticism from Bernard of Clairvaux—the content being that mystical theology is experience, not, in the first place, dogma. The young Luther spoke about Bernard, the mystic, as a friend in the spirit, a friend who had experienced the Divine. He knew that "the soul has rest only in Christ's wounds," Luther said about Bernard, his spiritual kin. It was not dogma that made him think that this was the truth, but rather experience in his heart and soul. The mature Luther returned to the same Bernard and the same insight. Bernard and Bonaventura, wrote Luther, lived in the mystical faith; they knew what "Christ's incarnation" meant.[381]

Erwin Iserloh, a German Catholic, discovered in Luther's theology a "continuous mystical approach" that was in harmony with the Reformer's deepest religious experience. This emotionally tinged kinship excluded the time-honored method according to which one establishes dogmatic stages, where all the main points in the doctrine are mutually excluded by corresponding theological assertions of the "enemy" camp. Iserloh was especially struck by the mystical tone in Luther's notes to Psalm 85:8. In his meditations, Luther discerned the limitlessness of the truth that God speaks to us. "Only a quiet, contemplating soul can understand this," Luther wrote. Luther's "actually continuous mystical attitude" invalidated a categorical two-stage solution to the problem of his mysticism, in which **one** thought was eliminated and completely replaced by **another**. Such a premise does not have room for one of two realities that are interwoven in faith: objective justification and subjective love of God, with all that this means for feeling and will.[382]

In a pioneering and penetrating essay on Luther and mysticism, Heiko Oberman argues that Luther's attitude to mysticism did not change when he encountered Tauler's writings and the anonymously written *Theologia Germanica*. Nor did it change fundamentally in the struggle against "*die Schwärmer*," the Enthusiasts. His attitude remained constant, even though external events forced him into his work as a reformer, whether one places the decisive experience in 1514-1515 or in 1518. Luther remained positively inclined toward "the mystical" as the experience aspect of Christianity. Oberman refutes the frequently heard assertion that "the young Luther was a mystic, until he discovered the dangers of mysticism at his confrontation with the left wing of the Reformation."

In 1516 Luther wrote in a marginal note to a Tauler-sermon that he considered *theologia mystica*, when it concerns the spiritual birth from within the uncreated Word, as secondary to, and derived from, *theologia propria*, which is the term for spiritual birth facilitated by the created, incarnated Word. Not that Luther denied the power and validity of "high mysticism," Oberman continued. As we know, Luther pointed out that both Mary and Martha are parts of the whole truth. God in his hiddenness and Christ in his revelation are interlinked. But some people would prefer to be passively immersed in God to being active with Christ.

In 1538 (note the year), Luther pointed out, in a commentary to Genesis 19, that true thinking about God is directed toward God's omnipotence within the order of man, that is, within the incarnated Son, born as a human. A true mystical life was not questioned and was not considered to be an impossibility. One reads exhortations from Luther to study Gerson and other mystics. But he warned in 1538, just as he had in 1516, against the danger of placing spiritual ecstasy ahead of the way to Christ through faith. Here we have both the young Luther and the mature Luther speaking positively **for** genuine mysticism. It is hazardous to seek unity with God outside the Word made flesh. However, mystical theology was part of Luther's image of Christ. Frequently he wrote ***sic*** or ***non***, yes or no, in the margins of mystical writings that he studied. But at least one mystic had his unqualified appreciation: Johann Tauler. Oberman did not share the opinion that Luther's enthusiasm for Tauler was a passing fancy. I remind the reader about Oberman's reference to the not insignificant number of times that the mature Luther approvingly cites Tauler (Chapter 8). Merely this fact disproves the assertion that Luther, during the latter part of his life, put "faith" in opposition to "psychological immediacy" and, theologically speaking, pilloried his "younger" days. However, the Tauler friendship is not the only bridge to the realm of mysticism. Luther certainly disassociated himself from synergistic tendencies in mystical exercises—in other words, the tendency to take credit for the miracle of one's liberation. Nor did he have overly exalted thoughts about the possibility of strolling into the divine path by means of reasonable speculation. But all through his life he experienced and, theologically, reckoned with the *mystical affectus*—the presentiment and the feeling of the presence of Christ.[383]

However you twist and turn the matter, one thing is certain, you cannot deny that Martin Luther, as a younger man, and Martin Luther, as a more "established" leader of a movement, in the depth thought the same about mysticism's innermost concern, the certainty of both feeling and will about God's presence and about the love that pours from the heart of God. His *Erfahrung* (experience) of the closeness of God and Christ did not come from an intellectual process, per se, but was mediated through feeling and will. Since Western theologians, in general, find this distinction irrelevant, they tend to emphasize the difference between the young and the mature Reformer more than the facts would warrant. It bears repeating that Luther, as we are aware by now, did not become absorbed in the writings of mystics just because they could be placed under the rubric of "mysticism." The label meant little to him. He recognized a spiritual way to talk about God and acknowledged the kinship. But he did so with discernment. We saw that "mysticism of personality" describes him better than "mysticism of infinity." Luther research has long been talking about a threefold categorization of the mystical mentors, against the background of the doctrine of justification.

Threefold mysticism

If one dares to call Martin Luther a "mystic," as, for example, Nathan Söderblom does, one must draw some lines between different categories of mystics. As we have seen, those theologies that, for various reasons, treat mysticism as a homogeneous block with identical patterns, are so dependent on particular prejudices that they show little interest in any differentiation.

Erich Vogelsang made a great contribution to research when, in the 1930s, he suggested the following three forms of Christian mysticism, not least as influences in Luther's life and thought. They are: the Neoplatonic form, that originated with Dionysius the Areopagite or Pseudo-Dionysius; the Romanic type, represented by persons like Bernard, Bonaventura, and Gerson; and the Germanic form of Johann Tauler and the anonymous author of *Theologia Germanica*.

Professor Åkerberg, a psychology of religion expert previously cited, may retort that Vogelsang did not find any room for psychological aspects. Systematicians have raised questions about the correctness of Vogelsang's chronology, as well as about his classification of specific mystics and the place of bridal mysticism. Oberman asserted, rightly, that a positive reference to mystical authority did not denote that the mystic in question was totally accepted. Luther would, for instance, cite a medieval scholar with approval, yet by and large reject his theology. Like others who have taken seriously Luther's *sapientia experimentalis*, his "existential wisdom" and his "exegetical mysticism" (Oberman's expression), Oberman uses Vogelsang's typology, mutatis mutandis, with the above-mentioned reservations.[384]

The groupings are based on Luther's knowledge about Dionysius the Areopagite or Pseudo-Dionysius (the sixth century), Hugo of St. Victor (1079-1141), Richard of St. Victor (?- 1173), Bernard of Clairvaux (1090-1153), Bonaventura (1221-1274), Johann Tauler (1300?-1344), St. Bridget, (1303?-1373), the Frankfurter in *Theologia Germanica* (around 1350), Gerson (1363-1429), and Wessel Gansfort (1419?-1489).

Dionysian Mysticism

Despite the fact that Martin Luther sometimes quoted the Dionysius Areopagite (Pseudo-Dionysius) with approbation, nevertheless, on the whole he repudiated Dionysic theology. In four accounts Dionysius treats the divine and the ecclesiastical hierarchy, in the name of God and in the name of "mystical theology." About God there is no complete knowledge. However, the divine draws man to itself through earthly symbols and through the hierarchy of the church, which is a reflection of the heavenly world. God is the center of the divine order, Jesus of the ecclesiastical world. Mystical theology is rooted in prayerful communion with God and, in this way, one penetrates beyond the outward signs to the measure of knowledge that man is able to absorb. Furthermore, such spiritual development means that one gradually gives up purely human conceptions and definitions and simultaneously moves toward the divine. Luther was of the opinion that Dionysius had not understood Christ's central role as the incarnated and risen Lord. He said that the person who seeks to elevate himself heavenward, with the aid of Lucifer, runs the risk of falling down. Dionysius' idea about a gradual ascent to heaven may lead to the false assumption that man is able to climb up to God by his own power. On the contrary, we must begin our ascent in Christ's humanity and humiliation. Sin can never be blotted out with the aid of deeds of penance. Therefore, the Christian life does not begin with an emulation of Christ as *exemplum*. It begins at the cross—in Christ as *sacramentum*.[385]

Romanic Mysticism

Most of the above-mentioned mystics belong to this category. The so-called Romanic mystics spoke sometimes as the Areopagites and sometimes like the Germanic mystics. Thus one would do well not to make the distinction too inflexible. Many of them laid considerable emphasis on Christ's humanity. That particular trait attracted Luther. He also felt at home with Romanic mysticism's emphasis on the experience of feeling. However, he found that some of them had little or no insight at all in what he called *Anfechtung*, the sense of being assaulted by demonic powers and of despair about salvation. Also, he regarded with suspicion all methods aimed at attaining union with the divine without mediation of the external Word. Furthermore, Luther felt that the claim of reaching contact with the "uncreated" word might be self-deception.

Romanic mysticism often described our life in God with biblical metaphors from the area of love between man and woman or of married life. Union with God is depicted as a wedding or a married relationship. Theological interpreters have had various opinions about the significance of bridal mysticism for Luther. Vogelsang tended to feel that one of the main reasons that Luther seemed to prefer Tauler over Bernard was the less frequent use of bride-bridegroom vocabulary with Tauler. As we saw in Chapter 6 in The Bride-bridegroom Analogues, Luther did not, in fact, appear hesitant when it came to describing the relation to God and Christ with the aid of images from the bond of marriage. Iserloh and Ruhland considered bridal mysticism a central element in the Reformer's experience of faith. How Luther's relationship to Romanic mysticism in this respect should be deciphered is presumably dependent on one's comprehensive dogmatic view. That the soul as bride is left alone in the bridal chamber with the bridegroom, Christ, becomes for those, with an "objective" view of faith, a veritable assertion of a poverty of merit. For those who experience faith "subjectively," the same scene elicits feelings of devotion that correspond to the bridal couple's feeling of devotion, and that which Luther occasionally called *conglutinatio*—that these two, the human and Christ adhered to one another, yes, were indissolubly "glued" or bonded to each other.

It is clear that Martin Luther desired that his readers would handle with caution what is termed "participation in God" (Chapter 6). This is the reason that, in his notes around Romanic mysticism, you will find both a yes and a no in the text, both an acceptance and rejection. As Luther saw it, one can take part in the Christ-life here on earth, but "the total Christ," all that he is, one can never possess.[386]

Germanic Mysticism

In his foreword to the first printed edition of the larger *Theologia Germanica* (1518), Martin Luther wrote the following:

> Now, some will perhaps say, as they have done before, that we are German theologians. This is quite all right with us. I thank God that I can hear and find my God in the German tongue, in a manner in which I and those with me have not found him anywhere, neither in Latin, Greek, or Hebrew.

In a letter to Spalatin, Luther commented on his discovery of Tauler as follows:

> If you want to read pure, solid theology, that is akin to the teaching of old, and that is available in the German tongue, you ought to get hold of the sermons of Johann Tauler. Here I am sending you a brief sample that may give you an idea of his whole preaching. For neither in Latin, nor in our language, have I seen a theology that is more sound and in keeping with the gospel.

The two mystics referred to above account for the total content in Vogelsang's representation of "Germanic mysticism." Two parenthetical ideas come to mind. First, it must be pointed out that Luther's emphasis on the German language hardly has anything to do "nationalism." We should not forget that Luther pioneered in the field of translating into and writing in German, after the prolonged period of the Middle Ages when Latin, the language of learning, dominated. The latter accounted for the fact that it was the relatively few educated people who wielded political power.

Secondly, as Oberman, among others, has pointed out, one must not delimit the distinctions too precisely. Much of the guidance and wisdom that Romanic mysticism conveyed fits well into the way that Germanic mystics speak of life in God and its connection to life in the world. One illustration that bears this out is Luther's numerous quotations from Bernard.

However, as far as the Frankfurter, anonymous author of the *Theologia Germanica*, and Johann Tauler are concerned, we do not find any *non* (no) in Luther's marginal notes, as is the case with other mystics where *non* is interspersed with *sic* (yes). We have observed that Luther's theological judgment has been questioned by later systematicians. We have also noticed that this criticism of the Reformer disregards Luther's innermost message from his study of the masters of mysticism, namely, his longing for co-pilgrims in the present or the past who, like himself, knew something about the subjective, the personal, yes, the experiential element in the justification that, through Christ, flows out of God's being.

It was in just this respect that Luther, almost as if seeking comfort in an intellectualistic desert, could read the words about life in God, as it came to him from the Frankfurter and from Johann Tauler. Thus it was not just a whim that he arranged the printing of this little pamphlet, which in the first and shorter version of 1516 was called *Eyn geystlich edles Buchleyn*. A second version, published in 1518, was longer, more authentic, and called *Eyn deutsch Theologia*. Since the end of the 1500's that book has been known under its Latin title, *Theologia Germanica*. That Luther often called the booklet "German" also had to do with the fact that, for him, it demonstrated the close link between the Wittenberg teachers and their contact with biblical-based, Catholic preaching through the centuries. Luther wrote in the foreword to the 1518 edition "Read this booklet, anyone, and determine for yourself whether the theology as we do it in Wittenberg is newfangled or in a solid tradition." Basically, he wanted to underscore that the Reformers preached and taught in German what many had previously said in Latin.

In several contexts, we have had occasion to mention Johann Tauler because he became, in a special way, Luther's friend, though long since departed from this life. As we have said, theological differences existed between them, mostly when it came to metaphysical premises that ruled the thought world of Tauler. But the differences were overshadowed by experiences of the inner encounter with the power and grace of Christ.

According to Luther, Germanic mysticism—and others outside this fold—spoke of the encounter with the incarnated Word, neither first and foremost as a training for more intimacy with God nor as a study of the cross-drama nor as an engagement in moral discipleship. Rather, it talked primarly, in a sound and true way, about communion in the depth of the soul. It described the man-God encounter in the name of Christ as experiential knowledge of the Savior's presence and as a union where outer, historical, and inner events are interwoven. When one says that Luther was a mystic in the sense that he "recognized" spiritual friends among the mystics, one does not say—I permit myself to repeat this—that he owed a debt to mysticism as far as intellectual notions were concerned. One rather says that he found mysticism's expressions about the "immediateness" of Christ's presence naturally akin to his own deepest certainty.

If Martin Luther were able to hear or read of the contemporary categorizations of his mystical connections, it would probably elicit hilarious laughter on his part. Neither "mysticism" nor "Germanic mysticism" belonged to his technical vocabulary. He used the adjective *mysticus* (mystical) as well as the terms *Christus mysticus* (mystical Christ) and *oculi mystici* (mystical eyes), for example. In the foreword to *Theologia Germanica,* Luther referred to "German theologians," not to mystical theologians. Not least for that reason, it is a mistake to put chronological limits for mysticism in his life. A pneumatic theological attitude discloses distinctions between various forms of mysticism but does not give us the right to discard mysticism from his thinking, neither theologically nor chronologically, even if the term may not occur in the context being considered. These distinctions were made from the perspective of the doctrine of justification, but also within the discovery of an essential "*Wesensverwandtschaft*" (spiritual kinship) to the mystics, as Iserloh called it. With the aid of only the intellect, one cannot penetrate and collectively explain this friendship or kinship, for here we deal with the meaning of life and personal spirituality, components in the Christian revelation and its personal appropriation. That is not translatable solely by way of abstract formulas and causal logic in theological service. In Luther's inner harmony with some mystics, faith and love become interchangeable—faith, as Luther experienced it, with love, the way many mystics experienced it. There are ecumenical overtones in this fact.[387]

CHAPTER TEN

EVANGELICAL VERSUS ROMAN CATHOLIC: CRITIQUE OF AN ANTITHETICAL APPROACH

The same holy church is now a holy place of sacrilege. . . . Yet, by means of his power and miracles, God has seen to it that under the pope there has nevertheless remained in the church: . . . holy baptism . . . the holy Gospel . . . the holy Sacrament of the altar . . . the Psalter, the Lord's Prayer . . . Now where such articles have remained, there surely the church and a number of saints have remained.

Martin Luther, *W* 38; 221, 18-35 (1535), *LW* 38; 177-178

One-sided dependence on the intellect and reason often lead Luther interpreters to undervalue mysticism's message and meaning in the Reformer's life and the lives of many other prophets. Such dependence on the exclusively intellectual creates confessional ramparts —or inspires their erection. Statements from Luther's writings were mobilized for the purpose of proving the absolute polarity between the evangelical and the Catholic positions. Examples of this phenomenon have been presented in this work. Both in traditional Lutheran orthodoxy and in Protestant analyses molded by the historical-critical method and liberal epistemology, one finds an apologetic confessionalism that systematizes the central articles of faith antithetically. The reader or the listener must choose between two contrary "trüths" of which the "proper" truth would be found on the Protestant side. (Catholic institutional traditionalism functions the same, inversely.) However, Luther's descriptions of religious "experience" contain elements that unite rather than separate the evangelical and Roman Catholic world.

On the preceding pages the conclusion has been drawn that the documentary material does **not** warrant the assertion that medieval Christian mysticism is unacceptable because it is and cannot be anything other than Roman Catholicism. Likewise, the corollary that Christian mysticism is heretical because it is not biblical and, hence, hardly Christian must be rejected. There are examples of these kinds of statements with Calovius and his comrades-in-arms among orthodox Lutherans and with Harnack and his followers among the Lutherans who have taken their theory of knowledge from modern science.

One may even turn the matter around and say that there is an "essential connection between Lutheranism and mystical religion." The words are Rudolf Otto's. Otto came to the conclusion that what he called the typical moments of mysticism—"creature feeling" before God and "oneness with God—are more possible on the basis of Luther's faith experience (as *fiducia*, trust; *adhaesio*, a spiritual cleaving to, a union with God; and, *conglutinatio*, bonding) than on the basis of *amor mysticus*, the mystical love, which may exude from the worshipping soul. One senses a mystical state of mind in Luther's words about the encounter with God in prayer, during meditation, at the reading of God's Word, and at the celebration of the Lord's Supper. Otto maintained, justifiably, that this osmosis to a great extent was similar to that of medieval mystics when they depicted the numinous world. Otto illustrates his point with a Luther quotation:

> He indeed who cleaves to God abides in light . . . Wherefore it is man's loftier perfection in this life so to be so united with God that the whole soul, with all its strength and all its powers, is gathered into its Lord and God and becomes one spirit with him.

Luther's faith was "ecumenical" in the sense that it tied him to an essential component of Roman Catholic thinking, which by its nature transcends institutional boundaries. The real Luther, Otto asserted, is to be found in his awe-filled reverence before God, an awe that could not, of course, be expressed in rational formulas. Vogelsang maintained that Luther recognized his own soul's mystical movements when he partook of mystical literature. All through his life, Luther expressed his gratitude to Bernard for pointing him to the Crucified One and to spiritual experience.

Luther came to regard Gerson and Tauler as spiritual kinsmen as far as a Christian's spiritual tribulations were concerned. Particularly in relation to Tauler, one can speak of spiritual kinship, not theological dependency, but kinship. It was Tauler who had convinced Luther that eternal life begins here on earth and that it ought not be linked with the matter of reward. From Bernard he received—as we have seen—his description of "mystical theology." Toward the end of his life Luther had the same feeling of closeness to Tauler and his message, as in earlier years. He also exclaimed once that he had found "sheer Jesus in Bernard." Luther and Tauler were one in the way in which they spoke of the personal certainty of salvation and grace in Christ, and they both knew that God was unfathomable majesty before whom man is reduced to a stammering dwarf.[388]

Thus there was potential ecumenicity in the manner in which Luther, and some mystics whom he studied, experienced God and Christ. Reliance on and unity with God in prayer and in worship, seen as mystical experiences, carry within them ecumenical possibilities that far surpass what can be expressed in a dogmatic discourse or debate.

Unfortunately, it is the case that theological conceptualizing—however essential—often leads to intellectualistic absolutism that juxtaposes Protestant and Roman theology in positions of combat. In this way the unity-in-Christ theme loses much of its vitality. Protestant theology has isolated certain notions in Luther's world of thought and has moved away from the central experience of the numinous, Otto wrote. One has made Christ into an **idea** and speaks about the Spirit as though the Spirit were present only on some special occasions, such as fixed institutional ceremonies, if I am permitted to extend that train of thought.

A great deal of the analytical investigation around the legacy of Luther has taken aim at Luther's moments of despair, at his times of distress, his periods of melancholy, his predestination theology—all in isolated doses, without the greater religious and mystical context. One has concentrated on Luther's conceptual terminology: "judgment," "punishment," "God's wrath," without setting it in the circumstances of the larger framework. Unity in God through Christ is enclosed in a very narrow confessional category and is limited to either Protestant or Catholic frames of reference.

Two works by Roman Catholic scholars may serve to illustrate the ecumenical incentives in Luther's theological style, but also the limitations that an exclusively rationalistic understanding of his doctrine can place on that style. The rational approach to interpretation is evident in McSorley's book on Luther's reply to Erasmus regarding the nature of the will, as expressed in *The Bondage of the Will*. McSorley's account was touched upon in connection with the discussion about the place of logic and the place of the numinous element in Luther's teaching (Chapter 9). Here we are concerned primarily with the question of the Catholic scholar's view of Luther's ecumenical significance.

McSorley, a good Scholastic and universal Christian, submitted that Luther abandoned tradition when he, in *The Bondage of the Will*, denied that we are equipped with a naturally free will. Luther introduced a necessitarian moment in his thinking about predestination, a deterministic theme that is not biblical and not to be found in Scholastic writing, nor in the documents of the Lutheran school. McSorley was of the opinion that Luther, with his incorrect and unbending view about the **necessity** or inevitability of events—as if some kind of mechanical process prevailed, had broken with the ecumenical legacy. In **this** respect, McSorley thought, Luther had gone astray.

But how would it be if the circumstances could be described as just the opposite? In his seemingly mechanistic and deterministic illustrations of free will before God *(coram Deo)*, Luther fetched water for his mill from a deep mystical well. That well was his numinous experience of God's dreadful majesty that prompts the theologically illogical statement that man has no free will whatever. Luther was giving expression to a religious experience that eludes ratiocination: man stands before God who knows all about him and foresees the choices man will make. To say that God, in his love for us, allows us freedom of choice, and, at the same time, knows what choices we will make, both positively and negatively, is a dual truth that does not jibe logically.

Yet, one ought to remember that Luther did not treat his theological determinism as part of a logically reasoned system. McSorley maintained, in an otherwise appreciative and thoughtful assessment, that Luther's assertion was a mistake because it was not logical. But at this point the American Catholic uses a misleading yardstick. Luther gave expression to a mystical experience that frustrates our *ratio*, our way of applying reason-bound logical discussion. The experience was this: man, in this case Luther, is standing before a God who knows everything about him and, who, in a manner that goes beyond theological logic, also knows what path the person will choose.

Mystical, numinous trustful dependency lay close to the center of Luther's thoughts in *The Bondage the Will*. Luther shared this fear-ridden and joy-imbued intuition with some mystics. One can, therefore, say that McSorley's suggestion did not go far enough. It continued to remain within the framework of dogmatic rational formulations. The basic assumption seems to be that, if theological patterns could be brought over to the same common denominator in regard to natural free will, the ecumenical potential would be augmented. In other words,

McSorley's account gives the impression that more rational discourses and dialogues would be the only avenue of ecumenical rapprochement.

Luther, on the contrary, spoke of a more essential mystical affinity when he chose the language of "necessitarianism." It was a question of the deeply unifying experience of the Unfathomable, all things unmasking God in whom we all live, move, and have our being.[389]

The Roman Catholic theologian, Jared Wicks, provides the second illustration of ecumenical stirrings in the discussion on Luther and mysticism. Wicks have scrutinized Luther's "earlier spiritual teaching." He asserted in his book, *Man Yearning for Grace*, that the Reformer was, in the first place, a man of spiritual stature rather than a dogmatic polemicist. Wicks declared also that the spiritual and the mystical themes in Luther's earlier works ought to be regarded as more central and more original than the categorical rational pronouncements of his later years. (Parenthetically, it ought to be mentioned that Wicks draws the conclusion that Luther's spirituality around 1518 was replaced by the dogmatic matter of certainty. In a later book, *Luther and His Spiritual Legacy*, he wrote "these new polemical notes of 1519 did not entail the rejection of the principles and concerns of Luther's early work"). In Wicks' interpretation one finds an awareness of the significance of Luther's mystical contacts, especially Tauler and *Theologia Germanica*. In McSorley's account, this awareness is conspicuous by its absence.

Both authors suggest potential areas for accord. McSorley recommends a partly revised and, logically, more consistent idea about free will than we find in Luther's *The Bondage of the Will*. Through this one might find a unifying link. Wicks points out that the ecumenical significance of Luther's work lies in the mystical spirituality that his work mediates.

McSorley puts considerable emphasis on "conception," "idea;" Wicks accentuates Luther's interest in *sapientia experimentalis*, "experimental spirituality," "existential wisdom." He maintained that Luther's theology was not primarily concentrated on intellectual penetration into the mystery of the revelatory deed but rather, in the first place, the "translation" of a radical spiritual experience. When a rationalistic theologian interprets Luther's thoughts about sanctification or "divinization," as the Reformer's attack against supernaturalism, Wicks declares this a distortion of Luther's intention. For Luther's world of thought embraced Christ's indwelling in the soul to the same intensive extent that it spoke of a more objective ascribing of Christ's deed "for you." Wicks concluded his analysis by expressing his satisfaction over the fact that Luther was speaking of God working in us.

> Both Catholics and Lutherans can learn much here. As we learn together from Luther's earliest spirituality, this too could well be a work of God, actively drawing us toward unity and reconciliation. [390]

We have here two instructive attempts by two Catholic scholars to distance themselves from the antithetical procedures that dominate much theological systematics around Luther's message. It looks as though McSorley's striving still moves inside the framework of a traditional intellectualism, whereas Wicks seems to be closer to the pneumatic interpretation which appears to carry the deeper ecumenical promise —seen from the perspective we have found useful for this book.

By that we have not said that ecumenical dialogues between Catholics and Protestants on various aspects of the Christian faith are useless. On the contrary, these theological dialogues—for instance, on baptism, the Eucharist, the nature of ordination and of the Church and the significance of the Nicene Creed—have doubtless brought theological thought, on both sides, closer together, or at least provided a forum for greater understanding. Nor is it insignificant that, for example, Lutheran theologians take a stand on the World Council's "universalistic" formulations concerning baptism, the Eucharist, and the preaching of the Word. One must, however, draw attention to the words in the Lutheran World Federation's summary of attitudes to the World Council of Churches proposal on questions of faith: "The overarching ecumenical goal, progress toward reciprocal recognition . . . may, unintentionally, encourage the churches to concentrate on unity in permanent separation rather than fellowship in reconciled division."

Behind this directional sign lies, of course, the remarkable fact that, during the latter part of the twentieth century after Christ, the people of the Reformation and of the old Church have begun to approach each other, more aware than previously of that friendly power that emanates from the Holy Spirit, promised us by the Risen and Living Lord. No opportunities for intellectual compromises or respectful assertions concerning unbridgeable differences would have been given if the mystical Christ-presence had not been allowed to make itself felt in the hearts of the estranged Christians. It may, at times, take four hundred years before the voice of the Spirit is permitted to make itself heard. One thing is certain, it was a matter of mystical presence before it came to intellectual analyses across the borders.

Our discussion about the frequently antipodal character of comments on mystical components in Luther's faith should consequently not hide the historical and theological differences between Luther's and Roman attitudes toward grace, the church, and the nature of man. My reminder of the fact that mere intellectual exchanges dealing with those differences can lead—and does lead—to theologically unrealistic absolutism ought not to be taken as an invitation to abandon distinctions in the world of ideas. Yet it is true that intellectualistic premises—prejudices—not infrequently cause "solar eclipses" in relation to Luther's mystical experiences. The premises are of both the epistemological and confessionalistic type. If one is aware of this unconscious exclusion or conscious omission, one also understands that there are theological minds that actually function on the assumption that theological conceptualization is **not** inspired by the supersensible and non-rational.

It turns out, namely, that if one consistently follows the antithetical method, placing "Catholicism-mysticism," on one side, and the "Reformation," on the other, Luther's thought is placed in an inauthentic framework. The origin of the antithesis-syndrome may very well lie with the Reformer himself in his angry or disputatious moods. Then his followers sharpened the distinctions with the intention of defending the fruits of the liberation against a tyrannical and still oppressive institution. But whatever one says in defense of drawing up confessional boundaries between law and grace, tradition and Word, the papacy and evangelical freedom, tradition and person, the theology of glory and the theology of the cross—the fact is that intellectual judgments and speculative, cognitive formulations prevail. There is no room for the immediate reality of the mystical experience and of spiritual knowledge called "the sense of the heart," to borrow a phrase from the writings of Jonathan Edwards, the American theologian.[391]

There is a bond between those who, in this latter sense, know that Christ in his supernatural glory was, and is, an eternal and omnipresent reality. This conviction or "knowing" continues to bind humans together across institutional and intellectual barriers. Jared Wicks, the American Jesuit and professor at the Gregorian University in Rome, wrote about Luther's "spirituality" and about Luther as a *homo religiosus*. He sheds light on one side of Luther that represents, in a special way, the ecumenical continuity of the whole of Christianity and the Christological bridge that permits one to encounter other "religions," namely, the numinous, intuitive, "heart-felt" and intimately private Christ-presence. This mystical element serves as a constant reminder of the limitations of antithetical polarization. But if this "privatization" —which is frequently the major accusation against everything "mystical"—would be interpreted as an exclusively inward turn, we are soon taken from this delusion by Luther's thoughts about the linkage between mystical faith and moral responsibility.

CHAPTER ELEVEN

MYSTICISM AND ETHICS WITH LUTHER

It is true that faith alone justifies, without works, but I am speaking about genuine faith, which, after it has justified, will not go to sleep but is active through love. . . . Inwardly it is faith toward God, outwardly it is love or works towards one's neighbor.

Martin Luther, *W* 40,2, 36, 4-5, 37, 26-28 (1535), *LW* 27; 30

Anders Nygren, the world-renowned Swedish theologian and ethicist, expressed his thoughts on Luther's relationship to the mystical and the ethical in the following way: German mysticism regarded ethical deeds as attempts to exert pressure on God, so that God would give man the blessedness for which he strove. Nygren asserted that this is the goal of all mysticism. How then could Luther use mystical terms and quote mystics with approval? Nygren answered that Luther's opinion of the positive, which he had taken from the mystics, was irrelevant. In other words, according to Nygren, the mystical and the moral had nothing to do with each other in Luther's theology, irrespective of what Luther himself might have thought on the subject.[392]

Nygren's younger colleague, the systematician Bengt Hägglund, to whose research I am greatly indebted, reached the opposite conclusion. He thought that it was a mistake to assume that the doctrine of justification by faith marks the most profound difference between Luther and mysticism. On the contrary, Hägglund continued, the fact is that "Luther regarded himself in agreement with the mystic Tauler and [with the author of] *Theologia Germanica*." With those mystics he found—despite, for example, differences in the question of the nature of the "Word"—corroboration for his belief that justification means that one does not trust in "deeds" to achieve salvation. Justification occurs "only through God's birth in the soul." This in turn inspires one to ethical responsibility, but one is not saved through deeds. Hägglund wrote that one ought "to take Luther's positive utterances on Tauler and *Theologia Deutsch* in earnest." This is not only a matter of "a similarity of thought," but of the "deep impressions and impulses from these writings," which Luther had received.[393]

Against this background—and with reference to the discussion about ethics in the Foreword of this book—let us examine Luther's way of linking the mystical and the moral, the experience of liberation through justification and Christian ethics. The central thesis becomes: the moral life is an integral part of life in the mystical Christ.

From my reading of Luther regarding mysticism and ethics, I have crystallized seven brief points, not least in order to substantiate that those mystics, to whom he adhered throughout his entire life, did not correspond to the image of escapism or detachment from life, which much traditional theology ascribed to them in particular and to mysticism in general.

1. The moral is anchored in the mysterious living presence of the Cosmic Lord, the Sun of Righteousness.

Thus Christian ethics is not rooted in speculations and concepts. It is grounded in a powerful, living, invisible Lord who, said Luther, "must be mightier than the devil, sin, death, the world and all creatures." His power is so tremendous that nothing could be compared with it.

This power, this might, flows through the sacraments and proclamation. It is much more than purely, and only, external signs. "God be thanked that I experienced a little of the essence and the power of this doctrine [about Christ's humanity and his divinity] and preserved it against other spirits." Theological "grammarians" have no idea of this. "And I also saw that this doctrine [about Christ] has been preserved for more than a thousand years over against all clever minds and devils in hell who assailed it. It will surely survive them all."

The works of Christ are, therefore, continuously being channeled through Christians. Christians are not, first and foremost, conveyers of good ideas. They are channels for divine power. "God has already 'made us sit with Him in the heavenly places'," Luther revealed in his comments on Ephesians 2:6. Work of an ethical nature continues in the mystical body of Christ. When the Lord was in a temporal body he could perform "only small and slight works." But after having been raised to rule over the entire invisible realm, he performs his wonders through Christians by their preaching, prayers, and works of mercy. "For in all Christians He will effect and produce these two things: First, He will convince and assure their hearts that they have a compassionate God; secondly, He will enable them to help others by their supplication."[394]

2. The inner union with Christ—the mystical element in justification through faith—is, at the same time, the wellspring of moral life.

Luther wrote in 1537—and I explicitly note the year since many have been taught that Luther did not speak mystical language after, shall we say, 1518—that observing the rules of the moral life

> depends on whether you feel and find that you love this Man [Christ]. . . . The heart must cleave solely to Christ and neither love nor fear anything else. . . . Where there is faith the works of love [charity] must follow.

One can be sure that the devil will attack every Christian who holds fast to Christ, yes, **firmly clings**, is perhaps closer to Luther's choice of words. For such a person does deeds of love, and nothing is more odious to the bold potentate. He is likely to say: How is it now, do you by any chance rely on your fine and good deeds as a means to your salvation? In such situations one should remember the promise that "The comforter is not from you." My own Christian experience must step in at this point and inform the devil that Christ "has rescued me" in similar situations and has let me know that he, Christ, has inspired my deeds of love.

It is, namely, a fact that one's acts and thoughts arise from the inner friendship with Christ and consequently are Christ's deeds. One can **experience** this, Luther maintained. It is more than a theological theory. We seek refuge in Christ with all our being: "Thus we must vault above ourselves and beyond ourselves to Him. Yes, we must become completely merged into Him." Then, in the most miraculous way, the burden of sin and feelings of guilt are lifted from us. Death and hell have vanished. There "is a descent from above. It is like this: Just as I am in Christ, so Christ, in turn, is in me." This Luther described as an inner conversation, audible in a mystical sense, and he continued

> Then there is a descent from above. It is like this: Just as I am in Christ, so Christ, in turn, is in me. I have taken possession of Him; I have crept into Him out of the power of sin, death, and the devil. Now He also manifests Himself in me and says: "Go forth, preach, comfort, baptize, serve your neighbor, be obedient, be patient. I will be in you and will do all this. Whatever you do will be done by me. Just be of good cheer, be bold, and trust me. See that you remain in Me. Then I, in turn, will surely be in you." . . . For if we are not convinced, do not believe, and cannot confidently assert that

whatever we say and do is done from above by Christ himself and is truly the work of Him who is in me and in whom I am, then the devil has already carried the day.

Yes, if one does not carry out Jesus' moral exhortation, one distances oneself from the love of the invisible Christ. The inner voice dies out and perhaps the unity is broken.

The necessary counterpart to "the Lord's dwelling in us," as individuals and as church, and our being his "dwelling place" is, consequently, moral obedience. "Christ is in us," and "we are in Him." "If you know this and make it your own, you will also be certain that whatever you say, preach, live, and do will be right and good, yes, will be, and will be called My own Word and work."[395]

3. The extraordinary anchorage of the moral does not exclude participation in the ordinary life of the world.

This truth about the Christian's engagement in the lives of humans, Luther expressed in the following words: "Thus a Christian uses the world and all its creatures in such a way that there is no difference between him and an ungodly man." After all, Christ himself came in ordinary human form. Yet, there is the "greatest possible difference. I live indeed in the flesh, but I do not live on the basis of my own self . . . That which you hear me say springs from another source." I have been touched by "the Holy Spirit." "The unspiritual man does not perceive this." He cannot surmise "where the words of the spiritual man come from." The fact is that the converted spiritual man is a conveyor of moral truth from God, although he, like all others, performs the common tasks of daily life and in spite of the fact that he lives in the "flesh" which resists.

The mystical participation in Christ, which occurs in, with, and under participation in the ordinary circumstances of life, must benefit the community and society, not just the individual supplicant.[396]

4. The formation of Christian life from within spiritual communion with Christ involves active service and an effort to effect social justice.

When justified in God by faith, man becomes "formed" in Christ, or Christ becomes "formed" in man, Luther points out. In this way Luther spoke about the shaping of the soul. He frequently used the verb *formare* in this connection, and this is alluded to in Chapter 6 of the present book. The "Soul, formed by Christ," as Luther expressed it, implies ethical responsibility and the formation occurs both within the individual and through the individual within the community. Luther paraphrased John 15: 10-12 in the following manner:

> "Therefore," says Christ, "if you are in Me . . . I must assign a task to you, and by your performance of this task you will be recognized as My branches . . . I remain in my Father's love by keeping His commandments. Consequently, if you keep my commandments, you also remain in my love."

Remember, Luther continues, that a Christian's deeds may be such that he denies his confession of faith in Christ. You can promote your neighbor's welfare as a reflection of abiding in Christ. If there are no such deeds in your life, you are not "fruitful branches" in Christ, "but decayed wood."

In this connection we might properly deal with the question of whether Luther considered works part of the salvatory event. In his more impassioned polemics, Luther often seemed to reject the necessity of human cooperation in salvation. From such remarks scholarly opinion has sometimes arisen that the Reformer's thought-world had no room for such cooperation in connection with conversion and salvation.

But, as we have seen, Luther's basic instructions followed a different path. Man is totally dependent on faith as a gift and as grace, which God-in-Christ grants him when he discovers his own sinfulness and smallness and simply surrenders. Here we have the first step and we must not forget that it is the first one. In situations of theological battle Luther often kept his silence about the continuation. And the continuation is this: although it is true that faith does not make us righteous before God **because of good deeds**, nevertheless there can be no faith **without the works of mercy**. From statements less negative and less polemical, it is quite clear that Luther's total view regarding the power of the gospel included the ethical component of man's will-oriented cooperation with God. We are branches of the tree, as John puts it. If we do not act morally-ethically, we become decayed wood, yes, dead wood. The power of justification by faith must, through love, be transformed into practical, edifying efforts. Otherwise "power" is just a word.

In a recent study of Luther's later commentary on the Galatians, a Roman Catholic scholar suggests that, as Luther's theology contained a *simul* (simultaneousness) of sin and righteousness—a *simul* of mendacious human and a soul formed in Christ—its explicit extension also embraces another *simul* of God-given faith and man's moral striving. Luther suggests this theological possibility when he uses an illustration from Bernard of Clairvaux about iron glowing in the fire. Luther adds that this is what happens to our moral life when Christ is permitted to provide the flame.[397]

5. Man's sinfulness is not the entire truth about humans, for in and through Christ we can speak about "the good in us."

Commenting on John 15:2 (on the branch and the fruit), Luther wrote that there are people who consider it both true and smart to say "Man can do nothing but emit his foul odor and stench; nothing but bad comes out of him." You really have to be "an evil worm or a stupid ass" to find fault with and despise the body because it purges what is bad. Luther went on:

> I must say that although sores and pus are in the body, the body is not evil because such things come out of it. For if these things were good, they would remain in the body as other things do. But since the body, together with its members, is sound and healthy, the filth must come out and be thrown away. If you want to reject your body because snot, pus and filth come out of it, you should cut your head off. Thus Christendom, too, is a living, healthy body of the pious little flock, God's children. Yet filth and stench are mixed in. They must be cast out.

Consequently, just as we carry the good with us both in the body and in the church, we, as individuals, must be able to see the good and not only search for and think about that which is evil in us.

As we have seen in the comments on the nature of man, we are presented with a biased interpretation of Luther when his thoughts on our deep-seated egocentricity are made into a kind of "gospel" about sinfulness. Luther also spoke about the inclination toward God that is a part of creation. Why would God totally destroy that which he has created? Like the prodigal son, man can come to himself. The image of God is not entirely destroyed. However, it is Christ who makes the great difference. He awakens the memory of God and creates "the good in us." Good moral fruit grows out of "abiding in Him," through prayer, through the celebration of the sacraments, and through the reading of the Word. Moral deeds outside Christ lack a source and a context. The person whose life is hidden in Christ radiates some of that Christian goodness through his societal contributions. The goodness is Christ's goodness, not the individual Christian's. One can consequently speak of the goodness in us in the sense that Christ has awakened life in the Divine Image that was never totally lost. Ethical goodness begins in humility—when one sees how much help one needs—and continues in disciplined action. About this Luther exclaimed: "Should God bestow on us all His grace and Christ, His Son, and then say: 'You need not do anything at all but follow your own inclinations and give free rein to all willfulness and knavery'?"

The moral outpouring in service among people is anchored in prayer-filled connection with Christ and immersion in him. In this turning to the invisible, our original alliance with our Creator is rejuvenated. This experience of oneness under the cross is more than a rationally derived appropriation of biblical information about Christ.[398]

That experience brings us to the question of the law.

6. In the spiritual union with Christ a paradoxical tension exists between the suspension of the law and a new confirmation of the law.

Luther said about the suspension of the law that the law is destroyed "when by faith we consciously take hold of Christ himself." We "die to the grave, i.e., the old law," and "rise with Christ."

However, the result of this mystical death is not lawlessness. Through the work begun and engendered by the Spirit in baptism, we enter a life of renewal. Luther explains:

> For in those who have been baptized a new light and flame arise; new and devout emotions come into being, . . . and a new will emerges. This is what it means to put on Christ properly, truly, and according to the gospel. . . . For when we have put on Christ, the garment of our righteousness and salvation, then we also put on Christ, the garment of imitation. . . . Then fruit and works follow.

Christ, "who is present particularly when he cannot be seen," brings forth in us a new moral attitude. "When by faith (the external as well as the inner, mystical faith) we consciously take hold of Christ himself, we enter into a kind of new law," Luther claimed. "Paul," he reminded us, "calls grace itself a 'law'."

In 1522 Martin Luther insisted that inner communion with Christ must precede this transforming of the moral commands from law, as an external command, to law as an inner obligation. Christ becomes a living, present power within you, a *sacramentum*, and an *exemplum*, example, in the realm of your ethical decisions.

Thirteen years later, 1535—again I call attention to the year since it has frequently been asserted that, in later years, the Reformer abandoned all things mystical—Luther developed this theme in some disputations against antinomian ideas. There is, he argued, an ongoing interaction between Christ as *sacramentum* and us as followers, as imitators of his *exemplum*. Consequently, this means that the law still exists, but that it is mystically inspired by a power from beyond—the gift of the Holy Spirit through Christ.

True, God liberates from the law. Yet, Paul certainly did not speak as an antinomian. Moral deeds and ethical thinking are, according to the epistles of Paul, part of the life of the Spirit. If you are guilty of certain actions or if you cling fast to thoughts that contradict the bidding of the Holy Spirit (Paul gives us entire lists of impious deeds), you cannot, according to Paul and Luther, "possess the Kingdom of God."

Within the range of God's forgiveness we appropriate the historical-dogmatic incarnation. But we also participate in "the mystical incarnation;" we sense, there, both contrition and joy. Christ fills the ensuing new humility with a law that is part of his love. "Those who reject this law crucify Christ and cast Him aside, just like those who cry out in the Psalm [2:3]: 'Let us burst their bonds asunder'." For after having bestowed the grace of forgiveness, Christ preached law.[399]

In order not to misinterpret the latter statement as a form of legalism, introduced through the back door, we must be clear about one thing, namely, that above and behind the new experience concerning the necessity of the law, there is a forgiving Lord and heartfelt conversation in prayer with him as a constant challenge to moral responsibility.

7. It is a mystical truth that the true Christian plays a central moral role in the world.

Christians who live in self-knowledge and humility (*humilitas*) and Christians who have lived in hell for three days, like Jonah, are vicarious bearers of mankind's sins. This was Luther's way of looking at the meaning of moral servanthood. The worldly person wants to have heaven directly with Christ, Luther asserts, but a Christian knows that it does not happen this way. First one has to go through hell with Christ.

Christian deeds in the world are the extension of the work that, to quote Luther, "Christ merely initiated." Consequently, one can say, "Christians do more works and more extensive works for God than Christ himself did. Yes, the works are identical; they are the same as his."

The solution to this enigma lies in Christ's words: "I go to my Father." Christ continues to be present with his followers through experienced power, because the resurrected and living Christ has all power in his hands. He is the Sun behind the sun. No wonder—or perhaps this is just the wonder, the miracle—that he can, in advance, give his support: "Whatever you ask, I will do it." In our practical deeds to help our neighbors, Luther encouraged Christians to "trustingly lean on Christ in faith."

Prayer more than **ideas**, the consciousness of the heart rather than **notions**, enable Christians to serve, unknown to the world, as the real upholders of life.

In the midst of all the talk about the flagging influence of Christians on this earth, it certainly ought to be encouraging to be able to reflect on Luther's words about the importance of the little flock. He explained that Christians, who in inner devotion are "bonded to God" and "trustingly lean on Christ," exert such an essential influence that "no city or country would enjoy peace;" grain would not grow in the field; people would not recover from illness; the world would be unprotected; if it were not for the hidden life of Christians in *Christus mysticus*, the mystical Christ. For, although it is invisible, Christians rely on Christ's power in the world. In other words, their strength is not found in theological formulations, but in Christ's power.

This entire situation is paradoxical. In the eyes of the world true Christian persons (*wahre Christen*) appear to be "miserable beggars" and, yet, they own everything. It is on account of their contributions that "power, honor and prosperity" exist among people. True Christians live in the midst of the unrepentant world, which does not understand this at all, and "thanks the Christians poorly for it."

"Christians are genuine helpers and saviors, yes, lords and gods of the world." (If they had not stood at the brink of nothingness and experienced grace that reduces the ego, they would indeed begin to suffer anew from pride upon hearing such language). When "the Christians' works and wonders cease . . . God will end it all; it will be consumed by fire." In Luther's exposition [on John 14:12] there follows some words on the intolerability, humanly speaking, of needing to observe the foolishness of ungodly people. Luther prepared his friends stating that, before the catastrophe of fire occurs, those who are spiritually "bonded" to the Lord must "suffer such filth and stench from them [those who do not know Christ] as do the legs that carry the paunch and the reeking belly." In this inimitable way Luther added extra color in his attempt to paint the Christian's ethical task in a sea of incomprehensibility.

He continues to speak on John 14:12:

> The world gapes only at that which appears to be great and glorious, what is rich and mighty, and what struts along in a

> pompous manner; but the world is ignorant of the source of its possessions. But Christ says: "If you are baptized and believe in Me, then you are the man who has more and can perform greater things, yes, can do the same works that I am now doing, and even greater works than these. I will make you who believe in Me such lords that your works will count and accomplish more than those of all the kings and lords on earth. You shall carry out whatever you will; you shall help Me rule spiritually over souls for their salvation, and you shall also obtain and receive by means of your prayer whatever physical goods there are on earth."

Here we have again the mystical thought that the godless are the unconscious beneficiaries of strength and blessings from the prayers of Christians. One could speak of both the ethical and moral significance of the little flock.[400]

In 1968, Mary McDermott Shideler, writing in the Christian Century, stated: "The churches ignore the contemplatives in their midst at their own peril, for only as man lives in the spirit can he live for others." She stressed that, in our pews, from our pulpits, in our political organs, and in our places of work, in one way or another, we announce "that we should live for others, and many of us want to. What we do not know is what we can live **from**." Intellectual argumentation, ethical exhortations, work on sociopolitical matters, analyses concerning one's own ego, self-forgetfulness in aiding others—nothing of this can in itself be the source of the moral life.

> Yet even today, and even in the churches that are most zealously oriented toward the world, almost certainly some people are there because they are hungry for something that is not promised by any other agency in our society. The traditional name for that something is "the grace of God." Goaded by heaven only knows what pressures from without and within, they have come to church for the bread of life. And we give them ethical pronouncements, political analyses, historical analogies—stones.

She averred that many secret yearners long for the life of the Spirit. Maybe the spiritual interest of many people is just a pretense, a façade to cover up ethical laziness and selfishness. But on the other hand, that which looks like a dearth of active engagement sometimes conceals a spiritual longing for an experience of God's grace:

> The Christian . . . is called primarily, not to morality, but to sanctity. His ultimate criterion is not the good but the holy. Obviously we need to revive the tradition that sanctity is the foundation and fountainhead of moral passion and ethical perception.[401]

Piety and holiness go deeper than theology and morality. From these deeper mystical and ecstatic fountains come ethical challenges and theological reflection.

After a long authorship in the area of social analysis, the French ethicist Ellul confessed, "My purely sociological and historical intellectual approach led me into a blind alley." Through what he regarded as a "miracle," his grasp on life changed. "Hope became near, living and all-embracing. No longer was it a theological formula." A new ethical attitude is developing, Ellul thought, not through new idea-bound combinations, but through what he termed "the secret places of the heart." The ethical concerns of the end of the twentieth century show clearly that "It is also important for the Christian to be willing to bring himself to believe in miracles."[402]

Martin Luther would have understood this kind of language. Like many of the mystics of the Middle Ages, he integrated moral action, and the ethics growing from it, with the Christian's hiddenness in Christ. Martha, he said, represents the moral birth. The created Word speaks thus. But Mary's longing for the uncreated Word must become part of Martha's deeds. The two "births" are woven together.

CHAPTER TWELVE

A LOOK BACK AND A LOOK FORWARD

Therefore beware of such misleading, shameful, and deceptive prattle, which represents Christ solely as a Teacher of works, as though He had taught and showed us nothing but proper conduct and behavior. In that capacity He could not be called the Way . . . His example is truly precious . . . But the walking and the way of which our text speaks no longer relate to this life. This is a walk and a leap by which one must enter and cross over into the life beyond . . . you can feel Christ's presence and He can say to you as He does to Thomas here: "Why are you seeking and looking for other ways? Look to Me," . . . [Christ] is and remains constantly at our side and within us, . . . who is so close that He alone is in our hearts. . . . For this walking is nothing but a constant growth in faith and in an ever-stronger assurance of eternal life in Christ.

Martin Luther, *W* 45; 497, 25-28, 33-35,498, 36-37, 499, 11-13, 21-23 (1538)
LW 24, 41-42

We have established that many interpretations of and discourses on God's self-revelation in Christ show an inability to deal with the Third Article of the Creed. To integrate the Holy Spirit's unpredictability with a solid system of thought meets with a certain resistance. The historical and phenomenological sides of revelation are registered with admirable consistency, whether this revelation is regarded as a specific event or as an enduring process. But a "linear" and "logical" mind does not know what to do with a "wind" that blows whither it wants or a Lord who, after his death promises to be with his friends, wherever two or three are gathered in his name. He speaks to each of them from the inaudible and from the invisible, yes, promises that in the strength of the Spirit they will do even greater things than He, Christ, has done.

Such claims—or some might say pretensions—are directly contrary to the testimonies of the five senses and sound reason, common sense. This is why they have been treated with careful skepticism in the history of Christianity ever since doubting Thomas insisted on tangible proofs. That is to say, man is equipped with the tendency to limit God's potentialities to the bio-physically determinable, the materially perceptible, and the "ordinary."

Furthermore, the so-called "exact" sciences and their philosophical counterparts have been permitted to influence what we ought to think about the power of the Holy Spirit. Due to osmosis from contemporary scientific materialism, theological systematicians have adopted the scientific codes of verification. Consequently, the gospel's evangelical and mystical aspects are not on the horizon. The church continues to repeat the Third Article of the Creed about the Holy Spirit as an account of bygone events or a present-day psychological truth, with some transcendental element baked in or a "promise" about redemption in the future. One has difficulty accepting the confession of faith as an invocation of and trust in a divine power, always present and ready, at our beckoning, to enter our consciousness. More often than not the church's thought has been shaped by theology seen as history, theology molded by anthropology, or theology presented as a promise of fulfillment in glory, without any links to present tasks, without any connection to God's messengers and saints in their earthly guise, as the Book of Revelation and the early church spoke of them: messengers seeking to do and present God's will in the destiny and consciousness of humankind.

One could say that on the preceding pages I have thrown down the gauntlet to challenge the theory of knowledge of the earth-bound, three-dimensional nature of Christian theology. The supernatural finds its own way into the consciousness of man, which the rational mind, shackled as it is to the five senses, is unable to comprehend. "Knowledge" in the mystical and spiritual sense requires an epistemology that finds room for inspiration in feeling and presentiment in prophetic ways, a reconnoitering service to the uttermost borders. Martin Luther cannot be understood if one continues to insist that the only valid model of cognition which one can and should apply to reports of mystical experience is the "scientific model," where physical causality rules like clock-work. Many of the theological treatments of Luther's relations to mysticism, which we have reviewed, bear this out.

When I, in this exposition, have submitted Martin Luther's way of conveying his experience of the invisible, and especially *Christus mysticus*, to our day and time, I have had three intentions in mind. The first concern is the question of the mystical experience in the Reformer's talk about justification. That experience was essential, not peripheral. Secondly, one can note that the mystical element was almost eradicated under the pressure of the worship of "reason" during bygone centuries. Thirdly, one can imagine that Luther's spiritual experience will be better understood and accepted with greater sympathy during the waning twentieth century's various revolts in the realm of science and religion against the aridity of intellectualism.

The piety of religious experience has, it must be admitted, sometimes resulted in legalism. But we run the risk of throwing out the baby with the bath water if we speak disparagingly about pietistic religion. "Pietism," derived from pietas (devout, God-fearing), has assumed the character of heresy in many of the theologies that now dominate the market. Practically every "mainline" Protestant theological student leaves his or her alma mater with the adjective "pietism" in its bag of forbidden or cursed items. ("Mysticism" is another, "Gnosticism" a third, and, often enough, "Roman Catholic" a fourth negatively toned adjective). But let us not forget that no faith and no true Christian ethic can be kept alive without prayer-filled spirituality, in one word, *pietas*, piety. Arndt, Spener, Francke—pietistic personalities in the history of Lutheranism—considered rightly that they had the experience of grace which Luther called *sapientia experimentalis*. Their piety, and that of many later Lutheran "pietists," lay within, not outside, Luther's opinion of the nature of faith. If mystical theology is, according to Luther, "experience"—that is the grace-filled presence of the gracious God—then, without a doubt, the *pietas* tradition, the nucleus of pietism, coincided with Luther's thought about life in God. But, alas, frightened by the outgrowth of judgmental legalism, the established church instead often chose the other extreme, dogmatic theology that transformed revelatory experience into doctrinal intellectualism.

If you place Luther's spirituality, that is to say, his experience and view of the work of the Holy Spirit in relief, you have thereby in no way made Luther a spokesperson for "emotionalism." Luther used the words *Gefühl* and *fühlen* (feeling and to feel) when he wrote about the accompanying element in the historical faith, namely, "true" or "inner" faith. To him the feeling component was not identical with emotionalism, if one by that term means prescribed, obligatory mental stages in an order of salvation. The feeling of faith was rather an experience of God's comforting presence. This experience was not registrable. As in the case of love, it has no catalog number. But the inner "knowing" established of itself a difference between an authentic—or, as Luther said, a "true"—theologian and an inauthentic one. In this sense the "Enthusiasts" (*Schwärmer*) embraced a false spirituality. They enjoyed psychological emotions in their immersion into God. They trusted in emotions and did not know overly much about the feelings that accompany the church's external symbols of the Spirit's work or about private meditation on the words of the Bible. That feeling, often termed "numinous," is the aura of the birth of humility, whereas the emotional state often becomes the soil for self-righteousness.

The soul's mystical rest in God—as Luther saw it—is the subjective side of the objective symbols. There are theologies that maintain that the history that they tell about and expound is limited to the **objective**, the **ordinary**, and the **public**. Our portrayal, however, emphasizes that the proclamation also must contain the mystical dimension without which one does slight justice to Luther's theological thought. This is to say that the story of Jesus is not simply a drama portrayed in objective terms, presenting ordinary conditions objectively and publicly so that everyone grasps them. When the gospel breaks into human consciousness as a spiritual presence, about which it heretofore had no inkling, it radiates a joy and reverence-filled awe that is experienced **subjectively**. It creates an awareness of the **extraordinary** dimension (that does not respect bio-physical causality) and belongs to the **personal-private** world that is you. It can be expressed this way: Martin Luther's thoughts about God, the Father, the Son, and the Holy Spirit cannot be reduced to mere verbalizations within an ordinary, empirical "common sense" framework, understandable to all, and, in that sense, public.

Yet, the objective and public side of the matter is always a necessary part of a theology of incarnation. Attention has here been drawn to Luther's emphasis on outward signs. But let me say—in the hope that the reader will not be too tired of the repetition—that Luther's thoughts on the justified sinner's situation reflected and counted with a supernatural world, a metaphysical reality beyond history and biophysical existence, experienced as a mystical Christ-presence. The evangelical **promise** of freedom does not possess spiritual meaning without the Lord's **presence**. In each prayer to God and in each response from God, the objective and the subjective are enlivened; ordinary existence is touched tangentially by extraordinary revelation; and, through personal, private impulse, meaning is given to the public face of the kerygma.

Through the mystical experience, including prayer, the non-rational is infused into the rational. It is a necessary theological-logical enterprise to bring a sensible clarity into the aspects around the kerygma of Jesus Christ. But the inspiration for such activity is mysticism and therefore transrational. When one perceives this, one also knows that the criteria of scientific knowledge are insufficient when it comes to theological reflection. As far as I can see, Martin Luther exhorts us to think theologically from spiritual experience as well as with the intellect, or not attempt to think theologically at all. Luther put much emphasis on the "mystical incarnation" and spoke often about the limitation of the historical faith.

Luther's view about God's grace was fired by mystical inklings. Numinous reality gave life to his thoughts, even during those periods when his mind was full of dogmatic controversy and his store of loving understanding was on the decline. "The supernatural" could not be distinguished from "the natural," in his thought-world. "The supernatural" was not a term for "God out there," but rather for an experience of a spiritual dimension, incomprehensible to merely the senses and logic. Let us scrutinize retrospectively another side of Luther's communion with the supersensible and the theological considerations arising therefrom.

It has frequently been pointed out in this book that Luther's numinous perception and his definitive "yes" to the reality of the transcendental cannot, with impunity, be separated from theological reflection. However, many Luther-interpreters have demythologized the Reformer in these respects, in the assumption that Luther shared with others of his epoch certain time-bound ideas regarding the supernatural and their effect on the human psyche. They assumed, and assume, that his thinking mirrored the superstitious folklore of his milieu, conceptions that mankind has abandoned, however, as its dominion over the natural world expanded.

It is true that Luther shared with his contemporaries the lack of knowledge about our physical world and existence that sometimes resulted in what we describe as superstition, which is a non-rational, magic-evoking attitude to the inexplicable. But, under the influence of scientific materialism in "modern" times, most of us in the "developed world" have classified as superstitious belief **all** accounts of visionary, clairaudial, and clairvoyant experiences—as well as dreams and poetical or prophetic inspiration. Such phenomena cannot be measured with conventional methods and are therefore rejected as sources of knowledge. The consequence of this "enlightenment" is that all manifestations of the supernatural in Luther's life and thought have been ignored—regarded only as time-bound superstition.

The same attitude is applied to the gospel. Exceptions must naturally be made. It is generally recognized that the resurrection of Christ—the main event in the history of the church—must have had a historical background and that Christ consequently "lives," at least in the sacraments. These two doctrines are considered essential for a respectable treatment of the gospel. Nevertheless, the two concessions do not, strictly speaking, fit into a theological frame where mystical theology is rejected as part of proper evangelical teaching. Because whatever the drawbacks that might be attached to the use of the adjective "supernatural," it undoubtedly benefits us to have in the musical score the transcendental overtones without which the interpretations of faith land in scientific materialism or skeptical scientism.

In the final analysis, perhaps the supernatural and the natural coincide. However, for pedagogical reasons, we are forced to return to the words "supersensible" and "supernatural" their theological dignity. The words in question testify to the fact that biblical revelation is, in the depth, an invasion from the paranormal into the normal.

The mystic has always known that his awareness of God's presence and power has been inspired by the Holy Spirit who works **for** and **in** the natural world, but also, for this reason, **beyond** man and nature. Luther's words about his closeness to mystics, his reference to mystical incarnation, his feeling of God's presence, and his trust in the power of healing through *Christus mysticus* should not therefore be censored or discarded in the false opinion that the entire supernatural aspect is in the category of medieval superstition. For Luther's statements about these things are reflections of biblical reality and are consonant with prophetic mystical experience throughout the ages.

We have asked whether Luther's terms about the mystical are essentially the same as those of the medieval mystics. Are not the theologians right who take it for granted that Luther's use of mystical terminology only seemingly depended on otherwise unbiblical and unevangelical symbols? The argument from my side against this has been that such a removal from the Lutheran agenda overlooks two circumstances.

First, Luther's way of describing mystical life consisted not only in attacks against the "Enthusiasts." In other words, one can say that theological analyses based on that assumption misconstrue Luther's attitude to the mystical.

Secondly, Luther evaluated mystical experience from within his own spiritual knowledge about how one is "justified" or is "liberated through faith." His instrument for evaluation was directed toward the question of God's taking command in a person's life. When this occurred, one knew it from this fact: the person in question stopped seeking to justify himself.

According to that measurement, one could say that some medieval mystics were more congenial to Luther and others less so. Luther declared openly his inner kinship with those who had tasted bitter sorrow at the reduction of the ego and the great joy, yes, ecstasy at the discovery that Jesus is a friend, is their friend. Luther experienced—like they—the divine presence and he sensed—like many of them—the absence of these feelings with Scholastics in general. He pointed out that justification is **more than** a not guilty verdict in a court proceeding, and he felt at one with mystics in this "more than." Like other mystical leaders, he was persuaded that God-in-Christ was present in such a way that the forgiven sinner could perceive it.

Consequently, Luther's gift of inner discrimination ought to be taken seriously when he confesses his kinship to authors who lived a hundred or more years before him. It is, it seems to me, uncalled-for to censor his positive referrals to mystics and their statements and thereby give some modern research preference in its negative evaluations of the Reformer's own opinions.

We have discussed attempts to place mystics whose experiences were similar to Luther's in theological frameworks that, it is asserted, do violence to the biblical truth about sin and grace. If one reads them in that light, two of Luther's especially good spiritual friends, namely, Tauler and the author of *Theologia Germanica*, do not pass muster. Luther is cordoned off in one theological camp and these mystics placed in another. The word for Luther's camp was "salvation" and the word for the mystics was "self-salvation." But instead of letting our own intellectual yardstick determine the answer, we should acknowledge that Luther really knew what he was talking about. At least, it has not convinced me when theologians, in some contexts and on the basis of rationalistic premises, have declared that Luther's positive evaluations of mystical fellow-pilgrims depended on his limited theological perspective.

That Luther knew whereof he spoke also on the subject of mysticism becomes clear from some sentences of Johann Tauler's lines added here to previously cited Tauler-remarks. They deal with the question of the Savior and the saved. In this quotation it is clear that one does not do justice to all mystics by indiscriminately assigning them to one large classification, which, in this case, Protestant Reformation-interpreters provide with the rubric "self-salvation." Tauler wrote:

> The father of the house is the Lord Jesus Christ. His house is heaven and earth, purgatory and hell. He saw that all of nature was in disorder and that his delightful vineyard lay fallow. The nature of man, who was created in order to possess this orchard, had gone astray . . . Jesus Christ is his Father's heir. We are co-inheritors. The Son has received everything from the Father. The Father has entrusted everything to his hands. . . . Whenever you attribute the divine to yourself, you change the divine to that which is created and darken the divine. (From pages 45 and 49, Georg Hofmann-edition of Tauler's sermons. Translated from the German by the present author.)

Parenthetically, it may be of interest to note that Luther would not have gainsaid Tauler even when he included purgatory in his faith. In his book *Defense of and Explanation to All the Articles* (*WA* 32:95, 1521; *LW* 32:95), Luther wrote that he personally was inclined to accept the belief in purgatory, although there is no "irrefutable" basis for it in the Bible. But the most important in the Tauler excerpt, cited above, is that we find in it both appreciation of God's "objective" deed in Christ and a strong consciousness of man's self-will. It was against such a background that both Luther and Tauler so eloquently described the joy-filled Presence. God is close, nearer than your clothes, yes, nearer than your skin, as Luther expressed it.

To be sure, one hears Neoplatonic strains with Tauler, for instance, about the "ground" of the soul, and Luther was never particularly fond of the kind of speculation about being that is called ontology. But he and Tauler were on the same wavelength when it came to life in God, "the feeling of the heart." They were also of one mind on the question of mysticism's basic paradox (expressed on pages 567 and 594 in the above-mentioned Tauler book): formation in God as growth, as a slow happening, occurs in a never quite ending tension between our nature, as God's creation, hence good, on the one hand, and our nature as rebellious will, hence evil, on the other. The compatibility between Luther and his spiritual kindred spirits among the mystics lies in the **experience** of gracious acceptance of righteousness as personal address *(Zuspruch).* Consequently, the emphasis is more on a Christ who is **in** me or on my resting **in** Christ, than on a Christ who is **for** me and whose vicarious deed I embrace with my intellect. In Luther's situation it was important also to place emphasis on an objective, historical fact that no tradition, nor institution, nor personal feeling, could shake, namely, that Christ suffered, died, and rose again for us. Yet, he added that this can be grasped and understood in the inner sense, only through the encounter of the will and feeling with the living friend and Savior. It was on this point that the encounters with mystics became meaningful and edifying for Luther.

In this book it has been argued that Luther's mystical experience permeated all his life. His later change of terms from the Scholastic *synteresis*, the highest form of knowing-with-God, to *fiducia*, grace-given trust, and his attacks against the Enthusiasts *(Schwärmer)*, mystics who advocated freedom from order, is more a change of tactics rather than reversing his position. Even after having become an "institution" as the unofficial leader of the Reformation and after many disappointments concerning God's possibilities in a person's life, Luther was aware of the power-filled Presence. All through his life Luther incorporated into his faith and thought the potential of the supernatural: angelic and demonic powers and their influence, Christ's mystical presence in Holy Communion, in baptism, and in prayers for protection and healing. It is thus questionable whether his changes in terminology can serve as affirmation for the theory that Luther abandoned the mystical shimmer around *sapientia experimentalis*, the existential God-wisdom, at the time that his mind was increasingly occupied with Reformation tasks. Luther, as a spiritual person, gives us, in fact, very little reason to devote much time to this theory.

The suggestion that mystical, emotional movements could be incorporated into systematic theology has been countered with the objection that certainly these movements are a part of the religious phenomenon, but that they are subjective and are therefore unregistrable. Furthermore, they do not meet the scientific standard of repeatability.

This objection overlooks the indisputable fact that all true revelation is ultimately grounded in data that are extraordinary and cannot be repeated in an identical manner—a standard that so-called exact science requires.

The revelation drama as a supernatural occurrence is the center around which dogma and dogmatics develop. We study our Bible and preach about its message **because of** paranormal events, on the basis of invasions into the physically confirmable and natural. Upon closer reflection we would find that the reason for the attraction which Jesus, Peter, Paul and other spiritual leaders, including Martin Luther, exert on us is precisely the "overtones" from the "beyond," from those dimensions that existed before us, co-exist with us, and will exist when the world of the five senses is gone. If the gospel of Christ and the gospel about Christ were only a recitation of observations that would wholly and fully fit into our ordinary existence—our "common sense"—both the adventure and the comfort would certainly disappear. It is precisely on the basis of these extraordinary, these numinous, these wonder-filled phenomena that our imagination and our longing soar. Even if ordinary spiritual curiosity were the incentive, that in itself would prove the validity of the assertion that the extraordinary, the supersensible, and the parapsychological are bells that call to matins in the gospel's summons to repentance and grace.

In our thinking about revelation we do not do justice to the subject if we exclude mystical incentive. One cannot repeat revelatory experiences in identical fashion. They are not a suitable subjects for precise scientific investigations. But in the theological search for truth they make all the difference. They are flashes of lightning in a dark night; suddenly they illuminate the landscape and disappear just as quickly. But the flash of lightning has allowed the pilgrim to see the lay of the land and how the road winds. The experience is fleeting and isolated and yet decisive for the comprehensive view and the direction to take.

Martin Luther had experiences of a mystical nature. They gave him an inner certainty about the presence of Christ. They occasionally brought him into out-of-body states. He never required such experiences as a condition for a Christian life. He never included them directly in his writings about the Christian faith. We can assure ourselves of this by referring to his Large and his Small Catechism. But experiences of the "Wholly Other" beyond the veil permeated his faith in the reality of God's grace. It was not mere words when he assured his readers that he not only interpreted doctrinal viewpoints but also relayed his experience of the living God. He was not, in the first place, an academic professor but one who spoke from experience, he pointed out (Not least in German Luther-research, Luther is represented as first and foremost a professor, whose main contribution was to systematize theological concepts). "You become a theologian in rapture and ecstasy (*raptus* and *ecstasis*)," he wrote, "that is what makes one a real theologian" (*WA* 3; 372, 23-95, 1513-1516). It is because of the experience of the heart that the dogma of the head comes alive.

In much the same way, although in less intensive cadences, each praying Christian makes the acquaintance of the mystical that charges external symbols with spiritual meaning and miraculously carries us through seemingly insurmountable distress. Most of the time we are hardly aware of the new knowledge. As true Westerners we rapidly explain away those manifestations of mystical presence that touch us. Yet, now at the end of the twentieth century, a sensitiveness toward the "still small voice," like that which reached Elijah's ears after the fire, the earthquake, and the storm, is becoming manifest. More frequently than during recent decades, one is prepared to recognize that "knowledge" also can be gained via non-rational hints.

A revisit with Martin Luther with special regard to his experiences of a spiritual-heavenly presence (in the midst of his often uninhibited earthiness) can count on greater understanding in the era that begins to listen to "drumbeats" from others than those who drum for the mechanistic epoch out of which we now are beginning to move. The new age brings forth more people who are willing to listen to the overtones of the gospel. They are ready to stretch the adventure of faith so that "their hearts may be encouraged as they are knit together in love, to have all the riches of assured understanding and the knowledge of God's mystery, of Christ, in whom are hid all the treasures of wisdom and knowledge"(Col. 2:2-3). There awaits us, namely, as Paul writes, a "knowledge" that grows out of faith and mystery. It surpasses everything and completes that "knowledge" which is limited by logical-causal argument.

At the end of the twentieth century, we are living in a sort of rebellion against the last offshoot of the Enlightenment, a revolution against the rationality that has a mechanistic key signature and has lured many to believe that man is the measure of it all. We see this revolt in many fields of secular research work. Its inner side faces the charismatic within the Christian borders; the outside faces a new, less mechanistic picture of knowledge in the scientific laboratories and centers of thought.

This does not mean to say that Christian evangelization and preaching should be dependent on a sudden change of wind direction in the scientific climate. Despite all, it may be, for example, that the growth of parapsychological insight into life's power and energy will be appropriated by a materialistic world-view (This happened on both sides of the "Iron Curtain," but was probably most conspicuous on the eastern side of it. Such research continues today). But, on the other hand, it is of considerable importance and a challenge to Christian evangelization that psychological, sociological, and philosophical investigations of the nature of the human abandon or step back from Enlightenment's exclusively rationalistic "confession of faith." This was a matter of belief in man's unlimited logical and rational potentialities that would gradually lead evolution from the primitive into a future where logic and sound reason would prevail.

However, in his revolt against this powerful utopia, the "post-modern" man says, paradoxically enough, that one ought to speak about an advance toward the primitive—a resurrection of powers, the annihilation of which one previously considered the prerequisite to becoming a proper human being. The question of the "whole human" is a subject that goes together with the degree of our openness to intuition, inspiration, and beckonings from the invisible, inaudible, transrational, and paranormal worlds. Here we get hints that no human wholeness, individual or social, comes into being without the cooperation of the unconscious and the divine. But, simultaneously, one must apply the inner yardstick about which I John 4:1 speaks: "Beloved, do not believe every spirit, but test the spirits to see whether they are of God."

Poetical, artistic, and prophetic insight has naturally always let it be known that "knowledge" is more than rational compendiums and analyses of external phenomena. However the citizens of the West have been suspicious of this revolutionary idea and considered it a threat against what Luther termed "*gefasste Gedanken*," rationally formulated thoughts.

Now when post-modern man questions the premises of rationalism, it does not mean that our attitude to the extra-ordinary should be "irrational." I have intentionally avoided that word when describing the effects of the invisible. With several of the pneumatically inclined theologians, I say that the non-rational or the transrational flows into the rational. Mystics, as we know, need to speak to their surrounding using "rational" language, even though it might be necessary to qualify that with "more or less rational." Criticism of rationalistic interpretation of the gospel's origin and growth in the world arises when rationalistic treatment of the non-rational becomes dogmatic.

The Swiss psychologist C. G. Jung has opened the door to the future, more spiritually-oriented age through his investigations of the role of the unconscious in our life, not least as it speaks to us in dream-symbols. Jung considered it important to point out that one should always respect generally accepted limits for scientific behavior and stuck as closely as he possibly could to the empirical surface. However, in some contexts, he moved the intellectualistic boundary outward. For instance, he answered a question about his belief in God in the following manner: "I do not believe, I know." Jung proposed that some intuitive knowledge has its origin not in the empirical depth of the self, but rather in worlds beyond the conscious and unconscious. His search pointed toward a scientific psychology liberated from Freudian naturalism. Jung maintained that the only and central drive is neither the sexually colored libido (Freud) nor the drive for power (Adler), but it is the religious impulse—an essential, autonomous force. This cannot simply be deduced from the libido, as Freud has done. In Jung's psychology we encounter a "modern person" who lives in a symbiosis between an objective, sophisticated, reason-bound attitude and a subjective, primitive religious feeling. The latter is by no means obsolete—neither can it, nor ought it, be.

In the field of parapsychology observations have been and are being made which nullify concepts of "reality" that hitherto were considered conclusive for evaluating the paranormal. Extra-sensory perception (ESP) is a term that seemingly contains its own contradiction, but it is increasingly filled with content. Manifestations of the spirit are being investigated as areas that augment our knowledge. In his book, *The Roots of Coincidence*, Arthur Koestler lays out facts that suggest that we cannot justifiably speak about "coincidences" or "chance." He pointed out that parapsychology more and more assumes the character of "science" whereas science more and more assumes the character of the "occult." The mechanical model for our existence, the clockwork model, is on the verge of losing its hold on us. Koestler cited the physicist James Jeans who declared that the universe should no longer be regarded as a machine. The universe, he said, is "a thought."

A biophysical reality resting on and possibly derived from a "reality" which is known as "thought" is a motif, which now is cautiously introduced, in scientific discussions. The mechanical must, in some measure, give way to the intuitive. In surprising ways the idea—"not a machine, but a thought"—sheds new light on long-held, traditional persuasions about the power of prayer and unity in God, which is also a unity in one global and one cosmic body. The study of thoughts as vibrations in an invisible "ether" can perhaps offer empirical proof for the biblical conviction that there is no neutrality. In no time, instantaneously, a thought always finds its goal and makes its mark. Scientific studies of para-sensible layers of life beyond the range and control of the five senses are in the process of liberating Western rationalism from its captivity in quantification of reality. With respect to the sources of knowledge, the climate changes do not occur mainly at theological schools, which one would probably be inclined to think. Instead, these occur in secular fields of research that previously led theology to adopt naturalistic and mechanistic premises that, to such a great extent, have dominated the interpreters of revelation.

The revolt against the "tyranny of reason" also includes our view of creation and the environment. Not only do we become more conscious of the chemical discharges and their destructive impact on air, water and forest, but we also begin to suspect that thoughts influence the physical. Although we once believed that we were dealing with insensitive material, we now discover life and an ability to respond deep within the smallest components. Thought and prayer have their bearing on a surrounding which, superficially seen, is totally lifeless. The emanations in a room for prayer and worship differ totally from the atmosphere in a dance hall, even when both are empty. Something has permeated the walls. Medical science—not so long ago mostly an engineering act for repair of bio-physical units—now speaks about the mind's significance for matters of health and calls the new way of approaching the sick "psychosomatic medicine." One has forgotten that, half a century ago, the ruling circles laughed at the idea.

Some decades ago one might have smiled skeptically and condescendingly at Peter Tomkin's book, *The Secret Life of Plants.* But on the verge of a new century we are prepared to accept the possibility that man operates on different levels simultaneously and therefore, through his consciousness, makes invisible imprints on nature and fellow humans around him. Benedict of Nursia, Francis of Assisi, and Pierre Teilhard de Chardin, representatives for that minority which takes a democratic attitude toward creation, may be the future mentors of those who are kindly disposed toward the environment. But, for now, the predominant belief is that of the Hebrew-Christian majority which regards man as a conqueror of nature around him, an autocratic-monarchical deputy to God, in an otherwise soulless and unfeeling creation.

Sociological research has also been affected by the change in the spiritual climate. As in theological studies, sociology, to the present, has used natural science as its model in its analyses. Hence the ideal has been objective, "value-free" investigations. In like manner, the effort to be objective in much theology has resulted in historicism. Sociology, in its attempts to find the truth by stepping away from the object under investigation, has depicted religious phenomena as projections of anthropological and social conditions. To put it differently, social conditions are seen exclusively as emanations of the material world, as crystallizations of the human ego, and as an object of investigations in which the individual researcher has no investment. One has consciously refrained from counting with two factors in mankind's wrestling with social problems: passion and religion.

During later decades, however, an ever-increasing number of sociologists have found academic neutrality to be insufficient, if one wishes to penetrate the innermost of the societal pathologies of our time. The involvement, the passion, has been allowed to color the investigations to a greater and greater degree. It is increasingly defensible in academia to permit an academic treatise to emerge as a defense of one particular notion or recommendation of a definite line of action, as long as personal bias is conceded. It is reported from recent American conferences of sociologists that the struggles around the question of the correct method have led to a division in two evenly divided camps: the traditionalists, who are of the opinion that all sociology can and must be "disinterested" (observations must be objective), and the activist camp, whose members believe that "passionate engagement" in favor of a certain course of action is legitimate, academically speaking.

Among the sociologists who introduce a religious explanation to the sociological discussion, one finds the American scholar Peter Berger. In his book, *A Rumor of Angels*, he thinks that he can "prove" that certain universal human postures are not only transcendent symbols, but also manifestations of transcendental, supernatural reality. Within the purely empirical he seems to find "prototypical human gestures" which point to a supernatural home: the inclination toward order, the need to play, the will to hope, the desire for justice, and the predisposition to humor.

A deeper view of "knowledge" is also provided by the charismatic revivals. It has raised some eyebrows in traditional Lutheran circles that I have used contemporary charismatics as illustrative of the slow veering toward mysticism and the supersensible. In an unusually biting document by a Lutheran theological professor, my 1976 account of Luther's relation to the mystics was characterized as one single long defense for the mid- and later-twentieth century Pentecostal-like charismatic movement. This was not the case. However, the contribution in question is evidence of the strong displeasure that traditional Lutheranism harbors against emotion-filled Christianity. For my part, I consider both the Catholic and Protestant charismatic movements of the nineteen-seventies a part of the revolt against enslavement to theological concepts as they appear in rationalistic dogmatic preaching. These charismatic currents have perhaps become institutionalized, as often happens with all enthusiastic beginnings. However, these movements are one of several signs that indicate how Western consciousness is beginning to abandon its proud ambition to make reason its God. And these charismatic renewals or religious revivals are one of the proofs that, to the extent that "thinking with the heart" is omitted from Christian commitment and "thinking merely with the head" prevails, a desert is created around our existence.

Present day charismatic experiences can be regarded as transcendental counterpoints to the new discoveries in the field of human transcendence. These experiences of divine address are more than a temporary mania. They confirm that we are called to be channels for the omnipresent Spirit. They help us to see the truth of Jesus' promise of his presence after his resurrection and assurance of aid when we pray in his name. They speak about the Spirit in the present, and they contradict, in a salutary manner, the often-heard dogmatic protest that the gifts of grace, as they are described in I Cor. 12, may have been experienced in the era immediately following Christ's resurrection, but they have little meaning for us in the present age. Many charismatic breakthroughs in the lives of modern Catholics and Protestants have been confirmations of the promise "I am with you always, to the close of the age."

In a biblical-theological encyclopedia (published by Herbert Haag), a writer about spiritual gifts declares that the church is "institutional," not "charismatic." This depicts a traditional view, rather than biblical experience. True, the church is called to serve as God's external medium and as a conveyor of grace through institutional orders: baptism, the Eucharist, and the preaching of the Word. For exactly that reason the church is committing itself to the charismatic power of the Holy Spirit, which is channeled through her media, but the presence and power of the Holy Spirit is not limited to the church's institutional orders.

We are often reminded about this in Luther's words about Christ's or the Spirit's presence during persecutions. An example, chosen at random, is the illustration of a Christian thrown into a cesspool by his tormentors (Luther did not choose such illustrations for insignificant or irrelevant reasons; his very existence was nearly always threatened). In any event, God would not be God, unless he would come to the rescue of the afflicted, right there in the cesspool. If that were not the case, Luther maintained, we must assume that God could reach us and become known to us **only** in the institutional premises, let us say, in a stately cathedral.

Another example comes from Luther's memories of the journey to Worms, 1521, where he was to defend the cause of the gospel before the parliament, which, as expected, declared him an outlaw. The certainty about the calling and presence of Christ made him blissfully unafraid. Even if the devils were as numerous as the roof-tiles on the houses in Worms, Christ was mightily present and he, Luther, would gladly jump into their midst. We can be sure of one thing, namely, that Luther relied on more than an influential memory, a fifteen hundred year old memory or the observance of a sacramental rite. His experience was "charismatic," if with this term one means inner knowledge about Christ and his presence.

I recognize that it is somewhat daring to include modern charismatics into the discussion about "mysticism." Hence another little section on the subject.

The charismatic renewal in some strata of Western Christianity is a symptom of the reaction against the deliberate, emotionless intellectualism that is the distinguishing mark of Western established society. It is also, in certain ways, a reminder of the feeling-tinged spiritual "gifts" in New Testament times. To the extent that charismatic renewal witnesses to Christ's immediate presence, it is a part of what we have described as "mysticism."

This said, we also have to point to the importance of discernment under the tutelage of Christ. Here, as when any "new" institution of spiritual weight is concerned, one has reason to meditate over the passage in I John about the stress one ought to put on inner testing in the name of Christ. The imparting of wisdom and knowledge, the power of healing, the miraculous, prophecy, discrimination of spirits, speaking in tongues and the accompanying interpretation—all of these, in various nuances, are linked to experience of divine presence. But none of these gifts, either innate or granted, has any value in itself unless humility serves as its frame. *Homo mendax*, the mendacious man, the self-aggrandizer and therefore the lying one, stands in ambush everywhere. He pops up even in the most devoted souls, perhaps as pride among theological gurus and ordained preachers and as self-contentment among the so-called "spiritually baptized." Please do not forget, says Paul at the conclusion of his enumeration of all the beautiful spiritual gifts, that **one** gift outshines all the others, love, streaming out God's being as the Father, mediated by the Son, "administered" by the Spirit (I Cor. 12-13).

This Pauline text on the body of Christ casts light on the contemporary interest in the "occult": astrology, extra-sensory perception, spiritualism, research in reincarnation, their meaning and their insufficiency from the perspective of the Christian faith. The same Pauline sermon also radiates a feeling for wise and appropriate latitude in dealing with various forms of charismatic activity: speaking in tongues, healing, the driving out of spirits, and so forth. Incomparable love pours from the heart of the solar system, Christ, whom Luther named "the Sun of Righteousness." "The Baptism of the Holy Spirit," or spiritual baptism, on which certain charismatic groups seem to believe they have a monopoly (especially those who place speaking-in-tongues at the center as the hallmark of salvation) does not concern a particular spiritual gift. Instead, this means that the seeker and supplicant, whether prodigal son or daughter, abundantly receives divine grace and, in a wholly new and decisive way, is granted certainty about his or her path in God. Spiritual baptism is to experience "Christ's births" in the soul, as Luther expressed it. Seen in this way, the work of the Holy Spirit becomes a function of Christ's presence as dynamic power and loving support.

It should not be a source of surprise that egotism rears its head, in one way or another, with those who are gripped by charismatic enthusiasm. The mendacious human within us remains a life-long problem, despite assurance about salvation. The slightest acquaintance with power struggles or dissension in Pentecostal congregations corroborates this observation. But this realism concerning the reality of sin is not a sufficient reason for "outside" Christians to reject the movement. It is, if nothing else, a significant manifestation. Martin Luther, who in truth took seriously the question of the egotistical bent of the soul, reminded his readers and listeners about the Spirit's work in the soul that can be perceived. To Luther, the Creed's third article, which many of us have intellectualized and institutionalized, was a formula for mystical-charismatic awareness. Think of his terms, *raptus* and *ecstasis*, for the encounter with God in prayer and meditation. He would hardly have been surprised at the charismatic gatherings within the Roman Catholic, Protestant, and Anglican churches of the waning twentieth century. Had he known more about Eastern Orthodox sacramental mysticism he would have felt quite at home there, too.

In her book, *Mysticism, Its Meaning and Message*, Georgia Harkness wrote that in our day and age many people are gripped and transformed by a vital experience of God's presence through the Christ whom they worship. This reality ought to be welcomed by every one who, like Luther, seeks and finds the God who is both the *tremendum*, before which we are reduced to nothing, and the *fascinosum*, that makes our spirit soar toward the beyond.

Both as a justification-theologian and as a mystic, Martin Luther has been accused of creating a gulf between religion and ethics. The American theologian Reinhold Niebuhr, among others, blamed Luther for Nazism. The doctrine of justification is supposed to have made a shambles of ethics, according to Niebuhr. Lutheranism's presumed lack of sensitivity to and engagement in societal concerns is blamed on the idea that faith is a purely intellectual notion, a "holding-this-to-be-true."

Because he was spiritually interested in the mystical life in God, Luther has also often been accused of what is popularly considered to be mysticism's greatest shortcoming, quietism—concentration on the contemplative life with the result that the practical-moral disappears from view.

As I hope I have shown in the chapter on Luther's ethics, the attackers are wrong in both instances. Let us concede that Lutheran orthodoxy, with its almost rationalistic emphasis on "objectivity" in matters of salvation in contrast to an emotionally laden sense of salvation, has led to socio-ethical insensitivity in many quarters. But then, at the same time, one must draw attention, for example, to the white Baptists of the American South that for theological and social reasons dissociate themselves from the blacks. We note also the Anglican colonizers' way of looking down on the "natives." The absence of living ethics and, consequently, the lack of social moral responsibility cannot be ascribed only to one theological or ecclesiastical group. It belongs to man's general tendency to build his religion around the interests of his own clan.

Let us also concede that some mysticism has expressed itself in escape from the world. It is perhaps especially true of the sort of mysticism that has been labeled "mysticism of infinity." But to the extent to which Lutheran pietism can be termed mysticism—and I call to mind the sympathy that Lutheran pietists felt for mysticism—to that extent it would be wrong to classify them as "quietists." The European continent's first Christian social contributions in modern times, the work of the inner mission, emanated from the pietists. In addition, Christian foreign missions from Lutheran regions have their beginnings in the circles of Lutheran pietism.

The typical assault against the mystic—that, by definition, he is a non-activist—is reduced to rather insignificant proportions upon closer acquaintance with the lives of mystics. The social work and foreign missions of pietists have just been mentioned. There the mystical encounter with God and the experience of union with Christ are translated into moral, socio-ethical obligations. In the Harkness work cited above, the author asserted that only deceptive theological and historical thinking calculates with a categorical difference between mystics and people who perform practical tasks for others. The following sentences paraphrase some of Harkness' thoughts on this subject. Mystical ecstasy, in the best sense, is found within and not in isolation from the mainstream of human events. The experience can come in visions, illuminations, yes, in a temporary but ecstatic feeling of unity with divinity and still be mysticism. But when the ecstasy radically breaks with our concrete world of reality, be on your guard! In any case, the best proof of ecstasy's reality is that which follows in the individual's daily life within his or her total universe.

In order to prove her point, Harkness devotes a chapter to persons of the twentieth century who did not isolate their mystical experiences from social realities. We meet Frank Laubach, the American missionary, who, after what he had experienced as deep disappointments in his work in the Philippines, felt Christ's presence and took courage again. He initiated a worldwide literacy campaign, "Each One Teach One." Next we meet Toyohiko Kagawa, the Japanese social reformer and labor-union leader. His sympathy for the exploited masses was aroused in mystical contemplation before the cross of Christ. Pierre Teilhard de Chardin is presented. He was a Jesuit and a paleontologist, who acquired his holistic theological view of the world while serving Christ in China. The Swedish General Secretary of the United Nations, Dag Hammarskjöld, is frequently mentioned as a present-day mystic. Hammarskjöld wrote that the mystical experience grants freedom to action and, in our time, the road to sanctification, of necessity, goes through action.

Many others could be added to the list, people that, to some degree, have had a "charismatic" or "mystical" experience have often been called to practical service. As Harkness properly said, "Out of the encounter with the divine arises the challenge to recreate a foundation for a better world."

This was the first objection to the assertion that the mystical grasp on life is irrelevant to the question of ethics. I now come to the second point. It concerns the tendency among Christian ethicists to view discussions of the moral to be correct only as a "rational investigation."

In an often exaggerated respect for run-of-the-mill academic attitudes, which can be described as scientific materialism or "scientism," some prominent moral theologians prefer to tone down many biblical passages in which it is taken for granted that the moral life—out of which ethical reflection grows—is an outflow of the mystical life in God. They undervalue contemplation of God's word and words about the Lord that engender moral power. After such toning down, one is left with generalizing themes, on the assumption, perhaps, that the underlying Bible passages must be known. Behind this method lies presumably a certain fear of being regarded a Biblicist, that is, one who uses the Bible's ethical exhortations as a kind of moral fundamentalism.

I am afraid that this ethical theme-thinking, closely linked to the results of sociological surveys (what the majority does is the basis for the prevailing moral maxim), tends to wipe out the biblical word's mystical character and leads us away from the nimbus, which the previously mentioned ethicist Ellul had rediscovered and called the experience of, and faith in, "miracles." Words in the Bible that speak about Christ radiate this same Christ. Luther spoke about divine words in the Holy Writ as "sacraments." He did this precisely because he had experienced their character as sacramental channels, bridges for divine presence and inspiration. If the analytical task consists only of intellectual efforts to formulate general themes, the analyst easily misses the Presence, which the Word communicates. By the way, that communication occurs straightforwardly and in defiance of form critical and redactionistic opinions of the text.

This is, naturally, not a question of biblical words as rigid principles, unchangeably applicable for all times and for all cultural situations. Biblical writers knew nothing about many of the moral problems and ethical dilemmas of modern times. Regardless of whether our ethics are goal-oriented, duty-determined, aristocratic-perfectionist, or a blend of these methods, they are always molded somewhat by historical circumstances. The latter provides us with **information**. But it is from Christ, by way of words from and about him and through prayer for his presence, that we get **inspiration**. We constantly hear about the poor, the disabled, the homeless, and the exiles. But the inspiration to vicarious deeds and sociopolitical decisions, often unpopular and poorly appreciated, comes from the power of the Cross and our cross bearing. One ought not to expect clear handbook-directives from the biblical word in regard to quite a string of complicated issues belonging to our time. The Bible's eschatological ethics must be translated to the social needs of our times. From this point of view, we are, of course, dealing with "analogies" and "themes" from the Scriptures. But hermeneutics—the interpretation of religious experience and its expression in worship, dogma, and society—grows out of fellowship with Christ, when he speaks to us through his words and through words about him. It becomes a dialogue between non-biblical and biblical sources. As an example of awareness of this kind of reciprocal influence, I want to mention B. C. Birch and Larry Rasmussen, *Bible and Ethics in the Christian Life* and Thomas W. Ogletree, *The Use of the Bible in Christian Ethics*.

The tendency to regard Christian ethics exclusively as a form of rational decision-making obscures for us the biblical experience that Jesus Christ is present in the sacrament and in personal worship. Many ethical expositions on moral questions suffer from precisely such rationalistic anemia. The mystical Christ is not acknowledged. Jesus is described as a model, a paradigm, a norm, a teacher, a principle, and a redeemer. Naturally, He is all of these, but, above all, He is the invisible but present one, in and among his friends. If one makes Christ only an "influential memory," whose legacy and teaching must be adapted to changing times with the aid of gifted intellects, one forgets what Ellul discovered: that Christ is a power and a force that gives both vision and strength for moral tasks, not least those tasks which would place one outside the conventional camp (Be aware that he who has been deeply moved by the moral responsibility of being human, seldom or never is accepted by the majority which follows the law of least resistance and therefore ridicules, persecutes, or even kills the one who threatens their comfort and security or troubles their conscience). In his book, *The Mystery of Being*, Gabriel Marcel (Ellul's fellow-countryman) maintains that we, unfortunately, have limited our epistemology—our thoughts on the nature of "knowledge"—and our opinion of reality to scientists' interpretations of what it is "to know." We have looked upon the world as a **problem** to be solved, where real matter can be touched and tested by the five senses. However, says Marcel, the world may also be viewed as a *mysterium*. We do **not** have the required evidence out there before us. We ourselves are part of the problem, the mystery. The only attitude ought to be **participation** and **communion**. Ethical inspiration arises, in the first place, from contemplation and prayer in the presence and awareness of mystery, not from intellectual reflection as such.

Doubtlessly, with the help of scientific codes of evidence, we must and should adapt our language with the use of terms that are available to the intellect. But statistical tables, and the analyses and the hypotheses based on them, do not lead to moral responsibility and are not the source of moral effort and achievement. The source is the Lord's mystical, inspiring, and life-giving presence.

Can this mystical acquaintance with the supersensible make any real difference? A look at the intimate connection, for practical mystics, between experience of the divine in Christ's name (Luther's manner of speech) and the tasks of this world give us the right to answer positively. The answer can be in the affirmative because the person who is united with the mystical Christ is in contact with a dimension that endows strength for the humanly impossible, instead of being guided entirely by calculating sophistry within the limits of the humanly possible.

In his classic book about Christian ethics, *Christ and Culture*, the American ethicist, H. Richard Niebuhr, gave an intimation concerning this latter truth. Toward the end of his book, he speaks about the origin of moral responsibility as a surd. Surd means "mute" or "voiceless." In mathematics, the word signifies an irrational number. In Greek, this inaccessibility is expressed by the word *alogos*, "wordless." In theological-ethical language, the term conveys that, in the last analysis, we must fall back on the surd, the irrational—or as I have called it here: the transrational. The surd beyond all human calculations is also, humanly speaking, the source of the unrealizable, impossible and, for most people, disturbing. We remold Christian ethics into the art of the humanly possible and, for our own comfort, suitable forgetfulness of the fact that our heroes in the annals of ethics belong to the derided and those rejected by the "average citizen."

We are back to Luther's vision of God, as we meet it in *The Bondage of the Will*. It is, one would think, not quite fair that God would keep in his hands the keys of both the elect and the damned and that he would, hence, know the fate of each individual without letting us know. This, God's "dreadfulness," is a mystical experience. One should not try to solve that riddle with the aid of logic. It is out of this tangential contact with the paradox of eternity that moral engagement grows because, in a singular manner, the experience in question is also bound to compassion—and moral engagement dies without compassion.

When everything seemed to collapse around Jesus and human self-sufficiency—on which we place such great value—failed, he turned in prayer to the heavenly "surd" and received power to carry the moral burden. It is only in this way that the unimaginable happens, and only against this background can one utter the, humanly speaking, senseless words: "For my yoke is easy, and my burden is light." How? Why? On account of the Christ-presence, Christ's power, and the devil's disappointment, as reported by Luther in relation to his arrival at Worms.

Ethics that is based only on cognitive considerations is easily changed into situation ethics, founded on social scientists' information and societal statistics. For instance, the Ten Commandments are described as projections of certain social conditions and are valid for nomads of the desert, but of little value for twentieth century people. They must develop a new ethics. The same holds true of Jesus' words on moral issues; in places where they address concrete circumstances concerning the dividing of property and rules of sexual conduct, they ought to be regarded, at most, as historically interesting projections of a different society—but modern man is forced to write new commandments within the commandment to love.

One contemporary Swedish theologian, Gösta Wrede, in writing about "Faith, experience, and mysticism" speaks of "liberation" as an alternative term for salvation. In statements that are only intellectual-dogmatic, there is no room for liberation. Liberation produces moral incentives, namely, vicarious deeds of service, which reason has difficulty in registering. The liberated is called upon to bear a smaller cross in the blessed shadow of the Large Cross; to turn the other cheek, a mode of behavior one hears a lot about, but which is seldom practiced; go the second mile after having been forced to go the first; continue to give a helping hand even though there is no sign of gratitude. As we said, we continue to theorize about the cross but unwillingly choose the perhaps little liked and cumbersome ethical alternative of private charity or social-moral action.

To complete Christ's completed deed—yes, it must be formulated paradoxically—is an undertaking that can be achieved only through incessant prayer (I Thess. 5:17). And incessant prayer is a mystical undertaking. New visions soar from that. Atmospheres change through it. Strength from incessant prayer supports the moral challenges that surpass all sophisticated summations of the possible.

Power for the cross-bearing life does not come from doctrines of imputed grace or from a conceptual outline of the meaning of revelation, but rather from personal communion with God, from God's living Presence in the sacrament, and from the Holy Spirit.

It was precisely in this sense that Martin Luther spoke about moral fruits emanating from the liberated or justified life. The liberated-justified person's hiddenness in God is the fountainhead of the moral life and hence the beginning of ethical thinking. Luther was persuaded that there was no great difference in the manner in which Christians and non-Christians discharged their daily duties or "used the world." But there is the "greatest possible difference" (See chap. 11). By dint of his "collaboration" with God through prayer and supplication, the Christian becomes a conveyor of moral power from the Almighty in a way that the consciously, or unconsciously, indifferent cannot. This viewpoint of Luther's, as we have seen, is obvious not least in his large commentary on the Epistle to the Galatians. And the power is not less potent and palpable because of its invisibility. Luther constantly stressed the importance of realizing that one who lives by faith must reckon with the world that is *invisibilis*, invisible, and Christ's eternal home.

We touch here the mystery about the grain of wheat that must be planted in the soil and suffer death for the sake of life. In this context we remind the reader of the Reformer's words in his book on John 14-16: A Christian's contemplation and invocation are so essential that "no city or country would ever enjoy peace," and life all around in all its aspects would disintegrate without the uniting and under girding power that Christians draw to this world through their imploring and invocation. I repeat that this could be of comfort for the little flock because in this way its central mission is confirmed. Of course, one can and ought to accept this confirmation without falling for the temptation to become over-confident, without letting the sin of pride get the upper hand.

Others rightly speak about Martin Luther as the renewer of our theological vocabulary, a wordsmith, poet, a musician, a politician, a realist, a Germanic hero, a man of modernistic cut, a down-to-earth, combative anti-saint. He was like a many faceted crystal. In this book we have met him foremost as a spiritual person, living in Christ, longing for Christ's advent in the soul, apprehending God's presence, experiencing God's healing grace.

Our focus on "the mystical Christ" and "the mystical Incarnation" in Luther's testimony has brought us to the central point and the secret in his battle for his own and the church's liberation. Although he, at least on the surface, fought against a clericalism that ossified the message, whereas we fight against a secularism that dissolves it, perhaps we recognize here our own longing after wholeness in God and to be useful among men. What is more, perhaps there is confirmation of our feeling that Christ, in friendship and majesty, is never far from us.

NOTES

Introduction

[1] *W* 40, 1; 289-290 (On Galatians 2:20, 1535). *LW* 26: 171-172. *W* 45; 535-536 (On John 14:12, 1537). LW 24; 82-83. Luther writes that the "unspiritual man cannot understand" what happened to Paul, how Christ took control of his heart "through the Holy Spirit . . . and how He works in everything through the spirit, although the flesh still resists."

[2] *W* 1; 335-345. From two sermons preached on Good Friday, 1518, on Isaiah 53 and Psalm 45.

[3] Gösta Wrede, *En väg till Gud, om Johann Tauler (d.1361), mystiker* [A path to God, about Johann Tauler, mystic] (Stockholm: Katolska teologföreningen) 1981, p. 89 (hereafter cited as Wrede, *En väg* . . .).

[4] *W* 1; 341, 3 (1518). Concerning Luther's expression "mystical theology," see *W* 9; 98, 20 (1516) and *W* 7; 546, 27-29 (1521). *W* 1; 341, 1-3 (1518). Erich Vogelsang treats Luther's Bernard-influenced definition of "mysticism" in "Luther und die Mystik," *Luther-Jahrbuch* XIX (1937): 32-54 (hereafter cited as Vogelsang, "Luther . . ."). The problem treated in this Introduction is also discussed in two articles of mine: "Luther and the Mystical," *The Lutheran Quarterly* XXVI (August 1974): 316-329. Also "On the Relationship between Mystical Faith and Moral Life in Luther´s Thought," [Lutheran Theological Seminary, Gettysburg, PA, USA] *Bulletin* 55 (February 1975): 21-35.

[5] On Melanchthon's "intellectualism," see Holsten Fagerberg, *A New Look at the Lutheran Confessions* (St. Louis; Concordia Publishing House, 1972), pp. 47-48. Also Robert Stupperich, *Melanchthon* (Philadelphia: Westminster Press, 1960), p. 13: Luther was moved by the mystical inwardness of Tauler and *Theologia Germanica* but "we hear of nothing similar from Melanchthon." See also Michael Rogness, *Reformer without Honor* (Minneapolis: Augsburg Publishing House, 1969), p. 138: Melanchthon stressed "imputed righteousness," made justification abstract, and separated justification from sanctification. Erich Vogelsang maintains that what the church lost through Melanchthonian intellectualism was, in a sense, recovered by the nature-mysticism of Goethe and romanticism. In the twentieth century the realities of "mystery," as direct experience of the Divine, "again knock at the doors of the church. Will we receive power both to conquer the mystical errors and the Melanchthonian one-sidedness . . . ?" See Erich Vogelsang, "Die Unio mystica bei Luther," *Archiv fur Religionsgeschichte* XXXV (1938): 80 (hereafter cited as Vogelsang, "Die Unio . . .").

[6] The philosopher-physicist James Jeans wrote: "Today there is a wide measure of agreement . . . that the stream of knowledge is heading toward a non-mechanical reality; the universe begins to look more like a great thought than a great machine. Mind no longer appears as an accidental intruder into the realm of matter: we are beginning to suspect that we ought rather to hail it as the creator and governor of the realm of matter." James Jeans, *The Mysterious Universe* (New York: Macmillan Co., 1932), p. 186.

[7] Rudolph Otto, *The Idea of the Holy*, 2nd ed., trans. John W. Harvey (New York: Oxford University Press, 1960), p. 108 (hereafter cited as Otto, *The Idea . . .).*

Chapter I. About angels as helpers and spoilers

[8] *W* 5; 45, 30-33 (1519-1521).

[9] *W* 5; 3-7, 506, 20-30 (1519-1521).

[10] With Luther one finds many references to Heb. 11:1, all on the theme of the "invisible." Among them are: *W* 3; 498, 27-36 (1513-1515). *LW* 10; 440. *W* 14; 692, 2-6 (1525). *LW* 9, 203. *W* 43; 554, 30-35 (1535-1545). *LW* 5; 183. *W* 44; 377, 33-37 (1535-1545). *LW* 7, 105-106. *W* 44; 700, 19-21 (1535-1545). *LW* 8; 166.

[11] *WB* 1; 224, 13-14 (1518).

[12] *WT* 2; 146, 16-19 (1532).

[13] *WB* 2; 336, 9-10 (1521). *LW* 48; 221. *WB* 2; 357, 18-19, 359, 123-124 (1521).

[14] *WB* 2; 348, 44-48 (1521). *LW* 48; 232.

[15] Johannes Lapaeus, *Doctor Martin Luthers Prophetior* [Doctor Martin Luther's Prophecies] (Söderhamn: Hamberg, 1851), pp. 27-28 (hereafter cited as Lapaeus). In this Swedish translation by Lapaeus from German, the translator reveals his cautious orthodox Lutheran *Sitz im Leben* by footnoting to the Lutheran public's comfort: "The intention is naturally not to claim that Luther, like the Prophets, had immediate inspiration from God's Spirit, he was only indirectly inspired and guided by the same Spirit, even as a Prophet."

[16] On obsession and possession by demonic spirits Luther spoke in his *Table Talks*, *WT* 1; 403-404 (ca. 1530). The relative power of the "bad angels" is described, for instance, in *WT* 2; 386 (1531) and *WT* 6, 120-121. In the latter instance the liberated will is depicted as redeemed from the captivity of extra-terrestrial demonic power.

[17] *WB* 2; 455, 50-54 (From a letter to Elector Fredrick, March 5, 1522).

[18] *W* 8; 177, 13-17 (1521). *WT* 2; 503, 20-24 (1532). *WT* 6; 83, 13-19 (Christ's power over Satan). *W* 4; 597, 26-30 (On guardian angels, 1514-1520).

[19] *WB* 11, 264, 16-19 (From a letter, January 17, 1546).

[20] Emanuel Hirsch, *Das Wesen des reformatorischen Christentums* (Berlin: Walter de Gruyter & Co., 1963), especially pp. 47-65. For a more detailed analysis of Hirsch's theology see Bengt Hoffman, *Luther and the Mystics* (Minneapolis: Augsburg Publishing House, 1976), pp. 48-50, 68-75 (hereafter the former will be cited as Hirsch, and the latter as Hoffman, *Luther*).

[21] Martin Luther, *Ein Predigt von den Engeln* (Wittenberg, 1535). *W* 32; 111-121 (1530). In English: Martin Luther, *On the Angels*. A sermon by Martin Luther of 1530. Trans. by Bengt Hoffman (Gettysburg: Lutheran Theological Seminary Bookstore, 1985).

[22] *Ibid.*

[23] Karl Barth, *Church Dogmatics* (Edinburgh: T & T Clark, 1960-), III, 3; 380, 369, 485, 500, 479 (hereafter cited as Barth).

[24] Ingemar Franck, *Mikaelidagens predikan* [Sermon for St. Michael's Day] (Lund: CWK Gleerups förlag, 1973), pp. 87-89. The reader is also referred to fn. 14 above. The mystics with whom Luther felt kinship spoke of angels in the same manner. See also Bengt Hoffman, trans., *The Theologia Germanica of Martin Luther* (New York: Paulist Press, 1980), pp. 79, 111 (hereafter cited as *Theologia . . .*). *Johann Taulers Predigten*, Georg Hofmann, compiler (Freiburg: Herder, 1961), pp. 519-520 (hereafter cited as *Johann Taulers . . .*).

[25] *W* 38; 358-375 (*Wie man beten soll, für Meister Peter Balbirer*, 1535). Author's translation. See also *LW* 43; 193-211.

[26] *Ibid.*

[27] *Ibid.*

[28] In this and the following quotations Luther speaks about experiences of the demonic. *WT* 6; 209, 20-34. *WT* 5; 87, 16-22, 88, 1-3 (1540).

[29] *WB* 2; 397, 17-21 (1521).

[30] *WT* 6; 204-222.

[31] *W* 10, 3; 9, 15-20 (1522). *LW* 51; 73.

[32] *WT* 1; 399, 25-400, 23 (1530's). *WT* 3; 9-10 (1532). *WT* 4; 254, 36-39 (1539). *WT* 5; 443, 38-444, 1-2. *WT* 6; 203, 32-204, 11. *WT* 4; 85, 8-86, 16 (1538). *WT* 4; 668, 9-10 (1540). *WT* 5; 63, 21-25 (1540). *WT* 5; 211, 27-28 (1542-43). *WT* 5; 552, 1-7 (On angels, n.d.). *WT* 6; 69, 1-12 (On relation to Christ, n.d.). Nathan Söderblom, *Humor och melankoli och andra Lutherstudier* [Humor and melancholy and other Luther studies] (Stockholm: Proprius, 1919 1983) p. 81 (hereafter cited as Söderblom, *Humor . . .*).

[33] Söderblom, *Humor . . .*, p. 366. Söderblom, who cites this conversation, does not provide any documentation. I have not succeeded in tracing the quotation.

[34] John Gottlieb Morris, *Quaint Sayings and Doings concerning Luther* (Philadelphia: Lindsay & Blakiston, 1859), p. 260 (hereafter cited as Morris, *Quaint Sayings . . .*). With reference to the precognition incident: *WT* 1; 74-75, No.157 (1532). *LW* 54; 23.

[35] *LW* 8; ix-x.

Chapter 2. Occultism and spiritual healing

[36] *W* 9; 98, 33-34 (1516). *W* 9; 100, 28-30 (1516).

[37] *WT* 1; 302, 30-35 (1533).

[38] *W* 2; 589, 37-590, 9 (Reference to Gal. 5:20, 1519). *LW* 27; 369. See also *W* 10, 2; 381 (1522). *LW* 43; 17.

[39] *W* 45; 528-530 (1537). *LW* 24; 75-76.

[40] *W* 45; 532-533 (1537). *LW* 24; 79.

[41] *W* 56; 60-61 (1515-1516). *LW* 25; 53.

[42] *W* 7; 337, 14-20 (On Matt. 10:7-8, 1521). *LW* 32; 24. See also Chapter 6, "Participation in God."

[43] *W* 23; 657, 34-658, 3 (1527). *LW* 20; 340. About Christ as the spiritual Sun behind all physical manifestations see also *W* 31, 1; 176, 25-35 (On Psalm 118:24, 1529-1530). *LW* 14, 99. *W* 54; 95, 25-96, 13 (On II Sam. 23: 1-7; Mal. 4:2, 1543). *LW* 15; 347.

[44] *W* 5; 549, 1-9, 548, 5-17 (1519-1521). *LW* 12; 140-141.

[45] *WB* 4, 319, 7-11 (1528).

[46] Dorothy Kerin, *Fulfilling* (London: Hodder & Stoughton, 1969), p. 52.

[47] Heinrich Gelzer, *The Life of Martin Luther and the Reformation in Germany*. Intro. and trans. by Theophilus Stork. (Philadelphia: Lindsay and Blakiston, 1854), pp. 74-75. August Nebe, *Luther as a Spiritual Adviser*, trans. Charles A. Hay and Charles E. Hay (Philadelphia: Lutheran Pub. Soc., 1894), pp. 54-55. (This incident is reported in both books.)

[48] *Ibid.*

[49] M. Michelet, *The Life of Luther*, 2nd. ed. (London: George Bell & Sons, 1878), p. 437.

[50] Morris, *Quaint Sayings* . . . , p.262

[51] Lapaeus, pp. 20-23.

[52] *WB* 11; 112 (1545).

[53] *W* 32; 111-121 (1530). See also chap. 1.

[54] Luke 20:38, Matthew 22:31-32.

Chapter 3. Luther on life after death

[55] *WB* 2; 422, 4-17 (1522). Luther added that he felt the same would apply to the damned: some feel their punishments immediately upon death; others are "separated until that day." *WB* 2; 422, 18-19. Luther's reference: Luke 16:24.

[56] *W* 10, 1, 2; 388, 30-31 (Sermon, the 16th Sunday after Trinity on Luke 7: 11-17, 1526). The previous Luther quote, reflecting an Old Testament concept of life after death as shadowy darkness and complete amnesia, is found in Osmo Tiililä, *Döden och odödligheten* [Death and Immortality] (Helsingfors: Församlingsförbundets Bokförlag, 1964), see especially p. 122.

[57] *W* 45: 494, 21-35 (1537). *LW* 24: 37-38

[58] *W* 45; 19-27 (1537). *LW* 24; 42-43.

[59] *WT* 5; 190-191 (1542). Partly in *LW* 54; 430-432.

[60] Ibid.

[61] *W* 42; 87, 17-18 (1535-1545). *LW* 1; 115.

[62] *W* 57, 3; 215, 8-14 (On Hebrews 9: 23-24, 1517). A similar thought is expressed in *W* 56, 324-328 (1515-1516). *LW* 25; 312-315.

[63] *W* 57, 3; 231 (On Heb. 11:4, 1517). *LW* 29; 233.

[64] *W* 42; 93, 38-39 (1535-1545). *LW* 1; 124-125.

[65] *W* 47; 434, 36-41. *W* 47; 435 (1537-1540).

[66] *W* 42; 556, 1-7 (1535-1545). *LW* 3; 10-11.

[67] *W* 40, 1, 428, 29-30; 429, 1-3 (On Gal. 3:12, 1535). *LW* 26; 274.

[68] *W* 7; 349-350, 451-455 (About purgatory, especially 451, 11-18, 1521). *LW* 32; 31-32, 95-98. *W* 45; 498, 34-499, 4 (About Christ as bridge, on John 14: 5-6, 1537). *LW* 24; 42-43.

[69] *W* 45; 501, 19-21. *W* 45; 502, 1-4 (1537). *LW* 24; 45.

[70] Peter Meinhold, *Die Genesisvorlesung und ihre Herausgeber* (Stuttgart: Verlag von W. Kohlhammer, 1936), pp. 100-103, 392-393 (hereafter cited as Meinhold, *Die Genesisvorlessung* . . .). Luther's lectures on Genesis are found in *W* 42-43. Meinhold suggests that these lectures, having been published in transcribed form, may contain ideas not germane to Luther, especially views on "natural immortality." However, there is sufficient evidence in other contexts to support the suggestion that a belief in immortality was an important component in the Reformer's thought.

[71] *W* 2; 695, 16-38 (1519).

[72] *W* 2; 696, 11-19 (1519).

[73] *W* 2; 696, 24-27 (1519).

[74] *W* 2; 697, 22-24 (1519).
[75] *W* 51; 194, 4-30 (1546). *LW* 51; 391-392 (Some changes in translation by author).

Chapter 4. On God and God in Christ

[76] *W* 17, 1; 437, 3-38 (1525).
[77] *W* 17, 2: 192, 28-31 (1525). *W* 18; 709, 18-22 (1525). *LW* 33; 176. *W* 19; 219, 31-33 (1526). *W* 23; 133, 26-29 (1527).
[78] *W* 40, 1; 287, 8-12 (1535). *LW* 26; 170.
[79] *W* 18; 633, 7-8: "Ut ergo fidei locus sit, opus est, ut omnia creduntur, abscondantur."
[80] Otto, *The Idea . . .*, p. 102.
[81] *W* 57, 3; 185, 1-8 (1517-1518). *LW* 29; 185. *W* 56; 368, 9-31 (On Psalm 69:13, 1515-1516). *LW* 25; 358.
[82] *W* 7, 548, 2, 8-11 (1521). *LW* 21; 300. Birgit Stolt in "Bister, mörk och sammanbiten: den svenska vrångbilden av Martin Luther" [Stern, Dour, and Cheerless: the Distorted Swedish View of Martin Luther], *Svensk Teologisk Kvartalskrift* 66 (1990): 14-22, comments on this Luther interpretation of the Magnificat. Prof. Stolt also quotes from one of Luther's *Table Talks, WT* 1, No. 494 (1533) [*LW* 54; 84], in which Luther gives advice on how to preach on the festival of the Annunciation of Mary: "This day one should preach . . . so that we may rejoice over the incarnation of Christ. . . . Intellectual discussions stand in the way of joy because they bring forth doubts. . . . But a Christian leaves discussions aside and concerns himself with feelings." (Translation by B. Stolt.)
[83] Otto, *The Idea . . .*, pp. 102-108. *W* 40, 3: 27-543, 13 (Comments on Ps. 90:7, 1535). *LW* 13; 110-111.
[84] Wrede, *En väg . . .*, p. 85.
[85] Gösta Wrede, *Unio Mystica:Probleme der Erfahrung bei Johannes Tauler* (Uppsala: Acta Universitatis Upsaliensis, Almqvist & Wiksell, 1974), pp. 81-92 (hereafter cited as Wrede, *Unio . . .*).
[86] Johann Taulers . . . , p. 405.
[87] Wrede, *En väg . . .*, p.87.
[88] Steven E. Ozment, *Homo Spiritualis: A comparative study of the anthropologly of Johannes Tauler, Jean Gerson and Martin Luther (1509-1516) in the context of their theological thought* (Leiden: E. J. Brill, 1969), p. 42 (hereafter cited as Ozment . . .).
[89] See, for example, *Johann Taulers . . .*, pp. 328, 392.
[90] Söderblom, *Humor . . .*, p. 170.
[91] Vogelsang, "Luther . . . ," pp. 32-54.
[92] *Johann Taulers . . .*, p. 45.
[93] *Theologia . . .*, p.107.
[94] *W* 5; 549, 40 (On Psalm 19:7, 1519-1521). *W* 3; 254, 27-29 (1513-1516).
[95] *W* 40, 1; 284, 2, 6-7 (1535). *LW* 26; 167-168. *W* 40, 1; 235, 6-7 (1535). *LW* 26; 134. *W* 40, 1; 290, 10-11 (1535). *LW* 26; 172. *W* 17, 1; 187, 7-9 (1525). *W* 40, 1; 285, 5, 8-23 (1535). *LW* 26; 168-169. See also chap. 6. Compare also with a contemporary mystic: Mary C. Fullerson, *By a New and Living Way* (London: Stuart & Watkins, 1971), p. 39.
[96] *W* 19; 492, 22-493, 28 (Sermon on the Sacrament, 1526).
[97] *W* 3; 479, 16-18 (1513-1516).
[98] *W* 40, 1; 229, 2-6 (1535). *LW* 26; 130.
[99] *WB* 5; 668-669. *WB* 5; 684, 18-21, 685, note 3 (1530).

[100] *W* 2; 501, 34-39 (On Gal. 2:19, 1519). *LW* 27; 234-37. See Erwin Iserloh, "Luther und die Mystik," *The Church, Mysticism, Sanctification and the Natural in Luther's Thought*, Ivar Asheim, ed. (Philadelphia: Fortress, 1967), pp. 75-83 (hereafter cited as Iserloh, "Luther . . . ," *CM*).

[101] Bengt Hägglund, "Luther und die Mystik," *CM*, pp. 89-90 (hereafter cited as Hägglund, "Luther . . . ," *CM*.)

[102] Bengt Hägglund, *The Background of Luther's Doctrine of Justification in Late Medieval Thought* (Philadelphia: Fortress, 1971), pp. 14-16 (hereafter cited as Hägglund, *The Background* . . .). Wilhelm Preger, *Geschichte der deutschen Mystik im Mittelalter* (Leipzig: Dörffling & Franke, 1874-1893), III, pp. 184 ff.

[103] Regarding true worship, see Otto, *The Idea* . . . , p. 108.

Chapter 5. The nature of the human being

[104] *W* 7; 550, 19-551, 27 (1521). *LW* 21; 303-304.

[105] Wrede, *Unio* . . . , pp. 30-33, 153-202. Wrede, *En väg* . . . , pp. 84-85.

[106] *Johann Taulers* . . . , p. 41.

[107] *Theologia* . . . , p. 146: "When something of the perfect Good dawns upon and is revealed to the soul of man, . . . a desire to approach and unite with the perfect Good is engendered in it."

[108] *Johann Taulers* . . . , p. 51.

[109] I am indebted to Bengt Hägglund for these thoughts on Luther's concept of the whole person in relation to Tauler's ideas concerning the concept of the ground of the soul. See Hägglund, "Luther. . . ," *CM*, pp. 90-92.

[110] *WT* 5; 368, 20-36. See also *W* 3; 228-231 (On Psalm 41, 1513-1515). *LW* 10; 190-191.

[111] Otto, *The Idea* . . . , p. 137.

[112] *W* 4; 469. 5-10 (On Psalm 1, 1513-1516). Jared Wicks, *Man Yearning for Grace* (Washington: Corpus Books, 1968), pp. 145-146 (hereafter cited as Wicks, *Man*. . .).

[113] *W* 4; 7-11. *W* 4; 10, 35 (On Psalm 84, 1513-1516). *LW* 11; 162 on Psalm 85:8. See Wicks, *Man* . . . , pp. 74, 273-274.

[114] Herbert Olsson, *Schöpfung, Vernunft und Gesetz in Luthers Theologie*. (Uppsala: Acta Universitatis, 1971), p. 249 (hereafter cited as Olsson). Wrede, *En väg* . . . , pp. 41, 29.

[115] Christian Braw, *Bücher im Staube* (Leiden: E. J. Brill, 1985), pp. 88-82. Wrede, *En väg* . . . , p. 30.

[116] Fredrik Brosché, *Luther on Predestination* (Uppsala: Almqvist & Wiksell, 1978) pp. 30-34 (hereafter cited as Brosché). *W* 44; 549, 14-21 (on Gen. 43, 1535-1545). *LW* 7; 336.

[117] *W* 45; 494, 21-35 (1537). *LW* 24; 37-38.

[118] *Johann Taulers* . . . , pp. 489, 390.

[119] Ozment, pp. 2-4, 8-9, 32-33, 45-46, 202.

[120] *W* 9; 102, 13-14, 34-35 (1516).

[121] *W* 1; 32, 1-6, (1514). See Heiko Oberman, "Simul gemitus et raptus: Luther und die Mystik", *CM*, pp. 57-58 (hereafter cited as Oberman, "Simul . . . ," *CM*). Regarding conscience see also pp. 179-180 and fn. 336.

[122] *W* 1; 36, 15-19 (1514). Oberman, "Simul . . . ," *CM*, p.58.

[123] Oberman, "Simul . . . ," *CM*, p. 56. In Scholasticism *synteresis* was the ground of moral discrimination and *conscientia* its existential application, ordered by the church and often issuing in casuistry.

[124] Hägglund, *The Background* . . . , pp. 7-8.

[125] *WT* 1; 101, 27-37.

[126] The Tauler quotes are from Kurt Ruh, *Altdeutsche Mystik* (Bern: A. Francke, 1950), pp. 50, 52.

[127] Otto, *The Idea* . . . , pp. 139, 144-154.

[128] *W* 40, 1; 268, 12-15 (1535): "Si vis vivere Deo, oportet te omnino mori legi. Hanc doctrina ratio et sapientia humana non capit." *LW* 26; 156. Among an abundance of similar assertions: *W* 34, 2; 152, 18-24 (1531).

[129] *W* 30, 1; 87, 5-7 (1529): "Das ist die Meinung, das ich glauben sol, das ich Gotts geschöpffe bin, das er mir geben hat leib, seel, gesunde Augen, rationem."

[130] *W* 55, 2,1; 113, 1-7 (On Psalm 10, 1513-1515). For further information on Luther's treatment of reason see Karl-Heinz zur Muhlen, "Ratio," pp. 192-265 in *Luther: sol, ratio, erudio, Aristoteles*, ed. Heiko Oberman, Reprint from *Archiv für Religionsgeschichte* XV (1971): 1 (hereafter cited as Oberman, *Luther: sol.* . .).

[131] *W* 18; 719, 20-26 (1525). *LW* 33; 190-191. (Author's translation).

[132] *WT* 5; 368, 20-36. See also fn. 7 above. *W* 45; 14, 7-13, 15, 3-4 (1537). *WT* 2; 374, 17. *W* 39, 1; 108, 5 (1536). "Amitto" in *W* 45; 14 can mean "to let it slip out of your hands." *LW* 34; 194: "to lose." See Gustaf Ljunggren, *Synd och skuld i Luthers teologi* [Sin and Guilt in Luther's Theology] (Stockholm: SKDB, 1928), pp. 110-111 (hereafter cited as Ljunggren). See also Bengt Hägglund, *De homine* (Lund: CWK Gleerup, 1959), pp. 77-91.

[133] Ozment's Luther interpretation is an example of this bifurcation method (see fn. 119 above).

[134] *Johann Taulers* . . . , p. 97.

[135] *W* 57, 3; 153, 8-10 (1517). *LW* 29; 157.

[136] *W* 54; 186, 9. Nathan Söderblom, *Sundar Singhs budskap* [The Message of Sundar Singh] (Stockholm: Hugo Geber, 1923), p. 16.

Chapter 6. Salvation

[137] Bengt Hägglund, *CM*, pp. 92-93, points out that for Luther the Biblical stories were more than metaphors of inner experience. However, he added, it is incorrect to say that Luther and the mystics parted company on the justification issue. Luther felt at one with Tauler and *Theologia Germanica* on this score, despite all dissimilarities.

[138] *W* 18; 719, 20-26 (1525). *LW* 33; 190-191. This previously used reference is found in *The Bondage of the Will*, in which Luther both disparages the possibilities of reason and elevates reason as a seeker of God.

[139] *W* 39, 1; 108, 5 (1536): "By faith you become what you are, *imago Dei*, an image of God."

[140] Olsson, pp. 458-459, 491-492.

[141] *Johann Taulers* . . . , p. 257.

[142] Olsson, pp. 346, 286.

[143] *W* 14; 19, 7 (1523-1524). *W* 22; 336, 30-31 (1537).

[144] *W* 5; 144, 20-21 (1519-1521).

[145] *W* 1; 216, 1-2, 17-18 (1520).

[146] On this subject see Hermann Hering, *Die Mystik Luthers* (Leipzig: J. L. Hinrich, 1879), pp. 171, 175 (hereafter cited as Hering).

[147] *Ibid.*, pp. 19-21.

[148] *Ibid.*, p. 206.

[149] *W* 40, 3; 738, 6-13 (On Is. 53:11, 1544). Also *W* 57, 3; 231, 20 (1517).

[150] Otto, *The Idea* . . . , pp. 102-103.

[151] Johann Taulers . . . , p. 321, sermon 42.

[152] *W* 10, 1, 1; 387, 5-14 (1522). *LW* 52; 107.

[153] Oberman, "Simul . . . ," *CM*, p. 59. *W* 1; 196, 25-26 (1517): "The prayer is that he asks for Christ, the cry [of anguish] that he confesses his wretchedness."

[154] *W* 3; 372, 23-25 (1513-1516). *W* 5; 163, 28-29 (1519-1521). Oberman, "Simul . . . ," *CM*, p. 53.

[155] *W* 3; 372, 23-25 (1513-1516). *W* 1; 336, 10-12 (1518). Oberman, "Simul . . . ," *CM*, p. 53.

[156] *W* 8; 111, 29-35 (1521). Oberman, "Simul . . . ," *CM*, p. 54.

[157] Heiko Oberman refers to *W* 5; 144, 34-36 (1519-1521) and *W* 40, 1; 41, 3-5 (1535), in his analysis of the aspect of passivity in mysticism. Oberman, "Simul . . . ," *CM*. p.55.

[158] *W* 56; 299, 17-300, 8 (1515). *LW* 25; 287-288. *W* 4; 64, 24-65, 6 (1513-1516).

[159] *W* 9; 98, 21-22 (Marginal gloss, Tauler's sermons, 1516).

[160] *W* 11; 117, 35-36 (1523).

[161] *W* 9; 100, 38-399 (1516).

[162] *W* 56; 300, 5-8 (1515). *LW* 25; 287-288.

[163] Karl-August Meissinger, *Der katholische Luther* (München: Leo Lehnen, 1952), p. 126. Quotation from *Resolutiones* on the 25 theses of 1518.

[164] *Johann Taulers* . . . , p. 428, Sermon 55.

[165] *Ibid.*, p. 408, Sermon 55.

[166] *W* 22; 339, 30-31 (1541).

[167] Leif Erikson, *Inhabitatio—Illuminatio—Unio: En studie i Luthers och den äldre lutherdomens teologi* [Inhabitatio—Illumintio—Unio: A study of Luther's and Earlier Lutheran Theology] (Åbo: Åbo Akademi, 1986), p. 27 (hereafter cited as Erikson). *W* 40, 1; 285, 24-286, 17 (1535): "Membra sumus corporis Christi . . . Ita, ut haec fides Christum et me arctius copulet, quam maritus est uxori copulatus."

[168] Erikson, p. 35. *W* 39, 1; 389, 18-390, 5 (1537-1540).

[169] Erikson, pp. 24-25, 31.

[170] From an unpublished letter from Martin Lindström, May 19, 1988, in response to the publication of *Luther and the Mystics* by the current author. Dr. Lindström, bishop emeritus, dogmatician, has translated into Swedish Luther's *Commentary on the Galatians*. (Stockholm: SDKB, 1939). See especially pp. 128, 135. The word "present," used three times on the latter page, is mystical rather than intellectual. *W* 40, 1; 241, 229 (1535).

[171] *W* 40, 3; 738. . . , 6-20 (1544). The same reference is noted in fn. 149 above.

[172] *W* 22; 339, 9-20 (On Matt. 1-14, 1537).

[173] *W* 22; 337, 29-34 (1537).

[174] *W* 7; 54, 31-32 (From *The Freedom of the Christian*, 1520). *LW* 31; 351.

[175] *W* 40, 1; 241, 13-14 (1531-1535). *LW* 26; 137.

[176] *W* 57, 3; 224, 13-15. *LW* 29; 226.

[177] *W* 40, 2; 422, 23-35. *LW* 12; 378

[178] Heinrich Bornkamm, *Luther und Böhme* (Bonn: A. Marcus & E. Webers Verlag, 1925), pp. 234-237. A good source for Luther quotes on bridal mysticism is Friedrich Theofil Ruhland, *Luther und die Brautmystik nach Luthers Schrifttum bis 1521* (Giessen: Münchowsche Universitätsdruckerei, 1938), (hereafter cited as Ruhland).

[179] *W* 3; 212. 29-35. Ruhland, p. 38.

[180] *W* 42; 174, 6-13 (1535-1545). *LW* 1; 233. See Wilhelm Maurer, "Luthers Anschauungen über die Kontinuität der Kirche," *CM*, pp. 94-121 (hereafter cited as Maurer, "Luthers . . . ," *CM*). The Luther reference at this juncture is the *Lectures on Genesis*. Quotations from Luther's Genesis lectures (*W* 42-44) have to be considered against the background that these lectures, and most other commentaries on the Bible by Luther, were edited by friends and followers. For a discussion on the authenticity of comments attributed to Luther, see Meinhold, *Die Genesisvorlesung* . . , pp. 236-256. Citations in the present book from Luther's *Lectures on Genesis,* and other material not edited by Luther himself, are in harmony with thoughts that pervade the Reformer's total production.

[181] *W* 5; 548, 553 (On Psalm 19, second lecture series on the Psalms, 1518-1521).

[182] *W* 7; 597, 10-18 (1521). *LW* 21; 351.

[183] *W* 39, 1; 3, 24-29 (1536).

[184] *W* 39, 1; 166, 4-5 (1536).

[185] *W* 40, 3; 738, 9-10 (1544). On the continuity of the church, see Maurer, "Luther . . . ," *CM*, p. 105. Also Jaroslav Pelikan, "Continuity and Order in Luther's View of Church and Ministry, *A study of De instituendis ministris ecclesiae* of 1523," *CM*, pp. 152-154. Both authors tend to overlook the mystical element in Luther's discussion of the church. "Proclamation" and "vertical dimension of continuity" can and must not exclude the experience of "presence," as is evident in the above cited texts.

[186] *W* 12; 186, 1-8 (1523). *LW* 40; 29.

[187] *W* 43; 388, 5-8 (1535-1545). *LW* 4; 349.

[188] *W* 12; 191, 28-36 (1523). *LW* 40; 37.

[189] *W* 3; 150, 15-26 (1513-1516). *LW* 10; 125.

[190] *W* 3; 254, 24-31 (Author's translation). In *LW* 10; 210 "*Christus mysticus*" is translated as "Christ in a mystical sense."

[191] *W* 56; 379, 1-6 (Lectures on Romans, 1515). *LW* 25; 368.

[192] Iserloh, "Luther . . . ," *CM*, p. 70. *W* 40, 2; 422, 3-5 (1532). This passage from *W* 40 is translated freely in *LW* 12; 377. The *LW* translator omits Luther's word "*sentire*," feel, sense. Perhaps this is a reflection of the intellectual frame of interpretation within which much Western theological speculation takes place. "To feel" is not considered to be a part of "to understand."

[193] Hering, p. 50. *WB* 1; 424, 132-142 (1519).

[194] Hering, p. 52. *WB* 1; 160, 3-28. *Theologia Germanica*'s anonymous author is also frequently called "The Frankfurter."

[195] One should note that medieval mysticism refuted speculative Scholasticism. Leading systematicians often incorrectly assume that there is no difference between mysticism and Scholastic speculation.

[196] Hering, pp. 54-55.

[197] Hering, pp. 257, 259.

[198] *W* 7; 215-216, 218 (1520). Hering, pp. 259-260.

[199] *WB* 2; 425, 22-40 (On Exodus 33:20, 1522). *LW* 48; 366-367. Hering, pp. 67-68.

[200] *W* 4; 265, 30-36 (1513-1516). See Iserloh, "Luther . . . ," *CM*, p. 68.

[201] *W* 57, 3; 144, 10-13 (1517). *LW* 29; 149. Iserloh, "Luther . . . ," *CM* p. 68.

[202] *W* 57, 3; 185, 1-8 (1517). *LW* 29; 185. A modern mystic describes a similar experience: Dorothy Musgrave, *Dorothy Kerin: Called by Christ to Heal* (London: Arnold, Hodder & Stoughton, 1969), p. 20.

[203] *W* 40,1; 360, 5-6 (1555): "Fides creatix deitatis non in persona sed in nobis." *LW* 26; 226-227.

[204] *W* 57, 3; 153, 8-10 (1517). *LW* 29; 157. *W* 4; 273, 14-22 (1513-1516).

[205] *Theologia* . . . , pp. 120-130. *Eine deutsche* . . . , p. 170.

[206] Söderblom, *Humor* . . . , p. 327.

[207] *W* 9; 440, 2-19 (1519-1521).

[208] *W* 9; 440, 9-10: "Thus Christ's words are Sacraments, through which he carries out our salvation."

[209] *W* 12; 171, 17-21 (1523). *LW* 40; 9-19.

[210] *W* 40, 3; 200, 21-23 (1532-1533). This illustrates that Luther thought that the inner, spiritual event lay beneath and behind the outer sign. *W* 40, 3; 199, 2-13 (1532-1533). Compare also *W* 3; 388-389 (1513-1516) and *W* 47; 234-235 (1537-1540). The younger and the older Luther thought alike in this instance.

[211] *W* 40, 1; 251, 9-11 (1535). Wilfred Joest, "Das Heiligungsproblem nach Luthers Schrift 'Wider die himmlischen Propheten'," *CM*, pp. 189-193. About groups that were called "Schwärmer," see G. H. Williams. "German Mysticism in the Polarization of Ethical Behavior in Luther and the Anabaptists," *The Mennonite Quarterly Review* XLVIII (July 1974): 290-291. Oberman, "Simul . . . ," *CM*, pp. 44-45.

[212] Vilmos Vajta, *Luther on Worship* (Philadelphia: Muehlenberg, 1958), p. 186-187. *WB* 8; 625 (1539). *W* 12, 215.

[213] *W* 12; 300, 15-19 (1523). *LW* 30; 45. *W* 7; 546 (1521). *LW* 21; 299. *W* 21; 250, 4-7 (1544). Regarding inner sources for outer signs, see Rudolf Otto, *Die Anschauung vom heiligen Geiste bei Luther, Eine historisch-dogmatische Untersuchung* (Göttingen: Vandenhoeck & Ruprecht, 1898), pp. 60-61.

[214] Martin Luther, *De servo arbitrio*, *W* 18; 623 (1525), trans. by author. Also Martin Luther, *The Bondage of the Will*, trans. J. I. Packer and O. R. Johnston (Westwood, NJ: Fleming H. Revell Company, 1957), p.88. *LW* 33; 47.

[215] Vogelsang, "Luther . . . ," pp. 52-53. Vogelsang writes that Luther conceived of the Word both as mystical *generatio* [the process of bringing into being] and "the oral word of the Gospel," whereas the mystics had only the former. It is difficult to see how this allegation can be substantiated as a general judgment. The references in the text are to *Theologia* . . . , pp. 74-75 (chap. 12), p. 91 (chap. 23), pp. 92-93 (chap. 24), p. 135 (chap. 46). *Johann Taulers* . . . , pp. 358-359.

[216] Johann Tauler, *The Inner Way*, ed. A. W. Hutton (London: Methuen & Co., n.d.), p.178.

[217] See, e.g., *W* 19; 219, 31-32 (1526). *W* 23; 133, 29-30 (1527). *LW* 37; 57.

[218] See, e.g., *W* 4; 32, 3-5 (1513-1516).

[219] *W* 9; 69, 36-37 (1510-1511).

[220] *W* 1; 219, 34-36 (1517). *W* 18; 529, 17-18 (1525). *LW* 14; 204. Author's translation.

[221] Vogelsang, "*Die Unio* . . . ," pp. 63-66.

[222] *W* 7; 25-26 (1520). Iserloh, "Luther . . . ," *CM*, pp. 71-75. The passage used by Iserloh in his German article is found in an English translation by Bertram Lee Woolf, *Reformation Writings of Martin Luther, Vol I, The Basis of the Protestant Reformation* (London: Lutterworth Press, 1952), pp. 363-364. It is that translation that is used here.

[223] *W* 56; 343, 18-23 (1515). *LW* 25; 332.

[224] *W* 2; 145-152, esp. 145, 14-21 (1519).

[225] *W* 40, 1; 285, 24-27 (1535). *LW* 26; 168. E. Iserloh, "Luther . . . ," *CM*, p. 73.

[226] *W* 40, 1; 417, 12-40, 418, 1-9 (1535). *LW* 26; 266-267. Peter Manns, "Absolute and Incarnate Faith — Luther on Justification in the Galatians' Commentary of 1531-1535," Jared Wicks, ed., *Catholic Scholars Dialogue With Luther* (Chicago: Loyola University Press, 1970), pp. 154-156 (hereafter cited as Wicks, *Catholic* . . .).

[227] *W* 4; 11, 9-11 (1513-1516). Wicks, *Man* . . . , p. 75.

[228] *W* 5; 548, 5-8, 14-17, 549, 6-9 (1519-1521). About Christ as the "Sun," see Werner Bohleber, pp. 177-191, in Oberman, *Luther: sol*. . .

[229] *W* 4; 599, 21-23 (1514-1520).

[230] *W* 39, 1; 204, 12-13 (1537). *W* 14; 19, 1-7 (1523-1524). *W* 22; 336, 24-31 (1537). *W* 5; 144, 20 (1519-1521). *W* 4; 305, 31-34 (1513-1516). *W* 40, 3; 200, 21-23 (1532-1533): "Ideo crux est medium, quo Deus nos exerceri . . . vult, ut quotidie magis ac magis purificemur." *W* 54; 95, 29-96, 13 (1543): II Sam. 23:17. *LW* 15; 347.

[231] *Die Predigten Taulers aus der Engelberger und der Freiburger Handschrift*, ed. Ferdinand Vetter (Berlin: Weidmannsche Buchhandlung, 1910), p. 348 (hereafter cited as Tauler, *Die Predigten* . . .). *W* 9; 103, 40 (1510-1511).

[232] *W* 1; 436, 18-20 (1518). Oberman, *Luther: sol* . . . , pp. 258-259.

[233] Otto, *The Idea* . . . , p. 206. Gal. 2:20: "I have been crucified with Christ; it is no longer I who live, but Christ who lives in me; and the life I now live in the flesh I live by faith in the Son of God, who loved me and gave himself for me." 1Cor. 6:17: "But he who is united to the Lord becomes one spirit with him." See J. Arndt, *True Christianity* (Philadelphia: The Lutheran Bookstore, 1868), p. 14.

[234] Otto, *The Idea* . . . , p. 206.

[235] *Ibid.*, pp. 96-98. As pointed out, "the numinous consciousness" should be seen as the background to the statements about the unfree will in *The Bondage of the Will.* See also chap. 9.

Chapter 7. Traditional confessional views

[236] Erikson, pp. 37-45. A representative passage: *W* 40, 1; 142, 13-22.

[237] Abraham Calovious, *Hypomnemata* (Wittenberg, 1664), Section III. Calovius, whose family name was Kalau, assumed this Latin name. In English he is also referred to as Calov.

[238] In his works on the Reformation, Karl Holl, German theologian and scholar, frequently indicated that he saw no fundamental difference between the medieval mystics and the medieval Scholastics. As we shall see, the evidence in many cases leads to the opposite conclusion. Medieval mystics often openly looked askance at Scholastics.

[239] *Grundtlicher Beweis, dass die Calvinische Irthumb* . . . (Wittenberg, 1664), p. 109.

[240] *Ibid.*, pp. 674-675.

[241] *Ibid.*, pp. 712, 715

[242] *Ibid.*, pp. 721-722.

[243] *Die Religion in Geschichte und Gegenwart* I, 1587 (hereafter cited as *RGG*), "Calov, Abraham," by F. Lau. "Calovius equated faith and the doctrinal formula."

[244] Heinrich Schmid, *The Doctrinal Theology of the Evangelical Lutheran Church*, trans. and ed. by Charles A. Hay and Henry E. Jacobs (Minneapolis: Augsburg Publishing House, 1899, 1961), pp.21-38.

[245] *Ibid.*, pp. 480-486.

[246] Vogelsang, "Die Unio . . . ," pp. 63-64.

[247] Erikson, pp. 41-42.

[248] Schmid, p. 355.
[249] Ernst Luthardt, *Kompendium der Dogmatik* (Leipzig: Dürffling & Franke, 1865, 1900), p. 44.
[250] *Ibid.*, pp. 263, 268.
[251] Franz Pieper and J.T. Muller, *Christliche Dogmatik,* (St. Louis: Mussouri Synod, 1946), pp. 58-63. *W* 23; 28, 12-14 (1527).
[252] *Ibid.* See also *W* 34, 2; 527, 25-32 (1531).
[253] *Ibid.*, pp. 63-65.

Chapter 8. Liberal and Neo-orthodox views

[254] This refers to theological systems which attempted to mediate between Christ and culture, spoke of Christianity as an incentive for potential human development, and in more or less qualified terms reckoned with man's goodness. Neo-orthodoxy showed less optimism with respect to human nature but accepted the theory of knowledge of Biblical criticism. Among the group of so-called mediation-theologians we find Dorner, Rothe, Neander and Martensen. Ritschl belongs in part to this school. These thinkers had little understanding for "mysticism." However one might have thought that Schleiermacher would have shown interest. That was not the case. See Friedrich Schleiermacher, *The Christian Faith*, 2 vols., ed. by H. R. Mackintosh and J. S. Stewart (Edinburgh: T & T Clark, 1960), vol. 1, pp. 170-184, 425-431.
[255] Robert F. Davidson, *Rudolf Otto's Interpretation of Religion* (Princeton University Press, 1947), p. 42.
[256] Albrecht Ritschl, *The Christian Doctrine of Justification and Reconciliation*, trans. by H. R. Mackintosh and A. B. Macaulay (Clifton, N.J.: Reference Book Publishers, Inc., 1966), pp. 98, 112-13, 180-183.
[257] *RGG*, III: 433, "Holl, Karl," by Ernst Wolf.
[258] Holl, Karl. *What did Luther Understand by Religion*? eds. James Luther Adams and Walter F. Bense, trans. Fred W. Meuser and Walter R. Wietzke (Philadelphia: Fortress Press, 1977), pp. 27-29 (hereafter cited as Holl, *What*. . .).
[259] *Ibid.*
[260] *Ibid.*, pp. 37-38.
[261] *Ibid.*, pp. 26-27.
[262] *Ibid.*, p. 29.
[263] *Ibid.*, pp. 40-41.
[264] On Luther and Gerson see Hering, p. 9. On Luther's reference to Gerson as regards *Anfechtung*, see *WT* 1; 495, 26-43 (1530's).
[265] Holl, *What* . . . , pp. 53-54. Holl cited Luther from *W* 40, 1; 371, 13-372, 1 (1535). (*W* 40 is not cited in the English ed.)
[266] *W* 10, 1, 2: 388, 29-30 (1526).
[267] *Johann Taulers* . . . , pp. 361, 364.
[268] *Ibid.*, p. 321.
[269] Holl, *What* . . . , p. 68-69.
[270] *Johann Taulers* . . . , pp. 329. *Ibid.*, p. 405
[271] *Ibid.*, p. 41.
[272] *W* 9; 102, 10-14 (1516). Holl, *What* . . . , pp. 68-69.
[273] *Theologia* . . . , pp. 61-62, 67-68.
[274] Holl, *What* . . . , pp. 35-37.

[275] *Johann Taulers . . .*, pp. 403. See also pp. 124, 161, 178-179, 442. *Theologia . . .*, pp. 99, 100, 112-114. See also chapters 24, 25, 26 and 29 about mysticism's ethical teaching.

[276] *W* 45; 535 (1538). *LW* 24; 82.7-24.

[277] Holl, *What . . .*, pp. 49-52.

[278] *Johann Taulers . . .*, p. 209. *Theologia . . .*, p.90.

[279] Holl, *What . . .*, p. 91.

[280] *Johann Taulers . . .*, pp. 392, 344. *Theologia . . .*, pp. 112-114, 120-122.

[281] Holl, *What . . .*, 90-92. Holl's reference is *W* 14; 467, 20-23, 468, 1 (1523-1524). Also, pp., 96-97 and *W* 2; 754, 9-18 (1519). *LW* 35; 67-73. (On *Bruderschaften* [brotherhood].)

[282] Hoffman, *Luther . . .*, pp. 45-100.

[283] Erich Seeberg, *Grundzüge der Theologie Luthers* (Stuttgart: W. Kohlhammer Verlag, 1940), pp. 147-148 (hereafter cited as Seeberg, *Grundzüge . . .*).

[284] *Ibid.*, pp. 32, 33, 210.

[285] Hirsch, pp. 55-56, 53, 64-65, 67, 140, 87. References in that order.

[286] Heinrich Bornkamm, *Protestantismus und Mystik* (Giessen: A. Töpfelmann, 1934), pp. 13-14, 15-16 (hereafter cited as Bornkamm, *Protestantismus . . .*).

[287] Johann Tauler, *The Inner Way*, ed. Arthur Wollaston Hutton (London: Methuen & Co., 1900), p. 147. *Johann Taulers . . .*, p. 321.

[288] *W* 40, 3; 738, 4-36 (1544): An excellent interpretation of Is. 53:11 about faith as "historical," accepted also of the devil, and faith as *agnitio experimentalis*, "knowledge of the heart."

[289] *W* 40, 1; 285, 5 (1531). *LW* 26; 168. *W* 40, 3; 542, 31 (1534-1535). *LW* 13; 110.

[290] *Johann Taulers . . .*, pp. 403, 210, 519-520, 489, in that order.

[291] Heinrich Bornkamm, *Luthers geistige Welt* (Lüneburg: Heliand-Verlag, 1947), pp. 262-263. Bornkamm seemed preoccupied with the notion of the Gospel's "virility." Heinrich Bornkamm, *Luther's World of Thought*, tr. Martin H. Bertram (St. Louis: Concordia Publishing House, 1958). Bertramm's translation is not based on the original, as stated, but on the second edition of the book, *Luthers geistige Welt*, published by C. Bertelsmann, 1953. The passages referred to in our text are to be found in a chapter entitled "Luther and the German spirit" and contained in the original published by Heliand, 1947. This chapter is not found in Bertram's translation.

[292] *RGG*, IV, pp. 487-88, "Luther," by Heinrich Bornkamm.

[293] Gerhard Ebeling, *Evangelische Evangelienauslegung* (München: Lempp, 1942), pp. 157-158. See also Gerhard Ebeling, *Luther: An Introduction to His Thought*, trans. R. A. Wilson (Philadelphia: Fortress Press, 1970), pp. 21ff., 226 ff., 230, 256 (hereafter cited as Ebeling, *Luther . . .*). The only "recent critical work" which Ebeling used as an authority is H. Boehmer, *Der junge Luther* (Gotha, 1929).

[294] Oberman, "Simul . . . ," *CM*, pp. 37-38. Luther scholar Bernd Moeller contributed the statistical research that contradicts Ebeling.

[295] Hägglund, "Luther . . . ," *CM*, p. 86. Reference is made to O. Scheel who declared that Luther "erroneously" expressed dependence on Tauler. In the Foreword to the Swedish trans. of Holl's Gesammelte . . . (*Luthers etiska åskådning*, Uppsala: SKSF, 1928) on p. 5, A. Nygren wrote: "Luther's opinion . . . is irrelevant."

[296] *W* 1; 557, 33-558, 4 (1518). *LW* 31; 129.

[297] Ebeling, *Luther . . .*, p. 230.

[298] *W* 56; 299, 23-27 (1515). *LW* 25; 287.

[299] Ebeling, *Luther* . . . , p. 230.

[300] *W* 56; 299, 27-28-300, 8 (1515). *LW* 25; 287. See also footnote on p. 287 of *LW* 25.

[301] *W* 40, 1; 603-604 (1531). *LW* 26; 396-401.

[302] Barth, IV, 4; 15. IV, 3, 2; 540-541. IV, 4; 11. IV, 1; 337. IV, 1; 629. IV, 2; 360-361. IV, 1; 287, 31-32, 295. IV, 2; 11. IV, 1; 628-629. IV, 1; 103-105: "A feeling of enjoyable musing on God can—one should not be a too fanatic antimystic—be considered an element of the activity which love of God sets in motion (Barth)." References in that order.

[303] Reinhold Niebuhr, *The Nature and Destiny of Man*, 2 vols. (London: Nisbet & Co., 1941-1943), 1: 15, 17, 62-65, 84, 125, 218-19. 2: 25-26, 116-117, 187-198, 278.

[304] Bengt Hägglund discusses the question helpfully in "Luther die Mystik," *CM*, pp. 85-86. The problem is described as an alleged "uniformity" of all mysticism and a presumed "basic thought" behind all mystic writings.

[305] *RGG*, III, 79.

[306] Adolf Harnack, *History of Dogma*, Vol. I-VII. (Boston: Little, Brown, and Co., 1899, Trans. by Neil Buchanan from the third German ed.), VI: 97; VII: 181, 185-86, 210, 197-98, 182-83; VI: 102-105; VII: 181. References in that order.

[307] W 4; 265, 23-26 (1513-1516): On ecstasy, and being beyond oneself. W 40, 1; 591, 31-592, 11-15 (1531). LW 26; 389 (153): On the unspeakable sighs.

[308] Harnack, VI: 108.

[309] Holl, *What* . . . , pp. 41-46.

[310] *Ibid.*, pp. 41-43.

[311] Seeberg, *Grundzüge* . . . , pp. 31-32. On Luther's spiritual "method" see Luther's *Wie man beten soll: Eine einfältige Weise zu beten, für einen guten Freund* [How to Pray, A Simple Way to Pray for a Good Friend]. This was written at the middle of the 1530's (far removed from "young Luther's mysticism). It is found in *W* 38; 358-375 (1535). *LW* 43, 193-211. (Also noted in fn. 25, Chap. 1.)

[312] Hirsch, pp. 29-32, 39, 47. *W* 32, 111-121 (1530). Hirsch, pp. 39-48-49. Citations in that order.

[313] Heinrich Bornkamm, *Mystik, Spiritualismus und die Anfänge des Pietismus im Luthertum* (Giessen: A. Töpfelmann, 1926), pp. 5-9.

[314] Heinrich Bornkamm, *Luther und Böhme* (Bonn: A. Marcus & E. Webers Verlag, 1925), pp. 231-237. Bornkamm pointed out that there are "immediate lines from Böhme's Christ-mysticism to Luther." He remarked that Luther in his treatise on Christian freedom used expressions like "the soul unites with Christ like a bride with her bridegroom" (*W* 7: 25-28) and "by faith . . . Christ is born by" us.

[315] Bornkamm, *Luthers geistige* . . . , p. 263. Not translated in *Luther's World of Thought*, see fn. 291 above. The tendency toward absolute distinction between the Catholic-mystical and the Lutheran-evangelical is visible already in *Luther and Böhme*, p. 231 where Albrecht Ritschl's verdict is accepted.

[316] Bornkamm, *Protestantismus* . . . , pp. 7-10.

[317] *Ibid.*, 263: "Evangelical truth." "Protestant faith calls this [mysticism's] interpretation . . . untruth" (p. 8). "The plausible immediacy of mysticism is an untruth" (p. 15). The claim that Luther experienced the divine "immediately, . . . this . . . is fraud" (p. 12).

[318] Bornkamm, *Luthers geistige* . . . , p. 93. ET: p. 95.

[319] *Ibid.*, p. 264. This passage is not found in the Eng. version(See fn. 291 above).

[320] Ebeling, *Luther* . . . , p. 39. Luther's comment on the miracle of conversion: *W* 54; 185, 14-15 (1545). *LW* 34; 336.

[321] Ebeling, *Luther* . . . , pp. 24-26. "We wish . . . to try to push forward to the foundation from which they [the separate facts or thoughts] emerge." (Author's translation).

[322] *Ibid.*, pp. 21-24.

[323] *Ibid.*, pp. 33, 34, 32. Luther's words on experiences which create a theologian: *WT* 1, 16,13, 1531. *LW* 54; 7.

[324] *Ebeling, Luther* . . . , pp. 33-34. "Luther is like a musical instrument, which combines the tenderest and the loudest registers. Only a trained ear can do justice to the tonal modulation."

[325] *Ibid.*, pp. 226-227.

[326] *W* 10, 3; 348, 9-15 (1522). *LW* 51; 112. *W* 40, 1; 280-283, esp., 283, 14-32 (1535). *LW* 26; 165-67.

[327] *W* 5; 165, 21-23 (1519-1521).

[328] *W* 2; 501, 34-502, 4 (1519).

[329] *W* 3; 117, 30-32 (1513-1516). *W* 7; 574, 24-32 (1521). *LW* 21; 328.

[330] Ebeling, *Luther* . . . , p. 260. Cf. ibid., p. 262: Luther's theology of the cross confirms every true religious experience, according to Ebeling. "This is existential theology."

[331] *W* 56; 306, 26-307, 15 (1515-1516). *LW* 25; 293-294.

[332] Ebeling, *Luther* . . . , pp. 256, 260.

[333] *Ibid.*, pp. 258-259.

[334] *W* 18; 614, 22-26 (1525): "This I assert on the contrary, and you will surely agree, that God's mercy alone moves [activates] all and that our will moves [activates] nothing but rather surrenders" (Author's translation). Luther added that, if this were not so, "the totality" would not be ascribed to God. *LW* 33; 35.

[335] *W* 7; 20-31 (1520) [German version]. *W* 7; 49-73 (1520) [Latin version]: From section 29: "The good things we have from God should flow from one to the other and be common to all, so that everyone should 'put on' his neighbor and so conduct himself toward him as if he himself were in the other's place." *LW* 31; 371: This is to say, heartfelt trust in God transforms man into an acting person. He acts in the face of God because he is activated, moved by God.

[336] Ebeling, *Luther* . . . , p. 262. About *synteresis*, see Chap. 5, The Nature of the Human Being. A distinction should be made between *synteresis*, the conscience as an image of God, and *conscientia,* conscience as the seat of ethical norms.

[337] *Ibid.* Ebeling says that Luther's words about the conscience may suggest that he had in mind actual, inner, mental, psychological change. However, this is only apparently so, Ebeling holds. Luther is merely taking the existential pulse at the points of friction between God and the world.

[338] *W* 3; 479, 17 ff. (1513-1516). *LW* 10; 418-419.

[339] *W* 39, 1; 204, 12 (1537).

[340] *W* 40, 1; 360, 5 (1531): "Fides est creatrix deitatis non in persona sed in nobis." *LW* 26; 226-227.

[341] Ebeling, *Luther* . . . , p. 262. On p. 303 in the original, Ebeling wrote: "Gott und Welt müssen zusammengedacht werden." The English translation lessens the force of the original's perception of Luther's theological existence as primarily a conceptualization process.

[342] Ozment, p. 4, p. 9: "Our study will compare the anthropology of Tauler, Gerson and Luther within the full systematic context of their thought."

[343] *Ibid.*, p. 8-9, 45-46, 202.

[344] *Ibid.*, p. 4. *WT* 1; 101, 27-33 (1532): Luther on God's power and essence (*potentialiter and substantialiter*) in each creature, a significant statement in the discussion about salvation. Ozment's account seems overly logical at this point.

[345] Ozment, pp. 30-34. On Luther's spiritual friendship with Tauler, see *W* 1; 557,29, 1518, where Luther says: "In Tauler I have found more true theology than in all the university doctors lumped together." *Johann Taulers* . . . , pp. 405, 321, *Ibid.*, 542, *Ibid.*, 110.

[346] Ozment, p. 199. *Ibid.*, p. 202 passim, *Ibid.* Preface.

[347] Walter von Loewenich, *Luther's Theology of the Cross*, 5th ed. (Minneapolis: Augsburg Publishing House, 1976), pp. 217, 222.

Chapter 9. If one counts with the Spirit: the pneumatic school

[348] Ernst Benz, *Die Vision* (Stuttgart: Ernst Klett, 1969), pp. 639-40.

[349] Rudolf Otto, *Naturalism and Religion,* trans. J. Arthur Thomson and Margaret R. Thomson (London: Williams & Norgate, 1907), pp. 1-16, 23-24.

[350] Harry McSorley, *Luther: Right or Wrong?* An ecumenical-theological study of Luther's major work, *The Bondage of the Will* (Minneapolis: Augsburg, and New York: Newman Press, 1969), pp. 217-273, a chapter entitled "Luther's early reaction: from *Liberum Arbitrium* to *Servum Arbitrium*." Note esp. p. 218: "What follows is a sketch of his evolution from a doctrine of *liberum arbitrium* to one of *servum arbitrium*."

[351] *Ibid.*, pp. 222-229. Luther is quoted as saying in his *Lectures on the Epistle to the Romans*: "The gift of Christ was not due to any merits of human nature. . . . Nevertheless there had to be a preparation and disposition in order to receive him . . . ." It is rightly said that ". . . God infallibly gives grace to the man who does what he is able to do. . . ."

[352] *Ibid.*, pp. 250, 221, 21, 254-260.

[353] *Ibid.*, pp. 21, 247, 348-49, 352, 250. McSorley: Luther's "terminology is poor and misleading for he does not adequately distinguish between two realities . . . acquired freedom and natural freedom. . . ."

[354] *Ibid.*, pp. 14-15. McSorley quotes H. Bandt: "One must remember that . . . the intention of his [Luther's] sentences frequently do not unequivocally coincide with their naked, logical-grammatical sense. . . . Hence one has to examine in Luther's writings whether . . . he really desires to say what on first blush he seems to be saying." McSorley declares: "We seek to discover Luther's genuine intention by doing more — not less — intensive historical research."

[355] Otto, *The Idea* . . . , pp. 96-97.

[356] *Ibid.*, pp. 90-91, 98-100.

[357] *Ibid.*, p. 103.

[358] Harry J. McSorley, "Erasmus versus Luther—Compounding the Reformation Tragedy," Jared Wicks, ed. *Catholic Scholars Dialogue With Luther* (Chicago: Loyola University Press, 1970), p. 115 (hereafter cited as *Catholic Scholars* . . .).

[359] Otto, *The Idea* . . . , pp. 103-104.

[360] Brosché, pp. 60-63, 207.

[361] Vogelsang, "Luther. . . ," p. 34. *W* 56; 299, 25-300, 1-4 (1515). *LW* 25; 287. *W* 4; 64, 27-30 and *W* 4; 65, 1-3: On Psalm 91, 1513-1516.

[362] Vogelsang, "Luther . . . ," p. 35-38. *W* 5; 163, 17-29 (1519-1521).

[363] Nathan Söderblom, *The Nature of Revelation*, Authorized English trans. by Frederic E. Pamp of *Uppenbarelsereligion*, 2nd ed., 1930 (New York: Oxford University Press, 1933), pp. 89-102. Söderblom's terms in Swedish for the two types of mysticism are: *oändlighetsmystik* and *personlighetsmystik*. Dr. Yngve Brilioth, a scholar and a native of Sweden, translated these terms slightly differently from F. Pamp, namely, "mysticism of the infinite" and "mysticism of personal life." Hans Åkerberg, whose work is discussed next and who has published in both English and Swedish, used the English translations of Y. Brilioth. Consequently, both translations are found in this text when they appear in direct quotations; however, Pamp's translation more accurately conveys the meaning of Söderblom's terms.

[364] Ibid.

[365] Nathan Söderblom, *Humor och melankoli och andra Lutherstudier* (1919), Ed. and Intro. by Hjalmar Sundén (Stockholm: Proprius förlag, 1983), pp. 88-89 (hereafter cited as Söderblom, *Humor*...).

[366] Nathan Söderblom, "Tre livsformer" (1922) in *Till mystikens belysning*, ed. by Hans Åkerberg (Lund: Studentlitteratur, 1975), pp. 236-249.

[367] Hans Åkerberg, *Omvändelse och kamp. En empirisk religionspsykologisk undersökning av den unge Nathan Söderbloms religiösa utveckling 1866-1894* (Lund: Studentlitteratur, 1975), pp. 218-219. See also fn. 363 above.

[368] Hans Åkerberg, "Oändlighetsmystik och personlighetsmystik. Till belysning av premisser och möjligheter i Nathan Söderbloms mystikdistinktion." (Uppsala: *Nathan Söderblom-sällskapets årsbok*, 1981), p. 64.

[369] Hans Åkerberg, "On the Comparability of Religio-Psychological Data," pp. 129-172 in Olof Pettersson and Hans Åkerberg, *Interpreting Religious Phenomena: Studies With Reference to the Phenomenology of Religion* (Stockholm: Almqvist & Wiksell; Atlantic Highlands, New Jersey, USA: Humanities Press, 1981), pp. 162-163, 168-172 (hereafter cited as Åkerberg, *Interpreting*. . .). Åkerberg had found that my analysis in *Luther and the Mystics* (1976) of the literature on Luther and the "experts" usual dismissal of mystics, had much to be said for it. Yet, he suggested that my account lacked "a suitable instrument for a more precise definition of the place of the mystical elements in Luther's religiosity." Thanks to Hans Åkerberg's observation I introduced more directly Söderblom's distinction both in the Introduction to my translation of *Theologia Germanica* and in this present work.

[370] Hans Åkerberg, "Luther och mystiken. Några religionspsykologiska och systematisk-teologiska anteckningar," *Svensk Teologisk Kvartalskrift* LIX (1983):114-117.

[371] Hans Åkerberg, *Tillvaron och religionen. Psykologiska studier kring personlighet och mystik* (Stockholm: Almqvist & Wiksell International, 1985), pp. 213-216, 219-220.

[372] Hans Hof, *Scintilla Animae: eine Studie zu einem Grundbegriff in Meister Eckharts Philosophie, mit besonderer Berücksichtigung des Verhältnisses der Eckhartschen Philosophie zur neuplatonischen und thomistischen Anschauung* (Lund: C.W.K. Gleerup, 1952), p. 125. Reiner Schürmann, *Meister Eckhart, Mystic and Philosopher* (Bloomington: Indiana University Press, 1978), pp. 159-160, 62, 26, 219. References in that order.

[373] Harnack, VII: 182-86, 210; VI: 98-99: "If Mysticism is withdrawn from the Catholic Church and set down as 'Protestant,' then Catholicism is emptied of its character, and evangelical faith becomes deteriorated." References in this order.

[374] Holl, *What* . . . , pp. 41-42.
[375] Söderblom, *Humor* . . . , p. 186.
[376] Ljunggren, p. 45.
[377] Bornkamm, *Luthers geistige* . . . , p. 263. Bornkamm, *Protestantimus* . . . , p. 8.
[378] Ebeling, *Luther* . . . , pp. 21, 256, 262. "Still with borrowings from the language of mysticism." — "Seeming internalization and spiritualization." pp. 226-227; p. 24; pp. 41-42. *W* 54; 185, 14-186, 16 (1545): On Luther's spiritual illumination. Ebeling, *Evangelische* . . . , p. 158. References in this order.
[379] Wilfred Joest, *Ontologie der Person bei Luther* (Göttingen: Vandenhoeck & Ruprecht, 1967), p. 91. Olsson, pp. 561-562. The mystical presence often seems to escape the conceptualization process of Protestant theology. The contention with respect to a time boundary also loses its plausibility when we compare Luther's mystical Christology with the profound Christology of *Theologia Germanica*; pp. 100-101, 132, 143. Do we face only concepts that supersede one another, or themes that pervade?
[380] Otto, *The Idea* . . . , pp. 97-98.
[381] Vogelsang, "Luther . . . ," p. 52. Luther quotes are from *W* 18; 479 ff.: "But Christ is himself there, in the same way as the rays of the sun . . . are not found . . . where there is no sun." *W* 18; 529, 12-18. Vogelsang, "Luther . . . ," p. 38. Luther on Bernard: *W* 3; 640, 40 (1514). Also *W* 43; 581, 11-21 (1542).
[382] Iserloh, "Luther . . . ," *CM*, pp. 60-62. Luther's words in *W* 10, 1,1; 728, 14-16 (1522): "It is a limitless word and wants to be grasped in a serene spirit. No one but such a still contemplating soul can understand it anyhow." (Author's translation) A comparison between Ebeling's logical conceptual method and Iserloh's pneumatic interpretation is instructive if one wishes to study the question of what theological "knowledge" is. Due to lack of space only a suggestion can be given here. Cf. Ebeling, *Luther* . . . , p. 260.
[383] Oberman, "Simul . . . ," CM, pp. 34-38, 53-54. Luther references in the Oberman essay: *W* 9; 98, 20-34 (1516). *W* 4; 650, 5-15 (1514-1520): On Mary and Martha. *W* 43; 72, 9-14, 22-28 and 72, 31-73, 9 (1535-1545). *LW* 3; 275-277. (References in that order).
[384] Vogelsang, "Luther . . . ," pp. 32-33, 49. Åkerberg, *Interpreting* . . . , p.162. In Ruhland, we have an analysis of Luther's use of bride-bridegroom symbolism up to 1521. This mystical imagery is shown to have been an integral part of Luther's theology up to that time. In "Luther und die Mystik" in *CM*, pp. 60-83, esp. p. 73, Erwin Iserloh maintains that Luther employed the same notion of mystical unity and the same imagery throughout his life. Oberman, "Simul . . . ," *CM*, pp. 24-28, 30-33. On p. 24 Oberman by and large rejects Vogelsang's attempt to apply a strict chronology and says that, although Vogelsang's contributions to a necessary typology of mysticism are of lasting value, his chronological distinctions must be questioned, as well as his classification of individual mystics. Without naming any theologians, Oberman questions the assertion that Luther's interest for the mystical path terminated, for example, in 1519-1520. Oberman believes that throughout his life Luther kept his faith in mystical experience. One comes to think of Ebeling who took the opposite position that was that "later critical judgments show . . . a temporal (chronological) borderline in Luther's development." (See Ebeling, *Evangelische* . . . , p. 158.)
[385] *W* 9; 98, 33-34 (on the temptation of Lucifer (1516). *W* 2; 493, 12 (Commentary on the Galatians regarding justification, 1519). *W* 4: 647, 19-21 (1514-1520): On Christ as the ladder to God. *W* 6; 562, 8-10 (1520): On the destructive, false mystical Platonic theology and on Christ as *scala*, our ladder to God. *W* 16; 144, 3 (1523): "Ipse descendit et paravit scalam." (He himself [Christ] descended and

prepared the ladder). *W* 57, 3; 114-115 (1517). *W* 2; 501, 34-37 (1519): Christ as example and sacrament. *LW* 27; 238.

[386] Oberman, "Simul . . . ," *CM*, p. 24. Vogelsang, "Luther . . . ," pp. 49-50. Vogelsang, "Die Unio . . . ," pp. 63-80, including criticism of Ritschl, Holl, Barth, H. Bornkamm, E. Brunner for their lack of understanding for the significance of the mystical for Luther. "'The ecstatic love' of older mysticism" is replaced by "ecstatic faith" for Luther. See also Ruhland, pp. 136, 138 regarding Bornkamm's expression "The temptations of Romanic mysticism." *W* 4: 401, 25-30 (1513-1516): On our inability to embrace Christ entirely.

[387] *Theologia . . .* , p. 54: On Luther's understanding of the Frankfurter. *WB* 1; 79, 58-63 (Luther to Spalatin about Tauler, 1516). About "faith" and "love" as interchangeable see Vogelsang, "Die Unio . . . ," p. 70.

Chapter 10
Evangelical versus Roman Catholic: Critique of an antithetical approach

[388] See Chapter 8 regarding orthodox and liberal rationalism. Otto, *The Idea . . .* , pp. 206, 202, 204-205, 102. Vogelsang, "Luther . . . ," pp. 38-43. References in that order.

[389] See also Chapter 9 for comments about other aspects of McSorley's book.

[390] Wicks, *Man . . .* , pp. 8, 11, 271-273. Wicks, *Luther and His Spiritual Legacy* (Wilmington, Delaware: Michael Glazier, 1983) p. 88. Wicks, *Man . . .* , pp. 152, 332: on Wicks' rejection of a rationalistic interpretation of Luther's conception of sanctification. *W* 56; 279, 22, 1515 (quoted by the criticized theologian H. Hübner), and *W* 56; 279, 24-25 and *W* 56; 280, 2 (quoted by Wicks as refutation), p. 280. The texts are cited in this order.

[391] As an example of ecumenical interpretations of a less fruitful type, I refer the reader to the Danish theologian Regin Prenter, *Spiritus Creator: Luther's Concept of the Holy Spirit* (Philadelphia: Fortress Press, 1953), p. 16: *Luther* thought "theologically" to the virtual exclusion of the "anthropological" and his thinking was (like the purported thrust of Prenter's investigation) "biblical" and "realistic" instead of "metaphysical" and "supernatural." The Roman Catholic Louis Bouyer, *Orthodox Spirituality and Protestant and Anglican Spirituality* (London: Burns & Oates, 1969) deplored the dogmatic polarization and the Protestant caricatures of Catholic teaching of grace. However, largely influenced by Anders Nygren's theology, he accepted the judgment that "forensic justification by faith" made Luther immune to the thought of Christ living in the soul. Regarding Lutheran-Catholic dogmatic dialogues see Paul C. Empie and T. Austin Murphy, eds., *Lutherans and Catholics in Dialogue, I - III* (Minneapolis: Augsburg Publishing House, 1965) concerning the Nicene creed, baptism and the Eucharist, and IV (New York: LWF-USA, 1970) concerning the Eucharist and the priesthood. On the Lutheran response to the dogmatics of the World Council of Churches see Michael Seils, *Lutheran Convergence?* (Geneva: LWF, 1988), especially pp. 165-166. Re Jonathan Edwards see Robert Jenson, *America's Theologian* (Oxford: Oxford University Press, 1988), pp. 65-68. References in that order.

Chapter 11. Mysticism and ethics: their relation for Luther

[392] Anders Nygren, Foreword to Karl Holl, *Luthers etiska åskådning* (Uppsala: SKS, 1928), p. 5.

[393] Hägglund, "Luther . . . ," *CM*, pp. 93-94. Hägglund, *The Background* . . . , pp. 9,14.

[394] *W* 45; 542, 23-26 (1537). *LW* 24; 90. *W* 45; 560, 21-28 (1537). *LW* 24; 109-110. *W* 45; 537, 25-26, 539 (1537): From Luther's Commentary on John 14-16. *LW* 24; 85-87. References in that order.

[395] *W* 45; 594-596 (On John 14:21, 1537). *LW* 24; 146-147. *W* 45; 597-598 (1537). *LW* 24; 149. *W* 45; 590 (1537). *LW* 24; 142-143. *W* 45; 591 (On John 14:20, 1537). *LW* 24; 142-143. References in that order.

[396] *W* 40,1; 289-290 (On Gal. 2:20, 1535). *LW* 26; 171-172. *W* 45; 672 (1537). *LW* 24; 231.

[397] *W* 45; 688-689, 21-30 (On John 15: 10-12, 1537). *LW* 24; 249-250. *W* 40, 1; 266, 15-19 (On Gal. 2:19, 1535). *LW* 26; 155. *W* 40, 2; 37, 15-30 (On Gal 5:6, 1535). *LW* 27; 30. Peter Manns, "Absolute and Incarnate Faith — Luther on Justification in the Galatians' Commentary 1531-1535," in *Catholic Scholars* . . . , pp. 153-156.

[398] *W* 45; 649, 15-650, 21 (On John 15:2, 1537). *LW* 24; 206-208. *W* 45; 672 (1537). *LW* 24; 231. *W* 45; 693-694 (On John 15:13-14, 1537). *LW* 24; 254.

[399] *W* 40,1; 270, 14-27 (On Gal. 2:19, 1535). *LW* 26; 157-158. *W* 40, 1; 540-542 (On Gal. 3:27, 1535). *LW* 26, 352-353. *W* 10,1,1;11 (1522). *W* 39; 1, 527, 1-4 (1538). *W* 2; 501, 34-37 (On Gal. 2:20, 1519). *LW* 27; 238.

[400] *W* 3: 433, 2-4 (On Psalm 69:16, 1513-1516). *W* 45; 531, 23 to 532, 24 and 535, 27 to 536, 29 (1537): Luther discusses John 14:12, which reads, in part: "he who believes in me will also do the works that I do; . . .". *LW* 24;77–86.

[401] Mary McDermott Shideler, "The Man for Others and the Man for God," in *The Christian Century*, April 10, 1968, pp. 448-451. An excellent analysis of dependency on intellectual arguments and a moral program that excludes reference to spiritual life in God.

[402] Jacques Ellul, *Hope in Time of Abandonment* (New York: Seabury Press, 1973), pp. vii-x.

BIBLIOGRAPHY

BOOKS

Åkerberg, Hans. *Omvändelse och kamp. En empirisk religionspsykologisk undersökning av den unge Nathan Söderbloms religiösa utveckling 1866-1894*. Lund: Studentlitteratur, 1975.

———. *Tillvaron och religionen. Psykologiska studier kring personlighet och mystik.* Stockholm: Almqvist & Wiksell, 1985.

Aland, Kurt. *Hilfsbuch zum Lutherstudium*. Gütersloh: Bertelsmann, 1957.

Archiv für Reformationsgeschichte. Gütersloh: Bertelsmann, 1951.

Arndt, Johannes. *Förklaring över Catechismum*. Åbo, 1728.

———. *True Christianity*. Philadelphia: Lutheran Bookstore, 1868.

———. *Vier Bucher vom wahren Christentum*. Berlin: Trowitsch & Sohn, 1831.

Asheim, Ivar, ed. *The Church, Mysticism, Sanctification and the Natural in Luther's Thought*. Philadelphia: Fortress, 1967. *(CM)*

Barth, Karl. *Church Dogmatics*, 4 vols. Edinburgh: T. & T. Clark, 1960-1969.

Benz, Ernst. *Der Heilige Geist in Amerika*. Düsseldorf-Köln: Eugen Diederichs, 1970.

———. *Die Vision, Erfahrungsformen und Bilderwert*. Stuttgart: Ernst Klett, 1969.

Benz, Ernst, and Zander, L. A. *Evangelisches und orthodoxes in Begegnung und Auseinandersetzung*. Hamburg: Agentur des Rauben Hauses, 1952.

Berger, Peter L. *A Rumor of Angels*. New York: Doubleday, 1969.

Billing, Einar. *Ett bidrag till frågan om Luthers religiösa och teologiska utvecklingsgång*. Uppsala: Akademiska Bokhandeln, 1917.

Birch B. C. and Rasmussen L. L. *Bible and Ethics in the Christian Life*. Minneapolis: Augsburg Publishing House, 1976.

Boeke, R. *Divinatie, met name bij Rudolf Otto*. Leiden: F. Dijkstra, 1957.

Bornkamm, Heinrich. *Luther und Böhme*. Bonn: A. Marcus & E. Webers Verlag, 1925.

———. *Luthers geistige Welt*. Lüneburg: Heliand-Verlag, 1947.

———. *Luther's World of Thought*. Translated by Martin H. Bertram. St. Louis: Concordia, 1958.

———. *Mystik, Spiritualismus und die Anfange des Pietismus im Luthertum*. Giessen: A.Töpfelmann, 1926.

———. *Protestantimus und Mystik*. Giessen: A. Topfelmann, 1934.

———, ed. *Imago Dei. Beiträge zur theologischen Antropologie*. Giessen: A. Töpfelmann, 1932.

Bouyer, Louis. *Orthodox Spirituality and Protestant and Anglican Spirituality*. Translated by Barbara Wall. London: Burns & Oates, 1969.

Braw, Christian. *Bücher im Staube: Die Theologie Johann Arndts in ihrem Verhältnis zur Mystik*. Leiden: E.J. Brill, 1985.

Brosché, Fredrik. *Luther on Predestination: The Antinomy and the Unity between Love and Wrath in Luther's Concept of God*. Uppsala: Almqvist & Wiksell, 1978.

Calovius, Abraham. *Hypomnemata*. Wittenberg, 1664.

Davidson, Robert F. *Rudolf Otto's Interpretation of Religion*. Princeton: Princeton University Press, 1947.
Eine deutsche Theologie. Edited by Joseph Bernhart. Leipzig: Im Insel-Verlag, 1922.
Eyn deutsch Theologia. Edited by Martin Luther. Wittenberg 1518. See also Hoffman, Bengt R.
Ebeling, Gerhard. *Evangelische Evangelienauslegung*. München: Lempp, 1942.
____. *Luther: An Introduction to His Thought*. Translated by R. A. Wilson. Philadelphia: Fortress, 1970.
Eckhart, Meister. *Deutsche Predigten und Traktate*. Edited by Joseph Quint. München: Hauser, 1955.
Edsman, Carl-Martin. *Mystiker i Vällingby*. Stockholm: Sveriges Radios förlag, 1968.
Ellul, Jacques. *Hope in Time of Abandonment*. Translated by C. E. Hopkin. New York: Seabury Press, 1973.
Empie, Paul C. and Murphy, T. Austin, Editors. *Lutherans and Catholics in Dialogue*, I-III. Minneapolis: Augsburg Publishing House, 1965. IV. New York: LWF-USA, 1970.
Erikson, Leif. *Inhabitatio—Illuminatio—Unio: En studie i Luthers och den äldre lutherdomens teologi*. Åbo: Åbo Akademi Foundation, 1986.

Fagerberg, Holsten. *A New Look at the Lutheran Confessions*. Translated by Gene J. Lund. St. Louis: Concordia, 1972.
Filthaut, E., ed. *Johannes Tauler: ein deutscher Mystiker*. Essen: Hans Driewer, 1961.
Forster, Karl, ed. *Wandlungen des Lutherbildes*. Wurzburg: Echter-Verlag, 1966.
Förster, Th. *Luthers Wartburgsjahr. Schriften für das deutsche Volk*, XXV. Halle: Max Niemeyer, 1895.
Franck, Ingemar. *Mikaelidagens predikan*. Lund: C.W.K. Gleerups förlag, 1973.
Franzen, August, ed. *Um Reform und Reformation*. Münster: Aschendorff, 1968.
Fullerson, Mary C. *By a New and Living Way*. London: Stuart & Watkins, 1971.

Gelzer, Heinrich. *The Life of Martin Luther, and the Reformation in Germany*. Translated and Introduction by Theophilus Stork. Philadelphia: Lindsay & Blakiston, 1854.
Goertz, H.-J. *Innere und äussere Ordnung in der Theologie Thomas Müntzers*. Leiden: E.J. Brill, 1967.
Grundtlicher Beweis, dass die Calvinische Irthumb . . . Wittenberg, 1664.

Haag, Herbert, ed. *Bibel-Lexikon*. Zurich: Benziger Verlag Einsiedeln, 1956.
Haas, Alois. *Nim din Selbes war, Zum Selbstverständnis der Mystiker*. Freiburg: Universitätsverlag, 1971.
Hägglund, Bengt. *De homine. Människouppfattningen i äldre luthersk tradition*. Lund: C.W.K. Gleerups, 1959.
____. *The Background of Luther's Doctrine of Justification in Late Medieval Theology*. Philadelphia: Fortress, 1971.
Harkness, Georgia. *Mysticism: its Meaning and Message*. Nashville: Abingdon, 1973.
Harnack, Adolf. *History of Dogma*, I-VII. Translated by Neil Buchanan from the 3rd German edition. Boston: Little, Brown, and Company, 1899.
Hering, Hermann. *Die Mystik Luthers*. Leipzig: J.L. Hinrich, 1879.

Hirsch, Emanuel. *Das Wesen des reformatorischen Christentums*. Berlin: Walter de Gruyter & Co., 1963.
Hof, Hans. *Scintilla animae. Eine Studie zu einem Grundbegriff in Meister Echharts Philosophie, mit besonderer Beruchsichtigung des Verhältnisses der Eckhartschen Philosophie zur neuplatonischen und thomistischen Anschauung*. Lund: C.W.K. Gleerup, 1952.
Hoffman, Bengt R. *Luther and the Mystics: A re-examination of Luther's spiritual experience and his relationship to the mystics*. Minneapolis: Augsburg Publishing House, 1976.
_____. Translator of and Introduction to *The Theologia Germanica of Martin Luther (1518), The Classics of Western Spirituality Series*. Ramsey, N.J., USA: Paulist Press, 1980.
Holl, Karl. *Luthers etiska åskådning*. Stockholm. SKS, 1928.
_____. *What did Luther Understand by Religion?* Edited by James Luther Adams and Walter F. Bense. Translated by Fred W. Meuser and Walter R. Wietzke. Philadelphia: Fortress Press, 1977.

Inge, William Ralph. *Christian Ethics and Modern Problems*. London: G.P. Putnam's Sons, 1932.

Jeans, James. *The Mysterious Universe*. New York: Macmillan, 1932.
Jenson, Robert W. *America's Theologian: A Recommendation of Jonathan Edwards*. Oxford: Oxford University Press, 1988.
Joest, Wilfried. *Ontologie der Person bei Luther*. Göttingen: Vandenhoeck & Ruprecht, 1967.
Jung, Carl G. *The Portable Jung*. Edited by Joseph Campbell. New York: Penguin Books, 1982.

Kerin, Dorothy. *Fulfilling*. London: Hodder & Stoughton, 1969.
Koestler, Arthur. *The Roots of Coincidence*. London: Hutchinson & Co., 1972.

Lapaeus, Johannes. *Doctor Martin Luthers Prophetior*. Söderhamn: Hamberg, 1851.
Ljunggren, Gustaf. *Synd och skuld i Luthers teologi*. Stockholm: SKDB, 1928.
Loewenich, Walther von. *Luther's Theology of the Cross*, 5th ed. Translated by Herbert J. A. Bouman. Minneapolis: Augsburg Publishing House, 1976.
Löfgren, David. *Die Theologie der Schöpfung bei Luther*. Göttingen: Vandenhoeck & Ruprecht, 1960.
Luthardt, Ernst. *Kompendium der Dogmatik*. Leipzig: Dürffling & Franke, 1865, 1900.
Luther-Jahrbuch. Amsterdam: John Benjamins N.V., 1967.
Luther, Martin. *D. Martin Luthers Werke, Gesamtausgabe*. Weimarausgabe, Vols. 1 - 58. Weimar: Hermann Bohlaus, 1883-1989. (*W*)
_____. *D. Martin Luthers Werke*. Weimarausgabe. Briefwechsel, Vols. 1-14. Weimar: Hermann Bohlaus, 1930-1970. (*WB*)
_____. *D. Martin Luthers Werke*. Weimarausgabe. Tischreden, Vols. 1-6. Weimar: Hermann Bohlaus 1912-1921 (*WT*).
_____. *Ein Predigt von den Engeln*. Wittenberg,1535.
_____. *Luther's Works*, Edited by H. T. Lehmann and J. Pelikan, Vols. 1-54. St. Louis and Philadelphia: Concordia och Fortress, 1955-1986 (*LW*).
_____. *Ob man vor dem Sterben fliehen möge*. Wittenberg, 1527.
_____. *On the Angels*. A sermon by Martin Luther of 1530 (*W* 32; 111 -121). Translated

by Bengt Hoffman. Gettysburg, Pa., USA: Lutheran Theological Seminary Bookstore, 1985.
_____. *The Bondage of the Will.* Translated by J. I. Packer and O. R. Johnston. Westwood, NJ:Fleming H. Revell Company, 1957.
_____. *The Freedom of a Christian.* Translated by W. A. Lambert, Revised by Harold J. Grimm. *Luther's Works, Vol. 31*; Philadelphia: Muhlenberg Press, 1957; reprint, Muhlenberg Press, 1960.
_____. *Stora Galaterbrevskommentaren.* Translated and Introduction by Martin Lindström. Stockholm:
SKD, 1939.
_____. *Wie man beten soll; für Meister Peter Balbirer.* Wittenberg, 1535.

McSorley, Harry J. *Luther: Right or Wrong? An ecumenical-theological study of Luther's major work, The Bondage of the Will.* Minneapolis: Augsburg, 1969, and New York: Newman, 1969.
Marcel, Gabriel. *The Mystery of Being.* Translated by René Hague. London: Harwill Press, 1951.
Martin, Alfred v., ed. *Luther in ökumenischer Sicht. Von evangelischen und katolischen Mitarbeitern.* Stuttgart: Fr. Frommanns Verlag, 1929.
Meinhold, Peter. *Die Genesisvorlesung Luthers und ihre Herausgeber.* Stuttgart: Verlag von W. Kohlhammer, 1936.
Meissinger, Karl-August. *Der Katholische Luther.* München: Leo Lehnen,1952.
Michelet, M. *The Life of Luther*, 2nd ed. Translated by William Hazlitt. London: George Bell and Sons, 1878.
Mieth, Dietmar. *Die einheit von Vita Activa und Vita Contemplativa in den deutschen Predigten und Traktaten Meister Eckharts und bei Johannes Tauler.* Regensburg: Friedrich Pustet, 1969.
Morris, John Gottlieb. *Quaint Sayings and Doings concerning Luther.* Philadelphia: Lindsay & Blakiston, 1859.
Muschig, Walter. *Die Mystik in der Schweiz.* Frauenfeld : Huber & Co., 1935.

Nebe, August. *Luther as Spiritual Adviser.* Translated by Charles A. Hay and Charles E. Hay. Philadelphia: Lutheran Publication Society, 1894.
Niebuhr, H. Richard. *Christ and Culture.* New York. Harper & Brothers, 1956.
Niebuhr, Reinhold. *The Nature and Destiny of Man*, Vols. I & II. London: Nisbet & Co., 1941-1943.

Oberman, Heiko, ed. *Luther: sol, ratio, erudio, Aristoteles.* Archiv für Begriffsgeschichte, Vol. XV, 1. Bonn: Bouvier-Grundmann, 1971.
Ogletree, Thomas W. *The Use of the Bible in Christian Ethics.* Philadelphia: Fortress, 1983.
Olsson, Herbert. *Schöpfung, Vernunft und Gesetz in Luthers Theologie.* Uppsala: Acta Universitatis,1971.
Osiander, Andreas. *Ein Disputation von der Rechtfiertigung.* Königsberg, 1551.
Otto, Rudolf. *Aufsätze das Numinose betreffend.* Stuttgart: F. A. Perthes,1923.
_____. *Die Anschauung vom Heiligen Geiste bei Luther.* Gottingen: Vandenhoeck & Ruprecht, 1898.
_____. *The Idea of the Holy*, 2nd ed. Translated by John W. Harvey. New York: Oxford University Press, 1950; reprint, 1960.
_____. *Naturalism and Religion.* Translated by J. Arthur Thomson and Margaret R. Thomson. London: Williams & Norgate, 1907.

_____. *West-östliche Mystik*. Gotha: Leopold Klotz, 1929.
Ozment, Steven E. *Homo Spiritualis. A comparative study of the anthropology of Johannes Tauler, Jean Gerson and Martin Luther (1509-16) in the context of their theological thought*. Leiden: E. J. Brill, 1969.
Pieper, Franz and Mueller, J.T. *Christliche Dogmatik*. St. Louis: Missouri Synod, 1946.
Preger, Wilhelm. *Geschichte der deutschen Mystik im Mittelalter*, Vols. I-III. Leipzig: Dörffling & Franke, 1874-1893.
_____, ed. *Luthers Tischreden aus den Jahren 1531 und 1532 nach den Aufzeichnungen von Johann Schlaginhaufen*. Leipzig: Dörffling & Franke, 1888.
Prenter, Regin. *Spiritus Creator*. Philadelphia: Fortress, 1953.
Die Religion in Geschichte und Gegenwart. Tubingen: J. C. B. Mohr, 1957-1965. *(RGG)*
The Revised Standard Version of the Bible (RSV).

Ritschl, Albrecht. *The Christian Doctrine of Justification and Reconciliation*. English translation of 1882 ed. Edited by H.R. Mackintosh and A.B. Macaulay. Clifton, N.J.: Reference Book Publishers, 1966.
_____. *Geschichte des Pietismus in der reformierten Kirche*. Bonn: Adolph Marcus, 1880.
Rogness, Michael. *Philip Melanchthon: Reformer Without Honor*. Minneapolis: Augsburg Publishing House, 1969.
Ruh, Kurt. *Altdeutsche Mystik*. Bern: A. Francke, 1950.
Ruhl, Artur. *Der Einfluss der Mystik auf Denken und Entwicklung des jungen Luther*. Marburg: Marburg/Lahn, Philipps-Universität, 1960.
Ruhland, Friedrich Theophil. *Luther und die Brautmystik nach Luthers Schrifttum bis 1521*. Giessen: Münchowsche Universitätsdruckerei, 1938.

Schleiermacher, Friedrich. *The Christian Faith*. Translated and edited by H.R. Mackintosh and J.S. Stewart. Edinburgh: T. & T. Clark, 1960.
Schloenbach, Manfred. *Heiligung als Fortschreiten und Wachstum des Glaubens in Luthers Theologie*. Kuopio: Savon Sanomain Kirjapaino, 1963.
Schmid, Heinrich F. *The Doctrinal Theology of the Evangelical Lutheran Church*. Translated and edited by Charles A. Hay and Henry E. Jacobs. Minneapolis: Augsburg, 1899, 1961.
Schürmann, Reiner. *Meister Eckhart, Mystic and Philosopher*. Bloomington: Indiana University Press, 1978.
Schütte, Hans-Walter. *Religion und Christentum in der Theologie Rudolf Ottos*. Berlin: W. de Gruyter & Co., 1969.
Seeberg, Erich. *Grundzüge der Theologie Luthers*. Stuttgart: W. Kohlhammer Verlag, 1940.
Seils, Michael. *Lutheran Convergence?* Geneva: Lutheran World Federation, 1988.
Söderblom, Nathan. *Humor och melankoli och andra Lutherstudier (1919)*. Stockholm: Proprius förlag, 1983.
_____. *The Nature of Revelation*. Authorized translation from the second edition of 1930 by Frederic E. Pamp. New York: Oxford University Press, 1933.
_____. *Sundar Singhs budskap* [The Message of Sundar Singh]. Stockholm: Hugo Geber, 1923.
_____. *Tre livsformer: mystik, förtröstan, vetenskap*. Stockholm: Hugo Geber, 1922; reprint ed., pp. 165-276 in *Till mystikens belysning*, with a Foreword by Hans Åkerberg. Lund: Studentlitteratur, 1975.
Stork, Theophilus. See Gelzer, Heinrich.
Strauch, Philipp. *Meister Eckhart-Probleme*. Halle: E. Karras, 1919.

Stupperich, Robert. *Melanchthon*. Philadelphia: Westminster, 1960.
Tauler, Johann. *The Inner Way, being thirty-six sermons for festivals by John Tauler*. Edited by A. W. Hutton. London: Methuen & Co., 1900.
_____. *Johann Taulers Predigten*, ed. Georg Hofmann. Freiburg: Herder, 1961.
_____. *Die Predigten Taulers aus der Engelberger und der Freiburger Handschrift*. ed. Ferdinand Vetter. Berlin: Weidmannsche Buchhandlung, 1910.
Theologia Germanica. See *Eine deutsche Theologie* and Hoffman, Bengt R.
Tiililä, Osmo. *Döden och odödligheten*. Helsingfors: Församlingsförbundets Bokförlag, 1964.
Tomkins, Peter and Bird, Christopher. *The Secret Life of Plants*. New York: Harper & Row, 1973.

Underhill, Evelyn. *The Mystics of the Church*. London: J. Clarke, 1925.

Vajta, Vilmos. *Luther on Worship*. Philadelphia: Muehlenberg, 1958.
Vogelsang, Erich. *Der angefochtene Christus bei Luther*. Berlin: Verlag von Walter de Gruyter & Co., 1932.

Wicks, Jared. *Man Yearning for Grace*. Washington: Corpus Books, 1968.
_____. *Luther and His Spiritual Legacy*. Wilmington: Michael Glazier, 1983.
_____, ed. *Catholic Scholars Dialogue with Luther*. Chicago: Loyola University Press, 1970.
Wolf, Ernst. *Staupitz und Luther*. Leipzig: Heinsius Nachf., 1927.
Woolf, Bertram Lee. *Reformation Writings of Martin Luther, Vol. I, The Basis of the Protestant Reformation*. London: Lutterworth Press, 1952.
Wrede, Gösta. *Unio Mystica. Probleme der Erfahrung bei Johannes Tauler*. Uppsala: Acta Universitatis Upsaliensis, Almqvist & Wiksell, 1974.
_____. *En väg till Gud. Om Johannes Tauler (d.1361), mystiker*. Stockholm: Katolska teologföreningen, 1981.

ARTICLES

Åkerberg, Hans. "Oandlighetsmystik och personlighetsmystik," Till belysning av premisser och möjligheter i Nathan Söderbloms mystikdistinktion. Uppsala: *Nathan Söderblom-sällskapets årsbok*, 1981: 49-73.

_____. "On the comparability of religio-psychological data." in Pettersson, Olof and Åkerberg, Hans. *Interpreting Religious Phenomena*. Stockholm: Almqvist & Wiksell; Atlantic Highland, N. J.: Humanities Press, 1981. Chap. IV.

_____. "Luther och mystiken." *Svensk Teologisk Kvartalskrift*, LIX (1983): 111-122.

Beyer, Hermann Wolfgang. "Gott und die Geschichte nach Luthers Auslegung des Magnificat." *Luther-Jahrbuch* XXI (1939): 110-134.

Bigelmaier, Andreas, "Zum Verhältnis Luthers zur Mystik," *Luther in ökumenischer Sicht. Von evangelischen und katholischen Mitarbeitern*. Edited by Alfred v. Martin. Stuttgart: Frommann, 1929.

Bornkamm, Heinrich. "Luther," *RGG*, IV, pp. 480-495.

Hägglund, Bengt. "Luther und die Mystik," in *The Church, Mysticism, Sanctification and the Natural in Luther's Thought (CM)*. Edited by Ivar Asheim. Philadelphia: Fortress, 1967, pp. 84-94.

Hoffman, Bengt R. "Beyond the Intellectual," *Religion and Psychology*, XXI, 206, September 1970.

_____. "Luther and the Mystical," *The Lutheran Ouarterly* XXVI (1974): 316-329.

_____. "On the Relationship between Mystical Faith and Moral Life in Luther's Thought," *Lutheran Theological Seminary Bulletin*, Gettysburg, Pa. 55 (1975): 21-35.

_____. "The Present Significance of Mysticism to the Christian Faith" in *Elevatis Oculis*, Festschrift für Seppo A. Toivonen. Helsingfors: Vammala, 1984.

_____. "Lutheran Spirituality" in *Spiritual Traditions for the Contemporary Church*. Edited by Robin Maas & Gabriel O'Donnell, O.P. Nashville, Tenn., USA: Abingdon Press, 1990.

Holsten, W. "Hirsch, Emanuel," *RGG* III, pp. 363-364.

Iserloh, Erwin. "Luther und die Mystik," *CM*, pp. 60-83.

Joest, Wilfried. "Das Heiligungsproblem nach Luthers Schrift 'Wider die himmlischen Propheten'," *CM*, pp. 189-193.

Lau, F. "Calov, Abraham," *RGG*, I, 1587.

McSorley, Harry J. "Erasmus versus Luther — Compounding the Reformation Tragedy," *Catholic Scholars Dialogue with Luther*, Edited by Jared Wicks. Chicago: Loyola University Press, 1970, pp. 107-120.
Manns, Peter. "Absolute and Incarnate Faith—Luther on Justification in the Galatians Commentary of 1531-1535," *Catholic Scholars Dialogue with Luther*, pp. 121-156.
Maurer, Wilhelm. "Luthers Anschauungen über die Kontinuität der Kirche," *CM*, pp. 95-121.

Oberman, Heiko. "Simul gemitus et raptus: Luther and die Mystik," *CM*, pp. 20-59.

Pelikan, Jaroslav. "Continuity and Order in Luther's View of Church and Ministry: A Study of De instituendis ministris ecclesiae of 1523," *CM*, pp. 143-155.

Ruh, Kurt. "Die trinitarische Spekulation in deutscher Mystik und Scholastik," *Zeitschrift für deutsche Philologie* LXXII: 24-53.

Shideler, Mary McDermott. "The Man for Others and the Man for God," *Christian Century*, April 10, 1968, pp. 448-451.
Söderblom, Nathan. "Fadern i det fördolda," *Svensk Teologisk Kvartalskrift* I (1925): 8-19 and 117-134.
Stolt, Birgit. "Bister, mörk och sammanbiten: den svenska vrångbilden av Martin Luther," *Svensk Teologisk Kvartalskrift* 66 (1990): 14-22.
_____. "Der Buchstab tödt — der Geist macht lebendig," *Festschrift zum 60. Geburtstag von Hans-Gert Roloff*, ed. James Hardin and Jörg Jungmayr. Berlin: Peter Lang, 1992, pp. 21-28.
Strauch, Philipp. "Zu Taulers Predigten," *Beitrage zur Geschichte der deutschen Sprache und Literatur*. Tübingen: Max Niemeyer, 1919.

Vogelsang, Erich. "Luther und die Mystik," *Luther-Jahrbuch* XIX (1937): 32-54.
_____. "Die Unio mystica bei Luther," *Archiv für Reformationsgeschichte* XXXV (1938): 63-80.
von Walter, Johannes. "Luthers Christusbild," *Luther-Jahrbuch* XXI (1939): 1-27.

Williams, G. H. "German Mysticism in the Polarization of Ethical Behavior in Luther and the Anabaptists," *The Mennonite Quarterly Review*, XLVIII (July 1974): 275-304.
Wolf, Ernst. "Holl, Karl," *RGG* III, pp. 432-433.
Wrede, Gosta. "Tro-erfarenhet-mystik," in *Luther idag*. Lund: Teologiska institutionen, 1983, pp.31-40.

Index of Subjects

H

I

J

K

L

M

N

O

Index of Names